THE AFRICAN NEXUS

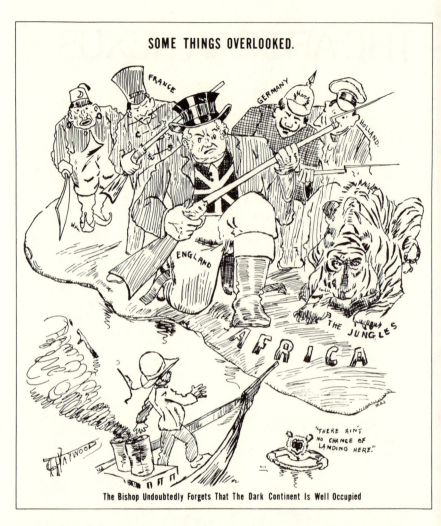

The Bishop Undoubtedly Forgets That The Dark Continent Is Well Occupied

A cartoon that appeared in the *Indianapolis Freeman* (Indiana) on 9 November 1907 illustrated the perceptions that literate and middle-class black Americans of the late nineteenth and early twentieth centuries had toward emigration to Africa and the European partitioning of the continent. This illustration referred to the futility of Bishop Henry M. Turner's African emigration scheme of Afro-American repatriation because so many European colonialists were present on the continent.

THE AFRICAN NEXUS

Black American Perspectives on the European Partitioning of Africa, 1880–1920

SYLVIA M. JACOBS

Contributions in Afro-American and African Studies, Number 55

GREENWOOD PRESS
WESTPORT, CONNECTICUT • LONDON, ENGLAND

Library of Congress Cataloging in Publication Data

Jacobs, Sylvia M   1946-
    The African nexus.

    (Contributions in Afro-American and African
studies ; no. 55 ISSN 0069-9624)
    Bibliography: p.
    Includes index.
    1.   Africa—Colonization—Public opinion.
2.   Public opinion—United States.   3.   Afro-Americans—
Attitudes.   I.   Title.   II.   Series.
DT31.J27   325'.34'096   80-660
ISBN 0-313-22312-2 (lib. bdg.)

Library of Congress Catalog Card Number: 80-660
ISBN: 0-313-22312-2
ISSN: 0069-9624

First published in 1981

Greenwood Press
A division of Congressional Information Service, Inc.
88 Post Road West, Westport, Connecticut 06881

Printed in the United States of America

10 9 8 7 6 5 4 3 2 1

To the memory of my beloved brother,
Rickie Jerome Jacobs

CONTENTS

Acknowledgments   ix

Methodological Note   xi

1. Introduction: Black Americans and Africa—
   A Historical Overview Before 1920   3

2. The European Presence in Africa Before 1880   17

3. The Meaning and Significance for Black Americans
   of the Scramble and Partitioning, 1880-1900   35

4. West Africa Leads the Way, 1880-1914   65

5. Europeans in Central Africa: The Congo
   Basin, 1880-1914   81

6. The Contest for East Africa, 1880-1914   113

7. British and Boer Rule in South
   Africa, 1880-1914   135

8. European Interest in North and
   Northeast Africa, 1880-1914   169

9. Ethiopia: Victory Over European
   Imperialistic Aggressions, 1880-1914   187

10. Liberia: Struggle Against European
    Domination, 1880-1914   205

11. Africa, World War I, and the Paris Peace
    Settlement, 1914-1920   235

12. Conclusion: The African Nexus   267

Bibliography   275

Index   301

ACKNOWLEDGMENTS

The subject of this research originated from the writer's keen interest in the respective attitudes and perceptions that Afro-Americans and Africans have held about one another. I am indebted to Clarence G. Contee for suggesting to me the topic under consideration. I am also grateful for the assistance given me by many librarians and libraries, including the Schomburg Center for Research in Black Culture (New York City), the Missionary Research Library (New York City), the Union Theological Seminary Library (New York City), the New York Public Library (New York City), the Library of Congress (Washington, D.C.), the National Archives (Washington, D.C.), the Moorland-Spingarn Research Center at Howard University (Washington, D.C.), the Morgan State University Library (Baltimore, Maryland), the Historical Foundation of the Presbyterian and Reformed Churches (Montreat, North Carolina), and Duke University Library (Durham, North Carolina). In addition, sincere thanks goes to Ernest Mason and Earl E. Thorpe for reading and critiquing the manuscript, and George W. Reid for reading portions of the manuscript. Finally, I would like to thank Linda Fenner and Helen A. Fuller for typing parts of the manuscript.

METHODOLOGICAL NOTE

This study attempts to assess the extent and possible impact of the views and attitudes of black Americans on the European partitioning of Africa during the late nineteenth and early twentieth centuries. Initially, organizing this manuscript created the most perplexing problem, but for several reasons, it was finally decided to categorize Afro-American ideas according to regions. Since blacks generally referred to European colonialism in Africa according to country, section, or colonial power, geographical divisions seemed the most appropriate. Though Afro-Americans were concerned with all the regions of Africa, there were instances where degree and intensity were greater for certain areas. So, for example, events in West, Central, and South Africa were widely discussed throughout the American black community; while, to the contrary, East and North Africa received only scant consideration, probably because fewer Afro-Americans had visited or were familiar with these areas, or possibly because Afro-Americans identified with them less.

Nonetheless, extant materials were examined, as much as possible, for each section, but sometimes a lack of available documentation or discussion of a specific area resulted in a presentation more brief than desired (indeed, there were historiographical gaps). It was felt, however, that to some extent the paucity or limitation of information on attitudes toward certain regions represented another kind of historical truth, or (to coin another historian's phrase) that "absence of evidence is not evidence of absence." Finally, all regions of Africa were included in order to compile a complete and comprehensive continental study, since the partitioning process cannot be fully understood unless interregional diplomacy is discussed, and also to end the practice, common among some African historians, of omitting North Africa when considering continental trends.

Originally, this examination hoped to answer the questions: How did black Americans view Africa from 1880 to 1920? Were the masses of black people aware of what was going on in Africa? Were they concerned with events on the continent? If so, to what extent? If not, which group of black Americans were aware, and what was their response to the partitioning of Africa? In addition to traditional sources of this period, such as manuscripts, newspapers, and auto-biographies, nontraditional sources were examined. These included literary works, religious and secular music, cartoons and illustrations, histories of black universities, fraternities, sororities, and Masons, among others. This was done to tap the folk expressions of the masses, although they seldom proved fruitful.

Furthermore, because some occupations attempted to appeal to the masses for support more so than others, it was assumed that such enterprises would reflect the feelings of the rank and file. Most partic-ularly were those groups that required some general approval or financial backing for continuation, such as members of the religious, journalistic, or political community. Often, however, these groups attempted to shape mass attitudes rather than echo them. Finally, it was believed that the documented views of the masses on distinct African issues, such as racial identification or emigration, could be used as an index of their general attitudes toward the continent and, by inference, an indication of views on other specific topics, such as the European partitioning of Africa.

However, the majority of blacks during the years under study concerned themselves with everyday subsistence and existence. Issues that affected the masses or majority of the southern black population centered around escape from the daily burdens of the sharecropper or cash tenancy systems, political and social oppres-sion, and racial discrimination. As a result of these concerns, these blacks considered internal migration within the United States or emigration to Africa. In fact, with rare exception, during the years 1880 to 1920 the multitude of blacks expressed opinions about Africa that were not for or against emigration. There were no public demonstrations by the masses of blacks on the European partitioning of Africa. Moreover, during these years and beyond World War I, the scope of most Afro-Americans was not international.

The partitioning of Africa was an issue about which these blacks were probably not well informed. Additionally, in 1880 (when this study begins), 70 percent of the black population was illiterate, and that figure was still almost one-quarter, or 22.9 percent, in 1920 (when the study ends). Only in a few cases did this number leave some form of documentation of their attitudes. The difficulty, then, of understanding the viewpoints and positions of the masses of blacks is one that, because of the high illiteracy rate among this group, sometimes is lost to history. While ideally history should reflect the attitudes and activities of all classes, we cannot proceed without adequate documentation, and lack of documentation was the problem faced in this investigation. Even among the majority of literate blacks it was not a practice to record attitudes and events in their lives, or to keep personal letters and manuscripts.

Thus, this inquiry became a study of the thought and perspectives of the articulate members of the black community. These included leading and well-known blacks as well as lesser-known blacks. It was from this group that comments and protests about the European partitioning and the excesses of colonialism came. As African emigration was a concern of the masses during these years, the development and missionizing of the continent was a concern of the articulate. This examination deals with the image of Africa in the mind of literate blacks from 1880 to 1920 and looks at how they viewed the continent during the years of "Jim Crow" in America and European colonization in Africa. This study reinforces the now current theory that, historically, blacks as a group have been interested in Africa but also proposes to show that different classes of blacks have expressed different concerns.

Finally, only Afro-Americans who spent the major portion of their lives in the United States were considered in this investigation. These were individuals who immigrated to the United States and remained for the greater part of their lives and those who traveled or worked in Africa or elsewhere and then returned to the United States. An individual neither had to be born nor die in the United States to be counted but must have been an American citizen who was outspoken on the European partitioning of Africa. This accounts for the fact that many well-known Afro-Americans who emigrated to Africa or elsewhere were not discussed. An attempt was made to reconstruct the life and thought of each of the leading personalities included. However, in some instances, information on that individual was scarce or nonexistent.

This study is comprehensive in its survey of how one segment of black Americans viewed the partitioning of the African continent by the European powers. Although much has been written about Afro-American perceptions of Africa and mass support of emigration to Africa, this is the first attempt to appraise the attitudes of literate and articulate blacks about probably the most dramatic event to occur on the continent. It also gives insight into how these blacks during this period viewed their fatherland and their responsibility to its development.

THE AFRICAN NEXUS

INTRODUCTION: BLACK AMERICANS AND AFRICA— A HISTORICAL OVERVIEW BEFORE 1920

1

I am an African, and, in this country, however meritorious my conduct and respectable my character, I cannot receive the credit due to either. I wish to go to a country where I shall be estimated by my merits, not by my complexion.

Miles Mark Fisher, "Lott Carey, The Colonizing Missionary," p. 389.
Lott Carey, 1780-1828.

We are of [the] opinion that the *free* colored people generally mean to live in America, and not in Africa. . . . For two hundred and twenty-eight years has the colored man toiled over the soil of America, under a burning sun and a driver's lash—plowing, planting, reaping, that white men might roll in ease, their hands unhardened by labor, and their brows unmoistened by the waters of genial toil; and now that the moral sense of mankind is beginning to revolt at this system of foul treachery and cruel wrong, and is demanding its overthrow, the mean and cowardly oppressor is mediating plans to expel the colored man entirely from the country. Shame upon the guilty wretches that dare propose, and all that countenance such a proposition. We live here—have a right to live here, and mean to live here.

"Colonization," in *Apropos of Africa*, comp. and ed. Martin Kilson and Adelaide Cromwell Hill, p. 45.
Frederick Douglass, 1817-1895

Return to the land of your Fathers. . . . There is no more doubt in my mind that we have ultimately to return to Africa than there is of the existence of God.
Yes, I would make Africa a place of refuge, because I see no other shelter from the stormy blast, from the ride tide of persecution, from the horrors of American prejudice.

Edwin S. Redkey, *Black Exodus*, pp. 29, 33.
Henry McNeal Turner, 1834-1915

From their beginnings in America, Afro-Americans have had to wrestle with the contradiction of their existence in a society that oppressed and rejected them. This factor has been a source of confusion for blacks and has left them with the complex inconsistencies of being black in a white society along with the accompanying dualisms and ambivalences associated with their desire to be treated as equals in American society and their constant rejection by that society. The overriding theme of the black experience in America has centered on how blacks have adapted in a predominantly white civilization and how that same culture has affected and been affected by black thought and behavior. The black experience in America, then, is not completely separate from the white one. Basically, Afro-Americans have been influenced by some of the same social, economic, intellectual, political, and cultural forces as whites, but in a more pronounced manner since blacks rarely controlled these phenomena. Their responses represent reactions to and creative initiatives from the basic tenets of the American experience.[1]

The history of Afro-American-African relations has also abounded in paradoxes. Not only have black Americans been ambivalent about their anomalous position in American society, they have also expressed mixed feelings about the continent of their forefathers. Africa has represented many things to various groups of Afro-Americans. Historically, the sentiment of American blacks toward Africa has been dependent upon their status in American society. During years of severe political and economic oppression, blacks have looked longingly at the continent and, conversely, during jubilant periods, the African link has been rejected. Furthermore, the complexity of Afro-America's relationships with Africa cannot be viewed out of the context of the forces operating on white American organizations and institutions or events on the continent. Black attitudes and feelings about Africa must be seen as one aspect of their struggle for survival and acceptance in American society.[2]

Finally, negative European and white American images and stereotypes of Africa, plus their debased attitude toward the continent and its people, affected black opinion. Although American authors of the nineteenth century were generally less informed about Africa than Europe, both were influenced by racial motivations and the assumption of cultural superiority in their writings. Hence, blacks were faced with the image of Africans as barbarians and shared many of the same repugnant images of Africa as did whites. Obviously, the negative portrayal of Africa and Africans was bound to create mixed feelings about Africa in the mind of blacks as they attempted to reconcile these ambivalences.[3]

In spite of attempts by Europeans and white Americans to represent Africa in a derogatory manner, however, there has always been a feeling for Africa among all classes of Afro-Americans and a small group who have attempted to retain links with Africa, in one form or another, and who did not abandon their ties with the continent. Neither the masses nor their leaders have ever forgotten Africa.

Within the antebellum black community, slave and free, Afro-Americans certainly did identify with Africa, as is evidenced by the names they took for themselves and their organizations. Before 1865, black Americans formed many organizations and institutions and labeled them "African."[4] This inclusion of the word "African" in the names of their organizations was not, as some writers have suggested, an acceptance of their inferior position in American society, but rather an open acknowledgment of their love for their fatherland.[5] Antebellum blacks did not hate Africa. Skin color, which left an indelible mark of difference on blacks, also identified them as descendants of Africans, and, frequently, whites referred to them as African. For some Afro-Americans, a knowledge of Africa was personal and recent, since many had arrived not long ago from the continent. For others, memories of Africa had been passed down orally from one generation to another. (A contemporary example of this is Alex Haley's extensive revelations on how he traced his "roots" back to Africa.) For all Afro-Americans, then, no matter how educated or remote from Africa or Africanness, there was the bond of race and tradition; blacks had little opportunity to forget the African nexus.[6]

The supply of newly imported Africans into the country continued well into the nineteenth century (despite the Foreign Slave Trade Act of 1808 forbidding the importation of slaves), thereby guaranteeing a little Africa in America. There developed a Pan-African environment, a mixing of recently arrived Africans from the continent with diaspora Africans located in the United States. It is obvious that the essentials of Pan-Africanism as an ideology existed in America years before the word was ever entered into dictionaries.[7]

Yet, Africa has always presented a dilemma for black Americans. Edwin S. Redkey has maintained that blacks looked to Africa with mixed emotions. Some of their responses are perfect examples of these feelings. Afro-Americans viewed Africa with both pride and humiliation, attraction and repulsion, hope and fear.[8] It would appear that, on one hand, for Afro-Americans to reject Africa would have been to reject themselves and their own self-worth. On the other hand, to accept Africa was to accept the prevailing views of barbarianism, heathenism, and savagery. This ambivalence is most important in understanding the different reactions to and attitudes toward Africa from the different classes of Afro-Americans. The masses of lower-class black people, not always aware of all the negative propaganda circulated about Africa, held out the greatest hope for Africa and its future and were the greatest supporters of the back-to-Africa movement. Middle-class blacks, their leaders, and spokesmen were consistently anti-emigrationist and instead suggested missionary activity and developmental projects as their contribution to the continent.

Among lower-class Afro-Americans, the desire to return to Africa increased proportionately to their exclusion from American institutions and their economic oppression in American society. Afro-American interest in emigration to Africa had a long antebellum history. Possibly the first repatriation scheme was proposed by the Quakers in 1713. Still, it was not until the late eighteenth century that efforts were made to organize such a movement. By this time, "back-to-Africa" had become a catch-all phrase for all emigration movements.

One of the first-known slave petitions, submitted in 1773, proposed manumission so that Afro-American slaves could emigrate to Africa. In addition, at the end of the Revolutionary War, thousands of American blacks who had fought on the side of the British were dispersed throughout the British colonies, some eventually making their way back to Africa. Moreover, in 1787, a small group of Bostonian blacks expressed an interest in emigration to Africa. Two years later, on 17 October 1789, forty members of the Free African Society of Newport, Rhode Island, which included Paul Cuffee, proposed to the Philadelphia parent body "the return of Africans to

Africa." Although the Philadelphia society was unreceptive to the idea of emigration to Africa, the Newport group requested permission from the British government to emigrate to the colony of Sierra Leone and in 1795 did send a delegate to Freetown, Sierra Leone, to survey the region. Eventually, however, they decided to remain in the United States.[9]

However, the first Afro-American individually to organize and implement a program of emigration to Africa was Paul Cuffee, a self-made Quaker fisherman, whaler, and merchant. Cuffee successfully transported thirty-eight American blacks to Sierra Leone in December of 1815, sailing into the Freetown harbor on 3 February 1816. Unfortunately, his plans for a second voyage, in which no fewer than 2,000 blacks would have been transported to Africa, was aborted by his untimely death in September 1817.[10]

The American Colonization Society was founded in late 1816 and immediately presented a plan for the colonization of free blacks on the west coast of Africa in what eventually became Liberia. The body hoped to rid the country of its burdensome problem of how to assimilate blacks into American society. But the colonization movement was seen by most blacks as an attempt by whites to eliminate the free black population and thus leave slavery secure in the United States. Therefore, the majority of Afro-Americans labeled the society as racist, and most had little to do with it. Colonization and emigration eventually came to represent two different things. Colonization was seen as a solution by whites to the racial issue and emigration was seen as a black nationalist answer to a racist society. The majority of antebellum free blacks generally opposed both colonization and emigration and decided instead to remain in America and fight for equality.[11]

Because of this skepticism among the group to whom the American Colonization Society was appealing, by 1835 the cause of African colonization was failing. During the period from 1835 to 1850, more blacks emigrated to Canada, Haiti, or the British West Indies, where they believed they would be better able to influence the government.[12]

But the Fugitive Slave Act of 1850 revived the debate over emigration, and, during the 1850s, it found new life. This is evidenced by the many letters written by lower-class blacks to the American Colonization Society during this decade requesting passage to Liberia. However, with the coming of the Civil War and its resultant optimism of equality for blacks in America, the emigration movement again appeared to be moribund.

Before 1865, the American Colonization Society transported approximately thirteen thousand black Americans to Liberia. Most free blacks, however, felt that emigration was too great a price to pay for equality and remained in the United States. Almost all slaves before 1865 were illiterate and, therefore, there is some paucity of documentation on their desire to return to Africa. The letters written to the American Colonization Society do suggest, though, that the majority of hopeful emigrants were lower-class blacks and former slaves. For many, black emigration became synonymous with black nationalism. Hollis Lynch has pointed out that antebellum Pan-Negro nationalism had a preoccupation with and concern for emigration, although the nationalists never succeeded in creating a mass exodus to Africa.[13]

It was in the late 1870s and the decade of the 1890s that the last serious nineteenth-century attempts were made to stimulate an interest in emigration. During the Reconstruction years, last-ditch efforts of the American Colonization Society were directed toward carrying out its initial goal of mass black colonization. The society was never successful and by the end of the nineteenth century had transported only about sixteen thousand blacks to Liberia. From 1893 to 1899 the numbers sent were less than six each year. Of the total dispatched from 1816 to 1900, Virginia had supplied the largest number, with declining amounts coming from North Carolina, Georgia, Tennessee, South Carolina, and Kentucky. At least twenty-seven states and the District of Columbia had contributed emigrants.[14]

A revived black-led emigration movement swept many parts of the South in the 1890s. In this movement, as in the back-to-Africa movement of Marcus Garvey in the 1920s, the most enthusiastic supporters were among lower-class blacks, most of them southern, illiterate, and poverty-stricken. For the masses of these blacks, Africa continued to hold a certain mysticism, romanticism, and hope. They saw emigration as a means of escaping oppressive economic, social, and political conditions in the United States. It can thus be inferred that, in spite of all the negative reports about Africa from travelers, missionaries, and returnees, probably if there had been a well-organized and adequately funded emigration project in the late nineteenth or early twentieth centuries, much of the lower-class southern Afro-American population would have returned to Africa. Bishop Henry McNeal Turner of the African Methodist Episcopal (AME) church claimed in 1900 that 2 million lower-class blacks, or 25 percent of the black population, had shown an interest in African emigration. The small number who did emigrate to Africa in no way reflects the extent of emigration sentiment during this period among southern blacks. For the poor farmers of this group, there remained a romantic vision of free land and a new life in Africa.[15]

As in earlier years, most articulate, middle-class blacks in the 1890s definitely opposed emigration as a solution to the racial problem, although they did sustain an ethnic identification and sympathy with Africa. With much more at stake in the American system than the masses of lower-class blacks, this group desired to wage its battle in the United States. They accepted the current ideology of taking up the "white man's burden," the *mission civilisatrice*, in Africa and praised the "civilizing" influences of imperialism but also warned of the dangers of white domination of Africa. It was from this class of blacks that the cry for Christian missions and against European exploitation came. They believed that it was the "special duty" of black Americans to participate in the "civilizing" of the continent, but through missionary activity and business ventures, not emigration. To the black middle class, emigrationism was a romantic, if not unreasonable, attraction to the fatherland. Missions were an attempt to identify with Africa while at the same time keeping it at arm's length until it conformed to Western standards of civilization. These middle-class blacks strove not to return to Africa physically but to establish cultural, economic, and political links with the continent. The two dominant black institutions during this time, the church and the press, opposed emigration but supported missions and development.[16]

During the years after 1870, some blacks attempted to find a solution other than emigration to oppressive racial conditions in America. In 1870, the majority of blacks continued to live in the South. Because of reports of food shortages, unpleasant climate, and disease sent back from Liberian emigrants and the closer accessibility of

American land, a larger majority of southern blacks who wanted to escape poverty, discrimination, and exploitation in the South chose to migrate to other parts of the United States. The western internal mass migration, or, as George Washington Williams, black America's first historian, described it, "folk migration," was stimulated and led by Benjamin "Pap" Singleton of Nashville, Tennessee, and Henry Adams of Shreveport, Louisiana.[17]

The impetus for this migration likewise came from lower-class blacks and was also a result of their continued economic exploitation, political oppression, and physical abuse. With stories of a "promised land" in the midwest, Singleton and Adams are given credit for having led forty thousand "exodusters" from the southern states (Afro-American migrants from the South who went to Kansas in the exodus of 1879). Singleton later unsuccessfully attempted an emigration scheme to Liberia under the United Trans-Atlantic Company. Northern and southern middle- and upper-class and propertied blacks generally opposed this internal migration as much as they had disapproved of African emigration, although not necessarily for the same reasons.[18]

The relationship between the internal migrations and the African emigration movements is a source of speculation. In both movements, lower-class blacks were the major participants, and middle- and upper-class blacks opposed them. In each case also, economic and political exploitation were the stimuli. Yet it is not clear if the cost and uncertainty of African emigration caused the more realistic migration to the Midwest or if dissatisfaction with the economic benefits of the western migration of the 1870s prompted the renewed interest in African emigration in the 1890s. Nonetheless, it is certain that a large number of lower-class blacks wanted to leave the South.[19] Furthermore, migration movements did not cease at the end of the nineteenth century. The first decades of the twentieth century witnessed two mass internal migrations and one last African emigration scheme.

In the first decade of the twentieth century, approximately fourteen thousand middle- and upper-class professional northern blacks migrated to the South to find employment and a clientele in the segregated society that had evolved in America. Also, between 1910 and 1920, approximately half a million southern blacks left that area and migrated to the North in search of economic and educational opportunities.[20]

While these events were occurring, one final emigration attempt before 1920 was being organized, the ill-fated scheme of Alfred Charles Sam, "Chief Sam," supposedly an Asante chief from Ghana. Drawing largely from disillusioned and destitute lower-class blacks in Okfuskee County, Oklahoma, in 1914 "Chief Sam," through his Akim Trading Company, transported sixty Afro-Americans to Ghana, a number that in no way reflected the amount of willing followers. The expedition was a failure, and no more blacks were carried to Africa, but the project represented a short-lived hope for a few disfranchised and oppressed blacks.[21]

Historians have attempted to understand why the majority of Afro-Americans opted to remain in the United States in spite of continued oppression. The answer seems to lie in a statement made by W. E. B. Du Bois in the early twentieth century: "One ever feels his two-ness,—an American, a Negro; two souls, two thoughts, two unreconciled strivings; two warring ideals in one dark body." Historically, black Americans have consistently considered the United States their adopted country. Despite evidence to the contrary, Afro-Americans have clung to the belief that they were entitled to the same rights and privileges as other Americans. Besides, America was well known to them, and blacks were not willing to gamble their lives and livelihoods on a new and foreign land. In the final analysis, the Afro-American experience has been essentially an American and not an African one.[22]

By 1920, Afro-American emigration to Africa was no longer possible because the European powers had partitioned the continent among themselves. Also, those colonialists would have blocked any attempt at collaboration between Afro-Americans and Africans, since the European imperialists had come to see the black American presence as a disruptive element in African society. But by this date Africa had taken on a new meaning for black Americans. Slowly they came to realize that black people everywhere were similarly exploited by whites and that blacks had to stand together to denounce oppression and exploitation.[23]

Black Americans have never spoken with one voice about Africa. Attitudes before 1920 centered around several ideologies or strategies: emigration to the continent, a Pan-African alliance with the continent, support of the "Christianizing and civilizing" of the continent, or a nationalist defense of the continent. But regardless of their views toward Africa, the vast majority of Afro-Americans continued to demand equality in American society and generally expressed a desire to remain.[24]

Before 1920, then, various groups of black Americans had complex relationships with Africa. Lower-class, illiterate blacks demonstrated their interest in the continent through a desire to emigrate. Upper- and middle-class literate blacks viewed Africa from a distance. It was from this group of Afro-Americans that perspectives about the European partitioning of the continent and the late nineteenth-century cry for missions came. To them, it was a matter of developing Africa and making the continent more acceptable to the world.[25]

Regardless of their attitude toward Africa, however, most blacks realized that there was a connection between the image white Americans held about Africa and Africans and their image of black Americans, that perhaps if Africa were respected Afro-Americans would be also. Thus, with the partitioning of Africa in the 1880s, middle-class and literate black Americans began to protest the excesses of European imperialism there, believing that the exploitation of Africans would only provide an excuse for the continuation of discrimination against blacks in the United States. It was during the late nineteenth and early twentieth centuries that all classes of black Americans began to develop a new relationship with their fatherland, emphasizing similarities and encouraging unity, or Pan-Africanism.

Notes

1. Melville J. Herskovits, *The American Negro, A Study in Racial Crossing*, pp. 52-53, 58. Herskovits discussed these responses in Chapter 4, "White Values for Colored Americans," pp. 51-66.

2. Martin Kilson and Adelaide Cromwell Hill, comps. and eds., *Apropos of Africa*, p. 3.

3. Edwin S. Redkey, *The Meaning of Africa to Afro-Americans*, pp. 2, 32n; and Bernard Magubane, "The American Negro's Conception of Africa," p. 153.

4. Many black Americans obviously had no problems identifying with

Africa, as the names of their organizations founded before 1865 prove: Free African Society, Philadelphia, Pa. (1786); African Lodge No. 459, Boston, Mass. (1787); First African Baptist Church, Savannah, Ga. (1788); African Baptist Church, Lexington, Ky. (1790); Abyssinia Baptist Church, New York City (1800); Free African Meeting House, Boston, Mass. (1805); First African Presbyterian Church, Philadelphia, Pa. (1807); First African Baptist Church, Philadelphia, Pa. (1809); Union Church of Africans, Wilmington, Del. (1813); African Methodist Episcopal Church, Philadelphia, Pa. (1816); African Methodist Episcopal Zion Church, New York City (1821); First African Baptist Church, New Orleans, La. (1826); and First African Baptist Church. Richmond, Va. (1841). See St. Clair Drake, *The Redemption of Africa and Black Religion* , pp. 12-13; and St. Clair Drake, "The American Negro's Reaction to Africa," pp. 12-13.

5. This thesis is advanced in Felix Nwabueze Okoye's *The American Image of Africa*, pp. 129-30.

6. See Redkey, *The Meaning of Africa to Afro-Americans*, p. 2; St. Clair Drake, "Hide My Face?—On Pan-Africanism and Negritude," p. 78; "Black Is Black?," p. 6; and Drake, "The American Negro's Reaction to Africa," p. 12.

7. Okoye, *The American Image of Africa*, p. 2; and Ples Sterling Stuckey, "The Spell of Africa," pp. viii, xiv.

8. Redkey discussed this ambiguous relationship in *The Meaning of Africa to Afro-Americans*, p. 2.

9. Martin R. Delany and Robert Campbell, *Search for a Place*, pp. 2-3; Herbert Aptheker, *A Documentary History of the Negro People in the United States* 1; 8; Charles Wesley, *Richard Allen*, pp. 66-67; and Magubane, "The American Negro's Conception of Africa," pp. 63, 162.

10. For a discussion of Paul Cuffee's life, see Henry Noble Sherwood's "Paul Cuffe" or his "Paul Cuffe and His Contribution to the American Colonization Society." See also, Sheldon H. Harris, *Paul Cuffe*, pp. 13-72.

11. Edwin S. Redkey, *Black Exodus*, p. 16; Delany and Campbell, *Search for a Place*, pp. 3-4; and Wilson Record, "Negro Intellectuals and Negro Movements in Historical Perspective," pp. 8-9.

12. P. J. Staudenraus, *The African Colonization Movement*, p. 249; Robbin W. Winks, *The Blacks in Canada*, p. 161; and Delany and Campbell, *Search for a Place*, pp. 4-5.

13. Redkey, *Black Exodus*, pp. 16, 18; Delany and Campbell, *Search for a Place*, p. 6; Hollis R. Lynch, "Pan-Negro Nationalism in the New World Before 1862," pp. 178-79; and Edwin S. Redkey, "Bishop Turner's African Dream," pp. 287-88.

14. August Meier, *Negro Thought in America, 1880-1915*, pp. 63-64;

Edward W. Chester, *Clash of Titans*, p. 40; Redkey, *Black Exodus*, p. 74; Staudenraus, *The African Colonization Movement*, p. 251; Willis Dolmond Boyd, "Negro Colonization in the Reconstruction Era, 1865-1870," p. 362; and Earl E. Thorpe, "Africa in the Thought of Negro Americans," pp. 8, 10, 22.

15. Robert G. Weisbord, *Ebony Kinship*, p. 35; Arnold H. Taylor, *Travail and Triumph*, pp. 51-52; Meier, *Negro Thought in America, 1880-1915*, pp. 63-64, 68; Redkey, *The Meaning of Africa to Afro-Americans*, pp. 9-10, and *Black Exodus*, pp. 10-15; and Melvin Drimmer, "Review Article—*Black Exodus*," p. 250.

16. Immanuel Geiss, *The Pan-African Movement*, pp. 77-78; Redkey, *Black Exodus*, pp. 244, 287-89; Meier, *Negro Thought in America, 1880-1915*, pp. 66-67; Weisbord, *Ebony Kinship*, p. 23; Edwin S. Redkey, "The Meaning of Africa to Afro-Americans, 1890-1914," pp. 7-8; Willard B. Gatewood, Jr., "Black Americans and the Boer War, 1899-1902," p. 227; and Magubane, "The American Negro's Conception of Africa," p. 66.

17. Weisbord, *Ebony Kinship*, p. 32; Roy Garvin, "Benjamin or 'Pap' Singleton and His Followers," pp. 8, 10; Walter L. Fleming, "'Pap' Singleton, the Moses of the Colored Exodus," pp. 61-64; William Toll, "Free Men, Freedmen, and Race," p. 576; and Drimmer, "Review Article—*Black Exodus*," pp. 251-53.

18. Nell I. Painter, *Exodusters*, pp. 137, 141-42; Chester, *Clash of Titans*, p. 40; Weisbord, *Ebony Kinship*, p. 320n; Meier, *Negro Thought in America, 1880-1915*, pp. 61, 65; Taylor, *Travail and Triumph*, pp. 52-54; Toll, "Free Men, Freedmen, and Race," p. 576; Garvin, "Benjamin or 'Pap' Singleton and His Followers," pp. 7, 11-12; and Fleming, "'Pap' Singleton, the Moses of the Colored Exodus," pp. 63-66, 70, 78-79, 81.

19. For a discussion of the various interpretations, see Painter, *Exodusters*, p. 145; Meier, *Negro Thought in America, 1880-1915*, pp. 63-64; and Drimmer, "Review Article—*Black Exodus*," p. 250.

20. In 1900, 27,000 blacks born in the North lived in the South. By 1910, that number had increased to 41,000. See Emmett J. Scott, *Negro Migration During the War*, pp. 8-9. For a discussion of the migration northward, see Benjamin G. Brawley, *A Social History of the American Negro*, pp. 345-46; Weisbord, *Ebony Kinship*, p. 32; and Drimmer, "Review Article—*Black Exodus*," pp. 251-52.

21. William E. Bittle and Gilbert Geis, *The Longest Way Home*, passim.

22. Jacob Drachler, ed., *Black Homeland/Black Diaspora*, p. 11; Kilson and Hill, eds., *Apropos of Africa*, p. 3; Weisbord, *Ebony Kinship*, p. 32; W. E. B. Du Bois, "Of Our Spiritual Strivings," p. 17; and Drimmer, "Review Article—*Black Exodus*," pp. 251-53.

23. Redkey, *The Meaning of Africa to Afro-Americans*, pp. 1, 3, 19-20; Geiss, *The Pan-African Movement*, p. 172; and Clifford M. Scott, "American Images of Sub-Sahara Africa, 1900-1939," pp. 2-3, 262.

24. Weisbord, *Ebony Kinship*, p. 7; Kilson and Hill, eds., *Apropos of Africa*, p. 3; Drachler, ed., *Black Homeland/Black Diaspora*, pp. 8-11; and Gatewood, "Black Americans and the Boer War, 1899-1902," p. 228.

25. Geiss. *The Pan-African Movement*, pp. 77-78, 172.

THE EUROPEAN PRESENCE IN AFRICA BEFORE 1880

2

Whites have been colonizing themselves in Africa for nearly a century, and . . . they are at this moment, as they have
been for nearly a half century in mortal combat with the
natives, to drive them from the south, and west, across the
interior, to the extreme east.
"Colonization Scheme," *Proceedings of the Colored National Convention*, 1853, p. 55.
James W. C. Pennington, 1809-1871

Africa for the African race and black men to rule them.
Official Report of the Niger Valley Exploring Party, p. 121.
Martin Robinson Delany, 1812-1885

By an almost common consent, the modern world seems
determined to pilfer Africa.
*The Past and Present Condition, and the Destiny of the
Colored Race*, p. 6.
Henry Highland Garnet, 1815-1882

The European presence in Africa before the nineteenth century consisted primarily of a few trading stations along the coasts. During the first years of the nineteenth century, European explorers and geographers began to penetrate the interior. Missionaries concurrently crusaded, evangelizing Africans. Early missionary activity in Africa and the cry for a "civilized" Christian Africa paved the way for the "civilizing mission." This mission would later be used by European administrators as a justification for colonization. The presence of European merchants, explorers, and missionaries set the stage for the imperial expansion of Europe in Africa. These European invaders attempted to camouflage their goals of economic exploitation under the pretense of entering Africa as a religious and sociological experiment. By 1880, a large portion of the African coastline was under some form of European influence.[1]

Thus, by the time of the partitioning of Africa, European statesmen had come to accept the idea that colonization, commerce, Christianity, and "civilization" would provide the most effective formula for the "development" of Africa. Although the European conquest of Africa reached its climax after 1880, during the age of the "new imperialism," the mood had already been set justifying the attitude of Caucasian racial superiority, which crystallized in the belief in the "civilizing mission," the awareness of technological supremacy, and the vision of African natural resources waiting to be developed by European industry and expertise.[2]

Prior to 1880, different groups of black Americans viewed Africa either with regard to a pride in the achievements of ancient Africa, the need for the continuation of Liberian sovereignty, the advantages and disadvantages of Afro-American emigration to or colonization in Africa, or the special duty of Afro-Americans in the "civilizing mission." As the pace of the European penetration and colonization of Africa quickened, some American blacks began to identify more and more with the plight of their racial brothers on the continent.[3]

Generally, those blacks who addressed themselves publicly to the issue of the European presence in Africa, and later the European partitioning of Africa, consisted of a small literate and articulate group usually composed of newspaper editors, journalists, religious leaders, missionaries, educators, attorneys, physicians, adventurers, diplomats, lecturers, and the literati. Because of their education or travels, these individuals were familiar with a wide range of international issues and social problems and could, therefore, enunciate views on African events. From the middle of the nineteenth century onward, these black Americans increasingly considered the effects of the European presence in and colonization of Africa, not only for the Africans in Africa but also for Africans of the diaspora.

The majority of working- and middle-class black Americans who discussed the European presence in Africa before 1880, either supported European efforts of religious and social "development" and the accompanying commercial and economic "progress," or took a militant stance against European activity. Those who supported the European presence generally believed that Africa was in need of the "civilizing" influences of Western culture, although they did not necessarily condone exploitation. Conversely, those who denounced the Europeans in Africa usually were supporters or organizers of an emigration movement to Africa and believed that continued European activity would make such efforts futile. There were those, too, who advocated emigration while praising the European commercial and humanitarian "civilizing mission."

Within the black community prior to 1880, discussion of the European presence in Africa was scanty. Obviously, during the antebellum years with the majority of blacks in slavery and with abolition of slavery the concern of most free blacks, the question of what was occurring on the continent of Africa was of some irrelevance to their daily existence. After emancipation, most blacks were overwhelmed with adjustment to a new life. But there were a few blacks who did discuss this issue. These included newspaper editors, religious leaders, abolitionists, professionals, and, in a few cases, nonprofessional blacks who wrote letters to newspapers.

Before 1880, some members of the Afro-American press believed in the idea of carrying "civilization" to Africa to benefit the Africans. Frederick Douglass, the best-known black journalist and leader before 1880, was a member of that group of Afro-Americans who felt that the "civilizing and Christianizing" of Africa by the European nations would be beneficial to the continent. Douglass was personally against Afro-American emigration to Africa, however, because he predicted that blacks in Africa would soon be forced to live under the rule of the white European powers, which he saw as not substantially different from the rule of whites in America. Douglass, who had escaped from slavery in 1838, urged less racial concern and claims to racial recognition among blacks and more interest in the principles of justice, liberty, and patriotism in America. Thus, in his earlier years, he denounced any thought of emigration to Africa, although late in his life he modified his view. This feeling reflected neither a particular love for America nor a hatred for Africa but was a response to the evils in a society which supported black inferiority. Throughout this period, Douglass's publications, *The North Star* (Rochester, New York), *Frederick Douglass' Paper* (Rochester, New York), and *Douglass' Monthly*, gave extensive coverage to many aspects of Africa, including such issues as emigration and colonization, Liberia, Ethiopia, and the slave trade.[4]

In a speech given in the late 1850s, Mary Ann Shadd Cary, an orator and later editor of the *Provincial Freedom*, launched in March 1853, in Windsor, Canada West (two years later moved to Chatham, Canada West), commended European activities in Africa but observed that the white Europeans had adopted an attitude of "superiority" in establishing relations with Africans. Cary, who adhered to the idea of the necessity of "civilizing and Christianizing" Africa, insisted that it was the duty of Afro-Americans to aid Europeans in the "civilizing" of Africa. Cary, a self-imposed emigrant to Canada from 1851, until she returned to the United States at the close of the Civil War, was also the first black newspaper woman in North America. She believed that black Americans should maintain a relationship with Africa, if for no other reason than to safeguard their chances of emigration if the Europeans were ever to gain complete control of the continent. She could see that the domination of blacks in Africa would act as a rationale for the continued domination of blacks throughout the world. Therefore, she felt that Afro-Americans had a personal interest in the future of African "development" and growth because their status as a people was at stake.[5]

Afro-American religious leaders before 1880 also generally supported the idea of the European presence in Africa. Believing that European interests centered only around humanitarianism, these churchmen predicted that it would lead to the "Christianization" of Africans. Concerned with the evangelization of Africa, Afro-American religious leaders saw the presence of whites in Africa as a means that they would surely use to accomplish this end.[6]

One such individual was Richard Allen. In 1786, Allen along with Absalom Jones, founded the Free African Society, which later grew into the African Methodist Episcopal (AME) Church. In a speech given in 1817, Allen denounced the white American Colonization Society before an audience of 3,000 Philadelphians at Bethel Church. Thirteen years later, Allen started the first national movement for resettling free blacks in Canada. Although favoring Canadian emigration and serving as president of the Haitian Emigration Society, he was a foe of African colonization. Believing that the African "barbarians" needed to be "civilized," Allen praised the work of the Christian missionaries on the continent.[7] His comments about the Christianization of Africa suggest that he approved of the European "civilizing mission" there.

Prior to 1880, Alexander Crummell, Episcopal clergyman, educator, and founder of the American Negro Academy, was perhaps the strongest Afro-American supporter of the "civilizing" aspects of the European presence in Africa. Generally, Crummell was regarded by his contemporaries as the leading nineteenth-century black intellectual. He received the A.B. in 1853 from Queen's College, Cambridge, England, and went directly to Liberia, where he served as an Episcopalian missionary for twenty years. He became a close associate of Edward Wilmot Blyden, the West Indian-born Liberian intellectual who became a leading nineteenth-century proponent of the concepts of Pan-Africanism, the African personality, and Negritude. He also became Professor of Intellectual and Moral Philosophy and English Literature at Liberia College. Although Crummell and Henry Highland Garnet had been schoolmates together, upon his return to the United States in 1873, he rejected Garnet's scheme of emigration because of his unpleasant experiences in Liberia. He continued, however, to advocate racial solidarity and self-help and was proud of his pure black ancestry.

Crummell supported the "civilizing mission" concept almost in totality and acknowledged that missionaries from Europe and America who had gone to Africa for the "regeneration" of the continent had begun to take a greater hold.[8] He had a conception of Africa as a "dark" continent and believed that Christian "civilization" would save Africans from racial extermination. However, he advocated the establishment of a plan to provide protection for Africans under imperial rule.[9] Viewing the economic aspects of imperialism as exploitative, Crummell recollected that the history of European commercial development in Africa up to that date had been distressful and disruptive.[10] Crummell summarized the economic history of the European presence in Africa by stating that it was a history of rapine, murder, and widespread devastation of the African people. Despite these somewhat critical remarks concerning the economic motives of the Europeans in Africa, Crummell nevertheless exalted Victorian "civilization" and maintained that the Europeans would bring religious, social, and moral "development" to the continent.[11]

For twenty-two years, from 1873 to 1895, from his pulpit at St. Luke's Episcopal Church in Washington, D.C., Crummell exercised leadership over middle- and upper-class blacks and Afro-American intellectuals in their relation to Africa. Having spent twenty years in Africa, he had seen first-hand the problems that faced the continent and its people. He believed that the burden of responsibility for uplifting black people lay with the people themselves and that black Americans should "take up the white man's burden" in Africa. He felt, "It is the duty of black men to feel and labor for the salvation of the mighty millions of their kin all through this continent [Africa]."[12]

Both Crummell and another religious leader of this period, Henry McNeal Turner, an AME bishop and one of the most important black advocates of African emigration in the years between the Civil War and World War I, voiced the belief that it was the "duty," "destiny," and "obligation," of American blacks to aid Europeans in the "redemption" and growth of Africa. The two argued that the claim and call of "the land of their fathers" could not be rejected by Afro-Americans, and, hence, black Americans owed Africa their services. This theory of "providential design," popular among nineteenth-century, mission-minded Christians, taught that God had allowed Afro-Americans to be enslaved and "civilized" so they could return and redeem Africa.[13]

Black diplomats of this period also became interested in the events occurring in Africa and the possible future effects upon the continent. The first black Liberian minister, James Milton Turner, praised the European presence in Africa. Born a slave in St. Louis County, Missouri, Turner received his education at Oberlin College and founded

Lincoln Institute (later Lincoln University) in Missouri in 1866. In March of 1871, Turner was appointed the first black minister resident and consul general at Monrovia, Liberia, and served until May 1878. Like Crummell, his negative experiences in Liberia caused him to take a firm stand against emigration to Africa upon his return to the United States. Turner predicted that the European influence in Africa would result in the spread of religion, education, and commerce on the continent. Believing that "Westernization" would benefit Africa, Turner concluded that the European would "develop" Africa and make it over into a prosperous area like Europe and America.[14]

Finally, lesser-known Afro-Americans before 1880 also assessed the impact that the European presence could have on Africa. One decade after the founding of Liberia, an anonymous letter from a free black South Carolinian appeared in the *African Repository*, the official publication of the American Colonization Society, expressing the view that the European presence would have a positive impact on Africa. Believing in the "mission of civilization" in Africa, the writer portrayed the Europeans as "the heralds of the cross" in Africa and the purveyors of Western "civilization" and, thus, Western "advancement." Accordingly, since Europeans had been the first to call for the "salvation" and "redemption" of Africa, they offered hope to the Africans and to the "development" and growth of the African continent.[15] This writer, who may or may not have been reflecting the attitude of Southern free blacks, like many blacks during this period believed that European interests in Africa were only humanitarian. Also important was the fact that this writer supported black emigration to Africa. Since it was among lower-class blacks that we find antebellum emigration sentiment, possibly this individual echoed the opinions of this group toward European activity in Africa.

In discussing the presence of Europeans in Africa, the black author of another nameless article that appeared in the *San Francisco Elevator* declared that they would lift "the veil from hitherto darkened land." Nevertheless, while concluding that Africans would benefit from European activity in Africa, he regarded European intentions and interests there as more commercial than humanitarian or philanthropic.[16]

There were blacks before 1880 who did not support the European presence in Africa. They did not adhere to the idea that the Europeans would act as a positive force in the "development" of the continent. Although mistrusting European intentions, these militants also had a self-interest in Africa remaining independent from foreign control. At the meeting of the Colored National Convention in 1853 (the largest black national conference up to that time), held in Rochester, New York, the question of European activity in Africa received considerable attention. The participants concurred that since the Europeans had begun to colonize Africa, ethnic groups had been exterminated, Africans had been outlawed on their own continent, and their land had been taken from them. Viewing the economic aspect of the European presence, members of the convention declared that "the white man in the land of Ham had been cruel and rapacious." Throughout Africa, the European presence had brought disruption and disintegration, they charged.[17] In 1853, however, the impact of the European presence in Africa could hardly be ascertained.

James W. C. Pennington, Presbyterian minister and chairman of the Committee on Colonization, warned at this meeting, "Africa is destined to be the theatre of bloody conflict, between her native sons, and intruding foreigners . . . for a century to come." Pennington, an escaped slave, received the Doctor of Divinity degree from the University of Heidelberg (Germany) and served as pastor of the African Congregational Church in Hartford, Connecticut. He actively supported Garnet's African Civilization Society and African emigration. Pennington viewed all the activities of the Europeans in Africa as basically economic in nature and centered his opinions about their presence on the continent around the exploitative aspects.[18] The 1853 meeting and its declarations had no impact on European activity in Africa.

Henry Highland Garnet, abolitionist and black nationalist leader, maintained that Africa would surely be redeemed by Christian "civilization." However, he suggested, "The great work is to be chiefly achieved by the free and voluntary emigration of enterprising colored people." Garnet was an escaped slave who delighted in his royal African lineage and, following the publishing of his *Address to the Slaves* in 1843, second only to Douglass among recognized black leaders of antebellum America. Garnet had a varied career. He graduated from Oneida Institute in Whitesboro, Pennsylvania in

1840; assisted in the publication of the *Clarion* (Troy, New York), the *National Watchman* (Troy, New York), and the *Anglo-African* (New York City); served as a Presbyterian pastor in Washington, D.C., and New York; acted as president of Avery College in Pittsburgh; worked as a missionary to Jamaica; and, at the time of his death, was beginning his duties as minister to Liberia. Garnet was a cripple at the age of fifteen, and his leg was amputated when he was twenty-six, but he did not let this handicap interfere with his active life as a demonstrator for black rights. He declared his opposition to emigration in 1848, but ten years later, at the organizing meeting of the African Civilization Society, he supported it. The group, with Garnet as president, proposed a settlement of American blacks in the Niger area, currently Nigeria. According to a printed circular, its primary aim was "the Evangelization and Civilization of Africa, and the descendants of African ancestors wherever dispersed." Garnet's new stand on emigration was followed by a decade of proposals supporting emigration and programs designed to make it a reality. However, war in Yorubaland in May 1860 ended the society's efforts to settle immigrant cotton planters there. Garnet was unable to win the confidence of black leaders because they saw his programs as a call for mass migration to Africa. Douglass and other black intellectuals of the 1850s devoted their attention to economic and political conditions on the American scene. By 1864, Garnet had severed his connection with the white-supported African Civilization Society.[19]

In a speech delivered at Coopers' Institute in New York City in 1860, Garnet voiced the hope that as a result of "the diffusion of Gospel in Africa," "idolatry and superstition" would be overthrown, the African slave trade would be destroyed, and civil government by black men would be established.[20] In proposing the replacement of the illegal trade in African captives with legitimate trade, Garnet was unknowingly echoing the sentiment of the European imperialists. This idea of the need for developing indigenous trade was one of the arguments later used by Europeans as a justification for their presence and continued activity on the continent, and it became the basis of European colonialism.

Martin Robison Delany, antebellum abolitionist, editor, and physician, along with Robert Campbell, a West Indian chemistry teacher in the Philadelphia Institute for Colored Youth from 1855 to 1859, visited West Africa in 1859 to 1860 with the Niger Expedition. Dr. Delany was probably the best-known emigrationist before the Civil War. A Harvard University-trained physician, Delany dabbled in almost every profession. At one time or another in his life he was a dentist, orator, explorer, politician, and army officer, as well as a physician. Between 1843 and 1846, he published and edited a weekly paper, *The Mystery* (Pittsburgh, Pennsylvania), for a short time and helped Douglass with the editorial management of his papers, the *North Star* and *Frederick Douglass' Paper*. Delany was proud of his African heritage and proud of African people. He named all his children after famous black leaders. He was born free to parents who traced their ancestry to African chieftains, and he grew up with a great pride in all things black. He spoke of a "Negro Nationality" and coined the slogan "Africa for the Africans."

Delany and Garnet became rivals in an effort to explore the Niger area, and their African projects sometimes worked at cross purposes. Both men had opposed emigration early in their careers but came to see it as a legitimate alternative for black Americans. However, Delany's unwillingness to accept money from whites kept his programs in constant pecuniary distress. It was, in fact, Garnet's white-backed African Civilization Society which put up the necessary money to send Delany's companion, Robert Campbell, on the Niger Expedition.

Following the Cleveland meeting of the National Emigration Convention of Colored Men on 24 to 26 August 1854, where it was debated whether the condition of blacks could be worsened by emigration, Delany joined Cary and others in Chatham, Canada West (Ontario) in February of 1856, after twenty-five years in Pittsburgh, and remained there until 1864. This was his way of protesting American oppression.

Between 1854 and 1858, Delany and Theodore Holly, a Protestant Episcopal bishop, campaigned for a black empire in the American tropics. But as new interest in emigration began to center on a location in Africa, coupled with the 1858 decision of Garnet's African Civilization Society to settle in the Niger River area, and the fear that Garnet would be able to arouse the interest of the black community in his project, Delany transferred his efforts from the American tropics to Africa. At the third meeting of the convention, held in

Chatham, Delany demanded immediate and specific action on the issue of African emigration and was selected as a commissioner to explore a suitable area in Africa. He was also authorized to raise funds for this expedition. Like Garnet, Delany's objective in his exploring party was also to obtain land for black settlement where cotton could be grown to compete with the American southern market. His unwillingness to accept money from whites, his inability to collect the necessary funds from the black community, and his militant stance, which alienated both groups, got him into financial difficulties. In the end, Delany was forced to depend upon white philanthropy to finance his trip to West Africa and was unable to claim that the project was either totally black-controlled or black-financed.

In 1859, one year after the meeting, Delany and Campbell traveled to the Niger Valley in West Africa, where they remained until 1860.[21] Campbell, a native Jamaican, emigrated to Nigeria in 1862 and was active in cementing ties between Africans and Afro-Americans until his death in 1884.[22]

Delany believed that, although the Europeans had contributed to the Christianizing of the Africans, Africa should be left to the Africans. He saw black Americans as the only feasible salvation for African growth and "development." Delany's promulgation of the slogan "Africa for the Africans" before 1865 was later adopted by other disillusioned blacks who watched the European colonization and exploitation of Africa. Delany denounced colonialism almost twenty years before the official conference was held that led to the partitioning of Africa among the European powers. He supported *"Africa for the African race and black men to rule them."*[23]

One major event before 1880 that sparked some middle-class black American discussion about the widening European presence in Africa was the Brussels Conference in 1876. The Brussels Conference was the first formal event during the years before 1880, and it marked the beginning of the official scramble for Africa, which led to the eventual partitioning. In 1876, King Leopold II of Belgium invited a group of distinguished geographers, explorers, scientists, and philanthropists from Europe and America to a meeting at Brussels to discuss the methods by which equatorial Africa would be opened to European exploration and commerce. As a result of this first Brussels Conference, a formal organization was formed, the International Association for the Exploration and Civilization of Africa, also referred to as the International African Association. Based in Brussels, this group was essentially a Belgian organization. In October 1882, the name of the International African Association was changed to the International Association of the Congo, indicating the body's specific interests.[24]

Because of the narrow scope of the conference, wide international coverage was not given to this meeting. Consequently, only a few Americans were probably aware of this assemblage and its implications. Since the conference was held in the early years of the scramble for Africa, less emphasis has been given to it as a significant event. However, it was important in terms of its impact on the eventual partitioning of the continent, because it laid the groundwork for Leopold's later claim to the Congo basin area.

In an address before the American Geographical Society in New York on 22 May 1877, Crummell discussed Leopold's efforts in the Congo. Convinced that the efforts of the association were largely humanitarian, he asserted, "I have the deep conviction that this 'International' movement has its foundation in reasonable and thoughtful practicality."[25] British activities on the West African coast were commendable, according to Crummell, but Great Britain had lost a golden opportunity in not settling the interior. Hence, this task was assumed by the International African Association, and Leopold, as organizer of the association, exhibited intentions that appeared to be humanitarian. Crummell expected great results from the International African Association and affirmed that it would usher in the "regeneration" of Africa. Consistently critical of African culture, Crummell believed that the European presence in Africa would bring "civilization" to the African peoples, and he endorsed European religious, scientific, and adventurous activities on the continent.

George Washington Williams, who wrote the first published scholarly history of black Americans, also apparently endorsed the formation of the International African Association. Years after its establishment, Williams urged American recognition of the association. His views on the Congo and Africa generally were similar to those held by his contemporaries, and he traveled to Africa in 1890 to investigate the possibility of using college-trained blacks to staff governmental and commercial operations. In his first book, *History of the Negro Race in America*, Williams commented on the relationship that Afro-Americans should have with Africa. After blacks in America had been educated, he contended, they should turn their attention to the "civilization" of Africa. He believed that educated and skilled Afro-Americans would "civilize" Africa and that the continent would eventually be united under black rule, although he did not necessarily support mass emigration.[26]

Apparently, not all Afro-Americans regarded the activities of the association with favor. One letter to the editor of the *People's Advocate* (Washington, D.C.), a few years after the conference, expressed concern about European activities in Africa. The unidentified writer predicted that Africa would be exploited by the Europeans and described the continent as a land that had fallen victim to the rapacity of the European powers.[27] Despite these few sentiments, however, available evidence indicates that the black community gave less attention to the first Brussels Conference than to the events that followed.

Before 1880, various groups of Afro-Americans perceived the European presence in Africa with disparate perspectives. Some believed in the necessity of "civilizing" and "Christianizing" Africa, although they may have differed on how to achieve this objective. These blacks viewed the "civilizing mission" as encompassing many tenets, including religious and moral "uplift," as well as economic, commercial, social, cultural, educational, and political "development." Aside from this number, who echoed what whites were saying about Africa, racially motivated spokesmen denounced European "humanitarian" efforts as being primarily selfish. In the final analysis, it is almost impossible to distinguish what the majority of southern and northern free blacks, slaves, and later freedmen felt about the European presence in Africa before 1880. Aside from these middle- and working-class perceptions, the masses of blacks were either unaware of the events occurring in Africa, did not care, or continued to support emigration in spite of European activity.

Similarly, the masses of Europeans and white Americans viewed European expansion in Africa as dichotomous. Between 1880 and 1920, the empire builders in Europe formulated the justifications for their activities in Africa and evolved an argument for "progress" encompassing "the improvement of the human condition, and ulti-mately of man himself." Thus, Western "civilization" was "the cus-todian of Christianity" and "the dispenser of earthly salvation." But along with this humanitarian mission of "civilizing the backward peoples of the world" went the economic benefits the colonialists would gain. There was, as a British colonial administrator, Frederick Lugard, later asserted, a "dual mandate," that "the backward peoples owed to civilized society whatever natural bounties civiliza-tion required for its use, while the civilized world had an obligation to spread the blessings of progress among the barbarians."[28] To the imperialists, the civilizing process could be measured not in years but in generations or even centuries.

This was the argument used to justify imperialism by Europeans, and much of this same sentiment was held by their white American contemporaries. Americans also perpetuated the idea of the "super-iority of the white race," while at the same time pursuing their own selfish motives of imperialistic expansion into other areas of the world. There was, of course, anti-imperialist and anti-expansionist feeling on both sides of the ocean, but, in the end, white Americans, along with their European counterparts, realizing the economic benefits they could receive if they would "take up the white man's burden," forged ahead using the humanitarian goal as a pretense.

During the years between the American defeat of the North Afri-can Barbary states in 1830 and the convening of the Berlin West African Conference in 1884, American-African diplomacy was almost nonexistent, except for a few commercial treaties signed with several African powers or commercial and missionary activities in sections of the continent. American foreign policy, in general, was characterized by the isolationism advocated by George Washington, who in his famous Farewell Address warned against "permanent alliances" with foreign powers. America's African policy before 1880 paralleled its Far East policy in that it shied away from deep political involvement and instead allowed commercial and religious interests to prevail. Merchants and missionaries played leading roles in open-ing up Africa for the United States prior to 1880.[29]

The majority of literate black Americans, in formulating their per-spectives on the European presence in Africa before 1880 and European activity in Africa from 1880 to 1920, adopted the prevailing sentiments of the period. White Americans and Europeans constantly emphasized that it was the "manifest destiny" of black Americans to redeem Africa for Africans. Consequently, while before 1880 these blacks had begun to talk of their special duty and obligation to participate in the "civilizing mission" in Africa, during the years 1880 to 1920, a few assumed this duty, making Africa their "special mission."

Notes

1. Robert O. Collins, ed., *The Partition of Africa*, p. 1; and Lewis H. Gann and Peter Duignan, *Burden of Empire*, pp. 165, 170, 187, 191-92.

2. Robin Hallett, "Changing European Attitudes to Africa," pp. 490, 494-95.

3. John H. Franklin, *George Washington Williams and Africa*, pp. 14-15. This idea is also expressed by Badi G. Foster in "United States Foreign Policy Toward Africa," p. 49. See also, August Meier and Elliott Rudwick, *From Plantation to Ghetto*, p. 2; George Shepperson, "Notes on Negro American Influences on the Emergence of African Nationalism," p. 310; and Edwin S. Redkey, "The Meaning of Africa to Afro-Americans," p. 6.

4. See *North Star* (Rochester, New York), Editorial, "The Colonization Society," 25 August 1848; Editorial, "Liberian Colonization," 8 September 1848; and "Liberia and the Slavetrade [sic]," 29 September 1848. See also, "The African Colonization Society," *Frederick Douglass' Paper* (Rochester, New York), 8 July 1859; and *Douglass' Monthly*, Editorial, "Africa Recommended in Boston by H. H. Garnet" (October 1859), 151; Editorial, "The Republic of Liberia" (July 1861): 483; "The Future of Africa" (July 1862): 674; and "Letter from Rev. Alex. Crummell" (August 1862): 695.

5. Debate, "Reasons in Favor of Favoring the Scheme of African Civilization," n.d., Cary Papers (1).

6. Henry Allen Tupper, *Foreign Missions of the Southern Baptist Convention*, pp. 279-80.

7. Richard Allen, "Address to the Free People of Colour of These United States," p. 10.

8. Alexander Crummell, "The Progress of Civilization Along the West Coast of Africa," pp. 109-10. For a discussion of Edward Wilmot Blyden, see Hollis R. Lynch, *Edward Wilmot Blyden*.

9. John Henrik Clarke, "Africa and the American Negro Press," p. 65. See also, Kathleen Wahle, "Alexander Crummell," pp. 393-94.

10. Alexander Crummell, "The Regeneration of Africa," p. 436.

11. Alexander Crummell, Sermon, "The Progress and Prospects of Liberia," 9 May 1861, Crummell Papers (MSC 36).

12. Alexander Crummell to Charles B. Dunbar, 1 September 1860, "The Relations and Duties of Free Colored Men in America to Africa," in *The Future of Africa*, p. 257. Crummell saw this duty as a twofold process and discussed it in an earlier address in Liberia. See Alexander Crummell, *The Duty of a Rising Christian State to Contribute to the World's Well-Being and Civilization and the Means by Which It May Perform the Same*, pp. 7-11. See also, Wilson J. Moses, "Civilizing Missionary," pp. 229-43, 251; and William Toll, "Free Men, Freedmen, and Race," pp. 590-94.

13. See *African Repository*, Letter from Alexander Crummell, "The Call of Africa" (January 1872): 20-22; Alexander Crummell, "The Obligation of American Black Men for the Redemption of Africa" (February 1872): 55-61 (June 1872): 162-68, and (August 1872): 234-38. Turner made this point in "Duties and Destiny of the Negro Race," *African Repository* (September 1873): 282-83. Also consult Jacob Drachler, ed., *Black Homeland/Black Diaspora*, p. 6, for a discussion of this theory.

14. "Reception of the American Minister," *African Repository* (October 1871): 311.

15. Letter to the Editor, *African Repository* (October 1832): 241. The letter can also be found in Carter G. Woodson, ed., *The Mind of the Negro as Reflected in Letters Written During the Crisis, 1800-1860*, p. 7.

16. "Africa," *San Francisco Elevator*, 17 December 1869.

17. *Proceedings of the Colored National Convention*, 1853, p. 49.

18. J. W. C. Pennington, "Colonization Scheme," *Proceedings of the Colored National Convention*, 1853, pp. 55-56.

19. Joel Schor, *Henry Highland Garnet*, pp. 3-27; Sterling Stuckey, *The Ideological Origins of Black Nationalism*, p. 17; Martin R. Delany and Robert Campbell, *Search for a Place*, p. 7; and Hollis R. Lynch, "Pan-Negro Nationalism," p. 54. For a discussion of Garnet's role in the African Civilization Society, consult Richard K. MacMaster, "Henry Highland Garnet and the African Civilization Society," pp. 97, 104, 110-12.

20. Henry Highland Garnet, "Speech Delivered at Coopers' Institute, New York City, 1860," pp. 183-84.

21. Wilson Jeremiah Moses, *The Golden Age of Black Nationalism, 1850-1925*, pp. 35-36; Delany and Campbell, *Search for a Place*, pp. 13-16; and Martin Kilson and Adelaide Cromwell Hill, comps. and eds., *Apropos*

of Africa, pp. 5-6. See also, Howard H. Bell, "Negro Nationalism: A Factor in Emigration Projects 1858-1861," pp. 42, 42n, 43n; Inez Smith Reid, "Black Americans and Africa," pp. 654-55; and A. H. M. Kirk-Greene, "America in the Niger Valley," pp. 229-31.

22. Robert Campbell, *A Pilgrimage to My Motherland*, passim.

23. Martin R. Delany, *Official Report of the Niger Valley Exploring Party*, pp. 103, 107; Victor Ullman, *Martin R. Delany*, p. 221; and Howard Bell, *A Survey of the Negro Convention Movement, 1830-1861*, p. 241.

24. Jesse S. Reeves, *The International Beginning of the Congo Free State*, p. 17; Eric Rosenthal, *Stars and Stripes in Africa*, p. 155; Arthur B. Keith. *The Belgian Congo and the Berlin Act*, p. 33; Lewis H. Gann and Peter Duignan, *Burden of Empire*, p. 197; Josphat N. Karanja, "United States Attitude and Policy Toward the International African Association, 1876-1886," abstract and p. 9; and "The Opening of Africa," *Missionary Herald* 74 (March 1878): 88.

25. Alexander Crummell, "Address Before the American Geographical Society, On the King of Belgium's Congo State," 22 May 1877, pp. 313-15, 320-22.

26. George Washington Williams, *History of the Negro Race in America* 2: 552 and Franklin, *George Washington Williams and Africa*, p. 21.

27. Letter to the Editor, *People's Advocate* (Washington, D.C.), 16 August 1879.

28. David Healy, *US Expansionism*, pp. 12-33 and Frederick Lugard, *The Dual Mandate in British Tropical Africa*, p. 61.

29. Edward W. Chester, *Clash of Titans*, pp. 52, 113-15.

THE MEANING AND SIGNIFICANCE FOR BLACK AMERICANS OF THE SCRAMBLE AND PARTITIONING, 1880–1900

3

Let the [European] nations divide the continent of Africa and parcel it out, let them form colonial governments, . . . but after all this, as in the case of [the] America[n colonies] so will it be with Africa; they [the Europeans] owned all, now they own none; . . . their power [will be] broken.
A.M.E. Church Review (October 1894): 234-35.
Benjamin William Arnett, 1838-1906

There is a remarkable unanimity of feeling between the powers of Europe when a slice of Africa is the question.
Editorial note, *Indianapolis Freeman*, 21 March 1896.
George L. Knox, 1841-?

Africa is rapidly passing under the control of European powers.
"Letter From Africa," *Savannah Tribune*, 20 October 1894.
Alfred Lee Ridgel, ?-1896

Early nineteenth-century expansion and colonialism were the antecedents of the "new imperialism" that evolved in the late nineteenth century. In the last two decades of the nineteenth century this resurgent expansionist spirit resulted in the scramble for colonies by the major powers. By the end of the century, the idea that the world was divided between "civilized" and "uncivilized" peoples and that it was the responsibility of the "advanced" nations of the world to carry "civilization" to alien areas had been universally accepted. In his poem, "The White Man's Burden," first published in 1899, Rudyard Kipling fictionalized the philosophy of this period. European nations, motivated by nationalistic ambitions, commercial advantages, racism, and destiny, began their "assault on barbarism."[1] The period from about 1880 to 1920 has been labeled the age of the "white man's burden." These years closed with the partitioning of the world among the great powers.

By 1880, European imperialism in Africa had come to be identified with the concept of mission and trusteeship as "a sacred duty which a superior civilization contracts toward less advanced peoples." Africa was seen as new field for missionary work, in need of the "humanizing influences of Christian civilization," as well as an area ripe for economic exploitation. The scramble for and partitioning of Africa were inevitable consequences of the European powers' desire for overseas empires.[2]

Factors that historians have attributed to the origins of the scramble for Africa include: the beginning of diamond mining in South Africa in 1867; the opening of the Suez Canal in 1869; the British occupation of Egypt in 1882; Savorgnan de Brazza's treaties with Makoko in Gabon, West Africa, in 1882; the activities of King Leopold II of Belgium in the Congo Valley; and the entrance of Belgium and Germany into the African sphere. Although these are all possible causes, it appears that the scramble for and eventual partitioning of Africa resulted mainly from the fear that the balance of power among the major European nations in Africa would be destroyed by other minor countries entering the continent.[3]

For black Americans, the years between 1877 and 1900 were a transitional period between the full suffrage of the Reconstruction era and the total disfranchisement of the end of the century. These years saw the consolidation of white supremacy, as mainstream white

America finally united on the racial issue. There developed in the United States an attitude of white superiority, supported by the Social Darwinism concept of the cultural and social evolution of species. It slowly became clear that blacks in America were to be an inferior, dependent, nonpolitical, landless, and laboring class. By the beginning of the twentieth century, second-class citizenship was guaranteed for blacks,[4] and the more than occasional lynchings, disfranchisement, triumph of Jim Crowism, and consolidation of white supremacy cemented the black man's place in American society.[5]

Confronted by this rising tide of prejudice and discrimination, black Americans increasingly emphasized self-help, group loyalty, racial pride, and racial solidarity. They organized cultural societies, set up libraries and reading rooms, and promoted lecture bureaus, debating societies, and music and art clubs.[6]

In 1880, 70 percent of the black population was illiterate. By 1920, that figure had dropped to 22.9 percent. In 1920, the majority of blacks continued to live in the South.[7] Most of the college-educated blacks before 1920 were found in the professions as editors, journalists, educators, ministers, lawyers, physicians, and writers, and even that number was extremely small. As late as 1910, only 2.5 percent of employed southern blacks and 3 percent of northern blacks were in professions, and this number included many ministers and teachers who lacked even a high school education. Other members of the middle- and upper-class black community included farm owners, skilled artisans, agricultural and industrial workers, and self-made businessmen. Nevertheless, this small group played a crucial leadership role within the black community.[8]

As mentioned, the post-Reconstruction years found blacks abandoned by and disillusioned with the northern liberals who had promised equality with their victory in the Civil War. A number of lower- and middle-class blacks turned to Africa, considering emigration, offering sympathy to the Africans, and protesting the exploitative elements of the European presence there. Many saw the partitioning of Africa as another form of racial discrimination against blacks, and some, believing that Africa was in need of "civilization," felt that it was the duty and destiny of Afro-Americans to return to Africa to help in the "redemption" and "development" of the continent.[9]

After the Civil War, one of the major forces shaping the attitude of middle-class blacks towards Africa was the missionary tradition. White missionary societies, believing that Africans would be more receptive to Christianity brought by fellow blacks and that black missionaries could better withstand the African climate, practiced a kind of "missionary tokenism." Black American missionaries, in self-justification, helped to perpetuate a distorted impression of African life among black religious leaders and the multitude of black people. The masses of late nineteenth-century and early twentieth-century black Americans learned about Africa from church leaders and missionaries. Members of the Afro-American religious community concerned themselves with the collective missionary influence that Afro-Americans could have in Africa in cooperation with the Europeans.[10]

William T. Alexander, who emphasized racial pride and solidarity in his writings, noted in his *History of the Colored Race in America* (1887) that the religious community, in acknowledging their interest in Africa, believed that Africa's redemption would come from black people. So it was that through the strongest organization in the black community, the church, Afro-Americans maintained a link with the fatherland. Sometimes the tone of the relationship was patronizing, but it was always sincere, and it never had the imperialistic connotations of European missionary efforts.[11]

During the years of this study, religious leaders voiced various opinions about the role of blacks in the "civilizing and Christianizing" of Africa. Daniel Alexander Payne, senior bishop in the African Methodist Episcopal (AME) Church until his death in 1893, was against the efforts of the church during this period to take a more active role in shaping and influencing Africa's future.

Payne was devoted to black people, constantly arguing self-elevation. He joined the AME Church in 1841 and was ordained a bishop in 1852. The first president of a black university, Payne served Wilberforce University (Ohio) from 1863 to 1876. After his resignation, he became the AME Church historian and wrote the first history of the AME Church (*History of the African Methodist Episcopal Church*, 1891). When it was recommended to him that he go to Africa, Payne replied that he felt it his duty to labor for the salvation of his people in the United States. He did not endorse emigration to

Africa or anywhere else. Regarding the efforts of the church to bring Africa under its wing as comparable to the efforts of the Europeans to bring Africa under its control, he held in the mid-1880s that the AME Church's attempt to plant missions in Africa was "African Methodist imperialism."[12]

Reverend Benjamin F. Lee, editor of the AME *Christian Recorder*, noted in 1890 that the whole world was now interested in Africa. Lee claimed that the reasons for the interest were various, including desire for acquisition, satisfaction of a natural curiosity, the missionary zeal, and racial motivations. There was a great difference of opinion among Afro-Americans regarding methods for African "development," he contended, but at least blacks were beginning to take a greater interest in the "uplift" of the continent.

Lee constantly insisted that he was as concerned about Africa and its people as anybody else, but that he did not want to live there. He believed that for most Afro-Americans the United States would always be their home. He even suggested that all those who advocated emigration to Africa for others should go themselves. Lee, who had graduated from Wilberforce University in 1872 with an A.B., favored segregated institutions. From 1873 to 1875, he taught at Wilberforce and in 1876, assumed the position of president, after the resignation of Bishop Payne. He filled this office for eight years, until 1884, when the AME Church elected him editor of the *Christian Recorder*.[13]

In the August issue of 1893 *Voice of Missions*, Henry McNeal Turner, also of the AME Church, issued a call for a national convention of Afro-Americans to be held in Cincinnati in November of that year to discuss the worsening condition of blacks in America and the possibility of repatriation elsewhere. The *Indianapolis Freeman*, one of the most widely read black newspapers in the nation, asked for comments about the convention and emigration from black leaders. The results were published in the 25 November 1893 issue. Thirty-nine replies were published, of which only two uncategorically favored emigration as a solution to the racial problem, twenty-two categorically rejected emigration to Africa or elsewhere, and the remaining fifteen opposed any kind of forced mass exodus but agreed that qualified individuals could voluntarily go to Africa.[14] Black leaders and spokesmen basically had not changed their earlier attitudes about emigration to Africa according to the newspaper survey.

One respondent, Alfred Lee Ridgel, in an open letter to Turner from Freetown, Sierra Leone, urged "intelligent" emigration to Africa. He claimed that Africa was an inviting field for healthy, industrious, and economizing blacks and predicted that unless Afro-Americans embraced these opportunities to acquire wealth in Africa, Europeans and white Americans would seize them. Ridgel, an AME missionary in Liberia until his death from drowning in September of 1896, warned again in 1894 that, "Africa is rapidly passing under the control of European powers."[15]

On 14 August 1893, a congress on Africa convened in Chicago. The organizers hoped to create a sentiment for Africa and her people. Over one hundred papers were read by explorers, missionaries, scientists, anthropologists, and statesmen from Europe, America, and Africa. The World's Congress on Africa was held in conjunction with the Chicago World's Fair and sponsored by the American Missionary Association.[16]

On 11 September 1893, Benjamin William Arnett, bishop of the New York diocese of the AME Church, spoke at the meeting on "Africa and the Descendants of Africa." Arnett was active in Pennsylvania and Ohio politics and was widely regarded as President William McKinley's chief advisor on black appointments. He supported a self-help philosophy. He encouraged commercial relationships with Africa and limited emigration as a means of Christianizing the continent. Africa, though in the hands of Europeans, would one day be a continent ruled by blacks, Arnett declared. The European nations might divide Africa and parcel it out, but Africans would one day rule Africa; he believed that the "redemption" of Africa would depend upon Africans. Arnett perspicaciously saw European imperialism as a force which would drive Africans together to oust the imperial nations, but he did not go so far as to suggest that the Europeans leave.[17]

Turner also spoke at the World's Congress on Africa held in Chicago in 1893. He viewed the last years of the nineteenth century with pessimism and warned that Africa was the only hope for Afro-Americans.[18] Turner, although an advocate of European missionary and commercial activity in Africa, was against any kind of economic exploitation and optimistically maintained that the return of Afro-

Americans could alter the pattern of imperialistic development there. He remained adamant about his back-to-Africa stance until his death in 1915.

Alexander Crummell, rector of St. Luke's Church in Washington, D.C., gave considerable attention to the issue of foreigners in Africa until his death in 1898. After his return to the United States from Liberia in 1873, Crummell consistently addressed his sermons to the issue of the "regeneration" of Africa. In their quest for economic advantage, Europeans had marked their presence with piracy and bloodshed, he declared bitterly.[19] Crummell felt that Africa's "redemption" could not be brought about by white American and European missionaries in Africa. Although he believed that the "dark" continent had to be brought under the "civilizing" influence of the Christian world, he emphasized that "the sons of Africa themselves must be the agents of Christianity."[20]

Thus, by the end of the nineteenth century, the Afro-American religious community was adapting its attitudes toward the view that black Americans should also assume a "civilizing mission" rather than leave the duty entirely to Europeans. This attitude reflected the growing awareness of the exploitative nature of European imperialism in Africa and of a resulting concern that it be curbed.

By the 1880s, the Afro-American press had also begun to question the motives of Europeans in Africa. Never quite as optimistic as the religious community about European intentions in Africa, the press had reserved its judgment during the early years of the European scramble.

The late 1870s saw a revival of black newspapers; by 1880, forty-two black newspapers had been established. Armistead Pride has estimated that between 1865 and 1915, 1,976 Afro-American newspapers appeared, most of them for only a short period of time. The most widely read and influential of the black newspapers of the late nineteenth and early twentieth centuries were the *Colored Tribune* (4 December 1875-22 July 1876), changed to the *Savannah Tribune* (1876-1960), founded by John H. Deveaux; the *Chicago Conservator* (1878-1909), founded by Ferdinand Barnett; the consecutively published *New York Globe*, *New York Freeman*, *New York Age* (1881-1960), founded by T. Thomas Fortune; the *Washington Bee* (1883-1925), founded by W. Calvin Chase; the *Cleveland Gazette*

(1883-1945), founded by Harry C. Smith; the *Richmond Planet* (1884-1945), founded by John P. Mitchell, Jr.; and the *Indianapolis Freeman* (1888-1926), founded by E. E. Cooper, later bought by George L. Knox.

Newspapers were generally personal ventures, owned and published by one person. Not infrequently, the life of a paper coincided with the life of its owner-publisher, and its prosperity depended on his other sources of income to support the usually financially unsuccessful paper. What developed was a personal brand of journalism, with editorials sometimes reflecting the personal philosophy and prejudices of the articulate editor more so than general public opinion about an issue. Generally, black editors shared the prevailing Western views about Africa and Africans.

Although the vast majority of blacks (over 85 percent) before 1920 lived in the South, almost half of the newspapers (47 percent in 1910) were published in the North. The most profitable and prestigious papers were published in large urban areas. It was these papers that ventured into the discussion of foreign affairs. Most southern black papers were introduced into small communities with populations of 400 to 500. In parts of the South where illiteracy was high, lower-class blacks would gather in barber shops or other meeting places to hear the news read aloud. This helps to explain why there were many more illiterate blacks aware of African events than written documentation can support.

The black weeklies were limited in news content to blacks' racial struggle (this theme represented three-fifths of all articles) because of the lack of access to the news-gathering facilities available to the white press. The black papers were not admitted to membership in the Associated Press, and it was not until 1919 that Claude A. Barnet of Chicago organized the Associated Negro Press as a news-gathering press service. This accounts for the many reprint articles that appeared in black newspapers before this time. Nevertheless, because of their greater access to the news than the ordinary person, black newspaper editors and journalists many times helped to form public opinion on issues that many literate, middle-class blacks knew very little about, and thus the editors' views many times determined the perspective held by these blacks. Because of the high illiteracy rate among lower-class blacks well into the twentieth century, black editors may not have had as great an impact on the attitudes of this group.[21]

Timothy Thomas Fortune, editor consecutively of the *New York Globe, Freeman,* and *Age* (all published in New York City), saw Africa as the newest "find" of the European powers. Africa was being systematically colonized by the Europeans, Fortune asserted, and the Africans in Africa were doomed to extinction and subjugation. He argued that the only benefit the Europeans had brought to the continent was "European civilization." In reference to the impact that the Europeans had had in Africa up to that date, Fortune concluded, "European occupation and aggression are of too short duration . . . to enable anyone to draw a prognosis of the outcome of the issues."[22] Later, in the *A.M.E. Church Review* in 1892, Fortune contended, "European rule in Africa is no more advantageous than the rule of descendants of Europeans in the United States; and wherever the European goes in Africa, he subjects or exterminates the natives." Fortune depicted the Europeans as repressive to African growth.[23]

Fortune was the leading black journalist from 1881, when he made his bow as editor of *The Rumor* (New York City), until 1907, when he suffered a mental and physical breakdown and sold the *Age* to Fred R. Moore and Booker T. Washington. He described himself as racially conscious, but he was at the same time a conservative businessman, integrationist, and assimilationist. He was the leading late nineteenth-century promoter of the term "Afro-American." Throughout his career, Fortune rejected any proposal for emigration to Africa or elsewhere and frequently attacked Bishop Turner's emigration schemes.

But Fortune was not indifferent to Africa. He was deeply concerned about the exploitation of the continent by white colonial powers and during his years as editor wrote caustic anticolonial and anti-imperial editorials on the subject. But he also predicted that the ultimate "redemption" of Africa would come from its oppressors. He was receptive to proposals for missionary work in Africa. Interestingly, as early as 1896, Fortune suggested that the time was ripe for an "association of Africans and the descendants of Africa from all parts of the world," a Pan-African conference.

During the 1880s and the 1890s, Fortune represented the protest tradition. By the end of the nineteenth century, however, he had shifted from protest to accommodation, as he and the young black educational reformer, Booker T. Washington, developed a close relationship. The *Age* was never profitable, and Washington financially assisted the paper many times. Because of these monetary ties with Washington and his militant nature, Fortune was notoriously inconsistent. After selling the *Age* in 1907, Fortune, until his death in 1928, worked in various capacities for the *Philadelphia Tribune* (Pennsylvania), *Amsterdam News* (New York City), *Washington Sun* (Washington, D.C.), *Norfolk Journal and Guide* (Virginia), and, from 1923 to 1928, Marcus Garvey's *The Negro World*.[24]

In 1890, an article in the *Indianapolis Freeman* written by Henry Clay Gray of Montgomery, Texas warned that white men were parceling out Africa among themselves under false pretenses. The *Freeman*, later observing that the European whites were going to Africa in greater numbers, disclosed that Afro-American colonization in Africa was impossible because Great Britain, France, Germany, Belgium, Portugal, Spain, and Italy were omnipresent and ready to occupy all of Africa, by force of arms if necessary.[25]

In 1896, George Knox, editor of the *Freeman*, noted that the partitioning of Africa would soon cease to be a "mid-summer's night dream" and would quickly become a reality. He conceded that there was a remarkable unanimity of feeling among the Europeans when African territory was in question. By 1897, Knox was again warning that, "Africa [is] slipping away piece meal into the clutches of the landgrabbing countries." Knox predicted that the future of Africa was dismal. There was a war of extermination in the British colonies and rapine, plunder, and decimation in the Dutch, Portuguese, and French, he insisted.[26]

George L. Knox, editor of the *Freeman* from 1892 to 1926, was born a slave in Tennessee who went to Indiana during the Civil War and prospered as a barber. In the 1880s he became proprietor of a barber shop in a leading white hotel in Indianapolis with a staff of fourteen barbers, and his shop was considered one of the finest in the country. Although a champion of civil rights, Knox refused service to blacks in his barber shop, which he operated for whites. With his earnings from this enterprise, Knox bought the *Indianapolis Freeman* from E. E. Cooper in 1892. The *Freeman* regularly received small amounts of financial support from Booker T. Washington and subsidies from the Republican National Committee. Although the paper covered controversies over African affairs extensively, an article or editorial on Africa in almost every weekly issue, Knox, as editor, was extremely accommodating and conservative.[27]

At about the same time, John L. Waller, editor of the *American Citizen* and ex-consul to Madagascar, was predicting that within twenty-five years "all of Africa worth the having, will be in the hands of the European nations." Suspicious of European motives in Africa, he noted that all the discussion about "African evangelization" was simply "moonshine."[28] Waller's perspective, incidentally, was a reflection of his negative experiences with the European powers in Africa.

At the Congress on Africa, held under the auspices of the Stewart Missionary Foundation for Africa of the Methodist Church North's Gammon Theological Seminary from 13-15 December 1895, black and white leaders came together to discuss the future of Africa. The general purpose of the conference was to promote interest among American blacks for missionary work in Africa. Many of the participants had attended the World's Congress on Africa in 1893. Topics of discussion centered around the industrial, intellectual, moral, and spiritual "progress" of Africa.[29]

Journalists were particularly prominent at this conference. Fortune again expressed his concern about the economic exploitation of Africa by the white colonial powers. He warned that, if the trend continued, Africa would be completely under European control. Fortune, of course, adhered to the theory of the "civilizing mission" in Africa. Although he denounced some of the methods of the Europeans, he belonged to that group of Afro-Americans who felt that the colonization and Westernization of Africa would be beneficial to the people of that continent, and he continued to stress his allegiance to and desire to remain in the United States.[30]

Speaking at the congress on "The Methodist Episcopal Church and the Evangelization of Africa," Madison Charles Butler Mason, editor of the *Christian Educator* and assistant corresponding secretary of the Freedmen's Aid and Southern Education Society, concurred with Fortune's assessment of the European impact on Africa. Mason had graduated from New Orleans University, receiving the B.A. degree and later the M.A. In 1896, he was the first black elected corresponding secretary for the General Conference of the Methodist Episcopal Church. He held this position for sixteen years until 1912 when he was elected National Organizer of the National Association for the Advancement of Colored People (NAACP). Mason, like Fortune, was against emigration to Africa, also believing that America was the home of Afro-Americans. Echoing the sentiment toward Africa held by many of the black middle-class leaders of his time, he exclaimed, "not emigration, but evangelization."

However, Mason did maintain that Afro-Americans could not leave the "redemption" of Africa to others. "The burden, may I say the privilege, of African evangelization [is] upon the Negro." Commenting that Afro-Americans of all walks of life were beginning to recognize their relation to the evangelization of Africa, he disclosed, "I rejoice that a deep and increasing interest in the redemption of Africa is daily possessing the civilized Negroes of the world."[31]

At the same conference, E. W. S. Hammond, editor of the *Southwestern Christian Advocate* in New Orleans, the Methodist Church, North's publication, accused the European powers of seizing African territory from the Africans and leaving them "under a system of bondage far more appalling than the heathenism in which they were found."[32] Hammond, editor of the most accommodating of the church publications, was lending credence to the belief that Africans were "pagans" in need of the Christian influences of Western "civilization." This argument also didn't hurt the cause of missions in Africa and the continuing demand for more missionaries.

John H. Smyth, editor of *The Reformer* in Richmond, Virginia, and ex-minister to Liberia, spoke on "The African in Africa, and the African in America." According to Smyth, Europeans in Africa had brought "political disintegration, social anarchy, and moral and physical debasement." He alleged that the state of things in Africa was a result of the exploitative policy of Europe toward that continent. Declaring that the European explorers had not paved the way for "the blessings of civilization," Smyth held that destruction, rapine, and murder instead had characterized their activity there.[33]

Thus, the general consensus of the black journalists at this meeting was that exploitation had become the major concern of the Europeans in Africa, instead of their initial professed goal of "redeeming" the continent. Since there was little notice of the Congress on Africa outside of Atlanta, it can be assumed that the impact of the speeches was limited.

John Edward Bruce (pseudonym, Bruce Grit), a militant free-lance journalist and influential black leader, discussed European imperialism in many of his articles. During his lifetime, which spanned the latter career of Frederick Douglass, the age of Booker T. Washington, and the early years of W. E. B. Du Bois and Marcus Garvey, Bruce addressed himself to the black community and its problems. He was an editor before he was twenty-five and eventually edited three papers and wrote columns or articles for over twenty papers, working more than fifty years as a journalist. In 1884, Bruce began writing regular columns in the *Cleveland Gazette* and *New York Age* under the name given to him by Fortune, Bruce Grit ("grit" was a common slang word in the 1880s meaning courageous or resolute). From then on, Bruce was known to his audiences as Bruce Grit. His articles and editorials were reprinted in black newspapers across the country and in parts of Africa and Europe. Bruce also sub-scribed to overseas newspapers, including the *Lagos Weekly Record* (Nigeria), the *Sierra Leone Weekly News*, the *Gold Coast Aborigines*, and the *African Times* (London), in order to keep abreast of issues affecting blacks the world over.

Bruce is less well known than other journalists of this time because his entire life was devoted to black people. He ignored white America and therefore did not gain recognition in their circles. He criticized white hypocrisy, assailed intermarriage, espoused black political power and economic independence, and urged blacks to rejoice in their blackness and study their history. Bruce, along with his friend, Arthur A. Schomburg, Puerto Rican-born and collector of black literature, organized the Negro Society for Historical Research in 1911, to collect relics and facts related to black achievements. This society was the precursor of the Association for the Study of Negro Life and History, founded in 1915 by Carter G. Woodson.[34]

Africa always occupied a special place in Bruce's life. Bruce, like his associate Fortune, saw some advantages to European imperial-ism in Africa, specifically religious and economic "development." He encouraged Afro-Americans not only to "take up the white man's burden" of Christianization in Africa but also to join in African com-mercial investment.[35]

Several other race leaders before 1900 agreed with the assessment that Fortune and Bruce had made concerning the impact that European imperialism would have on Africa. They adhered to the "civilizing and Christianizing" theory and saw European imperialism as a justifiable method of accomplishing that end. Notable among these was Booker T. Washington, educator and acknowledged as the major black leader of this period.

Washington, a graduate of Hampton Institute, was appointed principal of Tuskegee Institute in 1881. After his famous Atlanta Compromise speech of 1895, he was heralded by whites as the spokesman for Afro-Americans. Washington shared Fortune's opposition to African emigration and also denounced Bishop Turner. He included Africa in his plans for the spread of industrial education but, like Bruce, also saw the continent as a profitable field for business development by blacks. Washington's conservatism was reflected in his attitudes toward Africa, and his encouragement of American investment on the continent helped to bolster the argument justifying colonialism. His perspective was obviously imitated by aspiring black leaders and disseminated by those leaders among the masses of black people. Black intellectuals adhered to Washington's view of Africa, although they disagreed with his educational philosophy.

Washington noted in the late nineteenth century that it was impossible to keep the European out of Africa because of the commercial advantages of settlement and control. All of Europe, especially Great Britain, France, and Germany, had been "running a mad race for the last twenty years, to see which could gobble up the greater part of Africa," he argued, and the tide could not be turned back. Washington advised that it was to the advantage of the African people to use European imperialism as a means of "uplifting" themselves and developing their resources.[36] Washington, involved in the early twentieth century in efforts for the economic "development" of Togo, Liberia, the Congo Free State, South Africa, and the Anglo-Egyptian Sudan and even in preliminary attempts in British East Africa (Kenya), helped shape a black middle-class view of Africa similar to that of the European colonists.[37]

Another educator, Charles Nelson Grandison, president of the Methodist Church North's Bennett College in Greensboro, North Carolina, viewed European efforts in Africa from a more pessimistic perspective than Washington. Grandison believed that the black man's destiny was in Africa. His long-cherished dream as the grandson of an African king was to found a Christian black republic in Africa. He felt that emigration was the only solution to the racial problem in the United States. When viewing the partitioning of Africa by the European powers, he grew desperate and began to fear that he would forever be "nothing but an American Negro," one of a helpless and despised people, unable to return to his fatherland. Grandison eventually resorted to drink, dying an alcoholic.[38]

In addition to the religious community, the journalistic community, and educators, other blacks pondered the implications of the European scramble and partitioning of Africa. David Augustus Straker, a distinguished Detroit attorney, commented on the possible impact of European colonialism in Africa.

Judge Straker was the most distinguished black man in Detroit during the late nineteenth and early twentieth centuries. He had been born free in Barbados, West Indies and had come to the United States in 1868. In 1870, he entered the law school of Howard University (Washington, D.C.), graduating the next year, in 1871. Among his classmates were John H. Smyth, later minister to Liberia. In 1876, Straker was elected to the South Carolina legislature. Actually, he was elected three times and each time denied his seat. As an alternative to politics, he formed a law partnership with Robert Brown Elliot and T. McCants Stewart. In 1882, he became dean and professor of law at Allen University in Columbia, South Carolina. Later, in 1887, he moved to Detroit. Straker encouraged racial pride and unity. He attended the 1899 preparatory session and the Pan-African Conference of 1900 and, in fact, was one of the leading men consulted by Henry Sylvester Williams before the conference.

In a series of articles entitled "The Land of Our Fathers," Straker asserted that the sudden interest that the "civilized" powers had taken in the "improvement" of Africa should be of no small concern to Afro-Americans, for these nations were about to reap economic benefits from African resources. Concerned with fairness to Africans, Straker feared that the Europeans would have a negative impact in Africa because of the prevailing Anglo-Saxon attitude of superiority over black people.

Yet, Straker was optimistic about the "development" of Africa.

He urged American blacks to assume their duty and return to Africa to help in its growth. Afro-Americans should not be strangers in their fathers' land, Straker insisted. Throughout this period and until his death in 1908, Straker held out the hope that the activities of whites in Africa would lead to that continent's "advancement."[39]

Archibald Henry Grimke, a Boston attorney who during the late nineteenth century was a strong anti-Bookerite, shared Washington's perspective on the European scramble for and partitioning of Africa. While agreeing with Washington's assessment of the future impact of European imperialism in Africa, Grimke also believed that the influence of Western "civilization" upon Africa would have the effect of "developing" the principle of racial unity and nationality in Africa. Assuming that unity and nationality did not exist in Africa before the coming of the Europeans, Grimke maintained,

> It is the seed of African and Christian brotherhood, ay, human brotherhood if you please, that the West is to plant in the dark bosom of darkest Africa, in spite of the white man's prejudice. The Anglo-Saxon, the German, the French, the Belgian, with their genius for organization, must begin the great work of organizing the African tribes into national units. This is the first step in the redemption of Africa.[40]

Thus, Grimke, like other prominent Afro-Americans, believed in the "civilizing mission" concept and felt that black Americans should help in the "development" of the continent.

Grimke was graduated from Lincoln University with an A.M. in 1870 and Harvard Law School in 1874. He served as consul at Santo Domingo from 1894 to 1898 under President Grover Cleveland's second administration. The first president of the Boston Literary and Historical Association (founded in March 1901), he was also president of the American Negro Academy from 1903 to 1916. During the 1890s, Grimke was one of the best-known and most widely respected of the "Boston radicals" and anti-Bookerites, but by 1905 he had moved into the Tuskegee camp. Still, his views on Africa differed little from those of Washington.[41]

Ida B. Wells-Barnett, noted antilynching crusader, black leader, and editor of the *Chicago Conservator* from 1895 to 1897, took exception to the late nineteenth-century pessimistic forecast of Africa's future. Wells-Barnett favored emigration to Africa for all those who wished to and were able to go. The white Europeans should not be the only ones to reap economic benefits from Africa, she announced. Afro-Americans could also profit by returning to Africa and helping to "develop" the continent.[42] Like Turner, Fortune, Bruce, and Washington, Wells-Barnett supported American commercial investment in Africa.

Finally, black literary and historical societies were also concerned with African events, although there were few debates over the impact of European imperialism there. Among the black cultural organizations established before 1900 were the Society for the Collection of Negro Folk Lore, formed in 1890 in Boston; the Negro Historical Society of Philadelphia, organized in 1897; and the American Negro Academy, also founded in 1897. All of these groups were a part of the black history and protest movement of the late nineteenth century designed to promote dignity and racial pride against insults and to challenge racism and prevailing white notions of black inferiority.[43]

Of the many societies that sprang up in cities all over the country as forums of black expression, best-known and best-documented was the Bethel Literary and Historical Society, organized by Bishop Payne in Bethel Hall, Metropolitan AME Church, in Washington, D.C. on 9 November 1881. The society opened its first meeting with a paper on "Who Were the Ancient Egyptians and What Did They Accomplish?" Papers read at subsequent meetings in 1881 discussed "Are the Present Inhabitants of Egypt Identical With the Ancient Egyptians?" "The Ethiopians—Who Were They?" and "What Causes Are in Operation for the Redemption of Egypt?" At the fourth meeting of the society in late 1881, Reverend R. M. Cheeks presented a paper on "The Racial Connection of the Zulus." After his speech, Robert J. Smith, first president of the organization, expressed sympathy for the Zulus, who had been defeated in 1879. Smith described the Zulus, who were attempting to limit the expansion of the British imperialists, as courageous defenders of their country. He reported that, in spite of their loss, the Zulus had outstripped the British in their military tactics. Smith aroused the audience with his descriptions of the Zulus' bravery and skill in this war. John H. Smyth spoke in 1882 on "African Experiences." During the year

1892-93, one Bostonian commentator observed that American blacks were not qualified to engage in either African emigration or evangelization because of their lack of knowledge of the events presently occurring on the continent, probably referring to the European partitioning. In the thirteenth year, 1893-1894, Alexander Crummell read a paper on "The Relations of the Scriptures to Africa." The society, it seems, tended to focus more on the relationship of Afro-Americans to ancient Africa than on the question of current European activities there.[44]

By the end of the nineteenth century, black Americans were beginning to express their discontent with European imperialism in Africa. In the early years of the scramble, most blacks had wholeheartedly supported most of the elements of the "civilizing mission" in Africa and had perceived of the European partitioning as helping in the "development" of the continent. However, by the end of the century, more blacks were beginning to question whether the advantages of colonialism really outweighed the disadvantages. Slowly, imperialism was becoming identified with exploitation and discrimination. Undoubtedly contributing to the black perspective on European imperialism in Africa was black reaction to American imperialism in the Philippines.

As a result of the Spanish-American War in 1898, blacks began to distinguish between the "rhetoric" and the "realities" of imperialism. Initially, they viewed the efforts of the United States in the war much as they had viewed the early intentions of the Europeans in Africa; they saw Americans spreading "civilization" among the peoples of Cuba, the Philippines, and the other areas under Spanish rule. Black troops, supported by the majority of the black population, traveled to Cuba and the Philippines to "take up the white man's burden." However, as was the case with Europeans in Africa, by late 1899, blacks began to question Americans' professed intentions for involvement in the war.

From the beginning of the war, the Afro-American community was divided about endorsement of American participation. E. E. Cooper, editor of the Colored American, came out early in support of American involvement, but he immediately differentiated between "expansion," which gave commercial advantages to the United States and took "civilization" to the peoples of the Spanish colonies, and "imperialism," which consisted of forcible annexation of territory. Throughout the war, Cooper remained confident that positive advantages would come from the war, not only for the Spanish colonies but also for blacks in the United States.

Other editors of black newspapers were not so optimistic as Cooper about the impact of American imperialism. T. Thomas Fortune of the *New York Age*, Harry C. Smith of the *Cleveland Gazette*, W. Calvin Chase of the *Washington Bee*, and John P. Mitchell of the *Richmond Planet* were all reluctant to give their complete support to America's imperialistic venture. Afro-American support of imperialism would depend upon the adjustments made in American society toward distribution of equality for all, they insisted.

Black leaders' perspectives varied from acceptance to rejection of American imperialism. Bishop Turner, for example, contended that blacks would gain nothing from fighting in the war and claimed that disloyalty would be better than participating in a war where only whites would benefit. Similarly, Washington believed that the people of the Philippines should be given an opportunity to govern themselves and voiced the opinion that "until our nation has settled the Indian and Negro problems, I do not think we have a right to assume more social problems."

Black attitudes toward the cause of American expansion thus changed from "reluctant acceptance" to "belligerent opposition." Fortune, who visited the insular possessions in 1903 as special commissioner investigating possible black emigration to these areas, returned to the United States to an unresponsive black community that had decided to remain and fight their battle in America.

Considering their inferior position in American society at the end of the century, it was not surprising that Afro-Americans responded favorably to American imperialism initially because of their belief that this humanitarian spirit would have reverberations within this country. Blacks viewed American and European imperialism from a more personal perspective than did whites. By the beginning of the twentieth century, however, blacks had come to view imperialism, both the American and European kind, as only another element in the ideology of white supremacy.[45]

Black Americans were forced to make a choice in the election of 1900 between the white supremacist Democratic party, which was rapidly disfranchising them in the South, and the Republican party, which had become the party of imperialism. The leader of the Republican party, Theodore Roosevelt, carried racial ambivalences toward black Americans. The policies of Roosevelt's presidential administration witnessed—and actually encouraged—a decline in the status of black Americans.[46]

Black Americans were thus ripe for the more encouraging events to follow. The twentieth century was inaugurated by a conference that culminated nineteenth-century Pan-African thought. The meeting laid the foundation for the pattern of activity that was to characterize black involvement and interest in Africa during the first half of the twentieth century. This gathering was the Pan-African Conference of 1900. Pan-Africanism rested upon the belief that all peoples of African descent had a common cultural root and should work together in the struggle for their freedom. Henry Sylvester Williams, a Trinidadian student, and Alexander Walters, a bishop of the African Methodist Episcopal Zion (AMEZ) Church, organized and called the Pan-African Conference.

Williams was a law student at Gray's Inn in London. Three years earlier he had organized the African Association in London. Williams contacted several Afro-American leaders concerning "the greatest gathering our race as a people has ever witnessed." He wrote Washington, who, along with Bishop Turner, Judge Straker, and Professor William Scarborough, had attended the preliminary conference held in London on 12 June 1899, asking him to influence others to attend the meeting. Washington encouraged black attendance, declaring, "I beg and advise as many of our people as can possibly do so, to attend this conference. In my opinion it is going to be one of the most effective and far-reaching gatherings that has ever been held in connection with the development of the race."[47] Walters, who with Fortune had founded the Afro-American Council in 1898, and had been elected its first president, had become minister of one of the largest churches of the AMEZ Church in 1888. He encouraged missionary activities in Africa but opposed wholesale emigration.[48]

The Pan-African Conference was held in London, 23 to 25 July 1900, at Westminister Hall, with the objectives of bringing the peoples of African descent into closer contact with one another and starting a movement for securing full rights for all African peoples.

The conference was called at this time because some blacks were present at the Paris Exposition, which began in April of 1900, and others had just attended the second annual World Christian Endeavour Conference in London, and were therefore already in Europe. Thirty-one or thirty-two persons attended the meeting: twelve or thirteen from the United States; ten from the West Indies; three from Great Britain; and one each from Canada, Haiti, the Gold Coast, Liberia, Sierra Leone, and Nigeria.[49]

At this Pan-African meeting, appeals were made to the nations of the world, particularly the European powers, that they consider the welfare of the colonial peoples in their drive for Africa's economic exploitation. W. E. B. Du Bois, chairman of the Committee on the Address to the Nations of the World, explained that it was important that Africans not lose their identity because of European rule. In the address, Du Bois asked the Europeans to remember that "the true worth of colonies lies in their prosperity and progress, that justice, impartial alike to black and white, is the first element of prosperity" and that a colonial power was counted "not simply in cash and commerce, but in the happiness and true advancement of its black people." He also put forth the idea in the address that the Europeans should give "as soon as practicable, the rights of responsible government to the black countries of Africa." Du Bois concluded, "Let not the cloak of Christian missionary enterprise be allowed in the future, as so often in the past, to hide the ruthless economic exploitation and political downfall of less developed nations, whose chief fault has been reliance on the plighted faith of the Christian Church."[50]

Walters suggested that the concern in Africa should be "to civilize and Christianize heathen Africa." The Pan-African Conference and the Afro-American Council could be helpful in bringing about this result, as well as contributing to the "amelioration of the conditions of Africans," he maintained.[51] Williams condemned British rule in South Africa and accused the government there, embroiled in a war with the Boers, of mistreating the Africans.[52]

As a result of this conference, a memorial was prepared and sent to Queen Victoria condemning the acts of injustices committed against Africans in South Africa. In addition, the Address to the Nations of the World was sent to all the European powers engaged in activity in Africa.[53] Bishop Walters was elected president, to serve for two years. Du Bois was elected vice president for America, and Williams was elected general secretary. Frederick J. Loudin, S. Coleridge Taylor, and Anna J. Cooper, all of the United States, were among those elected to the executive committee. The African Association, founded earlier by Williams, was merged with the new Pan-African Association. The conferees agreed that the association would convene every second year in some large city in Europe, America, or an independent black state. The next meeting was to be held in the United States in 1902.[54]

Although the words of the conference were bold, the results were more symbolic than real. The second meeting was never held. Williams began practicing law in London in 1902; in 1903 he emigrated to South Africa returning to London in 1906; finally, in 1908 he returned to Trinidad to practice law, but late in 1910 he was struck down by a severe kidney ailment and died in March of 1911. Walters and Du Bois returned to the United States and began to concentrate their energies in other areas. Both were prominent in the Niagara Movement and the founding of the NAACP. Walters died in 1917. It was left to Du Bois to pick up the banner of Pan-Africanism and carry it to greater heights. This he did in the revival of the Pan-African meetings with the calling of the Pan-African Congress of 1919, and the subsequent meetings of 1921, 1923, 1927, and 1945.

From 1880 to 1920, most American contacts with Africa were unofficial. During the scramble for and partitioning of African territory by the European powers, the United States neither sought colonies for itself nor objected to European colonization. The U.S. government did not become involved in the partitioning because traditional American foreign policy forbade involvement in European political questions and because it had no economic interest in Africa. Official government relations continued to be limited until midway into the twentieth century, and it was not until after World War II that the United States evolved a foreign policy for the African continent as a whole. Before this date, the government assumed unofficial paternal protection of Liberia, established irregular consulate services in African seaports to protect American missionaries and business interests, signed several treaties with individual countries, and endorsed two commercial treaties with Ethiopia granting extraterritorial rights.[55] Compounding this equivocal relationship with Africa was America's austere discrimination against its own black citizens.

Ambivalence about Africa was also characteristic of most black commentators on the African scene during the years before 1900. Regardless of their role in the black community, whether religious leaders, secular leaders, back-to-Africa supporters, journalists, visitors to Africa, educators, or diplomats, black Americans in the early years of the scramble for and partitioning of Africa believed that Africa needed to be "developed." Most also believed that Afro-Americans should play a role in this "civilizing" process. However, black Americans differed in how they perceived European intentions in Africa. Some adhered to the "civilizing mission" concept, while others viewed European interests as purely and selfishly economic. Afro-Americans regarded trade and economic "improvement" as well as religious, educational, social, and political "development" as instruments of the "civilizing mission." These blacks, like their white counterparts, felt that the Europeans in Africa would develop legitimate indigenous trade and commercial activities to replace the illegal traffic in African captives and liquor. Many felt that blacks themselves should "take up the white man's burden" in Africa. Aspects of this "burden" involved the religious, educational, cultural, social, and political "development" of the continent. Yet these black spokesmen understood that the "burden" defined by whites had racist connotations. Most middle-class blacks of the late nineteenth century saw the "redemption" and Westernization of Africa as their "special mission." This attitude was another manifestation of the universal black brotherhood theme prevalent during this period and present in earlier years.[56]

By 1900, articulate members of the black community began to differentiate between European colonialism in the various regions of Africa and began to assess the impact the individual European nations were having on the continent. For example, blacks could support colonial rule in one area of Africa and reject it in another. Although Afro-Americans could debate the actual role of Europeans in Africa or the effect they were having on the continent, they all came to realize that the European was on the continent of Africa to stay.

Notes

1. Rubin Weston, *Racism in U.S. Imperialism*, p. 5; David Healy, *US Expansionism*, pp. 12, 16, 18, 129; James O'Conner, "The Meaning of Economic Imperialism," p. 101; and Magubane, "The American Negro's Conception of Africa," pp. 47, 51, 54.

2. Robert O. Collins, *The Partition of Africa*, p. 5; Lewis H. Gann and Peter Duignan, *Burden of Empire*, pp. 34-35, 208; and "American Missions in Africa," *Missionary Herald* 72 (April 1876): 110-11.

3. Roland Oliver and John Fage, *A Short History of Africa*, pp. 182-84; Collins, *The Partition of Africa*, p. 6; and Gann and Duignan, *Burden of Empire*, pp. 195-96.

4. Rayford W. Logan, *The Betrayal of the Negro*, pp. 23, 105; George M. Fredrickson, *The Black Image in the White Mind*, pp. 201, 254, 325; Stanley P. Hirshson, *Farewell to the Bloody Shirt*, pp. 251-58; Lewis H. Carlson and George A. Colburn, eds., *In Their Place*, p. 57; and Edwin S. Redkey, *Black Exodus*, p. 2.

5. C. Vann Woodward, *The Strange Career of Jim Crow*, p. 7; and Robert G. Weisbord, *Ebony Kinship*, p. 27. Between 1889 and 1918, 3,224 persons were killed by lynching mobs; 702 whites and 2,522 blacks (2,472 men and 50 women). See National Association for the Advancement of Colored People, *Thirty Years of Lynching in the United States, 1889-1918*, pp. 7, 29.

6. *The American Negro Academy Occasional Papers*, p. 1.

7. U.S., Department of Commerce, Bureau of the Census, *Negro Population, 1790-1915*, pp. 33, 404, and *Negroes in the United States, 1920-1932*, pp. 14, 231. In 1880, 90.5 percent of the black population lived in the South. This had only declined to 85.2 percent by 1920. See also Arnold M. Taylor, *Travail and Triumph*, p. 126.

8. Sidney Kronus, *The Black Middle Class*, pp. 2-3; Harold Cruse, *The Crisis of the Negro Intellectual*, p. 4; Taylor, *Travail and Triumph*, pp. 185-88, 194; August Meier, *Negro Thought*, p. 207; Wilson Jeremiah Moses, *The Golden Age of Black Nationalism*, p. 29; and August Meier, "Negro Class Structure and Ideology in the Age of Booker T. Washington," pp. 260, 265-66.

9. J. Abramowitz, "Crossroads of Negro Thought," p. 117; Willard B. Gatewood, Jr., "A Negro Editor on Imperialism," p. 43; and Robert Weisbord, "Africa, Africans, and the Afro-American," p. 307.

10. Jacob Drachler, ed., *Black Homeland/Black Diaspora*, p. 5; and Weisbord, "Africa, Africans, and the Afro-American," p. 307.

11. William T. Alexander, *History of the Colored Race in America*, pp. 530-31; and St. Clair Drake, "The American Negro's Reaction to Africa," p. 13.

12. Josephus R. Coan, *Daniel Alexander Payne Christian Educator*, p. 113.

13. Redkey, *Black Exodus*, pp. 68-69; and Editorial, "Africa and the Afro-Americans," *Christian Recorder*, 24 April 1890.

14. Redkey, *Black Exodus*, pp. 184-85; and Letters to the Editor, *Indianapolis Freeman*, 25 November 1893.

15. Rev. A. L. Ridgel, "An Open Letter to Bishop H. M. Turner," *Indianapolis Freeman*, 25 November 1893; and "Letter from Africa," *Savannah Tribune*, 20 October 1894. See also, "How Ridgel Was Drowned," *Voice of Missions* (December 1896): 2.

16. Frederick Perry Noble, "Africa at the Columbian Exposition," *Our Day* 9 (November 1892): 786-88; Frederick Perry Noble, "The Chicago Congress of Africa," *Our Day* 12 (October 1893): 279-81, 299; and Editorial, "The African Congress," *Voice of Missions* (October 1893): 2.

17. Edwin S. Redkey, "The Meaning of Africa to Afro-Americans," pp. 15, 23; and "Africa and the Descendants of Africa," *A.M.E. Church Review* 11 (October 1894): 233-35.

18. Redkey, *Respect Black*, p. 167; Willard B. Gatewood, Jr., "Black Americans and the Quest for Empire, 1898-1903," p. 549; and Weisbord, "Africa, Africans, and the Afro-American," p. 310.

19. Alexander Crummell, Sermon, "The Regeneration of Africa," n.d., Crummell Papers (MSC 33); and Alexander Crummell, Sermon, "Gospel Missions Are the Only Hope of the Heathen of Africa," n.d., Crummell Papers (MSC 363).

20. Alexander Crummell, Sermon, "How Shall Africa be Redeemed," n.d., Crummell Papers (MSC 393).

21. Frederick German Detweiler, *The Negro Press in the United States*, pp. 53, 82; and Emma Lou Thornbrough, "American Negro Newspapers, 1880-1914," pp. 468-69, 471, 473, 476, 486-87.

22. Editorial, "An African Empire," *New York Freeman* (New York City), 15 January 1887; and Editorial, "The Future of the African Continent," *New York Age* (New York City), 21 July 1888.

23. T. Thomas Fortune, "Will the Afro-American Return to Africa," *A.M.E. Church Review* 9 (April 1892): 289.

24. Emma Lou Thornbrough, *T. Thomas Fortune*, pp. 131-32, 141-45; and William Toll, "Free Men, Freedmen, and Race," pp. 584-87. For Fortune's views on emigration, see *Black and White*, pp. 121-22, 143.

25. See *Indianapolis Freeman*, Henry Clay Gray, "Africa or America, Which?" 4 January 1890; "Will Gobble Africa Sure," 1 July 1893; and "Against the Bishop's Idea," 18 November 1893.

26. See *Indianapolis Freeman*, Editorial note, 14 March 1896; Editorial note, 21 March 1896; and Editorial, "Africa's View of the American Negro in Politics," 17 July 1897.

27. Emma Lou Thornbrough, *The Negro in Indiana*, pp. 264-65, 360-61, 387. See also, Willard B. Gatewood, Jr.'s biography of George L. Knox, *Slave & Freeman; The Autobiography of George L. Knox*.

28. Editorial, "All Moonshine African Evangelization," *American Citizen* (Kansas City, Kansas), 8 January 1897.

29. J. W. E. Bowen, ed., *Africa and the American Negro*, pp. 9-10. See Editorial, "Congress on Africa," *Savannah Tribune*, 7 December 1895, for announcement of the upcoming meeting.

30. T. Thomas Fortune, "The Nationalization of Africa," in *Africa and the American Negro*, pp. 200-1; Thornbrough, *T. Thomas Fortune*, pp. 144-46; and Walter L. Williams, "Black American Attitudes Towards Africa, 1877-1900," p. 181.

31. M. C. B. Mason, "The Methodist Episcopal Church and the Evangelization of Africa," in *Africa and the American Negro*, pp. 143, 145; and idem, *Solving the Problem*, pp. 10-11, 138.

32. E. W. S. Hammond, "Africa in Its Relation to Christian Civilization," in *Africa and the American Negro*, p. 205.

33. John H. Smyth, "The African in Africa, and the African in America," in *Africa and the American Negro*, p. 74.

34. Peter Gilbert, comp. and ed., *The Selected Writings of John Edward Bruce*, pp. 1-9; and Inez Smith Reid, "Black Americans and Africa," p. 657.

35. Walter L. Williams, "Black Journalism's Opinions About Africa During the Late Nineteenth Century," p. 229; and Redkey, "The Meaning of Africa to Afro-Americans," p. 23.

36. Booker T. Washington, *The Future of the American Negro*, pp. 159-60. See also Thornbrough, *T. Thomas Fortune*, pp. 133, 156-61; and Martin Kilson and Adelaide Cromwell Hill, comps. and eds., *Apropos of Africa*, pp. 125-26.

37. William B. Helmreich, comp., *Afro-Americans and Africa*, p. xvi; Louis R. Harlan, "Booker T. Washington and the White Man's Burden," pp. 441-42, 467.

38. James D. Corrothers, *In Spite of the Handicap*, p. 116.

39. D. Augustus Straker, "The Land of Our Fathers," *New York Freeman*. This three-part article is found in three issues: 23 January 1886, 30

January 1886, and 6 February 1886. See also, "The Congo Valley: Its Redemption," *A.M.E. Church Review* 2 (January 1886): 148. For a discussion of Straker's life, see Obituary, *Cleveland Gazette* (Ohio), 29 February 1908.

40. Archibald Grimke, "The Opening Up of Africa," pp. 17-19, Grimke Papers (24). This article can also be found in *The New Deal*, pp. 355-56.

41. Stephen R. Fox, *The Guardian of Boston*, pp. 14, 28, 43.

42. I. B. Wells, "Afro-Americans and Africa," *A.M.E. Church Review* 9 (July 1892): 42.

43. *American Negro Academy Occasional Papers*, pp. 1-11.

44. J. W. Cromwell, "History of the Bethel Literary and Historical Association," pp. 3-5, 8, 22-23.

45. Willard B. Gatewood Jr., *Black Americans and the White Man's Burden, 1898-1903*, pp. x, 321; George P. Marks, III, *The Black Press Views American Imperialism*, pp. 100-1, 172-73; and Gatewood, "Black Americans and the Quest for Empire," passim.

46. Marks, *The Black Press Views American Imperialism*, p. 172 and James E. Haney, "Theodore Roosevelt and Afro-Americans, 1901-1912," pp. iii-iv, vi, 263, 266.

47. Henry Sylvester Williams to Booker T. Washington, 29 June 1900, Washington Papers (187); and Immanuel Geiss, *The Pan-African Movement*, pp. 180-81.

48. Alexander Walters, *My Life and Work*, passim.

49. Ibid., pp. 253-55; Geiss, *The Pan-African Movement*, pp. 181-82; Redkey, *The Meaning of Africa to Afro-Americans*, p. 22; Clarence G. Contee, "The Emergence of Du Bois as an African Nationalist," pp. 48-49, 51, 53, 59; John A. Davis, "Black Americans and United States Policy Toward Africa," pp. 238-39; and "The First Pan-African Conference of the World," *Colored American Magazine* (September 1900): 223-31.

50. Walters, *My Life and Work*, p. 259; and W. E. B. Du Bois, *An ABC of Color*, pp. 22-23.

51. Walters, *My Life and Work*, pp. 172, 262.

52. Clarence G. Contee, *Henry Sylvester Williams and Origins of Organizational Pan-Africanism, 1897-1902*, pp. 13-15.

53. Ibid.; and Walters, *My Life and Work*, pp. 256-57.

54. Owen Charles Mathurin, *Henry Sylvester Williams and the Origins of the Pan-African Movement, 1869-1911*, pp. 68-69.

55. Chester, *Clash of Titans*, pp. 3, 52, 165, 174-75; and Clifford M. Scott, "American Images of Sub-Sahara Africa," p. 2.

56. This theme emphasized the similarity in the history and plight of black people worldwide and manifested itself in Pan-African activities and emphasis on the Pan-African link. See Okon Edet Uya, ed., *Black Brotherhood*, passim.

WEST AFRICA LEADS THE WAY, 1880–1914

4

During my meanderings along the West and Southwest Coast of Africa, and in its rivers, I was keenly observant of the present position of the several European Powers, wherever their unfurled flags betokened their supremacy. I confess that I had not the remotest idea that the European was so well entrenched in his African Possessions as I found him to be. Waiving the presentation of all incidental questions, I am prepared to state that, in my opinion, the European is in Africa to stay, and that there are no conditions likely to arise which will dislodge him short of miraculous interference.
Glimpses of Africa, p. 50.
Charles Spencer Smith, 1852-1923

This wonderful international interest [Berlin West African Conference], which takes mainly a commercial direction, is the forerunner of the moral and intellectual awakening which coming ages will bring to Africa along the line of a Christian civilization.
"All the World Gone After Africa," *New York Freeman*, 20 December 1884.
Thomas McCants Stewart, 1853-1923

The Berlin [West African] Conference representing the principal powers of the Globe [has created] the Congo Free State of Africa, . . . recognized as one of the families of the Nations by all the great powers of the earth.
Editorial, "The New Independent African State," *Huntsville Gazette*, 18 July 1885.
Charles Hendley, Jr., 1855-?

By the early nineteenth century, Europeans had been trading on the West African coast for almost four centuries, though they still knew very little about the interior. During the first half of the nineteenth century, a number of European groups, including traders, missionaries, and explorers, helped to increase Europe's knowledge of the West African hinterland. Nevertheless, European powers showed little interest in an empire in this region of the continent before 1880. By this date, the European presence in West Africa was confined to the coastal areas and the valleys of the navigable rivers—the Niger, Senegal, and Gambia. Apart from the southern Gold Coast, which Great Britain had annexed as a Crown Colony in 1874, the French colony of Senegal, and restricted areas of the colony of Sierra Leone, European flags flew only over isolated forts and settlements throughout West Africa.[1] However, between 1885 and 1906, West Africa, except Liberia, was formally occupied by four European powers: Great Britain, France, Germany, and Portugal.[2]

King Leopold II of Belgium and Chancellor Otto von Bismarck of Germany set the stage for probably the most important event in the scramble for and partitioning of West Africa. This event was a watershed in African history and gave white legitimization to European imperialism there.

As a result of the expansion of Leopold and Bismarck in Africa, five European nations found themselves engaged in activities on the continent: Great Britain, France, and Portugal, which had been in Africa for some time, and, suddenly, Belgium and Germany. On 8 October 1884, Germany joined France in issuing invitations to the leading white powers to take part in an international conference in Berlin to discuss freedom of commerce in the Congo basin and freedom of navigation on the Congo and Niger rivers. Fourteen powers were invited to this meeting, including the United States. Not surprisingly, no Africans were invited to participate in this conference which decided their future.

The Berlin West African Conference was the first colonial conference of its kind in modern times, according to Sybil Crowe, leading historian of the conference. Held in Berlin between 15 November 1884 and 26 February 1885, the conference produced a general act, which attempted to regulate imperialistic behavior in those parts of

Africa as yet unoccupied by whites. The conference was justified on the basis that there was a need for freedom of trade in Africa and an amelioration of the "conditions" of the African peoples. The General Act of the Berlin Conference resulted in provisions for freedom of trade in the basin and mouth of the Congo River, freedom of navigation along the Congo and Niger rivers, recognition of the International African Association, abolition of slavery and the slave trade in Africa, definitions of requirements and formalities to be observed in the effective occupation of the African continent by the European powers, and protection of the welfare of indigenous populations.

The conference, however, caused no basic changes in the policies of the European powers in Africa. The importance of this meeting has been exaggerated since all of its provisions failed in their purposes and the legal consequence was minimal. The real significance of the Berlin Conference lies in the legitimization it gave to collective colonialism in Africa.[3]

Having been the first major power to recognize officially the flag of the International Association of the Congo as that of a friendly government, the U.S. government participated in the Berlin Conference. Americans, however, were disturbed by their government's participation because they believed that the United States was becoming involved in European "entangling alliances." The ratification of the general act became a partisan political issue forcing President Grover Cleveland to refuse recommendation for ratification and to withdraw the act from Senate consideration. The general act was never ratified by the U.S. Congress.[4]

For the entire period under consideration, the U.S. government had no official African policy; none seemed necessary. American contacts with Africa were of a missionary or commercial nature and thus did not require governmental involvement. It was never American policy to occupy territory in Africa permanently, notwithstanding its paternal relationship with Liberia. Hence, although the threatened carving up of other parts of the world elicited American governmental response, the almost total colonial takeover of Africa provoked no reaction. The guiding principles were isolationism and noninvolvement.[5]

The Berlin West African Conference and the division of West Africa evoked some interest from four segments of the middle-class

black community in the United States: clergymen, journalists, professionals, and educators. Not surprisingly, Afro-American churchmen
were in the forefront of those who responded to the conference.[6] By
the 1880s, Afro-American religious groups had long-established ties
with West Africa and, through their missionary societies, direct contact with events in that region.

Bishop Henry McNeal Turner of the African Methodist Episcopal
(AME) Church and leading nineteenth-century promoter of the
back-to-Africa sentiment, was devoted to the "religious crusade" in
Africa. Turner, an advocate of emigration as early as 1874, was
elected a lifetime honorary vice president of the white American
Colonization Society in 1876. A sometime Democrat, Turner had a
varied career; during his lifetime he was chancellor of Morris Brown
University, editor of the *Christian Recorder*, founder of the *Southern
Christian Recorder* and *Voice of Missions*, and organizer of the AME
Woman's Home and Foreign Missionary Society. In 1872, he was
honored with the title LL.D. by Pennsylvania University and with the
degree of D.D. by Wilberforce University in 1873. Turner made his
first trip to West Africa in 1891 when he visited Liberia and Sierra
Leone. He established AME churches in both countries. In 1898, he
opened the first AME Conference in South Africa.

In 1885, Turner warned that the European partitioning of West
Africa could be disastrous if the Europeans resorted only to exploitation. As a result, Turner advised that, if necessary, Afro-Americans
would have to speak out against European economic exploitation
and join with their African brothers in holding back the white invaders.
He promoted the idea that it was the "manifest destiny" of black
Americans to redeem Africa because they were better suited than
any other missionaries for the task. Turner constantly emphasized
the brotherhood theme and the need for unity among blacks throughout the world.[7]

During his visit to West Africa in 1891, Turner commented on his
perceptions of how Africans viewed the European powers in Africa.
The British, French, and Germans were hated in the interior of West
Africa because they robbed the Africans of their lands, he reported,
although the Africans preferred the British to the other Europeans.
Turner (always promoting his back-to-Africa program) emphasized
that Africans welcomed blacks returning to Africa. The blacks per-

sisted in wanting absolutely nothing to do with the whites.[8]

Immediately after the Berlin West African Conference, a series of articles appeared in the *A.M.E. Church Review* raising the question of what the policy of black Americans toward Africa should be. Several churchmen were asked to respond. These ministers discussed the attraction of Africa for the European powers and concluded that the policy of black Americans should be centered around shaping and influencing the future of Africa. They believed that black Americans could have a significant impact on the "development" of the continent if they would only "take up the white man's burden" in Africa.[9]

Among those expressing their individual views were Reverends John Bunyan Reeve of Pennsylvania, Rufus Lewis Perry of New York, and Solomon Porter Hood of New Jersey. Even within this small group there was no unanimity about the impact of the Berlin West African Conference on Africa or the role that blacks should play in African growth.

Reeve graduated from New York Central College in 1858 and later that same year was the first black to enter Union Theological Seminary in New York City. He graduated in 1861, and was ordained and installed as a pastor of Lombard Street Central Presbyterian Church in Philadelphia. Lincoln University honored him in 1870 with the first honorary degree of Doctor of Divinity. In 1871, he organized and became the first dean of the theological department at Howard University. After four years, he returned to the congregation at Central Presbyterian Church, where he remained until his death.

Perry was a Baptist minister and journalist in Brooklyn. He was editor of the *Sunbeam* (Brooklyn) and the *People's Journal* (Columbus, Ohio), coordinate editor of the *American Baptist* (later the *Baptist Weekly*, New York), and editor and publisher of the *National Monitor* (Brooklyn). For ten years, Perry served as corresponding secretary of the consolidated American Baptist Missionary Convention and, later, corresponding secretary of the American Educational Association and of the American Baptist Free Mission Society.

Hood graduated from Lincoln University in 1876 and four years later finished its theological course. He taught in the public schools, served as pastor of several churches, and spent four years as a missionary in Haiti. In October of 1921, he was appointed minister to

Liberia. Hood served in that post until 1927.

Reeve and Perry believed that black Americans should strive to "civilize" and "Christianize" Africa, whereas Hood contended that, because of the economic and commercial activity of European nations already in Africa, the continent would not be "redeemed" by Afro-Americans. Apparently, Hood believed that the Europeans would not easily forfeit their advantages in Africa.[10]

Perry was almost adamant in his belief that the "duty" of Afro-Americans was to help in the "development" of Africa. He maintained that, under the guise of philanthropy, the European rivals were plotting to gain a foothold on the continent. But Perry had no doubt that God had reserved Africa for the Africans and that in the end Africa would be a black man's continent. However, Afro-Americans could help shape Africa's future through Christian missions, commercial investments, and business enterprises, Perry averred.[11]

Some religious leaders were less concerned with missionary efforts and commercial endeavors in Africa than with the European economic exploitation of the continent. Theodore Holly, first black Protestant Episcopal bishop and representative of the American Episcopal Church in Haiti for twenty-eight years, maintained in 1885 that the Berlin West African Conference had been called because of the lust and rivalry of the European nations to possess the resources of the Congo basin. "They have come together to enact into law, national rapine, robbery and murder," he declared.

Holly, a shoemaker, was devoted to the idea of a "Negro nationality" and loyal to Africa and her descendants. Between 1854 and 1858, Holly and Martin Delany worked together, through the Board of Commissioners of the National Emigration Convention, on several expatriation schemes. At the 1854 meeting, Holly, who had investigated the possibility of migration to Liberia in 1850, emerged as the major proponent of emigration to Haiti. His efforts for mass black removal to Haiti bore little fruit, however.

Holly had little respect for the European nations in Africa. He felt that the European powers were making decisions and passing laws among themselves that robbed Africans of their possessions. He warned that imperial aggrandizement by the nations of Europe would result in the subjugation of Africans. Up to this point, Great Britain had been unrivalled in this business of "wholesale plunder,"

Holly contended, but now France and Germany were moving fast to gain territory in West Africa. According to Holly, this "territorial grabbing" emphasized the anti-Christian spirit among the so-called Christian nations of Europe. Holly, who believed that Africa should be "civilized," nonetheless questioned the motives of the Europeans there.[12]

Another churchman, Charles Spencer Smith, Methodist clergyman and AME bishop in South Africa from 1904 to 1906, in a voyage in 1894 along the west and southwest coast of Africa as far as Angola, recorded his impressions of the events occurring on that continent. He maintained that the European powers at the Berlin Conference had carved out the richest and most fertile parts of West and Central Africa and, without even consulting the Africans, had partitioned them among themselves. Thousands of miles from Africa, inspired by King Leopold of Belgium, the European "land-seeking Caucasians" had decided on Africa's future, he declared.[13]

Smith further observed that the years after the Berlin West African Conference had seen a great territorial advance of Europeans in Africa. Many "spheres of influence" had now been formally defined, he explained. But he saw European rule as having brought some "progress" to Africa and Africans because of the introduction of Christianity and the development of natural resources.

Thus favoring certain aspects of European rule, Smith remarked that he had always wondered if the partitioning of Africa was merely a scheme on paper rather than an actuality, but after traveling along the west and southwest coast of Africa he knew that the European powers intended to possess all of Africa. He concluded, "I confess that I had not the remotest idea that the European was so well entrenched in his African Possessions as I found him to be. . . . I am prepared to state that, in my opinion, the European is in Africa to stay."[14]

Smith was born in Canada West in 1852. He served as a Reconstruction member of Alabama's House of Representatives from 1874 to 1876. He was licensed by the AME Church to preach in 1871, ordained deacon in 1873 and bishop in 1900. Through his efforts, the AME Church in the early twentieth century moved away from the literal interpretation of the Bible. After his visit to West Africa in the autumn of 1894, he criticized any African emigration plan. He

had been displeased with what he had seen, in spite of the fact that
his "explorations" had only consisted of watching harbor activities
and recording weather phenomena from the ship deck. During his
entire three-month trip, he had gone ashore for only fifteen days,
and then not beyond the sound of the ship's whistle. In 1895, Smith
made a tour of the West Indies and South America because of his
continuing interest in the conditions of blacks all over the world.
Smith later became the historian of the AME Church (*A History of
the African Methodist Episcopal Church*, 1922).[15]

During these years, the journalistic community also exhibited a
curiosity in the events occurring in West Africa. Charles Hendley,
Jr., editor of the *Huntsville Gazette* (Alabama), discussed the results
of the Berlin West African Conference. Hendley, educated in the
schools in Huntsville and at Rust Institute (Holly Springs, Mississippi),
was editor of the oldest black journal published in the South. The
Gazette was published from 1879 to 1894. In an editorial, Hendley
registered support for the provisions of the meeting and claimed that
the world was particularly interested in the future of the Congo Free
State, which had been created by this gathering of the principal
powers of the globe. Hendley obviously believed that the assemblage
would result in the "redemption" of Africa.[16]

Other members of the press also concerned themselves during the
years after the Berlin West African Conference with the final partitioning and establishment of colonial rule in West Africa. T. Thomas
Fortune announced in 1906 that West Africa had been completely
partitioned and that the whole continent was being taken over and
exploited by Europeans. He proposed that the descendants of Africa
all over the world come together as a body to protest imperialism and
colonialism. The suggestion that blacks come together for a Pan-
African meeting had been advocated by Fortune ten years earlier in
1896, but apparently he was still calling for such a meeting despite
the Pan-African Conference of 1900.[17]

In an article in the *Cleveland Gazette*, a writer discussed the
predictions that Fortune had made previously at the Congress on
Africa in 1895. Fortune's prediction had come true, the writer
admitted, and all of Africa had been divided among the European
powers. The rights of Africans were ignored in this scramble for territory, it was reported. Indeed, all of West Africa had been divided up

as a result of European aggrandizement.[18]

Journalist John E. Bruce warned about this time that the white man's burden was largely of his own making and would cause his downfall if he did not begin to consider the rights of colonial peoples. Great Britain, France, and Germany in West Africa and throughout the continent were expanding their culture to alien peoples, he claimed, believing that God had called them to this duty. In September of 1913, Bruce formally organized the "Loyal Order of the Sons of Africa," a society whose objective was the unification of black peoples all over the world.[19]

A handful of professional blacks who had visited or lived in West Africa before 1914 also considered the impact the European presence was having in that area. Thomas McCants Stewart, a New York attorney, discussed the Berlin West African Conference in a letter to the *New York Freeman* from West Africa. Stewart was a freeborn Charlestonian who attended Howard University from 1869 to 1873. Leaving Howard before completion, he entered South Carolina University, where he graduated in 1875, receiving the A.B. degree. He then entered the law department of the same institution, graduated the same year (1875), and was given the title LL.D. He practiced law in South Carolina (with D. Augustus Straker) while at the same time teaching mathematics at the State Agricultural College. In 1877, Stewart entered Princeton College to study theology. After AME ordination, he was given pastoral charge of Bethel African Methodist Episcopal Church in New York City. There he combined a law practice with a pastorate. Stewart became the closest friend of the leading journalist of this period, T. Thomas Fortune.

In 1882, Stewart joined the staff of Liberia College as the Charles Sumner Professor of Belles Lettres, History and Law. In a letter to Fortune from Liberia, he discussed the events occurring in West Africa as he saw them. Stewart believed that the Berlin Conference was momentous because it would help in the development of "civilization" in Africa. Understanding that the European interest in Africa was a commercial one, he also saw it, however, as forerunner of the moral and intellectual "awakening" of Africa.[20]

In late 1885 Stewart returned to the United States and resumed the practice of law in New York. He recounted his bad experiences in Liberia. Actually, for all his criticism, Stewart was not hostile to Liberia, and he emphasized that it had played a useful function in African history and could help to serve as a starting point for a great African republic. After his return from Liberia, he encouraged commercial relationships with Africa and missionary efforts as a means of Christianizing the continent, but he did not favor African emigration.[21] Nevertheless, Stewart himself was a constant emigrant. In 1898, he moved to Honolulu, and it was his reports that stimulated Fortune's interest in the Pacific and thus his visit to the insular possessions in 1903 to investigate possible black emigration there. Stewart also lived in Liberia and Great Britain and died in St. Thomas in the Virgin Islands in 1923.

In a book on his personal observations and experiences in West Africa, Stewart wrote that black Americans had good reason to be interested in the affairs of Africa. The "elevation" of Africa and the "advancement" of American blacks had a direct influence on one another, he contended, and Afro-Americans could not forget Africa's claims upon them. Stewart maintained that American blacks could not ignore Africa and her pleas for sympathy and service.[22]

Finally, black diplomats were also interested in European activity in West Africa. William J. Yerby, an Afro-American consul for over twenty-five years, served in Sierra Leone from 1906 to 1915 and was later transferred to Senegal, where he worked for ten years, and then to France. In a letter to the secretary of state in 1913, Yerby commended the European governments for developing the resources of West Africa. Yerby, who was at that time consul for all the West African colonies, suggested that because of the partitioning and increased activity a consular agent should be placed at the capital of the German and French West African colonies, as well as in British Lagos, Nigeria, and Accra, Gold Coast.[23]

The attitude of some blacks toward European colonial rule in Africa was much more militant after 1900 than earlier. This was probably a result of the greater exposure to African affairs in the media and a growing awareness among blacks of the exploitative nature of imperialism. This knowledge even led a few blacks to advocate African violence against European imperialism.

Quite another response, however, was proposed by Afro-American educators. It was in West Africa that colonialists first experimented with industrial education. The importance of industrial training to

Africa had been underlined in one of the resolutions of the Brussels Anti-Slavery Conference of 1890, and the idea was extended to the continent in the late nineteenth and early twentieth centuries. The colonial powers were obviously receptive to an educational philosophy that would result in black subordination to whites. Thus, with the establishment of colonial rule, industrial education was initiated.

Tuskegee students, "captains of industry" as Washington called them, were welcomed throughout West Africa. The German government applied to Tuskegee for four persons to go to German Togo as technical assistants in the development of cotton culture. James Nathan Calloway, a Fisk University graduate with a knowledge of German who had supervised one of the Tuskegee farms, and three Tuskegee graduates arrived in Togo on 1 January 1901, with their teaching equipment, plows, wagons, a steam cotton gin, and a cotton press. Eventually, nine Tuskegee graduates were employed over a ten-year period by the German colonial development company. Four of them died in Togo, and five others returned to the United States after a few years. In 1909, only John W. Robinson, class of 1897, one of the original party, was left in Togo. Their work attracted considerable attention from missionaries and other colonial governments. Tuskegee Institute gained the trust of the colonial powers because of its positive attitude toward European activity in Africa and was constantly called upon by these powers to aid in the "development" of the continent.

Other West African countries were introduced to industrial education, including Nigeria and independent Liberia. Although Washington was too busy to go to Africa, he sent Tuskegee agronomists in his place and was rewarded with schools established in his honor. In fact, Washington's philosophy was so admired that in 1929 the International Education Board of the Rockefeller Foundation and the Phelps-Stokes Fund joined with the New York Colonization Society to establish the Booker T. Washington Agricultural and Industrial Institute in Liberia to provide workers for the Firestone Rubber Company's operation there.[24]

In an article in the *Kassai Herald* in 1906, Washington advocated industrial training as an aid to missions. In that same year, he talked with James E. K. Aggrey of Livingstone College about establishing Tuskegees in Africa and discussed the need for an international

conference in order to construct a model for the extension of industrial education to Africa. The idea was to hold a conference attended
by missionary societies and colonial governments to discuss the
possibility of these two groups establishing such educational activities.
Washington also believed that black Americans could play a major
role as educators and technical assistants.

Washington did not call his conference until 1912. The International Conference on the Negro was held at Tuskegee from 17 to 19
April 1912. Most of the conferees were missionaries and theologians.
Twenty-five attended, mostly white, representing twelve denominations and eighteen countries or colonies. There were three Afro-West
Indians present and a few Afro-Americans and Africans. The conference demonstrated the number and variety of people and governments who believed that the Tuskegee system of industrial education
could be adapted to Africa. Questions were raised concerning how
Afro-American educators and missionaries could best serve Africa
within the framework of white colonial rule.[25]

Because of events in the Congo Free State, South Africa, and
Liberia and earlier events in Ethiopia, Madagascar, and Egypt, black
American interest in West Africa waned after 1900. After all, it was in
this region that the European "model colonies" (German Togo,
French Senegal, and British Sierra Leone) developed, where ex-
amples of abuses were far less frequent than in other areas. Thus
during these years blacks looked to West Africa as an indicator of
African "progress" and change.

But by 1914, the black American groups that discussed West
Africa disagreed about the impact European imperialism was having
there. Since West Africa was one of the first regions formally partitioned by the European powers, Afro-Americans generalized about
how the partitioning would affect the rest of Africa. However, the
situation in West Africa was somewhat distinct from the other areas.
Because of centuries of contact, Europeans had already developed a
commercial relationship with this section. A strong European economic base already existed because of four centuries of European
involvement in the trade in African captives and because of efforts in
the first half of the nineteenth century to replace the illegitimate slave
trade with legitimate indigenous goods. Exploitation of land, labor,
and resources in West Africa had already begun before the partition-

ing, and the abusive exploitation that characterized other regions of the continent during the partitioning and establishment of colonial rule were not found here. Also, because of black missionaries, diplomats, and travelers in West Africa, more was known among the general black population about this region than any other. As the scramble for and partitioning of Africa continued, black Americans broadened their knowledge of the continent and began to assess the events occurring in the other areas being partitioned by the European powers, including Central, East, South, and North Africa.

Notes

1. Throughout this study, the contemporary names of African countries, rivers, peoples, and so on will be used for the sake of accuracy and consistency.

2. J. B. Webster and A. A. Boahen, *History of West Africa*, pp. 214-15; Michael Crowder, *West Africa Under Colonial Rule*, pp. 3, 47-48, 55, 59; Elizabeth Isichei, *History of West Africa Since 1800*, p. 159; and John D. Hargreaves, "The European Partition of West Africa," p. 402.

3. Sybil Crowe, *The Berlin West African Conference, 1884-1885*, pp. 3, 5, 7; W. E. B. Du Bois, *Dusk of Dawn*, p. 52; John D. Hargreaves, *Prelude to the Partition of West Africa*, p. 338; George Martelli, *Leopold to Lumumba*, p. 107; Robert O. Collins, ed., *The Partition of Africa*, pp. 10-12; Lewis H. Gann and Peter Duignan, *Burden of Empire*, pp. 199-201; Arthur B. Keith, *The Belgian Congo and the Berlin Act*, pp. 55, 57, 62; Roland Oliver and John Fage, *A Short History of Africa*, pp. 184, 186; and Jesse S. Reeves, *International Beginning of the Congo Free State*, pp. 1, 8, 26-27, 30-32, 34-36, 41, 45, 50-51, 66-67.

4. Edward W. Chester, *Clash of Titans*, pp. 146-48; U.S., Congress, Senate, *Independent State of the Congo*, S. Ex. Doc. 196, 49th Cong., 2d sess., pp. 1, 7-9, 12, 139-40, 188-89, 321-22, 326-27, 331; and *A Compilation of the Messages and Papers of the Presidents*, vol. 10, p. 4823.

5. Rupert Emerson, *Africa and United States Policy*, p. 15; and Roy Olton, "Problems of American Foreign Relations in the African Area During the Nineteenth Century," abstract, pp. 3-4.

6. "The Congo Conference," *Missionary Herald* 81 (May 1885): 206.

7. Edwin S. Redkey, ed., *Respect Black*, p. 55; idem, "Bishop Turner's African Dream," pp. 271-90; and Immanuel Geiss, *The Pan-African Movement*, pp. 138-39.

8. Henry McNeal Turner, *African Letters*, p. 39; Redkey, ed., *Respect Black*, pp. 109-11, 115; Letter to the Editor, "Bishop H. M. Turner's Travels in Africa," *Christian Recorder*, 13 December 1891, p. 1, and 14 January 1892, p. 1; "Bishop H. M. Turner, Letters from Africa," *A.M.E. Church Review* 8 (April 1892): 472; and "Bishop Turner on Africa," *New York Age*, 20 February 1892.

9. "What Should be the Policy of the Colored American Toward Africa," *A.M.E. Church Review* 2 (July 1885): 68-75.

10. Ibid., pp. 69, 72.

11. Ibid., p. 69.

12. Rev. Theodore Holly, "Sacred Chronology and the Inspired Arithmec [sic] of Divine Revelation," *A.M.E. Church Review* 2 (July 1885): 13. See also Howard H. Bell, "Negro Nationalism," p. 44, 44n.

13. Charles Spencer Smith, *Glimpses of Africa*, p. 23.

14. Ibid., pp. 27, 50, 53, 63; and Editorial, "Glimpe [sic] of Africa," *Indianapolis Freeman*, 12 October 1895.

15. Edwin S. Redkey, *Black Exodus*, pp. 206-07.

16. Editorial, "The New Independent African State," *Huntsville Gazette* (Alabama), 18 July 1885.

17. Editorial, "A Pan-African Congress," *New York Age*, 22 March 1906.

18. "France in Africa," *Cleveland Gazette*, 6 January 1912. This sentiment had been expressed in earlier years. See Editorial, "Social Problem in Africa," *Indianapolis Freeman*, 3 October 1903; "All Africa Appropriated," *Savannah Tribune*, 12 August 1905; and Editorial note, *Alexander's Magazine*, 15 December 1908.

19. Peter Gilbert, comp. and ed., *The Selected Writings of John Edward Bruce*, pp. 97, 101.

20. T. McCants Stewart, "All the World Gone After Africa," *New York Freeman*, 20 December 1884.

21. See *New York Freeman*, Letter to the Editor, "Will Not Return to Liberia," 24 October 1885; and "Resumes His Law Practice," 9 January 1886.

22. T. McCants Stewart, *Liberia*, pp. 101-04.

23. Letter, W. J. Yerby to Secretary of State, 19 August 1913, Department of State, Record Group 59, Decimal File (1910-1929), Box 1755, National Archives.

24. Kenneth James King, *Pan-Africanism and Education*, pp. 14, 46; William B. Helmreich, comp., *Afro-Americans and Africa*, p. ix; Donald Spivey, "The African Crusade for Black Industrial Schooling," pp. 1-2, 11; Louis R. Harlan, "Booker T. Washington and the White Man's Burden," pp.

442-43, 445; Editorial note, *Cleveland Gazette*, 17 November 1900; "A Tuskegee Graduate in West Africa," *Colored American Magazine* (May 1906): 355-59; "Speech of John W. Robinson," *Alexander's Magazine* (May 1906): 66-67; Booker T. Washington to Baron Herman, 20 September 1900, Washington Papers (282a); and Booker T. Washington to George Washington Carver, 11 September 1910, Washington Papers (604).

25. Edwin W. Smith, *Aggrey of Africa*, p. 146; Geiss, *The Pan-African Movement*, p. 219; King, *Pan-Africanism and Education*, pp. 17, 19-20; "International Conference on the Negro at Tuskegee," *Indianapolis Freeman*, 20 April 1912; "The Negro Conference at Tuskegee Institute," *African Times and Orient Review* 1 (July 1912): 10-12; and Robert E. Park, "The International Conference on the Negro," *Southern Workman* (June 1912): 345-52. For Washington's opinion on industrial training and missions, see Booker T. Washington, "Industrial Schools as an Aid to Missions," *Kassai Herald* (July 1906): 30-31. See also Inez Smith Reid, "Black Americans and Africa," p. 656.

EUROPEANS IN CENTRAL AFRICA: THE CONGO BASIN, 1880–1914

5

All the crimes perpetrated in the Congo have been done in *your* name [Leopold II], and *you* must answer at the bar of Public Sentiment for the misgovernment of a people, whose lives and fortunes were entrusted to you by the august Conference of Berlin, 1884-1885.

"An Open Letter to His Serene Majesty Leopold II," in *Apropos of Africa*, comp. and ed. Martin Kilson and Adelaide Cromwell Hill, p. 123.

George Washington Williams, 1849-1891

There are armed sentries of *chartered* trading companies [in the Congo Free State], who force the men and women to spend most of their days and nights in the forests making rubber, and the price they receive is so meager that they cannot live upon it.

"From the Bakuba Country," *Kassai Herald*, 11 January 1908, p. 15.

William Henry Sheppard, 1865-1927

At last the world is waking to the shocking truth that King Leopold's pretended philanthropy in the Congo is in reality a ghastly lie. The whole Congo country is recklessly exploited for private gain by this human monster. The report of a commission appointed by the Belgian Chamber of Deputies showed that the natives had been flagrantly robbed of their rights, [and] that shocking and revolting cruelties were practiced in forcing the natives to gather rubber for the government. . . . Leopold in the Congo is a stench in the nostrils of modern civilization.

Editorial, "The Congo Infamy," *Voice of the Negro* (December 1906): 541.

Jesse Max Barber, 1878-?

In the first three quarters of the nineteenth century, European nations had little or no interest in the Congo basin region. However, as the resources of this area—ivory, rubber, and palm oil—became more important to commercial and industrial development in Europe, and as explorers began to stimulate interest in this section, more Europeans entered the scramble for territory there. Portugal had been in this area for centuries and wanted to control the mouth of the Congo River. In 1884, it signed a treaty with Great Britain in which the British recognized Portuguese supremacy along the mouth of the Congo River and in turn were guaranteed freedom of navigation on the river. By 1884, France had claims to the northern territory at the head of the Congo. Another power, Leopold II of Belgium, was also vying for territory in the Congo basin. In 1879, Leopold had taken Henry Morton Stanley, an American reporter and explorer, into his service after Stanley's scheme for the opening up of the Congo basin had been rejected by the British government. Thus, Portugal, France, and Leopold II insisted that they had legitimate claims in the Congo. Eventually, Great Britain and Germany recognized Leopold's claims in the area to check French initiatives there, and all powers agreed to block Portuguese ambitions. France finally gave up its claim to territory with the assurance that it could assume control if Leopold and his International Association could not afford to administer the area.[1]

The formation of the International African Association in 1876 had simply been an instrument to facilitate the realization of Leopold's dream of a colonial empire in the Congo. The organization was believed to be dedicated to "humanitarian and philanthropic" pursuits, and this accounts for the formal recognition of the association as a friendly power by the U.S. government on 22 April 1884. The international position and prestige of the association was widely strengthened by this acknowledgment, since the United States was the first power to accept its sovereignty. Leopold, the silent manipulator behind the organization, saw this as a personal triumph.

By the time the Berlin West African Conference opened on 15 November 1884, the International Association had been sanctioned by three powers: the United States, France, and Germany. This was followed by its official recognition by all the Berlin Conference participants on 23 February 1885. During the Berlin Conference, the Independent State of the Congo (commonly known as the Congo Free State) was established as an "independent" area under the dominion of King Leopold II of Belgium.

On 29 May 1885, Leopold proclaimed by royal decree the formal existence of the Congo Free State and in August 1886 named himself sovereign ruler. President Grover Cleveland was the first world leader to recognize the Independent State of the Congo as a government under the control of Leopold II. In his extensive discussion of the beginnings of the Congo Free State, Jesse Reeves maintained that the Congo became an appendage of Leopold as he took upon himself the character of an absolute, autocratic ruler.[2]

According to Jean Stengers, "The Congo State, both in its genesis as well as in its policy of expansion, represented imperialism in its truest form."[3] The Congo Free State had originated from the whimsical megalomania of King Leopold II of Belgium. From its inception, it was the model of a European-dominated imperialist state. During this period of European territorial expansion, Leopold wanted a colonial empire and seized upon the Congo. The Belgian people did not share the expansionist dreams of their ruler, however, and Leopold personally took up this task.

Unfortunately for Leopold, the Congo Free State proved to be an unsuccessful economic venture in the early years. It suffered from lack of capital, lack of financial resources, and ineffective administration of such a large territory. As a result, Leopold embarked upon a policy of monopolies and concessions, which later proved to be very unwise. The issue of forced labor and the ensuing atrocities followed upon the heels of the introduction of concessionary companies in the Congo. The Congo was soon described by many observers as a giant slave plantation run by Leopold and his administration for the profits to be gained. Leopold's attempts to make the Congo profitable resulted in a marked improvement in its financial status, but this was made possible only through cruelties inflicted upon the African population.[4]

Leopold instituted his new policy of granting monopolies and concessions in the early 1890s. International opinion concerning incidents of cruelty to the Congolese appeared almost simultaneously.

A critical attitude toward Leopold's rule also arose among Afro-Americans. The initial protest against his rule in the Congo came from two black Americans, George Washington Williams and William Henry Sheppard.

Williams, who in 1884 had recommended the recognition of the International Association by the U.S. government because of his belief in its humanitarian motives,[5] spent four months in 1890 traveling in the Congo on a fact-finding tour for President Benjamin Harrison and railroad tycoon, Collis P. Huntington, to investigate a proposed Congo railroad and, at the request of the Belgian Government, to study the conditions of the Congolese. Williams also hoped to explore the feasibility of using college-trained Afro-Americans to staff government and commercial operations in the Congo.[6] From his behavior, Williams seems to have supported missionary activity in Africa, limited emigration for skilled blacks, and, initially at least, the European partitioning of Africa for commercial and economic reasons.

Williams graduated from Newton Theological Seminary in Massachusetts in 1874, delivering the valedictory address on "Early Christianity in Africa." He attended Cincinnati Law School and in 1881 was admitted to the bar in Ohio. Later he was admitted to the Massachusetts bar. He was nominated as minister to Haiti in 1885 but did not receive Senate confirmation. Williams had several careers during his lifetime, scholar, minister, politician, editor, and lawyer.

After he settled in Worcester, Massachusetts, Williams took an unusual interest in Congo affairs. During the winter of 1883-1884, he wrote a series of articles on African geography. In 1884, he urged the Senate Committee on Foreign Relations to recognize the International Association. Williams's trip to the Congo in 1890 resulted in three reports, one on the proposed Congo railroad, an account to the president, and an open letter to Leopold II.[7]

On 18 July 1890, Williams wrote an open letter to Leopold II publicly denouncing his rule and charging him with misrepresentation and abuse in the Congo Free State.[8] Williams, who also represented the Associated Literary Press of the United States, charged that Leopold had made no attempt to better the welfare of the African people. Announcing that all the crimes perpetrated in the Congo were under Leopold's name, Williams demanded that the king "answer at the bar of Public Sentiment for the misgovernment of a people." He appealed to the powers of the Berlin Conference to create an international commission to investigate his charges against the Leopoldian government.[9] He emphasized that certain aspects of European rule in Africa were retarding "development" and constantly reiterated that "my cry is *Africa for the Africans!*"[10] Williams, who had played a role in gaining American support for the Congo Free State, died on 2 August 1891, as one of the most critical opponents of Leopold's rule in the Congo.

William Henry Sheppard, an Afro-American Presbyterian missionary in the Congo from 1890 to 1910 who adhered to almost all of the elements of the "civilizing mission" concept, also became an outspoken critic of Leopold's regime. Sheppard, along with Samuel Lapsley, set up the earliest Presbyterian mission in the Congo, on the Kasai River.[11] Sheppard made a report to Leopold on the conditions in the Congo in October of 1899, but when no action was taken on the part of the Leopoldian government to alter these conditions Sheppard presented his allegations to the world in an article which appeared in the January 1908 issue of *Kassai Herald*, a mission paper. In this article, Sheppard accused the Leopoldian government in the Congo and the Kasai Company of forcing the Congolese to work under the threat of death. Sheppard did not mention the Kasai Company by name but only stated that armed sentries of chartered trading companies were forcing Congolese men and women to spend most of their time in the forests gathering rubber and thus preventing them from religious, social, and familial activities. The terminology and accusations in this article were phrased in such a manner that the Kasai Company would later be unable to prove that Sheppard was naming them specifically. Sheppard commented, "This is the article that started the great conflict."[12]

Sheppard, who had become interested in Africa at a young age, continued his denunciation of the Leopoldian regime throughout the early years of the twentieth century, giving accounts of the atrocities committed in the Congo. In these reports, he chronicled "heartrending evidence of the horrible cruelties inflicted by Africans indeed, but under authority given them by officials of the Free State." Sheppard regularly registered formal complaints with King Leopold and brought these offenses to the attention of the British and American governments whenever possible.[13]

Williams and Sheppard were among the first to initiate the Congo controversy, which came to a head at the beginning of the twentieth century. By 1900, the situation in the Congo had become scandalous. International protest movements began to develop. These protestors declared that, because of the granting of monopolies and concessions to big companies in the Congo, there had been a violation of the international agreement made at Berlin. The concessionary system and the alleged cruelty to the Africans in the Congo, they charged, openly violated the two sections of the Berlin Act of 1885 providing for free trade and securing the welfare of the indigenous population.[14]

As a result of the allegations made against the Leopoldian regime, Roger Casement, British consul at Stanley Pool in the Congo, was sent into the interior by the British government in 1903 to make an official investigation into the conditions in the Congo Free State. Casement's inquiry verified the reports of oppression, exploitation, and maladministration by the government in the Congo. His report, published on 12 February 1904, confirming what critics had been saying, aroused public feeling against Leopold's government in the Congo.[15]

Because of Casement's report and international concern over Leopold's administration in the Congo, movements for reform eventually developed throughout the Western world. The major center of protest was in Great Britain. On 13 March 1904, the Congo Reform Association was organized in Great Britain, with Earl Beauchamp as president and Edmund D. Morel as honorary secretary. The association eventually played a major role in developing world opinion on the conditions in the Congo.[16]

In October of 1904, Morel, of the British Congo Reform Association, spoke at the International Peace Congress in Boston, Massachusetts, on the reported atrocities in the Congo. Almost immediately afterwards, an American Congo Reform Association was established under the leadership of Dr. G. Stanley Hall, president of Clark University.[17]

The national headquarters of the American Congo Reform Association were located in Boston. Throughout the Congo controversy, the association attempted to pressure the U.S. government through the use of petitions, mass meetings, distribution of news-letters, lobbying, publications in journals, and resolutions calling for reform in the Congo. The association was interested in alleviating the conditions of the Congolese by forcing Leopold to bring about reforms and, if not, by Belgian annexation.[18]

Senator John T. Morgan of Alabama, a supporter of the association, was also helpful in bringing administrative attention to this issue. Morgan, a racist southern Democrat, had supported a colonization scheme in 1890 to settle American blacks in the Congo basin.[19] Within the Senate he became the spokesman for the Congo reform movement. His interests in the Congo, however, were twofold. While primarily concerned with reform, he again proposed to solve the "Negro problem," and thus continued his futile attempt to get a bill passed in Congress to provide funds for Afro-American emigration to the Congo. Considering the reports of atrocities in the Congo, it was not surprising that blacks did not react favorably to this "solution." Furthermore, Booker T. Washington, one of the vice presidents of the Congo Reform Association, while calling for reforms in the Congo, did not address himself to the question of possible Afro-American emigration to the area.[20]

With the inception of the Congo Reform Association in the United States, more attention was given to the conditions in the Congo throughout this country. The reports that seeped out of the Congo Free State continued to indicate incidents of extortion, torture, mutilation, and mass murder by the authorities in the Congo. As Americans became aware of these conditions, reformers and journalists demanded that there be an end to the atrocities and that reforms be initiated.[21]

The Congo controversy occurred during the era of muckraking journalism in the United States, and this could account for much of the exposure it was given in this country. The "Congo horrors" were illustrated in papers throughout the country, with pictures of Africans whose limbs had been severed and who had suffered physical abuses. Press agitation in the United States was led by the William Randolph Hearst newspaper, the New York American (New York City), which consistently contained articles discussing the Congo atrocities.[22]

Many black Americans were also concerned with the Congo

situation. Black journalists, religious groups, and educators became interested in conditions in the Congo Free State and offered several proposals to help alleviate the alleged conditions there. Their solutions were similar to those offered by the larger white population. Initially, they urged the U.S. government to intervene and assume administrative responsibility in the Congo; later they suggested that Americans pressure Belgium to help bring about changes in the Congo. Finally, they demanded that King Leopold give up his sovereign rule in the Congo and recommended Belgium's annexation of the region. By the end of the Congo controversy, moreover, many blacks, unlike most white critics, were beginning to urge the Congolese to resist openly the Leopoldian government.

Black Americans had already developed many of their attitudes about European imperialism in Africa by the beginning of the Congo controversy. This was a result of their growing knowledge of the events occurring in Africa and their direct exposure to imperialism during the Spanish-American War.[23] Consequently, many elements of the Afro-American community responded to this discussion, which focused on an unmistakable case in point of some of the exploitative elements of imperialism.

Throughout the controversy, the Afro-American press played an important role in keeping the black community informed of developments in the Congo and in influencing Afro-American opinion on the issue. Articles and editorials frequently appeared in black newspapers and periodicals during the height of the controversy, 1904-1908. Intensive publicity about the Congo scandal by Afro-Americans began almost immediately after the formation of the American Congo Reform Association, although journalists had noted the activities in the Congo earlier. While the black press did not mention Morel's visit to the United States in October of 1904, nor the formation of the association, elements of the press promptly began discussion of the role that blacks should play in this obvious example of the maladministration of an African colony by a European power.

In November 1904, the editor of the *Southern Workman*, a white journal published at Hampton Institute in the interest of black Americans, articulated one of the major themes that blacks were to emphasize throughout the Congo controversy. He predicted that the black race in America would play a significant part in the deliverance of

Africa from the hands of the white Europeans and in securing free-dom for the Congolese.[24] Black journalists of this period, such as Harry C. Smith, Fred Moore, T. Thomas Fortune, and W. E. B. Du Bois, were to reiterate this theme and express the need for racial solidarity concerning the issue of European imperialism in Africa. In expressing these views they were continuing a tradition that had been set in the late nineteenth century.

The *Cleveland Gazette*, a black newspaper edited by Harry Clay Smith, began serious coverage of the conditions in the Congo in November 1904. A month after the establishment of the American Congo Reform Association, Smith, one of the most militant journal-ists of this period, commented that the inhumanity and cruelty exhibited by the "Christian and civilized" Belgians in the Congo only helped to confirm his belief in the white man's obsession with exploi-tation of other peoples under the guise of "civilizing the peoples of the world."[25] Because Smith adhered to the religious, social, and economic missionizing of Africa, he felt that black Americans should assist in this "development" and that Africa would eventually be ruled by Africans. However, he was against any plan of emigration or African colonization.

Smith, an active politician in Ohio, served three terms in the state legislature. In the protest tradition, he was critical of any form of accommodation or segregation and constantly agitated against out-rages. He was a consistent critic of Washington. In August 1883, Smith, who had only a high school education, in connection with three others launched the *Cleveland Gazette* and eventually became sole proprietor. The paper was a success because of his outside source of income to help support the expenses of operation; Smith was an accomplished composer and band leader. Throughout the period under discussion, the *Gazette* was a conscientious paper conducted with integrity and consistency.[26]

Continuing its established militant stance toward the conditions in the Congo Free State, in 1906 the *Cleveland Gazette* carried a series of articles on the Congo issue. On 10 March, the writer of an article on the Congo reported that the Belgians were still mutilating the Congolese. The Leopoldian government in the Congo was de-scribed as in a deplorable condition, and "the trend of the farce of government instituted by the Belgian protectorate is apparently to legislate the natives off the earth." The writer complained that, although protests had been made to the powers of the world concerning the alleged "cruelties" committed in the Congo, nothing had been done to alleviate those conditions.[27] A second article recalled reports from missionaries who had witnessed these "Congo crimes."[28] The *Gazette* apparently believed that publication of such articles on the Congo would act as proof of the maladministration in that country. Many Americans, both white and black, felt that the United States had adequate basis for intervening in the affairs and conditions of the Congo because of such reports.

An article entitled "The Story of the Congo Free State," in the December 1905 issue of *Alexander's Magazine*, a black magazine published and edited by Charles Alexander, briefly discussed the reports of atrocities in the Congo. These reports of inhumane treatment of the Africans called for a black commitment to efforts to help bring international attention to this issue, contended the magazine.[29]

Alexander was a Tuskegee graduate who became editor of the *Colored Citizen* (Boston) in 1904. Washington heavily subsidized the paper to counter the anti-Bookerite *Boston Guardian* (William Monroe Trotter, editor), but it proved a financial failure. In April 1905, Alexander turned the weekly paper into a monthly magazine, named after himself. Washington continued to support the magazine until Alexander proved to be disloyal and the magazine folded in 1909.

Alexander had not endorsed emigration to Africa until October 1906. In January 1907, he advertised for young men trained in agriculture and mechanics to go to Liberia, and thereafter *Alexander's Magazine* was an active supporter of African emigration. Francis H. Warren, a Detroit intellectual, Walter F. Walker, Alexander's assistant, and Alexander organized and headed the Liberian Development Association, founded in 1907 for emigration purposes, although nothing ever came of it.[30]

In 1906, *Alexander's Magazine* announced that not only were the Congolese exploited and oppressed but the Belgian imperialists were also engaged in such gross atrocities as cutting off their limbs. In this article, Alexander illustrated these offenses with pictures taken of mutilations and maimings.[31]

Walter T. Walker, in his column in *Alexander's Magazine*, "News About Liberia and Africa Generally," warned that a revolt among the

Congolese against the system of forced labor was inevitable. This rebellion, he predicted, would reach alarming proportions.[32] Other newspapers also commented that Europeans could not continue to steal Africa from the Africans without meeting resistance.[33]

The Afro-American press constantly reiterated that the Congo was only one example of the oppressive results of European imperialism in Africa, and the so-called civilized nations of Europe were denounced for exploiting the countries and peoples of Africa. The press was particularly critical of the events in the Congo because of the obvious mismanagement. These journalists strongly denounced Leopold's government and urged American leaders to pressure Belgium to help bring about changes in the Congo.

Most blacks believed that Leopold's only concern in the Congo was the financial rewards and not the humanitarian treatment or "uplift" of the Congolese peoples. In the December 1906 issue of the *Voice of the Negro*, edited by Jesse Max Barber, readers were reminded that even the commission appointed by the Belgian Chamber of Deputies in 1904 had revealed that the Congolese were abused and denied their rights, and yet Leopold remained the sovereign ruler in the Congo. This editorial declared that Leopold had pretended since the Berlin Conference of 1885 that he wanted the Congo for philanthropic reasons, but it was now known that this was indeed no more than a pretense. There was growing international indignation against Leopold's rule in the Congo, Barber contended, and many groups were rightfully calling for the resignation of Leopold as sovereign ruler. The Congo Reform Association was congratulated for its work in promoting the investigation into the conditions in the Congo. Barber concluded that Leopold's actions in the Congo were repulsive to modern "civilization."[34]

In September of 1903, Barber signed a contract to edit the *Voice of the Negro*, moved to Atlanta, and took charge of the magazine. Following the Atlanta pogrom of 1906, the magazine moved to Chicago. The venture was never a financial success and was abandoned in 1907, but during its short existent the *Voice* was viewed as a progressive paper.

In an editorial of the *Voice* in 1907, Barber insisted that it was up to Americans, both black and white, to "create a wave of international indignation that will culminate in an international conference" to investigate the alleged atrocities in the Congo. Barber urged blacks to become involved in the movement for reform because "these are our brethren across the sea."[35]

On 10 December 1906, Senator Henry Cabot Lodge of Massachusetts submitted a resolution to the Committee on Foreign Relations asking for an American inquiry into the affairs in the Congo and advising that the president had the support of the Senate in any steps he took.[36] Lodge's resolution was reinforced by a series of articles in Hearst's *American* published between 10 and 14 December, charging the U.S. government with participation in a cover-up of the Congo scandal.[37]

An article in the *St. Louis Palladium*, a black newspaper, discussed the Lodge resolution and recommended its adoption. The passage of the Lodge resolution would go a long way toward bringing about amelioration of the conditions in the Congo, the paper explained.[38]

Although few reforms were made in the Congo, black newspapers and periodicals of the period commended the American Congo Reform Association on its attempts to bring about more changes in the Congo. The association pressured the U.S. government by various methods. The purpose of all of these forms of protest was to develop public opinion to the extent that it would demand American participation and intervention in bringing about reforms in Leopold's Congo.[39]

In the November 1906 issue of the *Colored American Magazine*, Fred R. Moore maintained that public opinion in Belgium would soon bring about changes in the rule in the Congo. He voiced the hope that the Belgian people eventually would demand an end to these acts because they were beginning to hear of the Congo atrocities. Moore also asserted that the position of blacks in the Congo could be compared with that of blacks in the United States. Blacks all over the world were furnishing the white man with the labor to develop industries, Moore upheld. As a result, he insisted that it was time for American blacks to unite against imperialism and the oppression of blacks in all parts of the world. In concluding, Moore declared "down with Leopoldism in Africa" and called for the immediate removal of Leopold from the Congo.[40]

Throughout the Congo controversy and, in fact, the entire period under study, one of the themes constantly emphasized by articulate blacks was the similarity between the exploitation of blacks in Africa and the discrimination against blacks in America. In his comment on the exploitation of black labor, Moore emphasized the need for racial solidarity. This theme of brotherhood reappeared in many of the discussions about Africa by literate Afro-Americans during this period.

The *Colored American Magazine*, which had been published in Boston since 1901, was moved to New York in 1904, with Moore as editor. Washington had been instrumental in bringing the publication to New York, and he invested $3,000 in the enterprise. Moore was editor of the magazine from 1904 to 1907. In 1907, he and Washington bought the *New York Age* from Fortune. Moore was editor of the *Age* from 1907 to 1930. He constantly appealed to racial pride, self-help, racial solidarity, and economic chauvinism. Moore was appointed minister to Liberia on 1 March 1913, but he never went to his post and was replaced by George W. Buckner.[41]

Reports of atrocities continued to seep out of the Congo. Incidents of soldiers raiding villages, assaulting Congolese women, burning down villages, and mutilating the Congolese peoples were numerously chronicled. In the wake of these events, black journalists began to predict or advocate that the Congolese people openly resist the oppressive rule of Leopold.

By almost the end of the Congo controversy, some Afro-American publicists were advocating total Congolese resistance to Leopold's rule if reforms were not made. The *Colored American Magazine* finally announced in 1907 that the Congolese could no longer expect justice or humane treatment from the Leopoldian government and must arm themselves against the "civilized nations that are raping their women and murdering their men."[42]

In a series of editorials in December 1906, T. Thomas Fortune commented on the progress of reforms in the Congo. The Congo issue had passed from the stage of sentimental discussion into a serious international issue, Fortune alleged.[43] He accused Leopold of converting the Congo into a large plantation run by slave labor. The Belgians had awakened, however, to the truth about the Leopoldian form of government, he asserted, and were beginning to recognize their duty to the Congolese. He maintained that it was unfortunate that Leopold has been unaffected thus far by international appeals to humanity and decency and that he had been allowed to continue the atrocities committed in the Congo.[44] Fortune felt that the United States should cooperate with the other European powers so that changes could be brought about in the conditions in the Congo.[45]

Fortune finally declared in January of 1907 that the rights of life and liberty could no longer be denied to the people of the Congo. These rights had been denied by the Congo authorities long enough, and it was time for the U.S. government to cooperate with the European powers in order to bring about changes in the conditions of the Congolese. Fortune explained, "None of the European governments have any right in Africa" but were only there for what they could get out of the continent. Fortune called for immediate intervention in the Congo.[46]

Fortune concurred with Moore's declaration that the Congolese themselves should help bring about changes in the Congo, but he suggested that they simply stop working. He asserted, "A recognition of the right of the natives to refuse to work for the Belgian exploiters would destroy at once the foundations of the enormous structure of profit which has been built up in the Congo during the past dozen years." The Congolese could best regain their independence by asserting their natural rights, Fortune exclaimed editorially.[47]

W. E. B. Du Bois, editor of Horizon: A Journal of the Color Line, a black periodical published in Washington, D.C. from 1907 to 1910 as an unofficial organ of the Niagara Movement, commented in 1907 that it was a matter of racial importance that blacks unite to denounce the atrocities being committed in the Congo.[48] Du Bois, like Alexander, Barber, and Fortune, saw the important role that black Americans could play in helping to bring about changes in the conditions of the Congolese. They all urged black participation in the reform movement.

In light of Sheppard's role in exposing conditions in the Congo, it was not surprising that leaders of the Afro-American religious community also exhibited interest in developments in the Congo and in the movement for reform. Like Sheppard, Clinton C. Boone, an Afro-American medical missionary in the Congo from 1901 to 1906, had also observed the atrocities inflicted by Leopold's agents upon the Congolese. Boone was the first missionary appointed under a plan of cooperation of the Lott Carey Baptist Home and Foreign

Mission Convention and the American Baptist Foreign Mission Society of Boston. Years later, in an autobiographical sketch of his stay in the Congo, Boone recalled that he had seen Congolese whose limbs had been severed and that, upon questioning them, he found that this practice was used as a punishment by the Leopoldian government.[49]

While both the Afro-American press and missionaries played an important role in publicizing the developments in the Congo, the religious community was also active in petitioning the U.S. government to use its influence in bringing about reforms. As early as 1904, the *Voice of Missions* had suggested that since the United States had been the first government to grant recognition to the International Association and had participated in the Berlin Conference it should be the first to act, with the aid of Great Britain, in making an appeal for the people of the Congo. The situation called for public denunciation, the *Voice* asserted.[50]

As a result of a missionary conference held at Kinchassa (Stanley Pool) on 11 January 1906, a memorial containing the signatures of fifty-two missionaries in the Congo was sent to the U.S. government and referred to the Senate Committee on Foreign Relations. Henry P. Hawkins, a black missionary in the Congo from 1894 to 1916 representing the Southern Presbyterian Church, was among the signers of this memorial, which protested against the continued disregard for appeals in behalf of the Congolese for humane treatment from the Belgian exploiters. Earlier, in 1904, Hawkins, as editor of the *Kassai Herald*, cautioned that "European civilization" was bringing to Africa things that tended to demoralize rather than "civilize."[51]

Memorials and petitions were sent to the U.S. government from various sectors of the Afro-American religious community. Members of the Charles Street African Methodist Episcopal (AME) Church in Boston sent a petition to the president and Congress of the United States on 30 September 1906 protesting the intolerable oppression of the Congolese. The adverse conditions in the Congo had been proved beyond question by the report of Leopold's Commission of Inquiry, the petitioners contended. The petitioners continued, maintaining that the ten million black citizens of the United States could not endure this injustice in the Congo without coming to the defense of the Congolese. The congregation urged the U.S. government to cooperate with Great Britain in an attempt "to rescue our Congo brothers from their immeasurable misery."[52]

In other instances, Afro-Americans not affiliated with the religious community sent letters and petitions to the Department of State. Much of this latter activity was encouraged by the efforts of the Congo Reform Association. In December of 1906, for example, as a result of an intense campaign on Howard University's campus by the Congo Reform Association to gain Afro-American assistance for the Congo reform movement, members of the university addressed comments to the State Department concerning the Congo controversy.

Ethel O. Hedgeman, a sophomore at Howard University, in a letter to Secretary of State Elihu Root in December 1906, expressed astonishment that the "so-called Christian nations" permitted the atrocities to continue in the Congo. She explained that she was disappointed that the U.S. government was not taking steps toward helping to ameliorate the conditions in the Congo and appealed to this country to right the wrongs being committed in the Congo.[53]

On 12 December 1906, a committee of students from Howard submitted a petition to the State Department. They demanded that immediate changes be brought about in the Congo Free State and called upon the U.S. government to assert its influence to help in the movement for bringing about reforms.[54]

George W. Cook, dean of the Commercial Department at Howard University, also voiced his opinion of U.S. policy with the Congo in a letter to Secretary Root. He felt that the United States should interfere in the Congo as long as it was consistent with official practices and asked that the United States intervene in the political and commercial affairs of the Congo so that justice would be given to the Congolese.[55]

Several weeks following this barrage of letters and petitions to the State Department, Edward L. Blackshear, principal of Prairie View State Normal and Industrial College in Texas, and second only to Washington as an educator who supported industrial training, suggested that this method be used as a way of informing the U.S. government of Afro-American concern for the conditions in the Congo. In discussing the "Congo horrors" in the *Age*, he contended that "the members of our race" in the Congo Free State cried out to black Americans for redress. He reported that the misdeeds that the Belgians and Germans had inflicted upon Africans were numerous and stated that the present Leopoldian policy seemed to be aimed at the extermination of the Congolese people. Blackshear advised black Americans throughout the country to circulate petitions in their churches and communities and forward them to the U.S. government and to the national headquarters of church groups so that these committees could present these petitions to King Leopold.[56]

Another educator, William Sanders Scarborough, president of Wilberforce University from 1908 to 1920, commented in an article in the *Voice of the Negro* that the end of Leopold's rule in the Congo was inevitable. According to Scarborough, it was just a matter of time before world pressure would force the Belgians to realize that the Congo situation reflected upon their world image and to annex the country.[57]

All of the previously discussed methods of responding to the Congo scandal, including publications in newspapers and periodicals and letters and petitions to the U.S. government, were employed by Booker T. Washington. Washington was so prominent in the Congo debate that his activities in the reform movement stand apart from the other sectors of the Afro-American community. Washington was constantly consulted because whites looked to him as the leader of black people. He subscribed to the idea of the "white man's burden" and the "civilizing mission" concept.

Washington dedicated a great amount of attention to African affairs. He felt that it was the duty of the more "civilized" nations and peoples of the world to help "uplift" the "less fortunate" members. He saw Africans as "savages" who needed to be "civilized and Christianized." Washington was very active in the Congo controversy; he gave speeches, presented petitions to the State Department, wrote articles, and even served as an officer in the American Congo Reform Association.[58]

At the International Peace Congress in October 1904, Washington attacked the government in the Congo and accused it of sanctioning the alleged outrages in the colony. He claimed that he had written testimony from Sheppard of the atrocities committed in that country, and he called upon the nations of the world to rise up against such cruelties. Asserting that he spoke for blacks in Africa and America

when he denounced the policies of Leopold's government, he concluded that most blacks in the United States were particularly interested in the outcome of the events in the Congo Free State.[59]

During the same month, Washington was credited with an article
in *Outlook* entitled "Cruelty in the Congo Country."[60] In making a
comparison between blacks in Africa and blacks in other parts of the
world, he declared that the oppression of blacks in one part of the
world led to the oppression of blacks in other parts. Even considering his belief in the "inferiority" of Africans, Washington nonetheless
adhered to the theme of brotherhood among blacks and the need for
solidarity. He denounced Leopold's government and concluded
that, if the administration of the Congo did not change, "civilized"
nations would have to intervene in behalf of the mistreated Congolese.[61]

Washington was closely associated with the activities of the Congo
Reform Association, and served as a spokesman for gaining approval
from black leaders and organizations. In November 1905, H. P.
McCormick, corresponding secretary of the association, wrote to
Washington informing him of an extensive campaign that the organization was undertaking regarding the conditions in the Congo and
requesting Washington to act as one of the association's vice presidents. McCormick commented that the association was interested in
arousing the awareness of all blacks in America on the Congo situation and gaining their support.[62] Washington accepted the position as
vice president of the American Congo Reform Association. His
name appeared as vice president on the letterhead of the association
in 1905 and 1906, along with that of one of his ghost writers, advisors, and later press agent, Robert E. Park, the white sociologist, as
recording secretary.[63] Washington made many personal attempts,
through his office, to persuade the U.S. government to use its diplomatic influence with Belgium to help bring about changes in the
Congo.

In November 1905, for example, Washington, representing the
American Congo Reform Association, presented a memorial to
President Theodore Roosevelt indicating the association's concern
for conditions in the Congo and urging the U.S. government to put
diplomatic pressure on the Belgian government and Leopold to help
bring about reforms in the Congo.[64] He was accompanied by a com-

mittee from the National Baptist Convention, the largest black organization during this period.[65]

Washington was also constantly called upon by the Congo Reform
Association to write articles protesting the conditions in the Congo.
Park wrote to Washington for the association in 1906, asking him to
write an article in the newsletter emphasizing that Afro-Americans
should become involved in the work of the organization and suggesting that black Americans assist in helping to pressure the U.S. government to intervene in the Congo. Apparently, the Congo Reform
Association felt that there was not enough involvement by the Afro-
American community in the Congo question. Park even suggested
that the association had begun to question Washington's interest and
stated that he was not taking an active enough role in the group.
Park mentioned that he would help Washington write the article.[66]
Washington completed this article and submitted it for publication.[67]

The article appeared in the August 1906 issue of *The Congo News
Letter* (Boston). Washington addressed himself to the issue of the
future of the Congo reform movement. He charged that, in partitioning Africa, the European powers had not given much attention to the
welfare of the African people and that, in the Congo, Belgian capitalists had encouraged a system of forced labor. Washington recommended that a permanent international society of scientists, explorers, and missionaries be established to exercise influence upon the
colonial policy of the European nations to protect the interests of
Africa and its people.[68] This suggestion would later be partially realized under the mandate system of the League of Nations.

Washington's influence in the Congo reform movement was felt to
be so effective that his opponents began to solicit his advice for bringing about reforms in the Congo.[69] Leopold attempted to interest
Washington in the Congo throughout 1905 and 1906 and exerted
pressure upon him to break with the Congo Reform Association.
Leopold offered Washington a free trip to the Congo, which he refused, and his representatives in the United States flattered Washington and tried to convince him that unscrupulous people were using
him to attack a just and humane government.[70]

In all these cases, the U.S. government failed to respond officially
to these appeals. Indeed, the U.S. government was supposedly
reluctant to comment on or interfere in the Congo, supposedly fear-

ful of "entangling alliances." Intervention might later require military enforcement, and the U.S. government was involved in foreign affairs in other parts of the world that took precedence over those in Africa. President Roosevelt, for example, commented that he did not wish to make the United States appear as meddling with what did not concern it.[71] John Hay, secretary of state when the Congo controversy began, commented in his diary after a visit from Morel that he saw no reason why the United States should intervene in the Congo, particularly considering that it had recognized the Congo government and entered into relations with it and especially in view of the fact that it had declined to sign the Congo agreement of the Berlin Act.[72] Later, Secretary of State Elihu Root maintained this policy. Root attempted to avoid discussion of Congo affairs[73] and consistently followed a policy of urging Great Britain to be the initiator of reforms.[74]

Further investigation demonstrates that U.S. foreign policy in the Congo from 1880 to 1914 was also based on economic considerations. The Congo was one of the important areas for American investment in Africa during this period. Leopold had granted commercial concessions to American citizens, and the American Congo Company, a syndicate of American millionaires, was one of four monopoly companies formed for the exploitation of that region. This could further explain America's reluctance to interfere in the affairs of the Congo Free State.

But persistent pressure from American and British reformers, a shift in American public opinion toward favoring some form of intervention, and the scandal arising from the exposure of King Leopold's American Congo lobby organized to influence Congress pushed the U.S. government closer to action. By 1906, President Roosevelt felt that he had adequate popular support to inform the British government that the United States was ready to attend any international conference to discuss the affairs of the Congo.[75]

In September 1906, the U.S. government expressed the desire to seek reforms in the Congo and, in conjunction with a declaration from Great Britain, officially protested the abuses of the Leopoldian government in the Congo.[76] In changing its position, the United States was not only bowing to pressure from the Congo Reform Association and from spokesmen like Washington but was responding to the entreaties of the British government as well.

Because of the worldwide condemnation of Leopold's rule in the Congo, the Belgian government began seriously to consider annexation of the Congo Free State. A commission of inquiry sent to the Congo in 1904 had confirmed the rumors of abuses in the government there.[77] Beginning in February 1906, the Belgian House of Representatives held debates on Leopold's administration in the Congo. The Belgian House debated the future of the Congo Free State on 20, 27, 28 February and 1, 2 March 1906. During these initial debates, the Leopoldian government in the Congo was criticized, and the House recommended Belgian annexation of the Congo.[78] This debate over the annexation of the Congo was not settled at this time, and the discussion continued for the next two years.

However, on 15 November 1908, sovereignty over the Congo Free State formally passed from King Leopold II to the reluctant Belgian government.[79] During the years of the Congo controversy, the movement for reform reached full strength and was largely stimulated by the Congo Reform Association. The association contributed immensely to Belgium's annexation of the Congo.[80] Although annexation ended discussion of the Leopoldian government in the Congo and the international movement for reforms in his administration, it did not end the issue of imperialism in the Congo.

Several black newspapers approved of the transfer of control of the Congo from Leopold to Belgium. They saw Belgium's annexation as an act of mercy. But these journalists were reluctant to accept Belgian imperialism without question. The *New York Age* stated that, with Belgian annexation of the Congo, "Africa is completely divided among the European nations." Belgium promised justice and "development" for the Congolese, but blacks maintained that the world would be watching to see that it fulfilled this pledge.[81]

One final incident marked the close of international discussion of imperialism in the Congo during this period. In February 1909, Louis Napoleon Chaltin, director of field operations for the Kasai Company (Compagnie du Kasai), a concessionary company located in the Kasai region of the Congo, filed a complaint against William M. Morrison and Sheppard, missionaries in the Congo, for "having sullied the respectability and injured the credit of the Company by means of certain publications in the 'Kasai Herald.'" Sheppard's article, published in 1908, was said to contain "lying affirmations."[82]

After several postponements, the trial began in Leopoldville on 20 September 1909. Sheppard was tried alone and found not guilty of malicious intent to injure the Kasai Company, and the company was fined court costs, $8.11.[83] Soon after, Sheppard returned to the United States permanently, and thereafter the Belgian government discouraged black missionaries in the Congo.[84] This dissuading of blacks from missionary work in the Congo was only one example of the policy that white imperialists throughout Africa were beginning to implement. Although blacks did not comment on this restraining tactic in the Congo, there was a mild outcry when it happened in South Africa.

Some blacks saw Sheppard's acquittal as an admission by the Belgian government of the crimes allegedly committed in the Congo. Now that Sheppard and Morrison had been acquitted, explained the *Colored American Magazine*, the knowledge of these heinous crimes should be acted upon and brought to an end.[85] Even by the end of 1909, though, the black press was reporting that atrocities, mutilations, and forced labor were still going on in the Congo.[86]

King Leopold II of Belgium died on 7 December 1909. Since the annexation of the Congo by the Belgian government, blacks had not really devoted any discussion to the effect of Leopold's rule in the Congo, but the *Savannah Tribune* saw his death as a blessing since he had much of the world against him because of his administration there.[87]

The annexation of the Congo by Belgium in 1908, the end of the Congo controversy that same year, and Leopold's death in 1909, brought to a close a brutal period in the Congo's history. Nevertheless, many observers viewed the fate of the country with apprehension. Commenting on the future of the Congo in 1910, Sheppard still held the view that the Congolese people were "uncivilized" and in need of the "Christianizing" influence of the Western world. He referred to them as "benighted brethren" who were superstitious and ignorant. But he felt that they could be "civilized" and "Christianized," and he saw hope for the "development" of the Congo and the Congolese under Belgian rule.[88] Other blacks agreed with Sheppard that reforms would be made in the Congo under Belgian rule to mitigate the horrors committed upon the Africans by the Leopoldian regime.

On 16 June 1913, the Congo Reform Association disbanded. The United States and the European powers regarded the Congo controversy as a dead issue.[89] The issue of encroaching imperialism was also inconsequential since by this time all of Africa, except for Ethiopia and Liberia, was under European control.

The early years of the twentieth century saw the final partitioning of Africa by the European powers and the entrenchment of imperialism there. Many black Americans who were aware of what was going on in Africa denounced imperialism in Africa when it centered around oppression and exploitation. They particularly denounced Belgian imperialism because of the obvious examples of maladministration. In this instance, blacks responded less to the question of European imperialism in general and more to oppressive Belgian imperialism.

The Congo scandal was one of the early publicized incidents of the exploitative nature of European imperialism in Africa. In his interviews of over one hundred Afro-Americans, Harold Isaacs reported that members of the panel frequently mentioned Leopold's atrocities in the Congo. One informant stated, "We heard of the Belgian Congo, the crimes of Leopold." Apparently, the Congo atrocities were discussed in black homes and churches, and in some families stories of the Congo outrages were passed down from one generation to another.[90] Since it was an example of abusive imperialism, the Congo developments resulted in a tendency for blacks to view European imperialism generally in a less positive manner. Although still believing in many of the tenets of the "civilizing mission" concept, middle-class Afro-Americans increasingly expressed doubts about the objectives of the Europeans in Africa, as they had done earlier in the case of the U.S. government in the Spanish-American War. And, as in the case of the war, these blacks rejected any idea of emigration, even though their position in American society was not improving.

Throughout the Congo controversy, many Afro-Americans emphasized the need for unity among blacks in elevating their position around the world. Because of their exposure to Western culture, these black Americans believed that it was their "duty" to help in the process of "development" in Africa. Increasingly, Afro-Americans began to hear of Africans being mistreated. At the same time that the atrocities were being committed in the Congo, for example, Africans throughout the continent were being relegated to an inferior position in their society. Thus, black Americans came more and more to question the benefits of European imperialism in Africa.

Notes

1. Roland Oliver and Anthony Atmore, *Africa Since 1800*, pp. 50-53, 108-10.

2. George Martelli, *Leopold to Lumumba*, pp. 107, 112; Jesse S. Reeves, *International Beginning of the Congo Free State*, pp. 17, 25, 53, 58, 68, 78; and Josphat N. Karanja, "United States Attitudes and Policy Toward the International African Association," pp. 9, 135.

3. Jean Stengers, "The Place of Leopold II in the History of Colonization," p. 30.

4. Ruth M. Slade, *King Leopold's Congo*, pp. 178-82; Harry H. Johnston, *George Grenfell and the Congo*, p. 415; and Jean Stengers, "The Congo Free State and the Belgian Congo Before 1914," p. 267.

5. John H. Franklin, *George Washington Williams and Africa*, p. 21.

6. See *Cleveland Gazette*, "King Leopold's Dilemma," 22 February 1890; and "To Go to Africa," 8 March 1890. Also examine, John H. Franklin, "George Washington Williams, Historian," p. 90; Paul McStallworth, "The United States and the Congo Question, 1884-1914," p. 198; and George Washington Williams to Robert Terrell, 13 March 1890, R. H. Terrell Papers (1).

7. McStallworth, "The United States and the Congo Question, 1884-1914," pp. 196-97.

8. George Washington Williams, "An Open Letter to His Serene Majesty Leopold II," in *Apropos of Africa*, comp. and ed. Martin Kilson and Adelaide Cromwell Hill, pp. 98-107; and Franklin, "George Washington Williams," p. 25.

9. Williams, "An Open Letter to His Serene Majesty Leopold II," p. 107.

10. George Washington Williams to Robert Terrell, 14 October 1890, R. H. Terrell Papers (1).

11. William H. Sheppard, *Presbyterian Pioneers in Congo*, pp. 62-63; Stanley Shaloff, *Reform in Leopold's Congo*, pp. 20-22; Robert D. Bedinger, *Triumphs of the Gospel in the Belgian Congo*, p. 205; and "The Negro as a Missionary," *Missionary Herald* 91 (July 1899): 292-93.

12. W. H. Sheppard, "From the Bakuba Country," *Kassai Herald*, 1 January 1908, pp. 12-15, Sheppard Papers. Also contained in the Department of State, Record Group 59, Numerical File (1906-1910), Cases 12053, 61-12074, book 793 National Archives. (Hereafter cited DS, with numerical case number.)

13. "In the Heart of Africa," *Southern Workman* (April 1900): 220-21; "Cruelties on the Congo," *Missionary Herald* 96 (June 1900): 246; and An Account of a Visit to the Zappo Zap Camp, September 1899, Sheppard Papers.

14. Sylvanus J. S. Cookey, *Britain and the Congo Question, 1885-1913*, p. 18.

15. Ibid., pp. 92-106; Robert O. Collins, *King Leopold, England, and the Upper Nile, 1899-1909*, p. 202; William Roger Louis, "Roger Casement and the Congo," pp. 101-2, 109; and William R. Louis, "The Triumph of the Congo Reform Movement, 1905-1908," pp. 270-71.

16. Cookey, *Britain and the Congo Question, 1885-1913*, p. 65. A discussion of the formation of the British Congo Reform Association is also given in Louis, "Roger Casement and the Congo," p. 117; and McStallworth, "The U.S. and the Congo Question, 1884-1914," p. 226.

17. See *Boston Herald*, Editorial, "The Congo Question," 5 October 1904; "Peace Delegates Discuss Congo," 8 October 1904; and "Leopold's Rule in West Africa," 9 October 1904.

18. See *New York Daily Tribune* (New York City), "Want U. S. to Intervene," 8 February 1906; and "Urges Interference in Congo," 9 March 1906.

19. See *American Citizen*, "Senator Morgan on the Race Question," 10 January 1890, and "Congo Valley Schemes," 17 January 1890.

20. Joseph O. Baylen, "Senator John Tyler Morgan, E. D. Morel, and the Congo Reform Association," pp. 118, 124; and Letter to John T. Morgan, 8 January 1907, Morgan Papers (22).

21. Editorial, "The Congo Atrocities," *Southern Workman* (May 1904): 261-62. See also, Stengers, "The Congo Free State and the Belgian Congo Before 1914," p. 269; "Leopold's Rule in West Africa," *Boston Herald*, 9 October 1904; and John Daniels, "The Wretchedness of the Congo Natives," *Voice of the Negro* (January-February 1907): 22-28.

22. William Roger Louis and Jean Stengers, eds., *E. D. Morel's History of the Congo Reform Movement*, p. 183; and Shaloff, *Reform in Leopold's Congo*, p. 101.

23. William B. Gatewood, Jr., "Black Americans and the Quest for Empire, 1898-1903," pp. 545-48.

24. Editorial, "Conditions in the Congo Country," *Southern Workman* (November 1904): 580.

25. Editorial, "Some African Editorial Opinions," *Cleveland Gazette*, 26 November 1904.

26. Percy E. Murray, "Crusading Editor, Henry Clay Smith," pp. 31-38.

27. "Cruelties," *Cleveland Gazette*, 10 March 1906.

28. "Congo Crime!" *Cleveland Gazette*, 17 March 1906.

29. "The Story of the Congo Free State," *Alexander's Magazine* (December 1905): 36-37.

30. Edwin S. Redkey, *Black Exodus*, pp. 281-8 ; and "Future of Liberia," *Alexander's Magazine* (January 1907): 127.

31. "As to the Congo Free State," *Alexander's Magazine* (April 1906): 7-21.

32. Walter F. Walker, "Revolt Among the Congo Natives," *Alexander's Magazine* (October 1907): 326.

33. Editorial comment, "Stealing Africa," *Rising Sun* (Kansas City, Kansas), 20 July 1907; and "Belgian Atrocities Proven," *Boston Herald*, 26 October 1907.

34. Editorial, "The Congo Infamy," *Voice of the Negro* (December 1906): 541.

35. Editorial, "More About the Congo," *Voice of the Negro* (January-February 1907): 14-15.

36. U.S., Congress, Senate, *Affairs of the Kongo Free State*, S. Res. 194, 59th Cong., 2d sess., 1906, p. 192.

37. See *New York American* (New York City), "King Leopold's Amazing Attempt to Influence Our Congress Exposed," 10 December 1906; "Belgian Lobby Exposé Stirs Washington, Lodge Offers Resolutions in Senate, Sec'y Root Now in Favor of Action," 11 December 1906; "How Thomas G. Garrett, Secretary of the U.S. Senate Sub-Committee Aided King of Belgian's Lobbyists," 12 December 1906; "Create American Vested Interest in Congo to Stop the Yelping of Agitators," 13 December 1906; and "Whitley's Name on List of Directors in Ryan's Congo Company," 14 December 1906.

38. "In the Congo Country," *St. Louis Palladium* (Missouri), 15 December 1906.

39. Examples of these methods of protest can be found throughout the Minor File (1906-10), vols. 32-34, Kongo, U.S. Department of State, National Archives. See for instance: John Daniels to Elihu Root, 7 March 1907, vol. 32; Congo Reform Association to Theodore Roosevelt, 13 March

1907, vol. 32; John Daniels to Elihu Root, 14 November 1906, vol. 33; G. Stanley Hall to Elihu Root, 17 December 1906, vol. 33; John Daniels to Elihu Root, 27 December 1906, vol. 33; and resolutions received by the Department of State, 12 December 1906, 26 December 1906, and 2 January 1907, vol. 32; Congo Reform Association to Theodore Roosevelt, 13 March President and Congress of the United States of America, 31 March 1906, Record Group 46, Records of the U.S. Congress, Senate 58th Cong., Committee on Foreign Relations Papers Related to Affairs in the Congo, National Archives. (Hereafter cited R. G. 46, Records of U.S. Congress, 58th Cong.)

40. Editorial, "Down With Leopoldism in Africa," *Colored American Magazine* (November 1906): 285.

41. Emma Lou Thornbrough, *T. Thomas Fortune*, pp. 261, 308-9.

42. "Denounces Congo Troops," *Colored American Magazine* (August 1907): 94.

43. "Hostility to Europeans," *New York Age*, 13 December 1906.

44. See *New York Age*, Editorial, "Leopold's Atrocities," 20 December 1906; and Editorial, "The White Man in Africa," 27 December 1906.

45. See *New York Age*, Editorial, "Belgian Congo Abuses," 3 January 1907; and "Leopold's European Rivals in African Atrocities," 10 January 1907.

46. See *New York Age*, Editorial, "Belgian Congo Abuses," 3 January 1907; and Editorial, "Germans in Africa," 31 January 1907.

47. Editorial, "Revolt Among Congo Natives," *New York Age*, 19 September 1907.

48. Editorial, "The Race Press," *Horizon* (March 1907): 19.

49. Clinton C. Boone, *Congo as I Saw It*, pp. 1-2, 76.

50. Editorial, "The Congo Atrocities," *Voice of Missions* (October 1904): 4.

51. Memorial, Kinchassa, Stanley Pool, Congo Independent State, 11 January 1906, R. G. 46, Records of U.S. Congress, 58th Cong. Editorial note, *Kassai Herald*, 1 April 1904, p. 31.

52. Negroes of the Charles Street African Methodist Episcopal Church of Boston, Mass., to the President and Congress of the United States, 30 September 1906. Signed for the meeting by Walter F. Walker and M. R. DeMortie, Minor File (1906-10), vol. 34, Kongo (S) to Lil.

53. Ethel O. Hedgeman, Miner Hall, Howard University, to Elihu Root, Secretary of State, 9 December 1906, Minor File (1906-10), vol. 33, Kongo (C-R). For expression of about the same sentiment, see also, P. F. Brooks, Howard University, to Secretary of State Root, 10 December 1906, Minor

File (1906-10), vol. 32, JE to Kongo (B).

54. Petition, Howard University, to Elihu Root, Secretary of State, 12 December 1906, Minor File (1906-10), vol. 33, Kongo (C-R).

55. George W. Cook to Elihu Root, Secretary of State, 14 December 1906, Minor File (1906-10), vol. 33, Kongo (C-R).

56. E. L. Blackshear, "[Congo] Horrors," *New York Age*, 17 January 1907.

57. W. S. Scarborough, "World Movements of 1906," *Voice of the Negro* (March 1907): 113.

58. See, for example, Telegram from Booker T. Washington to Brentano's Booksellers, 17 May 1905, Washington Papers (298).

59. Editorial, "At Home and Abroad," *Boston Guardian*, 15 October 1904; "Peace Delegates Discuss Congo," *Boston Herald*, 8 October 1904; "The Congo Their Home," *Baltimore Sun*, 9 October 1904; and Editorial, "The World's Peace Congress," *Voice of the Negro* (November 1904): 509-10.

60. The royalty check, however, was sent to Robert E. Park, the secretary of the Congo Reform Association. See Louis R. Harlan, "Booker T. Washington and the White Man's Burden," pp. 449-50. Fred H. Matthews in "Robert Park, Congo Reform and Tuskegee," p. 38, has stated that Park wrote a series of articles on the Congo Free State during the Congo controversy that were signed by well-known leaders (both black and white).

61. Booker T. Washington, "Cruelty in the Congo Country," Washington Papers (968). See also, Booker T. Washington, "Cruelty in the Congo Country," *Outlook*, 8 October 1904, pp. 375-77; Editorial, "Conditions in the Congo Country," *Southern Workman* (November 1904): 580; and Editorial, "Savagery in the Congo Country," *Springfield Republican* (Massachusetts), 12 October 1904.

62. H. P. McCormick to Booker T. Washington, 14 November 1905, Washington Papers (878).

63. Booker T. Washington to H. P. McCormick, 25 November 1905, Washington Papers (878).

64. Booker T. Washington to Dr. L. G. Jordan, 28 November 1905, Washington Papers (877).

65. Ibid. See also, Booker T. Washington to George E. Stevens, 18 November 1905, Washington Papers (881).

66. Robert E. Park to Booker T. Washington, 29 June 1906, Washington Papers (33).

67. Letter to R. E. Park, 17 July 1906, Washington Papers (33).

68. Booker T. Washington, "The Future of Congo Reform," *The Congo News Letter* (August 1906): 9.

69. "Kowalsky's Letters to Leopold," *New York American*, 11 December 1906.

70. Henry I. Kowalsky to Booker T. Washington, 1 March 1905, Washington Papers (303).

71. Alfred L. P. Dennis, *Adventures in American Diplomacy, 1896-1906*, p. 443; and *A Compilation of the Messages and Papers of the Presidents*, vol. 14, p. 7118.

72. Diary, 1904, 14 October 1904, Hay Papers (1).

73. G. Stanley Hall to Elihu Root, 15 December 1905, Root Papers (41).

74. Edward W. Chester, *Clash of Titans*, p. 151; Cookey, *Britain and the Congo Question, 1885-1913*, p. 206; and Shaloff, *Reform in Leopold's Congo*, p. 97.

75. Henry Lane Wilson to Secretary of State Root, 19 November 1906, DS, 2911-2927, roll 281; and James A. Smith to Robert Bacon, 29 June 1907, DS, 7872-7910, roll 584. See also, Cookey, *Britain and the Congo Question, 1885-1913*, pp. 171-77; and Harold E. Hammond, "American Interest in the Exploration of the Dark Continent," passim.

76. Chester, *Clash of Titans*, p. 149; and Cookey, *Britain and the Congo Question, 1885-1913*, p. 180.

77. *A Report of the Commission of Inquiry Appointed by the Congo Free State Government*, pp. 7, 146-47.

78. U.S., Congress, Senate, *Verbatim Report of the Five Days' Congo Debate in the Belgian House of Representatives, February 20, 27, 28, March 1, 2, 1906*, S. Doc. 139, 59th Cong., 2d sess., 1906, passim.

79. Martelli, *Leopold to Lumumba*, pp. 176-84. Discussion of the annexation is also given in Louis, "The Triumph of the Congo Reform Movement, 1905-1908," p. 298; and McStallworth, "The United States and the Congo Question, 1884-1914," p. 245.

80. Bernard Porter, *Critics of Empire*, p. 271; and Louis, "The Triumph of the Congo Reform Movement, 1905-1908," p. 269.

81. "The Congo Independent State," *Voice of Missions* (January 1908): 3. See also, *New York Age*, Editorial, "The Relief of the Congo," 1 October 1908; Editorial, "The Rule of the Congo," 26 November 1908; and Editorial, "Relief for the Congolese," 29 April 1909.

82. William Handley to Assistant Secretary of State, 26 February 1909, and 20 March 1909, DS, 12024-12053/60, book 792.

83. Telegrams, William Handley to Secretary of State, 20 September 1909, and 5 October 1909, DS, 12053/61-12074, book 793. See also, Judgment of the Court, Enclosed in William Kirk to Assistant Secretary of State, 19 October 1909, DS, 12053/61-12074, book 793. The two hundred-odd documents in case 12053 all deal with the trial of Sheppard and Morrison.

84. Horace Mann Bond, "Howe and Isaacs in the Bush," pp. 72-73. See also, George Shepperson, "Negro American Influences on the Emergence of African Nationalism," p. 305; Edwin S. Redkey, "The Meaning of Africa to Afro-Americans," p. 21; and "American Negro Hero of Congo," *Boston Herald*, 17 October 1909.

85. See *Colored American Magazine*, Editorial, "Congo Missionaries Acquitted" (October 1909): p. 248; and Editorial, "The Acquittal of Sheppard" (November 1909): 381. See also, Editorial, "William Sheppard, Christian Fighter for African Rights," *Southern Workman* (January 1910): 8-9.

86. See *Cleveland Gazette*, "Kill and Eat Natives at Order of King Leopold," 11 December 1909, and 18 December 1909.

87. "King Leopold II Dead," *Savannah Tribune*, 25 December 1909.

88. William H. Sheppard, "Yesterday, Today and Tomorrow in the Congo," *Southern Workman* (August 1910): 446-47.

89. Louis, "Roger Casement and the Congo," p. 119; and Louis, "The Triumph of the Congo Reform Movement, 1905-1908," p. 270.

90. Harold Isaacs, *The New World of Negro Americans*, pp. 147-48.

THE CONTEST FOR EAST AFRICA, 1880–1914

6

Now appears the eastern coat lines of the continent of Africa. On that continent, I learn, lie the ashes of my fore-fathers. Peace abide with them, and may peace crowned with justice come to such of their descendants as are still the victims of dishonesty and inhumanity by enlightened and professedly Christian nations.

Shadow and Light, p. 239.
Mifflin Wistar Gibbs, 1823-1918

Great Britain and Germany have just concluded negotia-tions by which their respective so-called rights in [East] Africa are defined; while France stands upon the outside of the ring of thieves and gnashes her teeth because she was not consulted and her so-called rights were ignored.

Editorial, "Robbers in Africa," *New York Age*, 28 June 1890.
Timothy Thomas Fortune, 1856-1928

Portuguese East Africa [is] a national home to which the wandering Ethiopians [blacks] the world over might come and live in peace. Who could tell? With such a foothold an enterprising colony might expand until it had recaptured the whole continent [from Europeans].

The Pedro Gorino, p. 116.
Harry Dean, 1864-?

From the beginning of the nineteenth century until the 1880s, European contacts with East Africa, as in West Africa, were concerned with exploration, Christianization, and the consolidation of strongholds along the coast. In East Africa, the preparation for the partitioning roughly paralleled the activities in the west. Spurred on by commercial, exploratory, and Christian groups, European governments laid the foundations for the division of East Africa. However, the European colonization of this region, although basically commercial, also had strategic concerns.

There were two events in the years before 1880 that sparked interest in the eastern region of Africa. First was the continuing dispute over the source of the Nile River. Many well-known explorers joined the search for the origin of the Nile. It was believed that this knowledge would lead to the opening up of the interior of East Africa and also to control of the most important waterway in that area. In 1862, when John Hanning Speke reported to the world that Lake Victoria was the source of the Nile, European explorers, scientists, traders, financiers, and missionaries scrambled for influence in East Africa. Second, with the opening up of the Suez Canal in 1869, Europeans envisioned the eastern coast of Africa as a bridge connecting trade with Europe and the Far East. From this date on, there was a sharpened European interest in East Africa as British, French, German, and Belgian groups joined the Portuguese in the quest for territory there.[1]

Up to 1880, Europeans had generally avoided annexing territory along the eastern coast of Africa. Five European nations had minimal interest and control in this area, but the major power here was Arabian. Throughout most of the nineteenth century, the sultans of Zanzibar exerted authority over the Swahili-speaking peoples of the eastern coastal towns and over the islands off the mainland of East Africa.[2]

Surprisingly, it is in East Africa that we see that largest number of Europeans showing an initial interest in colonization. Portugal, France, Germany, Great Britain, and Belgium were all drawn to the region before 1880. Strategic considerations account for most of this curiosity.

During this time Portugal, which had been on the East African coast since the sixteenth century, continued to maintain a weak position in Mozambique, whereas the French had nominal control over the island of Madagascar. Germany's involvement in East Africa dated back to 1844, when the first missionary arrived there. Sponsored by the British Church Missionary Society, other German missionaries followed and paved the way for the explorers and traders who later appeared. The unification of Germany in 1871 provided an atmosphere conducive to German expansion throughout the world.

British influence in East Africa had begun in 1861. The opening of the Suez Canal hastened the decision to make East Africa the center of British imperial strategy in that part of the world. Although the British Foreign Office initially was not particularly interested in this area of Africa, their commitment increased concomitantly with their denial of desiring colonies in East Africa. Finally, the other power to show an early interest in East Africa was Belgium. Between 1878 and 1879, even Leopold II of Belgium considered colonization in East Africa. The International African Association experimented with the idea of an East African colony and created stations along Lake Tanganyika. Because there were no real conflicting claims for territory there, Leopold believed that this area was still open to European colonization. However, after the announcement by Henry Morton Stanley of the course of the Congo River, Leopold's interests shifted to that region.[3]

The Berlin West African Conference of 1884-85 helped to precipitate the partitioning of East Africa. The same general rules for the partitioning laid down for West Africa at the Berlin Conference were repeated for East Africa, and the apportionment into spheres of influence followed much the same patterns as had dictated the division of the western and central regions of the continent. The actual scramble for territory in East Africa only lasted a few years. After that, the major European powers here came to an agreement about the partitioning of the area. The primary problem in East Africa, however, was the presence of so many colonial powers engaged in activity there.[4]

In late 1885, the three dominant European powers in East Africa, Great Britain, France, and Germany, formed an "impartial Commission" to deal with the delimitation of interests in that area. The commission announced its findings in June of 1886. By the agreement presented, the Sultan of Zanzibar was permitted to retain the islands of Zanzibar and Pemba, a few other dependent islands off the coast of East Africa, and a strip of mainland shore ten miles wide and about one thousand miles long. The hinterland of the East African mainland was divided into two zones, the smaller northern one passed to Great Britain (British East Africa) and the southern area to Germany (German East Africa). The French settled for recognition of their claims in Madagascar. Portugal retained control of Mozambique. The Anglo-German Agreement of 1886 can be said to have determined for East Africa what the Berlin West African Conference did for West Africa.[5]

Between the Anglo-German Agreement of 1886 and the Heligoland Treaty of 1890, then, the two dominant European powers in East Africa were Great Britain and Germany. Although the Sultan of Zanzibar, the French, and the Portuguese continued to exert some control in their areas of authority, the British and Germans expanded their spheres of influence throughout the region.

The British had no colonies in East Africa before 1886, and, in fact, had no serious commercial or national interest in that area up to that date except to abolish the slave trade and maintain routes to India. However, from this time on the British began to build a colonial empire in East Africa.

The British hoped that a commercial company could develop East Africa at little expense to the home government. In 1885, Harry Johnston's work became the basis of the British East African Association. A few years later, in 1888, William Mackinnon, the shipping giant, was given a charter for his Imperial British East Africa Company. The British government approved of the aim of the company, to expand British control into the region of the Buganda kingdom, and authorized the company to administer and exploit certain territories to promote trade, commerce, and good government.[6]

Germany was also concerned with widening its authority in East Africa to include Uganda. With this mounting interest, the Anglo-German contest for East Africa shifted to a new area. Uganda was seen by both powers as a coveted prize because the region was fertile, attractive upland country and, most important, it controlled the headwaters of the Nile River.

Like the British areas, the German territories were also first developed by commercial companies. Bismarck approved of this for the same reasons as the British and selected the commercial company as the agent of his expansionist policy. The German Colonization Society, founded in 1884, had the aim of obtaining land in East Africa. Treaties of "eternal friendship" were signed with chiefs of the region ceding an area of almost 60,000 square miles to German interests.

In 1885, the German East Africa Company grew out of the German Colonization Society. The company concentrated on plantations and settlement rather than trade. The Swahili inhabitants of this region resented German colonization because it resulted in the loss of their land and competition in trade. But the company proved to be inexperienced and lacked sufficient resources to develop that area.[7]

In 1890, the German East Africa Company obtained a questionable treaty from the kabaka (king) of Buganda, Mwanga. Because of British interest in the area, a conference was called to settle the Anglo-German conflict over territory there. On 1 July 1890, three months after Bismarck had been succeeded by Graf von Caprivi, Great Britain and Germany signed a treaty delineating their respective "spheres of influence." The Heligoland Treaty of 1890, although covering broad areas in Africa, made a definitive settlement of territory in East Africa. By the agreement, Great Britain expanded its control in East Africa and gained new territory. Buganda came under British control, which guaranteed for it control of the headwaters of the Nile. The sphere of the British South Africa Company was defined, and the boundaries of German Togo and British Gold Coast in West Africa were fixed. The islands of Zanzibar and Pemba became British protectorates; the Sultan was not given any say in the matter. The Germans gave up Witu, Nyasaland, and all claims in British East Africa. In return, Germany received Heligoland, a tiny island in the North Sea, which was to be converted into a naval base; recognition of her position in Southwest Africa, augmented by the Caprivi Strip, which extended the area to the Zambezi River; an addition to German East Africa westward to the Great Lakes and the Congo Free State; and an extension of the German Cameroons to Lake Chad.[8]

The Heligoland Treaty of 1890 ended the scramble between Great Britain and Germany for territory in East Africa. All that remained was the "effective occupation" of the colonies and the establishment of colonial rule. In both the British and German areas, this continued, for the next few years, to be under the jurisdiction of the commercial companies.

The Imperial British East Africa Company continued to have control over the development of trade in British East Africa, and the newly acquired area of Uganda was placed under its control in 1892, after the pacification of Kabaka Mwanga by a military expedition under the leadership of Frederick Lugard. However, administration of these two regions proved beyond the financial power of the company, and losses eventually forced it to withdraw. The British government reluctantly took over control of the interior area from the company and proclaimed the Uganda Protectorate in 1894. The company also withdrew from the coastal areas, receiving compensation from the British government. The British East Africa Protectorate was declared in 1895. These colonies were thus added to the British empire.

The German East Africa Company continued to administer German East Africa. But the company also proved to be financially and politically weak and unable to develop the resources in this region. Finally, it relinquished its rights there, and German East Africa passed to the administration of the German empire on 1 January 1891, becoming the German East Africa Protectorate.

Generally speaking, the initial groundwork for British and German control in East Africa both centered around development by commercial companies. But in each instance company rule failed, just as the concessionary companies in the Congo Free State had failed to make that territory self-sustaining without abusive exploitation. None of these companies were able to make these areas economically profitable and were only effective in delaying governmental administration temporarily.[9]

Hence, by 1895 four European colonial powers had control in East Africa: Great Britain, Germany, and, of course, Portugal and France. Portugal began to assert itself in the field in the 1870s. Although long-established in Africa, the Portuguese barely met the minimal requirements for colonial possession. In 1876, the Portuguese government secured a loan to pay for a public works project in Africa. The Lisbon Geographical Society was later formed to encourage Portuguese colonial exploration. Poor and unable to maintain a dominant position in Africa, Portuguese imperialism in East Africa suffered from this basic weakness. Nonetheless, Portugal continued, during the partitioning of East Africa, to hold Mozambique ineffectively and, in spite of little government there, maintained a colonial policy basically no different from that of the other European colonizers.

The French continued to keep a weak hold on their European-acknowledged protectorate of Madagascar, but military action proved to be inadequate in controlling the peoples of the island. Finally, in 1894, French West African troops were transferred to Madagascar to pacify the area. Fighting continued until the people ultimately succumbed to French rule. Madagascar was officially declared a French colony in 1895.[10]

The mid-1880s saw the entrance of another European power in East Africa that had not shown an earlier interest. Italy, disappointed in the French declaration of a protectorate over Tunisia in 1883, and thus unable to actualize immediately its vision of a colony in North Africa, sought compensation on the eastern coast of the continent. Italy seized the port of Massawa in Ethiopia in 1885. In 1889, Italy announced a protectorate over Ethiopia and, in 1890, over a thousand miles of the Somali coast south of Cape Guardafui. Italy's expansion on the east coast ended, however, when it was decisively defeated by the Ethiopians in 1896. As a result, the Italian government found itself with a heavy burden of expense and two vulnerable and worthless strips of seacoast in East Africa, Eritrea and Italian Somaliland.[11]

After 1896, the Europeans in East Africa devoted their efforts primarily to administering and exploiting their colonial possessions there. Following the British takeover of British East Africa, its initial concern was with militarily subordinating the Africans. After several displays of their military strength, they were able to rule through the political institutions that already existed in the city-states on the Swahili coast. The British were not as successful, however, in securing law and order among the stateless societies of the Nilotic-speaking peoples in the interior of East Africa.[12]

Germany's problem in East Africa was a little different. The German government attempted to rule German East Africa, which had a population of over six million, with only seventy German administrators. Traditional political institutions were disregarded, and new patterns of authority were established. German settlers set up farms, and workers for these plantations, as in the Congo Free State, were recruited through forced labor. This system of brutality resulted in discontent among the African inhabitants and made the Germans less successful than the British in maintaining control over the East African peoples.[13]

In fact, this colonial mistreatment resulted in many African uprisings during the years 1890 to 1910. In British East Africa alone there were three during these years. In German East Africa, seven major revolts against colonial rule occurred between 1892 and 1907. The largest one was the Maji-Maji (water-water) Rebellion of 1905-1907, which seriously threatened German rule in German East Africa. The revolt centered around forced labor, taxes, and German repression in that country.[14]

By 1914, European rule in East Africa had been effectively established. World War I temporarily suspended European interest there. At the end of the war, German East Africa became a British mandate as Tanganyika Territory. In 1920, British East Africa became the Kenya Colony and Protectorate.[15]

Afro-American interest in the idea of colonization in East Africa had developed before the actual division of the area by Europeans. Martin Delany, antebellum emigrationist, proposed a "Project for an Expedition of Adventure to the Eastern Coast of Africa" as early as 1836. Delany suggested appointing a board of commissioners whose duty would be to direct an expedition to the East African coast, research a suitable location for Afro-American settlement, and make a topographical, geographical, geological, and botanical examination of the area. He hoped that funds could be raised from Great Britain and France, since they would benefit from opening up this area to trade. Delany emphasized, "The Eastern Coast of Africa has long been neglected . . . but has ever been our [Afro-Americans] choice part of the Continent." Delany probably was attracted to East Africa because less European interest had developed in the area at this time and because he felt emigration and colonization by black Americans in this area would be less objectionable to the European colonialists. He was also interested in black commercial development of the area. Although Delany's dream did not reach fruition, he continued to believe that this area was the most valuable in Africa and would grow into a prosperous region under Afro-American supervision.[16]

Delany's idea of an Afro-American East African colony was again considered during the European partitioning of the area. In 1888, a letter from a black American visiting East Africa was printed in the *Fisk Herald.* The writer acknowledged that there were no Afro-American missionaries or travelers in East Africa and called for the establishment of a colony there of "educated, civilized, and chris-tianised Americo-Africans."[17] This suggestion that blacks could emigrate and build up a colony in East Africa was reiterated through-out the period of the European partitioning and colonization of the area.

Another Afro-American in the late nineteenth and early twentieth centuries had the same idea that had been put forth earlier. Harry Dean, in an autobiographical account written years later, discussed his plan. Dean, following in the steps of Paul Cuffee, was a sea captain and has been described as a black Trader Horn. His ancestors had been seamen, and he had learned the science of navigation in Great Britain. In his fifty years as an explorer, he had circumnavi-gated Africa eighteen times, crossed it from east to west three times, and from north to south once. He was ardently pro-African and boasted that he knew African history. Dean felt that black Americans should emigrate to East Africa and stated, "I had always been con-vinced that the Ethiopean [black] must return to Africa if his race was ever to reach world prominence." He visualized bringing Afro-Americans to East Africa to form, in conjunction with the indigenous Africans, a united black nation.

In a strange set of circumstances, a Portuguese government official offered Dean "the vast territory of Portuguese East Africa [Mozam-bique] including the city of Lorenco Marques for the ridiculously low figure of fifty thousand pounds sterling." Dean took this offer seri-ously and marveled at the idea of an East African colony for Afro-Americans. He saw Portuguese East Africa as a "a national home to which the wandering Ethiopians [blacks] the world over might come and live in peace." A prosperous colony would show the European imperialists that Afro-Americans could gain by legal means all that they (the Europeans) had gained illegally and immorally, Dean contended. He launched his "Ethiopian" empire scheme in 1906.

Unfortunately, Dean was unable to raise the necessary funds to secure this dubious offer. He did not have the money himself and tried unsuccessfully to collect it from affluent American blacks. Dean became discouraged and observed, "I began to despair of ever acquiring for my race the territory of Portuguese East Africa." Dean sadly commented, "Thus the bright bubble burst, and the greatest chance the 'negro' has ever had to rehabilitate Africa came to nothing." It seems obvious that the Portuguese administrators were playing a joke on Dean. The pity was that he earnestly believed the offer and was heartbroken at not being able to found an empire in East Africa for Afro-Americans.[18]

There was another opportunity in 1907 for black Americans to cooperate in a pioneering effort in East Africa, a British developmental project. Since Booker T. Washington had been successful in sending Tuskegee graduates skilled in cotton culture to different areas in Africa, he was asked by several British financiers to supply a number of experts for cotton experimentation in British East Africa. Apparently, nothing ever came of this project, and the Tuskegee students were not sent to the colony.[19]

Before 1914, black religious interest and involvement in the scramble for and partitioning of Africa centered around events in West, Central, and South Africa, and up to this date, with few exceptions, they concerned themselves with the more widely publicized activities of Europeans in these areas. Black church denominations sent missionaries to West, Central, and South Africa; purely practical and economic reasons dictated these decisions. White denominations hesistantly sent black missionaries to these same areas, while East and North Africa were usually reserved for white missionaries. One writer has claimed that generally the large white denominations shied away from sending Afro-American missionaries anywhere in Africa after 1910, because of the possibility of an incident with the European imperial powers.[20] Although there does not appear to have been a ban on the entry of blacks into East Africa, few traveled there as missionaries of white churches before World War I.[21] There is evidence, however, that some blacks did travel to East Africa before 1914 in individual capacities, as physicians and businessmen.[22]

The scanty discussion in religious circles about East Africa before

1914 centered around economic and commercial growth. The ecclesiastic community believed that the building of roads, construction of railways, and erection of telegraph lines would be invaluable toward "civilizing" East Africa.[23]

It was not until the middle of World War I that blacks were involved in any significant number in extended mission contact with East Africa. This was made possible by the role of the International Committee of Colored Men's Young Men's Christian Association (YMCA), in conjunction with the Native Carrier Corps in the Allied forces' East African campaign. Max Yergan, a young black graduate of Shaw University (Raleigh, North Carolina), answered a request to work as YMCA secretary in India and was later transferred to British East Africa. Eventually, six additional black secretaries were sent to East Africa, fulfilling a long-frustrated desire of blacks to work with Europeans in East Africa to improve conditions there. When Yergan accepted the national secretaryship of East Africa, serving under the English National Council but deriving his support from the black department of the International Committee, a permanent link between black America and East Africa was established, in spite of the fact that Yergan was later recalled and eventually stationed in another African country. Extensive postwar possibilities for Afro-American mission work were suggested by this event.[24]

By the 1890s, the press began a brief discussion of the impact of the partitioning of East Africa. T. Thomas Fortune discussed the Heligoland Treaty of 1890. Fortune noted that the treaty signed by Great Britain and Germany relating to their respective rights in East Africa only served to emphasize that the continent of Africa was fast being parceled out among the strong governments of Europe. He claimed that serious disturbances in Europe over the partitioning of African territory had only been avoided by chance and a collision between the European "thieves" was likely to occur at any time. The rights of Africans had not been considered, he announced, and the time would come when Africans would unite and drive the European robbers from their continent. This prediction was not far from actuality since, as noted, between 1890 and 1910, serious African uprisings did occur.[25]

In the mid-1890s, Harry C. Smith of the *Cleveland Gazette* discussed the ineffectiveness of European governments in East Africa.

A cause of uneasiness among the European powers at the end of the nineteenth century was the reports of slave-like conditions on the plantations in Zanzibar and Pemba. Smith protested that instead of taking "civilization" to East Africa, the colonialists had instituted a severer form of slavery than that of the earlier Arab traders on the coast. He observed that the system of forced labor on the islands of Zanzibar and Pemba, off the coast of East Africa, was allowed to persist with the full knowledge of the European imperialists. Smith insisted that this form of slavery also continued despite urgent protests from other nations of the world.[26]

By the early twentieth century, journalists began to complain about British and German rule in East Africa, which they depicted as oppressive to the indigenous populations. The Germans were particularly criticized because of uprisings in several of their colonies, including German East Africa and Southwest Africa. These editors revived Martin Delany's nineteenth-century cry of "Africa for the Africans" and expressed the belief that Africans would eventually rule their continent. Germans were accused of slaughtering Africans in East and Southwest Africa and inciting them to insurrection. The "Africa for the Africans" movement, which spread throughout the continent in the early twentieth century, was associated with the Ethiopian movement that had developed in South Africa in the late nineteenth century.

The *Colored American Magazine* commented in a series of editorials in 1905 that because of the European partitioning of Africa, the spirit of rebellion had taken root all over the continent and Africans had decided to die or kill those who would dominate them. "Africa for the Africans" was the war cry of a people resolved to reclaim their land, the paper asserted, and the white man must withdraw or perish. The magazine declared, "African for the Africans, and for the Africans now!" Fred Moore warned that Africans would soon rise up against the British and French colonialists as they had against the Germans. Commending blacks for their growing interest in the events occurring on the continent, Moore observed, "We cannot but express the complete satisfaction with which we view the intelligent and patriotic interest the black men of all countries are beginning to show in the status and future of Africa."[27]

The *Voice of the Negro* voiced the same sentiment, expressing

delight that Africans had finally raised the cry "Africa for the Africans."
J. Max Barber explained that the flags of the "civilized" nations of
Europe in Africa were in the hands of men devoid of every vestige of
principle. The magazine reported that severe conflicts were taking
place between Africans and German troops stationed on the continent. Barber mentioned that many uprisings were occurring in German East Africa, and the Germans feared that the entire section was
about to be set ablaze with an insurrection. Barber noted that Germany was also having trouble in Southwest Africa.[28]

Fortune supported East African resistance to colonial rule. He
insisted that "none of the European governments have any right in
Africa" and emphasized that they were only there for what they
could exploit from the continent and its people. He reported that the
Europeans were slaughtering East Africans but were still having a
difficult time dominating the inhabitants. Fortune maintained that
blacks in the United States praised the fight of the Africans and were
beginning to oppose strongly German rule in Africa because of its
exploitative features. He encouraged African rebellion against
oppressive rule. From the beginning of the twentieth century until
1907, Fortune continued to urge African insurrection in editorials in
the *Age*.[29]

The *Boston Guardian* and the *Indianapolis Freeman* also described German imperialism as oppressive. The German colonial
policy had deprived the Africans of all their natural rights, the *Guardian* asserted. In addition, the *Freeman* contended that the Germans
had implemented drastic measures throughout their colonies to
suppress any idea of rebellion among the indigenous peoples.[30]

The *Cleveland Gazette* concurred with this depiction of German
imperialism. Although arriving late in the partitioning of Africa, the
paper asserted, Germany had developed an exploitative African
policy that was similar to the policies of the other European imperialists. "Africa for the Africans" was a cry rightfully spreading throughout Africa, the paper concluded.[31]

Thus, by the beginning of World War I, most black journalists
viewed German imperialism in East Africa as exploitative and British
rule as only a little better. They supported "Africa for the Africans" in
East Africa and throughout the continent and suggested resistance to
colonial rule. The rising tensions in Europe that eventually led to

World War I, with Germany long seen as a threatening menace on the horizon, could also account for anti-German sentiment within the journalistic community.

Of all the groups in the Afro-American community before 1914, black diplomats stationed in East Africa were the closest to European imperialism in that region. Afro-Americans have been sent as diplomats to the African countries of Liberia, Sierra Leone, Senegal, Angola, and Madagascar. This limited representation is indicative of the lack of American interest in the continent.

The first black American consul to Madagascar was John L. Waller, lawyer, journalist, politician, and entrepreneur. Waller, born a slave in Missouri, eventually migrated to Kansas with Benjamin "Pap" Singleton's exodus. He was admitted to the Iowa bar in 1877 and later the Kansas bar. In 1882, he established the *Western Recorder* (Kansas City, Kansas) and published it until 1885. Three years later, he and his cousin established the *American Citizen* (Topeka, Kansas). A loyal Republican, in 1889 he applied to President Benjamin Harrison for a consular post, after his efforts had helped carry Harrison in the election of 1888. Waller was appointed U.S. consul at Tamatave, Madagascar, in February of 1891, assumed the post in August of 1891, and continued to hold office until January of 1894. He carried with him the idea that Madagascar might be a solution to America's racial problems. Like Delany before him and Dean after him, he attempted to found a black empire in East Africa. During his four years as consul in Madagascar, Waller tried to persuade American blacks of the available opportunites in East Africa and wrote over five hundred letters to blacks and influential whites expounding the benefits of that region.[32]

While consul, Waller indentified with the Malagasy (Hova) government as peoples of color under the domination of whites and constantly criticized French imperialism in Madagascar. Shortly after his arrival, he became involved in a dispute between the French colonialists and Hova leaders. American interest in East Africa was principally in Zanzibar and it had been the first Western power to establish a consulate there. The United States had concluded commercial treaties with independent Madagascar in 1867 and 1881, though the island was only of marginal importance to America. France's weakly held protectorate had not been recognized by the

United States when Waller arrived in 1891, and his attitude, although consistent with American policy, was a constant source of friction with the French. His behavior evoked intense hostility from French representatives in Madagascar, who eventually concluded that Waller was a threat to French interest there.

At the end of his term as consul, Waller was granted a land concession from the Queen of Madagascar. He immediately advertised in American and African newspapers for settlers. The French Resident General declared the land grant "null and void" and would not recognize Waller's claim.[33] Unknowingly, Waller had become involved in an issue more important than a few acres of land. His claim put in question the ability of a European colonial power to control its colony.

In December of 1894, the French bombarded and captured Tamatave, proclaimed martial law, and put the mails under surveillance. Waller was arrested on 5 March 1895 and charged, first, with dispatching a letter from Tamatave without it being viewed by French authorities, in contravention of an 18 January 1895 public order, and, second, with attempting to correspond with the enemies of France to furnish them information prejudicial to the military and political situation of France in Madagascar. After arguments on both sides, the court, using procedures contrary to French law, by a unanimous vote found Waller guilty on both charges and sentenced him to twenty years' imprisonment. Waller, shipped from Madagascar to France chained to the ship's floor for seven days, without food or water for two days and nights, arrived in France, his health broken. Later elucidating his prison experience, Waller recounted that there was not a piece of furniture in his cell and that he slept and ate off the bare floor. He described the walls of the cell as damp with only one ray of light coming in. By the end of his prison stay Waller explained that he was almost blind.[34]

If it had not been for Waller's poor health, U.S. officials might not have acted in his behalf, but the possibility of an American ex-consul dying in a foreign prison prompted them to intervene. The State Department, although believing the charges and sentence were justified, reached an agreement with France stipulating that the U.S. government would not pursue Waller's claims against the French for damages relating to his imprisonment. With this understanding,

Waller was released on 21 February 1896.[35]

After his return to the United States, Waller tried unsuccesfully to obtain compensation for his land concession in Madagascar, continued to devote attention in his speeches and journalistic activites to the question of black emigration to Africa, and finally attempted to found a colony of black Americans in Cuba. With the Waller affair fading from international attention, the real issue was lost to history. But in the course of the imposition of European colonial rule in Africa, the Waller incident demonstrated European certitude in holding its African colonies in check and also emphasized America's determination to stay out of the question of European activity in Africa.[36]

Several years passed before another Afro-American was appointed as consul to Madagascar, but in October of 1897, Mifflin Wistar Gibbs was chosen United States Consul to Madagascar. Gibbs was born in 1823 in Philadelphia but moved to California in the 1850s, going into business as an importer of boots and shoes. In 1858, he moved to Victoria, Vancouver Island, British Columbia, where he established a mercantile house. He read law while in Victoria. Reuniting with his family in 1869, he moved to Oberlin, Ohio, where he allegedly entered and received a doctorate in law from Oberlin College. In 1871, he moved to Little Rock, Arkansas, opening up a law office, and eventually becoming a judge. From 1877 to 1889, he worked as register of the United States Land Office for the Little Rock District of Arkansas.[37]

On 1 January 1898, Gibbs left New York City for Madagascar. While in Tamatave, he criticized French imperialism for not improving the conditions of the people there. According to Gibbs, the establishment of French rule in Madagascar represented the planting of a strong nation's authority over a weaker power under the guise of "civilization and humanity." He characterized the colonial rule of the "professedly Christian nations" in East Africa as dishonest and inhumane. Rejecting the so-called civilizing mission concept, he maintained that wherever there was a territorial plum ripe for picking there was always a wanting "grabber." The French and British in Africa were no more than robbers and thieves and he exclaimed, "O! civilization; what crimes are committed in thy name!"[38]

In a letter addressed to E. E. Cooper, editor of the *Colored American*, Gibbs discussed French colonialism in Madagascar. He was optimistic that with the building of railroads, telegraph lines, turnpikes, and canals, the French might develop the country. Despite France's "force and iron will" in acquiring this territory, he stated, perhaps the interest of "civilization" would be realized. Gibbs remarked that he particularly approved of the French establishment of schools for industrial training since "as you know industrial training is my pet."[39]

Gibbs remained in Madagascar until April of 1901, when he requested a leave of absence. After his leave expired, he decided not to resume his postion and returned to his law practice in Little Rock. Another Afro-American, William Henry Hunt, the vice-consul who had been left in charge, was appointed consul.[40]

Hunt was born in 1869, in Louisiana and educated at Groton Academy and Williams College, both in Massachusetts. In 1898, he was appointed vice-consul to Gibbs and was selected consul to Madagascar by President William McKinley on 27 August 1901. He served until 1906, when he was transferred to St. Etienne, France. In 1904, he married Ida Gibbs, an Oberlin College graduate and the daughter of Judge Gibbs. Mrs. Hunt was particularly interested in African affairs and was a participant at the first Pan-African Congress of 1919. Hunt was a career diplomat, serving not only in Madagascar and France but also in Guadaloupe, the French West Indies, the Azores Islands, and Liberia. He retired from the foreign service in 1932, dying in Washington, D.C., in 1951.

Because of his position as a representative of the American government, and more importantly because of the Waller incident. neither Hunt nor his Afro-American successor, James G. Carter, who served as consul to Madagascar from 1906 to 1916, discussed the issue of colonialism in Africa or French imperialism in Madagascar. During Hunt's five-year stay in Madagascar he remained aloof from the question of the pros and cons of European activity in Africa.[41]

By 1914, East Africa, like the other areas of Africa, had been partitioned. And, like the other regions, the partitioning was not without incident. The source of conflict in this region centered around Afro-

Americans' unsuccessful attempts at settlement. Delany in what became British East Africa, Waller in Madagascar, and Dean in Portuguese East Africa (Mozambique) all contemplated the founding of a black American empire. However, the European colonialists were also determined to maintain their control over those areas. The contest for East Africa resulted in another victory for Europeans in their quest for African territory.

Notes

1. Robert O. Collins, *Europeans in Africa*, pp. 54-58; and Reginald Coupland, *The Exploitation of East Africa, 1856-1890*, pp. 319-24, 348.

2. Halford L. Hoskins, *European Imperialism in Africa*, p. 63; and Collins, *Europeans in Africa*, p. 55.

3. Basil Davidson, *East and Central Africa to the Late Nineteenth Century*, p. 170; Mary E. Townsend, *The Rise and Fall of Germany's Colonial Empire, 1884-1918*, p. 131; Norman R. Bennett, *Africa and Europe*, p. 89; Roland Oliver and Gervase Mathew, *History of East Africa*, 1, p. 364; Collins, *Europeans in Africa*, pp. 55-57, 71-73, 97; and Hoskins, *European Imperialism in Africa*, pp. 63-64.

4. Collins, *Europeans in Africa*, p. 71; and Hoskins, *European Imperialism in Africa*, p. 63.

5. *British Imperialism in East Africa*, p. 6; John D. Anderson, *West Africa and East Africa in the Nineteenth and Twentieth Centuries*, p. 300; and Hoskins, *European Imperialism in Africa*, pp. 65-66.

6. Anderson, *West Africa and East Africa in the Nineteenth and Twentieth Centuries*, pp. 298-301; Hoskins, *European Imperialism in Africa*, p. 66; and *British Imperialism in Africa*, p. 7.

7. Anderson, *West Africa and East Africa in the Nineteenth and Twentieth Centuries*, pp. 303-5; Hoskins, *European Imperialism in Africa*, p. 65; and Townsend, *The Rise and Fall of Germany's Colonial Empire, 1884-1918*, p. 124.

8. Zoe Marsh and G. W. Kingsnorth, *An Introduction to the History of East Africa*, p. 115; John H. Wellington, *Southwest Africa and Its Human Issues*, p. 172; Anderson, *West Africa and East Africa in the Nineteenth and*

Twentieth Centuries, pp. 301-2; Hoskins, *European Imperialism in Africa*, p. 67; Davidson, *East and Central Africa to the Late Nineteenth Century*, p. 172; Robert O. Collins, *King Leopold, England, and the Upper Nile, 1899-1909*, p. 28; and D. R. Gillard, "Salisbury's African Policy and the Heligoland Offer of 1890," p. 632.

9. Anderson, *West Africa and East Africa*, pp. 302-3; Hoskins, *European Imperialism in Africa*, p. 68; Townsend, *Germany's Colonial Empire*, p. 141; and *British Imperialism in East Africa*, pp. 7-8.

10. Lewis H. Gann and Peter Duignan, *Burden of Empire*, pp. 174-84.

11. Hoskins, *European Imperialism in Africa*, pp. 85-86.

12. Collins, *Europeans in Africa*, p. 95.

13. Ibid.; and Anderson, *West Africa and East Africa in the Nineteenth and Twentieth Centuries*, p. 307.

14. Collins, *Europeans in Africa*, p. 95; and Anderson, *West Africa and East Africa in the Nineteenth and Twentieth Centuries*, p. 308.

15. Hoskins, *European Imperialism in Africa*, pp. 68-69.

16. Martin R. Delany, *The Condition, Elevation, Emigration and Destiny of the Colored People of the United States*, appendix, pp. 211-13.

17. Letter to the Editor, *Fisk Herald* 5 (January 1888): 5.

18. Harry Dean, *The Pedro Gorino*, pp. 114-16, 123-24, 255; and Clifford Scott, "Up the Congo Without a Paddle," pp. 18-19.

19. Letters, J. K. Jones to B. T. Washington, 5 and 23 September 1907, Washington Papers (35).

20. Harold Isaacs, *The New World of Negro Americans*, p. 124.

21. Kenneth J. King, "The American Negro as Missionary to East Africa," pp. 5-10.

22. Theodore Roosevelt, *African Game Trails*, p. 10.

23. See, for example, *Voice of Missions*, "East Africa" (April 1893): 2; and Note (March 1904): 2.

24. See King, "The American Negro as Missionary to East Africa," pp. 8-9; and his *Pan-Africanism and Education*, pp. 58-59, 63.

25. Editorial, "Robbers in Africa," *New York Age*, 28 June 1890.

26. See *Cleveland Gazette*, Editorials, "Slavery in Zanzibar," 24 and 31 October 1896.

27. See *Colored American Magazine*, Editorial, "Africa for the Africans" (September 1905): 470-71; and Editorial, "Still Fighting in Africa" (December 1905): 663-64.

28. Editorial, "African Unrest," *Voice of the Negro* (June 1906): 400-1.

29. See *New York Age*, Editorial note, 12 September 1904; "Africa for the Africans," 1 June 1905; "Africa for the Africans," 28 December 1905; Editorial, "Germans in Africa," 31 January 1907; Editorial note, 12 September 1907; and Editorial note, 19 September 1907.

30. "African Natives Made Serfs by Germany," *Boston Guardian*, 2 November 1907; and "Africans Made Serfs by Germany," *Indianapolis Freeman*, 16 November 1907.

31. See *Cleveland Gazette*, "To Rule Africa," 17 June 1905; "Will be Fight," 24 June 1905; and "Germany in Africa," 18 November 1911.

32. I. Garland Penn, *The Afro-American Press and Its Editors*, pp. 191-92; Allison Blakely, "The John L. Waller Affair, 1895-1896," p. 216; Randall B. Woods, "Black America's Challenge to European Colonialism," pp. 58, 62-65, 73-74; and Roy Garvin, "Benjamin or 'Pap' Singleton and His Followers," p. 18.

33. Edward W. Chester, *Clash of Titans*, pp. 114, 135; Blakely, "The John L. Waller Affair, 1895-1896," pp. 216-17; and Woods, "Black America's Challenge to European Colonialism," pp. 66-67, 70-72.

34. France, Case of John L. Waller, in *Foreign Relations of the United States*, 1895, pt. 1, pp. 252-54; Blakely, "The John L. Waller Affair, 1895-1896," p. 217; "John L. Waller's Story," *Indianapolis Freeman*, 11 April 1896; and "Waller's Talk," *American Citizen*, 26 June 1896.

35. Frederick L. Schuman, *War and Diplomacy in the French Republic*, pp. 122-23; *Foreign Relations of the United States*, 1895, pt. 1, pp. 314-16; and Blakely, "The John L. Waller Affair, 1895-1896," pp. 217-18.

36. Blakely, "The John L. Waller Affair, 1895-1896," pp. 217-18; and Woods, "Black America's Challenge to European Colonialism," p. 66. Waller's case and State Department action can be found in *Foreign Relations of the United States*, 1895, pt. 1, pp. 251-396.

37. J. Max Barber, *How They Became Distinguished*, pp. 35-36; Mifflin Wistar Gibbs, *Shadow and Light*, pp. 3, 85, 110-11, 126, 128, 136, 185, 222; and Robbin W. Winks, *Blacks in Canada*, pp. 274, 276, 285.

38. Gibbs, *Shadow and Light*, pp. 223-24, 239, 242, 284.

39. Ibid., pp. 244-46.

40. Ibid., pp. 311-12, 321.

41. Hunt briefly discussed conditions in Madagascar, in Letter, William Hunt to Ida Gibbs, 12 January 1901, Hunt Papers (2).

I grant you that British rule in South Africa is not all we wish it were but it is a thousand times better than Boer administration. Britain has her missionaries there and doing *something* to lift up the race while the Boers with all their religious hypocrisy dont [*sic*] believe we even have a *soul* to be saved and only seek to repress and further degrade us.

Letter to John E. Bruce, 29 April 1900, in *Apropos of Africa*, comp. and ed. by Martin Kilson and Adelaide Cromwell Hill, p. 143.

Frederick J. Loudin, 1840-1904

In South Africa and England, as well as in other portions of the world, there are those who are friendly to the Boers in their attempt to maintain their independence, believing their cause to be just. But it is quite certain that a considerable majority of sympathizers are on the side of England.

Observations of Persons and Things in South Africa, 1900-1904, Letter no. 17, p. 140.

Levi Jenkins Coppin, 1848-1924

The people [Boers] who are now asking the civilized world to sympathize with them, and, if need be, assist them, are those whose policy has been repressive, exclusive, ungenerous, and tyrannical.

Editorial, "The Boers and the English," *Washington Bee*, 21 October 1899.

William Calvin Chase, 1854-1921

America's initial contact with South Africa during the years 1784 to 1834 was primarily commercial. The United States sent its first consul to Cape Town in 1799. After 1834, white American missionaries began to be stationed in South Africa. Unquestionably, this missionary activity was oftentimes tied to the operation of trading activity. However, American diplomatic involvements in South Africa before 1880 were almost negligible.[1]

One significant aspect of South African history during this early period was the struggle between the British and the Boers (South African settlers of Dutch ancestry, who today call themselves Afrikaners),[2] for control of that area. The British first occupied Cape Colony in 1795. Later, they occupied Natal Colony. For generations, however, they followed a laissez faire policy of government throughout South Africa, finally recognizing the sovereignty of the Boer republics, the South African Republic (Transvaal) in 1852 and the Orange Free State in 1854. More intense problems involving rule in South Africa were created with the beginning of diamond mining in 1867, and the opening up of the gold fields after 1884. Both of these events brought an influx of British settlers and a change in the patterns of South African political life. The eventual annexation of the diamond fields by Cape Colony was one of the causes of the war between the British and Boers, which began at the end of the nineteenth century.

Organized Boer resistance to the British imperialists was led by Paul Kruger, president of the South African Republic from 1880 to the end of the Anglo-Boer War in 1902. He advocated complete independence from British control for the two Boer republics.

Meanwhile, the black South African population was also undergoing change. Systematically, through the years the South Africans were placed in a position of subjugation and servitude. In 1809, a proclamation issued by the British government abolished the "tribal system" and placed the South African Khoikhois (Hottentots) under colonial rule. Later that same year another proclamation marked the beginning of the pass system. The South Africans were dispossessed of their land, forbidden to practice their traditional methods of food gathering, taxed, and thus forced to supply the labor for Cape Colony. Although the Boers had not camouflaged their system of quasi-slavery among South Africans, the British used a more subtle method to subjugate the black population.[3]

The British found that their greatest opposition among black South Africans came from the Zulus. The main cause of dispute between the British government and the Zulus centered around the boundary between Zululand and the Transvaal. Because of the administrative and financial collapse of the Transvaal, Great Britain had annexed the area in 1877. As a result of this border question, the Zulu War began in January 1879, and the first battle ended in the victory of the Zulus at Isandhlwana. The British, however, were victorious later in July when the final battle was fought at Ulundi. To some historians, the Zulu defeat removed the final obstacle in South Africa to British control over the black South Africans and represented the first stage in British rule of all of South Africa.[4]

The question as to which white power would rule in South Africa culminated in the Anglo-Boer War of 1899-1902. On 9 October 1899, the South African Republic, or the Transvaal, presented an ultimatum to the British government demanding the withdrawal of British troops from the frontier. When Great Britain refused to comply with these terms, the armed forces of the Transvaal crossed the border into the British colony of Natal on 11 October. The Orange Free State joined its sister republic, the Transvaal, and thus began the struggle which would linger on for the next two years and eight months. The war centered around the question of who would control South Africa, the British or the Boers.[5]

On 19 October 1899, the Boers informed the U.S. government that a state of war existed between the British and themselves.[6] The war created nationwide interest within the United States.[7] The United States itself had recently become involved in imperialistic ventures with the colonial acquisitions from the Spanish-American War; so Americans were more attuned to international events.[8]

Boer sympathizers viewed American intervention as the only way of bringing an end to the hostilities. Early in the war, they sought to persuade President William McKinley to act as a mediator.[9] In addition, Boer representatives thought that, if they could influence popular sentiment, they could alter official policy and gain American support.[10]

Great Britain also attempted to influence American official policy and turned to the United States for sympathy and economic support.[11] The British and Boer campaigns in the United States differed, however, in that Great Britain, believing that the U.S. government would be impartial, did not attempt to launch a formal campaign to promote its objectives.[12]

The U.S. government did indeed adhere to a policy of neutrality in the Anglo-Boer War,[13] although it refrained from a formal declaration of neutrality and preferred to remain silent.[14] Yet, despite this official political stance, the U.S. government demonstrated a more benevolent neutrality toward the British cause than the Boer and furnished diplomatic aid and comfort wherever necessary to Great Britain. American officials, fearful of the international political effects of a British defeat in South Africa, quietly assured themselves that Great Britain would win.[15] A British victory was also desired by commercial and financial interests in the United States that had economic reasons for supporting the status quo.[16]

Through constant discussion in the press supplied by Boer delegates and American supporters, public interest in the war was maintained.[17] Anticolonial feeling, a part of the American tradition, was used to arouse sympathy for the Boers. Appeals were constantly being made to President McKinley to aid in mediation. In soliciting support, the Boers attempted to compare their struggle for independence with America's early years under British rule.[18] The pro-British policy followed by President McKinley and Secretary of State John Hay was not affected by public sentiment, however.[19] McKinley made it clear in his State of the Union address in 1899 that the U.S. government would remain faithful to the doctrine of avoiding "entangling alliances."[20]

The indigenous population of South Africa was not a prominent issue in the minds of most observers or critics during the Anglo-Boer War.[21] Concern for the black South African was seldom shown, and the question of their welfare, when raised at all in the debates over the war, was used simply as a mechanism for gaining support for one side or another in the discussion. The South Africans themselves seemed to have favored the British.[22] According to Marshal Maxeke, a South African attending Wilberforce University during the war, his people were entirely opposed to the Boers because of their lack of knowledge about right and justice, and they hoped for a British victory.[23] However, many blacks and whites indicated real doubt that British rule in South Africa would offer less injustice.[24]

During the early years of the war, the American public was bombarded with articles, editorials, and news items discussing the war. Because of this propaganda and the lack of information concerning the background to the war, Americans were not sure initially which side was the more just. Some Americans sided with the British, believing that Great Britain, because of its superior military strength, would naturally win. These supporters also pointed out that the United States and the cause of "civilization" would best be served by the victory of the British forces in South Africa.[25] Others contended that the Boer cause was worthy and that Great Britain had a long record of being a bully among nations. They believed that, as long as the Anglo-Boer War lasted, sentiment would be against the British because Americans admired the unexampled courage and devotion of these tiny republics fighting for their independence.[26]

Indeed, most white Americans saw the Anglo-Boer War as one between a strong monarchy and a small, determined republic. An appeal for sympathy was elicited by contrasting the small Boer republics to the giant empire of Great Britain.[27] The Boers eventually came to represent the unending quest for liberty, while the British represented tyrannical control. The most avid supporters of the Boers were the old enemies of the British: Irish-Americans, German-Americans, and Dutch-Americans.[28]

Boer sympathizers sent petitions, resolutions, and delegations to President McKinley and the Department of State attempting to solicit American mediation in the war.[29] Resolutions condemning British involvement in South Africa and expressing support and sympathy for the Boers were also passed by many state legislatures and introduced in Congress.[30] Americans hoped that these resolutions would demonstrate that American public sentiment was in favor of the Boers and would force President McKinley to adopt a more energetic role in negotiating an end to the war.[31] In addition, mass meetings were held throughout the country to demonstrate in behalf of the Boers, and thousands of dollars were raised for the Boer Relief Fund.[32]

However, the fact that the Senate Committee on Foreign Relations and the House Committee on Foreign Affairs were pro-British was a factor of significant consequence. Although resolutions were introduced periodically in these committees during the Anglo-Boer

War authorizing the U.S. government to offer its services as a mediator, they never gained any notable support and always died in committee.[33]

Despite the governmental policy of neutrality and the futile attempts to gain support in the U.S. Congress, the Boers continued throughout the war to work for American intervention. In January 1900, May 1900, and again in February 1902, Boer envoys came to the United States to gain support for their cause. On all three visits, the president and the secretary of state spoke with these emissaries but tactfully refused to promise any intervention on the part of the U.S. government.[34]

American sentiment in the Anglo-Boer War was put to a test in 1900. The Democratic party's overestimation of American public sentiment for the Boers was a significant issue in the presidential campaign and election of 1900.[35] The Democratic platform declared support for the Boers in their "heroic" and "unequal" struggle to gain independence and condemned British oppression in South Africa.[36] The strategy of the party was to use this issue in the election as a means of gaining votes. They also attempted to emphasize McKinley's partiality towards the British.[37] The Boer issue may have influenced a few voters in the election, but it was not important enough to win a Democratic victory. William Jennings Bryan's denunciation of British rule in South Africa, in conjunction with his denunciation of American imperialism in the Philippines, apparently aroused little interest.[38]

When Theodore Roosevelt, who was of Dutch ancestry, became president in September 1901, the Boers and their sympathizers felt that there might be a shift in American diplomatic policy as it related to the war.[39] Although Roosevelt was more sympathetic to the Boer cause than McKinley was, he did not make any changes in American policy. The Boers discovered that Roosevelt was no more supportive of their cause than McKinley had been.[40] Throughout the war, Secretary of State Hay also maintained a policy of neutrality.[41] Thus, in spite of the fact that the American press and people were overwhelmingly in favor of the Boers, and notwithstanding the strenuous efforts on the part of Boer agents and sympathizers to induce the American government to lend assistance to them, American officials throughout the war followed a policy of friendly neutrality with Great

Britain and in so doing prevented possible mediation of the war by other European powers.[42] Because of American economic and commercial investment in South Africa, the common Anglo-Saxon bond with Great Britain, and its own racially exclusive policy, the U.S. government supported the British in this war to avoid the possibility of the minority rule of the isolationist Boers.

It was during the post-Reconstruction years in America that black Americans established their formal contact with South Africa. These were especially grim times for American blacks. They had been given their civil rights at the end of the Civil War, and now Jim Crow segregation was taking hold in the southern states, depriving them of the liberty they had only just begun to enjoy. Those blacks who went to South Africa during this period were usually connected with missionary work or employed in commercial businesses, such as the mining industry, as skilled or semi-skilled workers. Some were sailors from American merchant ships.[43]

Because Afro-Americans during this early period generally viewed British imperialism as humanitarian, they worked with them during the 1880s and 1890s in efforts to bring about the "Christianization" of South Africa. The 1890s thus saw a movement among black Americans to aid in the "regeneration" of South Africa through missionary activity. Before and during the Anglo-Boer War, most Afro-Americans preferred British control in South Africa over that of the Boers for they saw Boer rule as oppressive.[44]

By the end of the nineteenth century, Afro-American opinions about imperialism hardened as a result of their disillusionment with the American imperialistic venture and their exposure to European imperialism in Africa. During all the activity by white Americans concerning British or Boer imperialism in South Africa, American blacks, although preoccupied with their own declining status, also reacted to the Anglo-Boer War. From the inception of the conflict, articles and editorials appeared in most black newspapers and periodicals discussing the issues of the war. Editors of black newspapers commented on the war and were evidently instrumental in formulating the position middle-class American blacks took concerning the war.

Most American blacks openly supported the British in their war with the Boers because it was believed that they would be more humane to South Africans. Afro-Americans saw the Boers, because of their past treatment of South Africans, as more abusive than the British. The black religious community and the Afro-American press, the most consistently articulate groups in the black community, expressed the viewpoint that in the war the British stood for equal justice for all, while the Boers represented oppression.

The religious community was particularly supportive of British rule during these years. The African Methodist Episcopal (AME) Church expanded into South Africa during the 1890s because of a rising interest in the "redemption" of Africa and a desire to affiliate with the separatist church movement developing among South African blacks during this period. The independent South African church movement triumphed in 1892 with the founding of the Ethiopian Church.[45]

In 1892, Bishop Henry McNeal Turner traveled to South Africa proclaiming the slogan "Africa for the Africans."[46] Turner, representing the AME Church, visited South Africa in an attempt to influence South Africans to establish a church of their own under the auspices of the American-based AME Church.[47] He rejected certain aspects of white rule in South Africa by both the British and the Boers and, in a series of letters that he wrote from South Africa during his visit, asserted that the South Africans hated the Europeans for robbing them of their lands.[48] Turner contended that throughout Africa, Great Britain, France, and Germany were earning millions of dollars that rightfully belonged to the black man.[49] Turner's perspective on British imperialism in South Africa, and European imperialism generally, obviously was colored by his emigrationist ideology and his desire to see black Americans colonize Africa. In 1898, he organized the Transvaal AME Conference. Turner, enthusiastically welcomed by the South Africans, alarmed whites with his inflammatory speeches extolling African separate development.[50]

Because of its religious connections with South Africa, within the ecclesiastical community the AME Church was the most vocal about events in South Africa. After his return from establishing a conference in that country in 1898, Bishop Turner spoke at the southwest Georgia annual meeting of the AME Church, held in Columbus, Georgia. Turner confessed that he, like many Afro-Americans, sympathized with the British because he felt that they would be more just to South Africans. He expressed some doubt, however, as to an ultimate British victory, for he feared that the Boers might win.[51]

Levi Jenkins Coppin, stationed in South Africa from May 1900 to May 1904, was the first resident bishop of the AME Church to serve in that country.[52] Coppin had joined the AME Church in 1877. From 1880 to 1896 he served as editor of the *A.M.E. Church Review*. In 1900 he was elected bishop. He was married three times, and his second wife was the renowned black educator, Fanny Jackson Coppin. Bishop Coppin expressed joy at being selected to go to South Africa in 1900. While there, his main responsibility was to cement ties between the Ethiopian Church and the AME Church and to establish new churches. In an autobiographical sketch of his residence in South Africa, Coppin observed that European policy there was designed to divide the blacks.[53] Coppin doubted that South Africans would reap any benefits from the Anglo-Boer War. He conceded that, as a nation, Great Britain had adhered to the theory of equal justice for all, but he suggested that "this whole South African condition is now a great problem."[54] Coppin further asserted that he was aware that in many parts of the world a considerable number of people sympathized with the Boers in their attempt to maintain their independence, but he contended that there was an equal number of people, like himself, who sided with the British.[55] Accepting the "civilizing mission" idea, he believed that the salvation of Africa was in the adoption of "Christian civilization."[56] Throughout the Anglo-Boer War, Coppin sent leters to the AME press describing the events and his opinions of the war.[57]

When Levi Coppin arrived in South Africa in 1900, he was denied a permit to visit some of the more volatile provinces in the country. During Coppin's residence in South Africa, AME Church activity was curtailed even more. By the end of the Anglo-Boer War, the British were beginning to perceive of Afro-American missionaries as threats to colonial rule because of a fear that they were fermenting revolt among South Africans. Due to the change from Boer to British rule in the Transvaal and Orange Free State colonies and because of British suspicions of AME motives in South Africa, the church lost its recognition and privileges in those two colonies. As a result, Bishop Coppin was unable to travel in the colonies where the chuch had originated and where membership was the strongest.[58] This provoked a mild outcry from articulate blacks, which will be discussed later.

The *Christian Recorder*, an organ of the Publication Department of the AME Church, took an unusual stance in its position
on the war. Henry Theodore Johnson, editor, felt that blacks
should not involve themselves at all with the war. "As in the case
of all wars, so in this," he editorialized, "we as a race are neutral."[59]
Actually, this attitude could have been expected from Johnson.
In a speech delivered at the Nova Scotia Conference in 1899,
Johnson began with a satirical poem. "Pile on the Black Man's
Burden," in which he condemned American imperialism and
demanded that whites deal with the racial question at home before
going to other areas of the world. Whites would eventually have to
answer to God's justice for the burdens they had heaped on blacks,
he insisted. This was a continuous argument for Johnson, that black
and white alike in the country could not divide or refocus their
attention elsewhere until they had successfully dealt with the "Negro
problem" in the United States. For this reason, he was against
emigration to Africa or elsewhere. And, of course, this also accounts
for his unconcern with support for either side in Anglo-Boer War.
Johnson did predict that the British, because of their numbers, would
be victorious over the brave Boers and that they would also be better
rulers to black South Africans.[60]

Another AME publication, the *Voice of Missions*, an organ of the
Missionary Department of the church, also took an interest in the
war. The paper predicted in 1901 that the British would defeat the
Boers. With the conclusion of the war, the paper seemed pleased
that Great Britain had finally secured peace in South Africa. The
Voice contrasted British and Boer rule, claiming that the Boers were
a menace to the progress of South Africa because their rule supported tyranny and slavery while British rule encouraged liberty,
education, and "civilization."[61]

A member of another black church denomination, Charles S.
Morris, was also concerned with white rule in South Africa. At the
Ecumenical Missionary Conference, held in New York, 21 April to 1
May 1900, Morris, representing the National Baptist Convention,
spoke on "A Work for American Negroes." Morris forewarned that
South Africa had been populated by European invaders who had a
bitter, unrelenting prejudice against the black South African. He
called for American blacks to go to South Africa to play a greater role

in the development of the country.[62] Morris, who had just returned from South Africa, naively believed that American blacks could alter imperialistic exploitation in South Africa.[63]

As these examples demonstrate, generally the Afro-American religious community viewed the Anglo-Boer War in an ambiguous manner. While they favored British rule over that of the Boers, they realized that black South Africans had not really had a say as to who would rule their country. Religious leaders wondered if British rule would really benefit blacks any more than Boer rule had.

The Afro-American journalistic community was likewise ambivalent about the war. Although most editors believed that the British would be better rulers to the South Africans than the Boers, some only reluctantly supported the British as the "lesser of two evils." A few were even pro-Boer, identifying with their fight for independence.

Before the outbreak of the hostilities in South Africa, George Knox of the *Indianapolis Freeman* observed that the Boers still condoned slavery and it was obvious that they were not friends of black South Africans. A few weeks later, after the declaration of war, Knox in an editorial urged blacks to support the British since the Boers were pursuing their established policy of inhumane treatment of the South Africans. The British must "righten these wrongs of generations," he asserted, and teach the Boers a long-deserved lesson. Despite Great Britain's refusal to accept the assistance of black Africans, Knox indicated that historically the British had nonetheless acted more humanely toward the black Africans than had the Boers. The *Freeman* remained pro-British throughout the war.[64]

One of the *Freeman's* competitors, the *Indianapolis Recorder* was also pro-British. The *Recorder*, which appeared in 1897, began a discussion of the war in October 1899. This was actually unusual since the paper ordinarily contained more local and state news than international news and devoted more attention than the *Freeman* to the affairs of Indiana blacks. George P. Stewart, founder and editor of the paper, in a series of articles at the beginning of the war, described the Boers as an ignorant, selfish, nonprogressive people who had enslaved South Africans. The paper predicted that the British would win the war, but Stewart expressed the hope that the South Africans, to whom the country rightfully belonged, would eventually realize their strength and unite against white rule.[65]

By early 1900, Afro-Americans, like white Americans, seem to have established their position in the Anglo-Boer War. While most whites by this time sympathized with the Boers, blacks swung to the side of the British. Edward Elder Cooper, editor of the *Colored American* (Washington, D.C.), claimed that a few noisy Irishmen and Germans were trying to suggest that there was widespread sentiment for the Boers, but he urged the black press to continue to speak out on the issues surrounding the war and to take the side of the British, who had always stood for the freedom of black people.

In 1883, Cooper and others began publication of the *Colored World*, issued at Indianapolis (it later became known as the *Indianapolis World*, which was published until 1924), and in 1888 founded the *Indianapolis Freeman*, which he sold to Knox in 1892. Ultimately, he went to Washington, D.C., where he edited the *Colored American* until its demise in 1904. Like many black newspapers, the *Colored American* received financial support from Booker T. Washington.

About his position in the Anglo-Boer War, Cooper was resolute. He contended that the tyrannical Boers were not the friends of progress, noting, "The Boers have no just title to the Transvaal territory. They stole it from the natives, and by a system of cruelty and barbarous oppression, brought the latter to a state of subjection." Predicting that the Boers would not win the war, he advised that the British, friends of the Africans, would be victorious because they were right. He concluded that blood was thicker than water and no rational black person could fail to be interested in the conditions of South Africans under oppressive Boer rule.[66]

The *Savannah Tribune* was also pro-British, applauding McKinley's refusal to intervene in the war. The paper explained that McKinley's action left no hope for the Boer cause in America and cleared away any misapprehensions about the real attitude of the U.S. government with reference to the South African war. But the *Tribune* also gave attention to the issue of the fate of black South Africans at the end of the war. The paper complained that, while many people were discussing the struggle between the two white groups involved, little attention was being given to the black South Africans whose rights and future were as much at stake as those of the British or the Boers. In discussing the treatment of the South Africans by the Boers, the *Tribune* pointed out that the Boers had adopted a system of law that served to subjugate the blacks through ill treatment, oppression, and denial of all civil rights.[67]

The *Washington Bee* echoed the *Tribune's* complaint that the issue of the black South Africans' fate was not being dealt with and also reproved the British for not accepting the aid of black South Africans. William Calvin Chase, editor, reluctantly supported the British, believing that the war was but another attempt by the Anglo-Saxon "to dominate the world under his hypocritical pretense of civilizing and christianizing it."

Chase was a prominent Virginia attorney who began publication of the *Bee* in 1883, which he published until his death in 1921. The motto of the paper, "honey for friends and stings for enemies," aptly described Chase's temperament. He has been portrayed as a critical, invective, vicious individual who used persuasive methods sometimes approaching blackmail. Chase's limited discussion of African events during his editorship of the *Bee* was a rumination of the middle-class ambivalence toward Africa. Obviously, he was opposed to black emigration to Africa or elsewhere. Chase, along with his fellow Washingtonian, Cooper, reflected the views of the black elite in the nation's capital.

Believing the Anglo-Boer War would be of short duration, Chase felt that it narrowed down to one between "generosity, universal brotherhood, and enlightened government on the one hand and selfishness, race prejudice, repressive ecclesiasticism and autocracy on the other," the British representing the former, the Boers, the latter. Chase therefore perceived the British cause to be one of humanity while the Boers were depicted as self-seeking and non-progressive. "The people [Boers] who are now asking the civilized world to sympathize with them, and, if need be, assist them, are those whose policy has been repressive, exclusive, ungenerous, and tyrannical," he insisted. Chase welcomed the defeat of the Boers by the British because he believed that British policy favored the "development" of South Africa and leaned towards the destruction of color distinction. Chase was one of a sizable group of middle-class Afro-Americans during this period who felt that European imperialism, and particularly the British kind, would benefit Africa and Africans in the process of "development."

When the Boer envoys came to the United States in 1900 to solicit American support for their cause, Chase noted that their situation must have reached a serious level since they had not done this before. Like the *Tribune*, he commended President McKinley for rejecting the Boer request for American intervention in the war in behalf of the two republics.[68]

At the beginning of the war, the *Topeka State Ledger* (Kansas) appeared to have been pro-Boer, claiming that the British had little justice on their side and that the Boers were defending their homes and fighting for their liberty. Fred L. Jeltz, in an infrequent editorial in 1899, claimed that American sympathy must go out for the "plucky and patriotic" Boers. Yet, after 1900, the paper apparently shifted its support to the British because the articles published after that date were biased in favor of a British victory. Most of the articles that Jeltz printed tended to focus on British successes, and the Boers were referred to as "the enemy."[69]

This indecisiveness was felt by many black editors. The *Richmond Planet* (Virginia) seemed to have been in favor of the British. The *Planet*, however, also admired the determination of the Boers and urged the U.S. government to remain neutral. John Mitchell, Jr., editor of the paper, found little reason for blacks to support either side.

Mitchell was an influential member of the Richmond community. In 1884, the *Richmond Planet* was placed under his editorship; from 1888 to 1896 he was a member of the Richmond City Council; during the 1890s he was twice elected president of the Afro-American Press Association; in 1902, he founded and became president of the Mechanics Savings Bank; and he served as Grand Chancellor of the Virginia Knights of Pythias. Mitchell, like Chase, viewed Africa with reserve and was against mass migration to Africa, believing that emigration was an individual choice.

During the Anglo-Boer War, although the *Planet* had a pro-British slant, most of the articles on the war were reprints from London newspapers and dispatches from white correspondents working in South Africa. Mitchell himself made no editorial comments, perhaps due to a belief that blacks would not affect the outcome of the conflict.[70]

Curiously, the *Cleveland Gazette*, one of the most mundane black newspapers of this period, with wide international coverage and scope, did not report the war as extensively and seemed less interested in the conflict than other black newspapers. Since the *Gazette* was aware of the events of the war, it can be postulated that Harry C. Smith, the paper's editor, similar to Mitchell, did not think it worthwhile for blacks to be concerned with a war that involved the balance of power between two white parties. Reprints of editorials and articles and news items from special correspondents of other newspapers were printed, but Smith, who usually expressed views on almost every issue affecting blacks the world over, made little editorial comment. The articles and news items that were printed about the war were slanted toward British rule over that of the Boers. In a rare editorial in February of 1900, Smith depicted the Boers as oppressive to the African people, while the British were described as a nation with a long-established reputation of liberality.[71]

Not all black American newspapers were pro-British, however. Early in the war, some editors other than Jeltz and Mitchell also expressed sympathy for the Boer cause, likening it to the black quest for freedom. Acknowledging that the U.S. government had an official policy of nonintervention in the Anglo-Boer War, the *Parsons Weekly Blade* (Kansas) emphasized that this policy did not "prevent the people of this country from sympathizing with these little republics." The *Blade* gave extensive coverage of the war in its initial period. In articles and editorials, it was obvious that this Kansas paper sympathized with the Boers. Unlike other black newspapers that favored the British, the *Blade* did not focus on the conditions and treatment of South Africans under Boer rule. The editor, A. E. Lide, readily commented on British defeats and blamed this on the strength of a brave, determined people fighting for their home and country.[72]

The *Broad Ax* (Chicago) was another pro-Boer paper. The paper claimed that it saw through the transparent guise of neutrality professed by the U.S. government and accused officials of secretly aiding the British. The *Broad Ax* criticized the McKinley administration for its policy in the war. The paper contended that the United

States could not afford to see "a grasping monarchial [sic] power like Great Britain deliberately conquer and take possession of two weak republics on another continent." Great Britain's developing strength would one day put it in a position too strong to hear protests, the paper predicted, and a limit should be imposed upon its expansion. American commercial interests, it charged, were aiding in the continuation of the war because of the profits they were gaining, as was evidenced by the increased demand for American products in South Africa. The paper explained that the British lack of success in ending the war was due to the sympathy and assistance that the Boers were receiving from all parts of the world. The *Broad Ax* periodically contained articles on the aid that the Boers were getting from sympathizers.[73]

These two black papers and others that identified with the Boer cause compared the Boer position in South African society with that of blacks in American society. They could somehow find a parallel in the minority Boer fight in South Africa and the fight of Afro-Americans in the United States.

The Afro-American press covered the events of the war until its conclusion. It reported who was winning and the anticipated end of the war. Some papers discussed the continuing efforts of the Boers to gain American support for intervention.[74] All of these matters were discussed with less intensity after 1900, however, as blacks become more preoccupied with their own decaying status.

Black journalists came under criticism in the early months of the war, when Sergeant E. D. Gibson of the U.S. Army, 10th Cavalry, 24th Infantry, in a letter to the editor of the *Colored American* in March 1900, reprimanded the black press for its lack of adequate coverage of the Anglo-Boer War. Gibson declared, "The silence of the Afro-American press on the English-Boer conflict—when our kith and kin is so deeply concerned; is criminal!" He proposed that blacks send resolutions sympathetic to the British cause to Great Britain. Gibson was sure that South Africans would receive better treatment under British rule than under that of the Boers. His letter concluded that black people should show "the world that the Negro race is not so thoroughly bereft of the clannishness that binds kind to kind" as to overlook the fate of their brothers in South Africa.[75]

Afro-American travelers in Africa during this period shared

Gibson's view that black people throughout the world should express sympathy for black South Africans. They emphasized the need for black Americans, particularly, to show unity with blacks in South Africa.

In 1900, the Jubilee Singers visited South Africa. Frederick J. Loudin, director of the singers, commented in a letter to black journalist John E. Bruce that white people all over the world were holding meetings and passing resolutions in sympathy with the Boers who would "enslave our people the very moment they free themselves from British rule." He maintained that, although British rule in South Africa was not the best, it was much better than Boer administration. Loudin's ambiguity about British rule reiterated what other black writers of this period were saying. The British deserved the support of black Americans, Loudin explained, and he advised black Americans to hold mass meetings and adopt resolutions expressing black support of the British. He felt that black opinion could have great weight in this issue.[76]

Loudin had joined the Fisk University Jubilee Singers in 1875 and traveled with them for three years. After the disbanding of the company in 1878, and its reorganization as the Loudin Jubilee Singers in 1882, he became manager and director. In 1888, the Loudin Jubilee Singers began a world tour, finally returning to the United States in June of 1900. Loudin attended the Pan-African Conference in July of 1900. He eventually made his home in Ravenna, Ohio, where he became the largest stockholder in a shoe manufacturing company, and died in 1904.[77]

Captain Harry Dean was one of the few black travelers in South Africa during the Anglo-Boer War to leave an extensive account of his impressions and opinions of the war. In his autobiographical novel, Dean criticized imperialism and echoed the various perspectives that middle-class black Americans of this period expressed about European activity in Africa. Dean believed that black people all over the world should unite against the partitioning and exploitation of Africa by the European powers.

When Dean arrived in South Africa, the country was in the midst of the Anglo-Boer War. Maintaining that the world was unaware of the manner in which black South Africans had been treated under Boer rule, he depicted the Boers as a God-forsaken bunch of mortals unequaled in their iniquities to Africans. He also charged the British with robbing and maltreating the South Africans. In the final analysis, Dean saw little difference between the two white rulers and declared, "I am fully convinced that the Boers and the English have the same attitude toward the natives," and aptly referred to South Africa as the "land of villainy, blood, and tears." Looking back to an African golden age, he reminisced, "I remember dreaming of Africa as it had been before the ships from Europe reached her shores." He seemed to long for those days.[78]

At least two black Americans are known to have participated in the Anglo-Boer War, H. A. Smith and Horatio L. Scott. Both joined the British forces. Although nothing is known about Smith other than the mention given to him by Scott, Scott wrote a small book about his experiences in Africa. Scott was California-born and had been a sugar grower in the South Sea Islands and a gold miner in Australia before arriving in South Africa in 1896. There he was employed as an explorer and ranger for Cecil Rhodes's British South Africa Company. When the Anglo-Boer War broke out, he joined the Imperial Light Horse, a corps of British mounted infantry. In a letter to the editor of the *Indianapolis Freeman* from South Africa in 1900, Scott predicted that the British would win because they were fighting for a just cause and equity was on their side. The Boer government, he noted, had no respect for black South Africans, and their whole aim was to humiliate Africans and keep them down. He was not completely confident that the British would be much better and cautioned black Americans to wait and see. In this letter, Scott mentioned that one other black American, H. A. Smith, was also fighting in the war on the side of the British.

Scott returned to the United States in 1901, and a year later published a book, *The Truth of Africa*, describing social and economic conditions in Central and Southern Africa. In his book, Scott extolled the British government as the friend of the black man and claimed that British rule in South Africa would mean that color would be no impediment to equal participation in South African society. Scott encouraged Afro-American emigration to South Africa as the best African country for agricultural and commercial prospects. He believed that for black people South Africa offered the best opportunities. In speeches across the country after his return to the United

States, Scott, seen as a hero by blacks, helped keep alive black American interest in the outcome of the Anglo-Boer War.[79]

On 12 April 1902, the Boer leaders agreed to discuss peace proposals, and on 15 May 1902, representatives from both governments met at Vereeniging to discuss peace. A treaty was agreed to and signed on 31 May 1902, bringing an end to the war.[80]

The Afro-American press seemed pleased that an end had finally come to this war. Many of these journalists doubted, however, that the conclusion of the war would really bring any changes in the lives of South Africans.[81] Like the rest of the literate black community, these journalists, regardless of which side they supported, basically saw the war as one between two white powers. The question of the future of black South Africans was largely avoided in this confrontation, and these black Americans seemed to have been aware of this omission. Therefore, when the war ended, black American perspectives on imperialism in South Africa remained basically unchanged; blacks viewed foreign rule in South Africa with reservation, whether it was the Boers or the British, and saw both as oppressive to black South Africans.

Accordingly, immediately after the end of the Anglo-Boer War and the settlement of the question of who would rule in South Africa, black Americans turned their attention to the issue of how the British would treat the South African people. This question dominated their discussion of South African issues for several years.

As early as 1903, Captain Dean, who was experiencing difficulties in his efforts to leave South Africa, complained to the State Department that British rule in South Africa was as tyrannical as that of the Boers. He accused the British of restricting not only the rights of black South Africans but also those of black American residents in South Africa as well. Dean was regarded as dangerous by the British because of his militant ideas and pronouncements. During his stay in that country there were several attempts made on his life. Eventually Dean was forced to leave South Africa without his ship, the *Pedro Gorino*, and penniless.[82]

The black press took up the same issue of the treatment of black South Africans. It continued to see the Boers as "barbarous" in their treatment of South Africans. Some journalists held that under Boer rule the South Africans had possessed neither political nor civil rights, and they printed articles demonstrating that blacks were enslaved, maltreated, and exploited under the Boer government. These editors implied that British rule would be different.[83]

The *Colored American Magazine* exhorted the British to allow black South Africans to participate in governmental activities. Great Britain should welcome any movement that inspired South African blacks to take an active part in political affairs, the magazine wrote. The publication contended that "the Negroes of South Africa have been knocked about, and trodden under foot, and ousted from their possessions, and rogued out of their earnings by tyrants and adventurers from every point," and the British should not be a party to such injustices.[84]

Other segments of the Afro-American press insisted that such offenses had to stop being meted out to South Africans. South Africa would one day be a black man's country, one newspaper explained, and the country was destined to come under black rule. According to this paper, attempts at disfranchisement and discrimination would only hasten the day of black supremacy in South Africa.[85]

T. Thomas Fortune saw the British form of government as more severe than that of the Boers. The British concern in Africa was for the "almighty dollar," he asserted, and their treatment of South Africans would eventually result in their expulsion from South Africa. Although Fortune conceded that under the Boer government blacks had no rights or opportunities whatsoever, he explained that it was becoming clear that the British were even more repressive because of their continued exploitation of African peoples.

Fortune believed that the British faced a dilemma in South Africa. They had to educate the South Africans in order to exploit their labor, but, in educating them, they created a situation of unrest. Educated South Africans would be less tolerant of prejudice and domination, Fortune averred.

Fortune was generally critical of all Europeans in Africa when their activities constituted exploitation of the African peoples. Fortune observed that in South Africa the rule and exploitation of the British, and the Boers before them, had kept the blacks in a state of perpetual degradation and unrest. He compared the events in South Africa with those throughout the continent. The British, French, German, and Belgian governments, with large possessions in Africa, were seen as having no other motive in Africa than greed. He further maintained, "Whatever the nationality of Europeans in Africa, they have robbed the natives of their land." They should have brought "the Gospel of Christian love and civilized methods of develop-ment," he declared, but instead they reduced the Africans to the lowest conditions of life. Fortune concluded by asking, "What have the Belgians, the French, the Germans and the British done in Africa but despoil the natives and teach them to hate the white man and the Christian religion?" In making this assessment of the impact of Euro-peans in Africa, Fortune echoed the sentiments of a large sector of the middle-class Afro-American community.[86]

In the limited ways available to them, black South Africans resisted British colonial rule. Protest methods ranged from efforts to gain greater participation in governmental affairs to outright violence, as in the case of the Bambata or Zulu Rebellion of 1906.

In 1906, the Natal administration imposed a poll tax in the colony, which was eventually adopted by all the South African colonies. The measure was a method of forcing Africans to leave their homes to work for whites. The Zulus refused to pay the tax, martial law was declared, and several incidents resulted in the death of whites. Gov-ernment troops finally suppressed the rebellion, and Bambata, the leader of the revolt, and 500 of his followers were executed. There was a total loss of 4,000 African lives.

The *New York Age* was one of the few black newspapers to report the Bambata Rebellion of 1906, which demonstrated black South Africans' desire to have a say in their country. In reporting the events, the *Age* boasted that "the natives showed amazing courage." The method of suppressing the Bambata uprising indicated the oppressive nature that British rule in South Africa was to take, Fortune insisted.[87]

The colonial administrators in South Africa placed part of the blame for growing unrest among black South Africans on the Afro-American missionaries stationed there. From the end of the Anglo-Boer War until the beginning of World War I, the Afro-American religious community, which had been active in South Africa since the 1880s, came under severe criticism by the colonial government. This sector of the Afro-American community had had the greatest opti-mism at the end of the Anglo-Boer War concerning British rule in

South Africa. Believing in Great Britain's humanitarian interest, missionaries in South Africa welcomed its rule.

By the end of the war, however, an image had already formed in the minds of colonial administrators which depicted Afro-American missionaries as subversives. Convinced that these missionaries were identifying too closely with the plight of the South Africans under colonial rule, the government began to discourage black American missionary work in that country. More and more disillusioned with British racial policies in South Africa, Afro-American missionaries began to support separatism there. The "race solidarity" and "race regeneration" ideologies that the black missionaries espoused alarmed British authorities. The South African government accused the black missionaries of the AME Church, particularly, of encouraging and stimulating revolt against the British among the South Africans. The British government feared that the black missionaries would aid in a plan to overthrow British imperialism in South Africa. Missionaries, on the other hand, accused the British government of suppressing all activity by black South Africans in an attempt to continue to subjugate them.

Black American missionaries of the AME Church were more militant in their outlook and much more outspoken than black missionaries of any other religious group in Africa. This militant stance was possible probably because the AME Church itself was black and their missionaries in Africa felt that their recalcitrant activities would be more readily supported by the home church than black missionaries of white denominations.

After the Bambata Rebellion of 1906, the British placed a restriction on Afro-American missionaries in South Africa. Even conservative black American missionaries were viewed with suspicion. By the time of the unification of South Africa in 1910, identification of Afro-Americans with African unrest was universal throughout the continent. Until the late 1920s, colonial authorities did their best to discourage black American contact with Africa because of the fear that they would drive Africans together to upset the colonial governments.[88]

The British government's concern about the development of the sentiment of "Africa for the Africans," which came to be known as "Ethiopianism" in South Africa, and their belief that AME missionaries had promoted it there evoked the interest of some segments of the black community in the United States and South Africa.[89] The *Age* suggested that the work of the church in South Africa had been hampered because of the European fear of revolutionary black missionary activity there. The *Wichita Searchlight* accepted the contention that American blacks were responsible for South African unrest but warned that the future of South Africans looked dismal if the missionaries were expelled. The purpose of all this activity, the paper explained, was to drive the whites out of Africa.[90]

Bishop Charles S. Smith of the AME Church, who had just returned from South Africa, delivered a paper at the 1 August 1906 session of the Negro Young People's Christian and Educational Congress, where he discussed South Africans and the activities of the AME Church. The European had addressed himself to the task of making South Africa a white man's country, he claimed, by oppressing the original residents. The British government, known in the past as the most liberal, was ruling South Africa with an iron hand. The system resembled slavery, Smith contended, and the British government "joins hands with exploiters in keeping the Africans subjugated." He concluded that, although Afro-American missionaries had been restricted in South Africa, "the spirit of liberty, independence and manhood that has been aroused among the natives can never die." Smith felt that Africans would continue to propagate the ideas disseminated by the Afro-American missionaries.[91]

Apparently, even some South Africans questioned the motives of Afro-American missionaries there. John L. Dube, South Africa's Booker T. Washington and principal of the Zulu Christian Industrial School in Natal, chastised American black missionaries for preaching "Africa for the Africans" to South Africans. He argued that American blacks were being educated and fitted for the part they would play in the evangelization of Africa, but they were making a great mistake in arousing the South African blacks, only creating a great racial hatred in South Africa.[92]

As in the case of the Congo, Booker T. Washington viewed European rule in Africa generally, and British rule in South Africa specifically, in a somewhat different light from his Afro-American contemporaries, but very similar to Dube. Washington felt, "Since the blacks are to live under the English government, they should be taught to love and revere that government better than any other institution." Because of his pro-European perspective, the British asked Washington's advice on the development of a racial policy for South Africa, and he encouraged self-help programs there. He also agreed with the British assessment of the role of black missionaries in South Africa. The colonialists saw black missionaries as fermenting dissent rather than developing skills, and Washington concurred. In commenting on the basic need for education and training for the "development" of South Africans, Washington contended, "It is not always true that the Missions teach respect for the rulers in power." Washington supported those colonial governments who saw black American missionaries as subversives.[93]

Aside from the exploitation of black labor, the British tended to view blacks in South Africa as expendable when it came to granting them equality within that society. This was evident in the settlement of the Anglo-Boer War. Because of British guilt over bullying the two Boer republics, in the final draft of the peace treaty the question of the African franchise and participation in the government was left to the individual white colonies. When Great Britain granted self-government to the Transvaal in 1906, and to the Orange Free State in 1907, the franchise was permanently limited to white adult males. The all-white convention that drafted the constitution for the Union also excluded blacks from the franchise, except those qualified in Cape Colony, and there they were forbidden to sit in the Union Parliament. On 31 May 1910, exactly eight years to the day after the Treaty of Vereeniging ending the Anglo-Boer War was signed, the Union of South Africa was inaugurated.[94]

In the period preceding the inauguration of the Union of South Africa, the black press discussed the possible effect that the Union would have on the position of black South Africans. The *Colored American Magazine* asserted that although there was no provision in the new constitution for the ballot for black South Africans, "the lot of the African should gradually improve under the United Government" and predicted that "the English Government will probably rule by giving the natives a large measure of self-government." The magazine naively assumed that the united colonies would not duplicate the exploitative methods that characterized Boer rule in the

Transvaal and in the Orange Free State colonies.[95]

Fortune also minimized the serious implications of the political restrictions of South African blacks under the constitution. The British had made no provisions for black representation in the legislature, but the condition of the Africans should improve under the Union, Fortune observed. He believed that, "the union of the colonies must redound eventually to the uplift of all the people of South Africa." Fortune felt that the British government would be the "salvation of South Africa" and would probably rule by giving Africans a larger measure of self-government.[96]

These blacks showed an obvious lack of understanding of the meaning of the Union. The racist Boers were determined to exclude blacks from equal participation in South African society. They were able to persuade the other two colonies to succumb to their prejudices. The British government accepted the Union constitution with its exclusive provisions, thereby accepting an inferior status for South Africans in their country. British rule was really no better than Boer for black South Africans.

In 1913, three years after the establishment of the Union, the Natives Land Act was passed. It had the effect of enforcing territorial separation and retaining white political domination. The act removed all rights of African sharecroppers, limited African ownership of land, and set up specific areas for African settlement, commonly known as "reserves." The year 1913 thus marked the first of the discriminatory legislation that would be placed on the statute books under the newly inaugurated Union of South Africa. Also in 1913, General James B. M. Hertzog founded the National party (precursor of the Afrikaner National party, which has been in power in South Africa since the election of 1948). The apartheid system, of course, had seen its origins in earlier centuries, but the 1913 act and the formation of the National party solidified once and for all the inferior position that blacks were to have in the Union of South Africa and set the pattern for the society which exists in South Africa to this day. Black Americans did not comment on either of these important events.

Middle-class Afro-Americans seemed to have been divided and ambivalent about the affairs in South Africa. Though for various reasons they supported either British or Boer rule in South Africa, in the final analysis most American blacks understood that they could not alter the imperialistic patterns in that country and would not have an impact on either the course of the Anglo-Boer War, the peace settlement, or the formation of the Union. What is bewildering is that some blacks could see a parallel between the minority position of the racist Boers in South Africa and blacks in America. In the end, black Americans had little impact on the destiny of South Africa. They could not even change their inferior status in the country of their birth. How could they hope to change the course of events thousands of miles away in a foreign country?

Thus the final settlement of the question of who would govern South Africa, the British or the Boers, resulted in a system that continued to oppress black Africans. Somehow it seems doubtful that black South Africans saw any real difference in British or Boer imperialism. And, simultaneously, although earlier differentiating between British and Boer rule, by 1914 even middle-class Afro-Americans realized that imperialism in South Africa was a single phenomenon.

Notes

1. Alan R. Booth's dissertation, "Americans in South Africa, 1784-1870," pp. 18, 69, 281, along with several other dissertations completed at Boston University, provides extensive information on American activity in Africa. Booth's dissertation discusses American involvement in South Africa during the early years of commercial development.

2. Throughout this chapter, when referring to the white residents of South Africa, the terms "British" and "Boers" will be used, depending on which applies; when referring to black South Africans, the terms "South Africans" or "Africans" will be used.

3. Leo Marquard, The Story of South Africa, pp. 179-81; Eric A. Walker, A History of Southern Africa, pp. 340-41; and J. Congress Mbata, "Race and Resistance in South Africa," pp. 216-17.

4. Marquard, The Story of South Africa, p. 197; and Walker, A History of Southern Africa, pp. 378-80.

5. Lewis H. Gann and Peter Duignan, Burden of Empire, pp. 36-38.

6. John H. Ferguson, American Diplomacy and the Boer War, p. 44, has devoted extensive discussion to this question.

7. Myra S. Goldstein, "The Genesis of Modern American Relations With South Africa, 1895-1914," p. 135.

8. Clarence Clendenen; Robert Collins; and Peter Duignan, *Americans in Africa, 1865-1900*, p. 103.

9. Goldstein, "The Genesis of Modern American Relations With South Africa, 1895-1914," pp. 131-32.

10. Walter Wellman to John Hay, 1900, Hay Papers, vol. 20, reel 13.

11. Goldstein, "The Genesis of Modern American Relations With South Africa, 1895-1914," pp. 132-33.

12. Ferguson, *American Diplomacy and the Boer War*, p. 176.

13. Clement Keto, "American Involvement in South Africa, 1870-1915," p. 245; and Olton, "Problems of American Foreign Relations," p. 7.

14. Edward W. Chester, *Clash of Titans*, p. 154.

15. Ferguson, *American Diplomacy and the Boer War*, pp. 44-50. See also Bradford Perkins, *The Great Rapprochement*, p. 97; John Hay to Reverend Edward Everett Hale, 13 January 1900, Hay Papers, vol. 3, reel 3; and J. W. Stowe to Thomas W. Cridler, 22 November 1899, Department of State, Record Group 84, Despatches from U.S. Consulate at Cape Town, National Archives (hereafter cited DS, Despatches from Cape Town).

16. J. W. Stowe to Thomas W. Cridler, 17 October 1899, DS, Despatches from Cape Town.

17. Goldstein, "The Genesis of Modern American Relations With South Africa, 1895-1914," pp. 136-38.

18. Rayne Kruger, *Good-Bye Dolly Gray*, pp. 148-49.

19. Goldstein, "The Genesis of Modern American Relations With South Africa, 1895-1914," p. 136. See also Alfred L. P. Dennis, *Adventures in American Diplomacy*, p. 127.

20. *A Compilation of the Messages and Papers of the Presidents*, vol. 13, p. 6371.

21. "The South African War," *Missionary Herald* 95 (December 1899): 517.

22. Bernard Porter, *Critics of Empire*, pp. 65, 67-68.

23. See Marshal Maxeke, "How the Boers Treat the Natives," pp. 2947-48; and his "Black Man's Side in the Transvaal War," p. 3287.

24. W. C. Wilcox, "How the English Treat the Natives," pp. 3288-89.

25. Editorial, "The Deplorable Reverses of the British," *New York Times*, 18 December 1899.

26. Harry T. Peck, "American Opinion on the South African War," pp. 530-32; and F. B. Nash, "America and the Transvaal War," pp. 236-37.

27. Sydney Brooks, "America and the War," pp. 339-44.

28. Ibid., pp. 341-42. See also Eric Rosenthal, *Stars and Stripes in Africa*, p. 127.

29. "Cannot Interfere," *Washington Evening Star* (Washington, D.C.), 12 October 1899; and R. A. Alger, "America's Attitude Toward England," p. 333. See also George D. Dowkonutt to John Hay, 26 February 1900; B. Odell Duncan to John Hay, 26 February 1900; James McMillan to John Hay, 29 June 1900, Hay Papers, vol. 19, reel 13; and D. J. Connell to John Hay, 9 April 1902, Hay Papers, vol. 23, reel 15.

30. Goldstein, "The Genesis of Modern American Relations With South Africa, 1895-1914," pp. 138-39.

31. Ferguson, *American Diplomacy and the Boer War*, p. 188.

32. Ibid.

33. U.S., Congress, House, *House Resolutions*, H. Res. 186, 57th Cong., 1st sess., 1902, p. 1. Similar resolutions can be found in U.S., Congress, House, *House Joint Resolutions*, H.J. Res. 84, 56th Cong., 1st sess., 1899. p. 1; H.J. Res. 193, 56th Cong., 1st sess., 1900, p. 1; H.J. Res. 27, 57th cong., 1st sess., 1901, p. 1; H.J. Res. 137, 167, 170, 57th Cong., 1st sess., 1902, p. 1; and U.S., Congress, Senate, *Senate Resolutions*, S. Res. 56, 56th Cong., 1st sess., 1900, pp. 1-2.

34. Goldstein, "The Genesis of Modern American Relations With South Africa, 1895-1914," p. 196.

35. Perkins, *The Great Rapprochement*, p. 92; Chester, *Clash of Titans*, p. 155; Keto, "American Involvement in South Africa, 1870-1915," p. 242; and Goldstein, "The Genesis of Modern American Relations With South Africa, 1895-1914," p. 139.

36. Goldstein, "The Genesis of Modern American Relations With South Africa, 1895-1914," p. 142. See also Kirk H. Porter and Donald B. Johnson, comps., *National Party Platforms, 1840-1956*, p. 115; and "The Boer Cause in American Politics," p. 145.

37. Rosenthal, *Stars and Stripes in Africa*, pp. 196-97; and Ferguson, *American Diplomacy and the Boer War*, p. 192.

38. Ferguson, *American Diplomacy and the Boer War*, p. 197; Healy, *US Expansionism*, pp. 48-49; and Goldstein, "The Genesis of Modern American Relations With South Africa, 1895-1914," p. 143.

39. Ferguson, *American Diplomacy and the Boer War*, pp. 206-7.

40. Chester, *Clash of Titans*, pp. 156-57; and Goldstein, "The Genesis of Modern American Relations With South Africa, 1895-1914," p. 132.

41. Ferguson, *American Diplomacy and the Boer War*, p. 221.

42. Ibid., pp. ix, 221; and Clendenen, Collins, and Duignan, *Americans in Africa, 1865-1900*, p. 101.

43. Keto, "American Involvement in South Africa, 1870-1915," pp. 158, 168-69. This discussion is continued in his "Black Americans and South Africa, 1890-1910," pp. 386, 390.

44. Thomas J. Noer, "The United States and South Africa, 1870-1914," pp. 69-71.

45. Josephus R. Coan, "The Expansion of Missions of the African Methodist Episcopal Church in South Africa, 1896-1908," p. 27; George Shepperson, "Ethiopianism and African Nationalism," p. 9; and Daniel Thwaite, *The Seething African Pot*, p. 36. Thwaite discusses the independent African church movement in chapter 2, "The Growth of Ethiopianism in Africa."

46. H. M. Turner, "The American Negro and His Fatherland," p. 196.

47. Harold Isaacs, *The New World of Negro Americans*, p. 125; and Robert G. Weisbord, *Ebony Kinship*, p. 38.

48. Henry McNeal Turner, *African Letters*, pp. 39, 47-48.

49. Ibid., p. 58.

50. Thwaite, *The Seething African Pot*, p. 36; and Shepperson, "Ethiopianism and African Nationalism," p. 9.

51. "Bishop Turner on Kruger," *Savannah Tribune*, 4 November 1899.

52. For a discussion of missions of the AME Church in South Africa, consult Coan, "The Expansion of Missions of the African Methodist Episcopal Church in South Africa, 1896-1908."

53. Levi Jenkins Coppin, *Observations of Persons and Things in South Africa, 1900-1904*, p. 28. See also Bengt G. M. Sundkler, *Bantu Prophets in South Africa*, p. 42; and Keto, "American Involvement in South Africa, 1870-1915," p. 203; and his "Black Americans and South Africa, 1890-1910," p. 400.

54. Coppin, *Observations of Persons and Things in South Africa, 1900-1904*, Letter no. 8, p. 76.

55. Ibid., Letter no. 17, p. 140.

56. See Levi J. Coppin, "The Negro's Part in the Redemption of Africa," p. 244; and his "The American Negro's Religion for the African Negro's Soul," pp. 748, 750.

57. See, for example, Letter to the Editor, L. J. Coppin, "Our Work in South Africa," *Voice of Missions*, 1 May 1901.

58. Keto, "Black Americans and South Africa, 1890-1910," p. 396;

Keto, "American Involvement in South Africa, 1870-1915," p. 187; and Coan, "The Expansion of Missions of the African Methodist Episcopal Church in South Africa, 1896-1908," pp. 423, 432.

59. Editorial note, "The Boer British War," *Christian Recorder*, 24 May 1900, p. 6.

60. Editorial, "The South African War," *Christian Recorder*, 7 June 1900, p. 2; and H. T. Johnson, "The Black Man's Burden," pp. 2-8. Johnson's poem can also be found in *American Citizen*, 3 February 1899.

61. See *Voice of Missions*, "Bishop W. J. Gaine's Great Speech," 1 February 1901, p. 1; and Editorial, "Peace in South Africa," 1 June 1902, p. 8.

62. Charles S. Morris, "A Work for American Negroes," pp. 469-70.

63. Discussion of Morris's observations in South Africa is given in Letter to the Editor, Charles S. Morris, "From Africa," *Christian Recorder*, 19 October 1899, p. 1. See also, Charles S. Morris, "Among the Zulus," *Cleveland Gazette*, 31 March 1900.

64. See *Indianapolis Freeman*, Editorial, "The Boers," 7 October 1899; Editorial, "The Boers and Slavery," 28 October 1899; and Editorial, "The Boers and the Negroes," 11 November 1899.

65. See *Indianapolis Recorder*, Editorial, "British-South African War," 21 October 1899; and Editorial, "Trouble in Africa," 28 October 1899.

66. See *Colored American* (Washington, D.C.), Editorial note, 18 November 1899; Editorial, "Should Stand for England," 20 January 1900; and Editorial, "The British and the Boers," 14 April 1900. For a discussion of E. E. Cooper's journalistic ventures, see Emma Lou Thornbrough, *The Negro in Indiana*, pp. 385-87.

67. See *Savannah Tribune*, "Boers Again Rout Britains," 3 February 1900; "Boers Meet Rebuff," 26 February 1900; Editorial, "Hypocrisy of the Boers," 12 May 1900; and "No Boer Sympathy," 2 June 1900.

68. See *Washington Bee* (Washington, D.C.), Editorial, "The Boers and the English," 21 October 1899; Editorial, "The English and the Boers," 28 October 1899; Editorial, "The Conflict in South Africa," 4 November 1899; Editorial note, 10 March 1900; Editorial, "Boer Envoys," 26 May 1900; and Editorial, "Pretoria," 16 June 1900.

69. See *Topeka State Ledger* (Kansas), Editorial, "Our Opinion," 16 December 1899; "Cape Colony Free of Boers," 15 March 1900; and "Boer Recruits From America," 8 May 1900.

70. See *Richmond Planet* (Virginia), "Will Remain Neutral," 14 October 1899; "How Boers Fight," 28 October 1899; Editorial note, 28 October

1899; "The War in Africa," 11 November 1899; "British Disaster," 17 February 1900; "Boers Concentrating," 24 February 1900; "Boers Have Left Natal," 10 March 1900; "Boer Peace Emissaries," 19 May 1900; and "The Boers Determined," 26 May 1900.

71. Editorial, "The Boer Government," *Cleveland Gazette*, 3 February 1900. Further discussion of the war is given in *Cleveland Gazette*, "The War in Africa," 4 November 1899; "The War in Africa," 13 January 1900; "South Africa," 28 April 1900; "The Boers and the Negroes," 19 May 1900; "Boers and Blacks," 14 July 1900; and "South Africans," 2 March 1901.

72. See *Parsons Weekly Blade* (Kansas), "Declaration of War," 13 October 1899; "War in Transvaal," 20 October 1899; Editorial note, 27 October 1899; "The South African War," 10 November 1899; "Will Join the Boers," 15 December 1899; and Editorial note, 15 December 1899.

73. See *Broad Ax* (Chicago), "Boer War Pays Us," 4 November 1899; "South Africa," 20 January 1900; "Boers Refusing Aid," 24 February 1900; "Fate of the Boer Republics," 31 March 1900; and "Cause of the Boers," 16 June 1900.

74. See *Topeka State Ledger*, "Boers Are Surrendering," 20 August 1900; "Boers Active Again," 25 May 1901; "Thinks African War Ended," 5 October 1901; and "Big Pro-Boer Meeting," 4 January 1902. Discussion is also given in "British Casualties," *Topeka Colored Citizen* (Kansas), 9 November 1900; "The War in Africa," *Parsons Weekly Blade*, 21 December 1900; "South African War," *American Citizen*, 5 January 1900; "The Boer Envoy," *American Citizen*, 8 June 1900; "How the War Began," *Western Enterprise* (Colorado Springs), 6 January 1900; "Transvaal War Items," *Detroit Informer*, 13 January 1900; "Boers Prepared for Fight," *Statesman* (Colorado Springs), 27 January 1900; "Boer Perseverance," *Wichita Searchlight* (Kansas), 27 October 1900; "Queen Victoria—The Friend of the Negro," *Colored American Magazine* (March 1901): 355; *Portland New Age* (Oregon), 1899-1902, passim; and *Wisconsin Weekly Advocate* (Milwaukee), 1899-1902, passim.

75. E. D. Gibson, Letter to the Editor, "The Boer-English War," *Colored American*, 17 March 1900.

76. Frederick Loudin to John E. Bruce, 29 April 1900, Bruce Papers (uncatalogued). This letter can also be found in *Apropos of Africa*, comp. and ed. Martin Kilson and Adelaide Cromwell Hill, pp. 122-25.

77. J. B. T. Marsh, *The Story of the Jubilee Singers*, pp. 112-15, 123-154.

78. Harry Dean, *The Pedro Gorino*, pp. 78, 212-13, 232, 253, 255.

79. Willard B. Gatewood, Jr., "Black Americans and the Boer War," pp. 236, 240-41; Letter to the Editor, "Foreign Shores," *Indianapolis Freeman*, 1 December 1900; and "Chalk-Marked His Back," *Cleveland Gazette*, 20 September 1902. For Scott's description of South Africa and the war, see his *The Truth of Africa*, pp. 2, 64, 65. I am indebted to Dr. Willard Gatewood for a copy of this book.

80. Ferguson, *American Diplomacy and the Boer War*, p. 44.

81. "Boers Accept Peace Terms," *Topeka State Ledger*, 10 May 1902; "Boers Give Up! War is Ended!," *Savannah Tribune*, 7 June 1902; Editorial "The Boers," *Washington Bee*, 7 June 1902; "Negroes in Africa," *Wichita Searchlight*, 7 June 1902; and Editorial note, *Richmond Planet*, 14 June 1902.

82. Harry Dean and James Brown c/o D. Martin to Secretary of State, 28 August 1903, Department of State, Record Group 59, Miscellaneous Letters of the Department of State, roll 1182, National Archives; and Dean, *The Pedro Gorino*, pp. 253-62.

83. Editorial, "What Do the Boers Want Here," *Boston Guardian*, 23 August 1902; Editorial, "Reconstruction in South Africa," *New York Age*, 4 May 1905; and Editorial, "Oom Paul Kruger," *Voice of the Negro* (August 1904): 303.

84. "Let the Natives of South Africa Have Justice and Education," *Colored American Magazine* (April 1904): 291.

85. "The Future of Africa," *Broad Ax*, 6 May 1905.

86. See *New York Age*, Editorial, "British Oppression in Africa," 13 April 1905; Editorial, "Statesmanship in South Africa," 29 March 1906; Editorial, "Troubles in South Africa," 5 April 1906; Editorial, "South African Affairs," 3 May 1906; Editorial, "The Labor Problem in South Africa," 20 September 1906; and Editorial, "The White Man in Africa," 1 November 1906.

87. See *New York Age*, "Chief Bambaata [sic] Slain," 21 June 1906; "350 More Natives Fall," 5 July 1906; "600 Natives Killed," 5 July 1906; and "British Soldiers Sicken As They Execute Orders," 19 July 1906.

88. George Shepperson, "The American Negro and Africa," p. 9; Horace Mann Bond, "Howe and Isaacs in the Bush," pp. 67, 72; Robert Weisbord, "Africa, Africans, and the Afro-American," p. 307; Edwin S. Redkey, "The Meaning of Africa to Afro-Americans, 1890-1914," p. 21; Coan, "The Expansion of Missions of the African Methodist Episcopal Church in South Africa, 1896-1908," pp. 368-70; Noer, "The United States and South

Africa, 1870-1914," pp. 220, 226, 239; and "Native Unrest in South Africa," *Independent*, 30 November 1899, p. 3240.

89. *Colored American Magazine*, Editorial, "Africa for the Africans" (July 1905): 350; and "South African Negro" (February 1909): 71. Also discussed in Editorial, "Africa for the Africans," *New York Age*, 29 June 1905; "Africa for the Africans," *Wichita Searchlight*, 12 August 1906; and Editorial, "Africa for the Africans," *Voice of the Negro* (March 1905): 156-58.

90. "The Redemption of Africa," *New York Age*, 28 February 1907; and "American Blacks Plot Uprising in Africa—To Drive Whites Into Sea," *Wichita Searchlight*, 28 December 1907.

91. "The Relation of England to the Natives of South Africa," *New York Age*, 16 August 1906; and "South African Conditions," *Alexander's Magazine* (September 1906): 15.

92. John L. Dube, "Are Negroes Better Off in South Africa?" pp. 583-84.

93. Booker T. Washington to Mrs. Theodore Luling (Grace Lathrop Luling), 28 January 1905, Washington Papers (303). Discussion of the attempts by the British government to have Washington visit Rhodesia and South Africa and make recommendations on how "to raise, educate, and civilize the black man" there can be found in William T. Stead to Dr. Albert Shaw, 11 February 1903; Albert Shaw to Booker T. Washington, 7 March 1903; William T. Stead to Booker T. Washington, 3 June 1903, Washington Papers (277); and Booker T. Washington to E. B. Sargant, 30 June 1909, Washington Papers (398).

94. L. M. Thompson, *The Unification of South Africa, 1902-1910*, p. 433.

95. See *Colored American Magazine*, Editorial, "The Constitution of the Transvaal" (June 1905): p. 294; "Salvation of South Africa" (July 1909): 10; "The Union of South Africa" (September 1909): 197-204; and "The South African Union" (October 1909): 249.

96. See *New York Age*, Editorial, "Resisting Injustice in South Africa," 22 June 1905; "Meeting in South," 1 April 1909; and Editorial, "Salvation of South Africa," 1 July 1909.

EUROPEAN INTEREST IN NORTH AND NORTHEAST AFRICA, 1880–1914

8

England's guns have battered down the forts of Alexandria. English troops have possession of what remains of the city. . . . Victorious England! To accomplish this she has indirectly caused the murder of over three hundred Christians, the destruction of millions of [dollars in] property, unsettled the peace of Europe, and brought about a crisis in her Cabinet.

Editorial, "Victorious England," *The Sentinel*, 15 July 1882.

R. Henri Herbert, ?-?

England will revoke lease of Equatoria [Sudan], now held by the Congo Free State. This is the natural outcome of the policy which aims at the complete control of the Nile from Uganda to Khartoum in the interest of Egypt and Great Britain.

Editorial note, *Broad Ax*, 25 February 1899.

Julius F. Taylor, ?-?

There are those who believe that a vast organized anti-European movement, extremely powerful and directed by a high intelligence, permeates the entire northern half of the Dark Continent, and that Morocco is one of its principal fields.

"A Wider African Movement," *Alexander's Magazine* (October 1907): 327.

Walter F. Walker, ?-?

North and Northeast Africa were significant in the nineteenth-century European partitioning of Africa. Beginning with the French occupation of Algeria in 1830, which precipitated the British and French delineation of "spheres of influence" throughout the continent, and ending with the Italian declaration of a protectorate over Libya in 1912, North and Northeast Africa have been tied to the European world in a dependent status. Some historians have also claimed that the British invasion of Egypt in 1882 helped to launch the "official" scramble for Africa. Because of its close proximity to Europe and its strategic linking potential to the Far East, Europeans have always considered North Africa and North African politics important to European diplomatic, strategic, and political decisions.

In North and Northeast Africa, Europeans encountered situations distinct from those in sub-Saharan Africa. First, and probably most important, the people of North Africa were religiously and culturally united under the umbrella of Islam and strongly opposed to Christian rule. Second, most North African rulers were tied in some way to the Ottoman empire. After 1800, the European powers attempted to undermine the sovereignty of these Islamic Maghrib rulers, an early indication of mounting European economic imperialism in Mediterranean Africa. The future direction of European activity in North Africa became apparent after the French invasion of Algeria in 1830. France had maintained commercial relations with North Africa for decades, but a minor incident in 1827 involving the French consul was used as the pretext for the French conquest of Algeria.

French troops left France in May 1830, landed in Algeria in June, and on 5 July the capital city of Algiers surrendered. Before the end of July all of the principal areas of Algeria were under French control. Algeria became a French protectorate. The French attack on Algeria set into motion forces which had far-reaching effects on the development of French colonial ambitions in the rest of the Maghrib and which magnified the conflicting claims of the other European powers in this area.

Even the French were surprised at the ease of their victory in Algeria, and for a decade afterward official French policy was one of limited occupation. After 1840, however, the policy shifted to total occupation. It took almost thirty years for the French to gain control of the interior of Algeria, but by 1857 the conquest was complete.

After the French defeat in the Franco-German War of 1870-71, the French sought compensation in Algeria for the loss of Alsace-Lorraine. From this time to the beginning of World War I, a French settler community emerged and began to build a French Algeria.[1]

After 1878, the relationship between the rulers of the other Maghrib countries of Tunisia, Morocco, and Libya with the European powers entered a new period. From 1830 to 1878, the rulers of the Maghrib countries surrounding Algeria were able to maintain their independence through compromises and concessions and by taking advantage of the rivalries between the different European powers. During these years, the three European countries interested in this region, Great Britain, France, and Italy, were unable to agree upon their respective spheres of influence, and the Maghrib countries felt confident that France would not expand outside of Algeria. After 1878, however, Great Britain gave up its policy of safeguarding the territorial integrity of the Ottoman empire in North Africa and began to negotiate with France and Italy over colonial territory in this region. After this date, the Maghrib countries were unable to use European dissent to preserve their independence.[2]

The section of North Africa adjoining Algeria on the east, Tunisia, had come under Turkish control during the sixteenth century, but it had achieved virtual independence in the eighteenth century. France had obtained special privileges in this area at the time of its invasion of Algeria, and other European powers sought the same benefits. Italy was particularly interested in Tunisia, because of its location, as an area for future national expansion. Unsound financial decisions and debts to European financiers presented Tunisia with threats to its sovereignty throughout the 1860s and 1870s. Suspension of interest payments on outstanding loans led the French government in 1869 to take over supervision of Tunisian finances. Protests from both British and Italian leaders resulted in a financial commission with representatives from all three countries. Finally, in 1871, Tunisia recognized Ottoman sovereignty.

The British occupation of Cyprus in 1878 ended its traditional policy of preserving intact the territory belonging to the Ottoman empire. At the Congress of Berlin in 1878, France was assured of British and German support of its future plans for occupation of Tunisia. Bismarck encouraged French initiatives in Tunisia so as to divert French attention from the loss of Alsace-Lorraine, which had been annexed by Germany in 1870. By this date, the prospect of an eventual partitioning of Ottoman territories among the European powers was viewed with equanimity.

The French were anxious to thwart Italian designs in Tunisia, and thus, with little thought of the difficulties entailed in the 1830 Algerian expedition, a French army was sent to Tunisia in April of 1881. Tunis was occupied on 12 May 1881. In order to minimize Italian hostility to the French occupation of Tunisia, no reference to a protectorate was made in the Treaty of Bardo. Under the settlement, Tunisia agreed to a "voluntary" and "temporary" limitation of its external sovereignty for an indefinite period of time. Two years later, in 1883, the abandonment of Tunisian autonomy was completed in the al-Marsa Convention, whereby Tunisian internal authority was placed under French supervision and control. In essence, Tunisia became a French protectorate.[3]

Since 1845, France had refused to delineate the southern frontier between Algeria and Morocco, in spite of the recurrence of frontier incidents. By the close of the nineteenth century, Morocco was surrounded by the territorial possessions of France. In the Anglo-French Declaration of 1899, settling the Fashoda incident in the Sudan, Great Britain recognized France's right to preserve order in Morocco. Secret agreements conceding Morocco as a French protectorate were frequent in the diplomatic relations of Great Britain, France, Germany, Italy, and Spain in the early twentieth century. The United States signed more treaties with Morocco before 1880 than any other African country but declined the 1871 offer to make Morocco an American protectorate.

In January of 1906, representatives of fourteen nations, including the United States, convened at Algeciras, Spain, to decide Morocco's fate. The Algeciras Conference resulted in a vague acknowledgment of French interest in Morocco. Morocco was recognized as independent but under international supervision, with its police powers controlled by France and Spain. A program of quiet military occupation of Morocco was undertaken by France. On 30 March 1912, the ruler of Morocco signed the Treaty of Fez instituting a French protectorate over that country for the next forty-five years. The Spanish continued to govern about one-twelfth of Morocco.[4]

Turkey reoccupied Libya for the second time in 1835. By 1843, the Ottoman administration of what was to become the state of Libya had taken shape. Unlike the other countries of the Maghrib, Libya was not subject to the threat of European imperialism during the nineteenth century. However, Italian ambitions in Libya, which had been encouraged by British and French hints at the Congress of Berlin in 1878, became a matter of defending national pride when the French occupied Tunisia in 1881. Compensation for the Italian disappointment at the loss of Tunisia was sought on the eastern coast of Africa. However, the failure of designs on Ethiopia in East Africa eventually brought Italian aspirations back to Africa's Mediterranean shores.

Incidents between Italian and Ottoman officials in Libya amplified after 1881. In 1887, Great Britain formally agreed to support Italian interests in Libya, and Spain followed suit. In 1900, France signed a secret agreement with Italy offering to aid in its plans in Libya with the understanding that Morocco would be regarded as a French sphere. By this time, Italy's only obstacle to annexing Libya was the Ottoman empire.

On 28 September 1911, an ultimatum was sent to Turkey listing Italian grievances in Libya and demanding guarantees of reforms within twenty-four hours. Although the Turks replied with a conciliatory acknowledgment, on 29 September, Italy declared war on the Ottoman empire. In November of 1911, Italy annexed Libya by royal decree. The Treaty of Lausanne ending the war was signed on 18 October 1912. The contested area was surrendered to Italy. Libya thus became the last country in North Africa to be partitioned among the European powers.[5]

In Northeast Africa, the British faced the same dilemma as Italy with the Ottoman empire, and, in addition, there were the complications presented by the Anglo-French contests over Egypt and the Sudan. The Turks had conquered Egypt in 1517. The Sudan became a dependent of Egypt in 1821. In the latter third of the eighteenth century, the British and French conducted negotiations with the rulers of Egypt to secure exclusive rights to the overland Suez route. British and French rivalry in Egypt, as in other parts of the Ottoman empire, originated with commercial competition but also had political and strategic motivations. Napoleon Bonaparte's ill-fated expedition to Egypt in 1798 and his adventures in the Near East introduced a new factor in Anglo-French rivalry. His regime in Egypt threatened the integrity of the Ottoman empire, which the British continued to support until 1878, and seriously endangered the British position in India. However, the French occupation of Egypt lasted only three years, and, after their defeat in 1801, Egypt was restored to the Ottoman empire. Muhammad Ali became pasha of Egypt and, assisted by French advisors, began to modernize the country. Until World War I Egypt remained nominally attached to the Ottoman empire.[6]

After 1825, Great Britain became particularly interested in Egypt as a necessary link in its Red Sea route to India, and thus the political condition of Egypt was considered vital to the British eastern campaign. During the 1840s, the French openly objected to the British building of the Cairo-Suez railway, and the British blocked the French project in the Suez Canal in the 1850s and 1860s. Both feared that any advantage would increase its rival's influence in Egypt. Nonetheless, despite British opposition, the Suez Canal was completed in 1869. By the mid-1870s, British and French competition in Egypt was so intense that there was danger that the country might be occupied by one or the other of the powers. In 1875, the British government purchased a large block of canal shares from the bankrupt Khedive Ismail in order to keep its balance of influence in the waterway equal to that of France. In 1876, Ismail declared bankruptcy. The khedive finally agreed to an international commission of inquiry to investigate Egyptian finances. The commission's report in August of 1878 sharply criticized Egyptian financial practices.[7]

On 26 June 1879, Ismail received a telegram addressed to "the ex-Khedive Ismail Pasha" informing him that he was deposed in favor of his son. The British and French took credit for having replaced the independent-minded Ismail with the more pliable Tawfiq and were now able to reorganize Egyptian finances. However, in the winter of 1881 to 1882, they were faced with a revolt, led by Colonel Ahmad Arabi, which gradually assumed a nationalistic character. Attempts to quell the uprising proved futile. An Anglo-French naval expedition in Egyptian waters precipitated an outburst of anti-foreign spirit in Alexandria, where on 11 June 1882, a number of Europeans were killed and property destroyed. Commercially and strategically, the Nile waterway was so important to British interests that its safety was generally accepted as of vital national concern, and the British government had already decided to take Egypt by force. Therefore, on 11 July, Alexandria was bombarded, a British army landed, and, on 14 September, Cairo was occupied and Arabi's forces defeated.[8]

The French reacted to the British occupation of Egypt with resentment and continued to do so until the Entente of 1904. France was unwilling to grant Great Britain a free hand in Egypt unless French preponderance in East Africa was recognized. France finally found compensation in Tunisia and Morocco.[9]

The British announced in 1882 that their occupation of Egypt was only a temporary measure intended to stabilize the finances of the country and restore law and order. They remained, however, for over half a century, until 1936. The fact of possession eventually produced its own justification for occupation and utlimately was accepted by the other powers, just as French control in Algeria had been. By the beginning of World War I, British control of Egypt was taken for granted. Though formalities of Ottoman sovereignty and khedivial authority in Egypt were preserved after 1882, the British Foreign Office possessed the real power. When Turkey joined the cause of the Central Powers at the beginning of World War I, the British "temporary" occupation was replaced in December of 1914 with a formal protectorate over Egypt.[10]

In July of 1821, an army led by Ismail Pasha, the youngest son of Muhammad Ali, conquered and imposed Egyptian rule on the people of the Sudan living between the cities of Wadi Halfa and Sennar. The Sudan thus became a colony of Egypt, itself a dependency of the Ottoman empire at the time. Muhammad Ali believed that the Sudan would pay its own way. In October of 1822, the Sudanese revolted and murdered Ismail but were only able to forestall the reinstatement of Egyptian rule. By 1824, the rebellion was over. The Egyptian regime in the Sudan resumed and lasted until 1885. This period of Turkish-Egyptian rule in the Sudan was known as the Turkiya.[11]

On 29 June 1881, Muhammad Ahmad, thirty-six years old, proclaimed himself the expected Mahdi, the savior of the Sudan. The governor-general of the Egyptian Sudan, Charles George Gordon, mistook Mahdism for a local religious fad and ignored it.

Within two years, however, the Mahdi had brought most of the Sudan completely under his control, breaking the Egyptian hold on the country. The defeat at Omdurman of Hicks Pasha, on 8 September 1883, awakened the British government to the interdependence of the Egyptian and Sudanese questions. Having occupied Egypt in 1882, the British were disinclined to extend their obligations to the Sudan. They had no present interest in the area and felt that Egypt's already weak finances would be drained by a large military expedition to defeat the Mahdi. Therefore, in January of 1884, the British decided not to get involved in fighting the Mahdi and withdrew their troops from the Sudan. With the fall of Khartoum to the Mahdist forces and the death of General Gordon in January of 1885, Egyptian administration also ended in the Sudan. The Turkiya was over. On 22 June 1885, the Mahdi died at Omdurman after a short illness. Abdallahi ibn Muhammad was elected the successor of the Mahdi. Khalifa Abdallahi remained head of the Mahdist state until his defeat in 1898.[12]

Various European nations held the position that British claims to the Sudan ended with its abandonment of the area in 1884 and denied the existence of any "effective occupation" as defined in the Berlin Act of 1885. Thus, in the 1890s, the southern Sudan was coveted by the French and the Belgians in the Congo Free State, but both were thwarted by the Khalifa's army. British public opinion began to favor an assault upon the Sudan to protect national prestige and the all-important Nile River. Thus, on 12 May 1896, the British announced their invasion of the Sudan. The sudden decision was prompted by the Italian defeat at Adowa on 1 March. Ethiopia's victory altered the balance of power in this region of Africa and suggested the possibility of a coalition between the Ethiopian and Khalifa's forces to defeat the European powers vying for territory there.[13]

The military followers of the Khalifa were overwhelmed near Omdurman on 2 September 1898, and the Khalifa was killed on 24 November 1899. The Mahdist was over. But a more serious problem presented itself a few weeks later. The French, anxious to acquire the southern Sudan as the final link in their trans-African possessions stretching from the Atlantic to the Indian Oceans, had occupied the city of Fashoda (now Kodok). On 19 September 1898, the British and French armies met at Fashoda. An armed clash was averted only by the two commanders' unwillingness to precipitate a major European war. The question was referred to the respective governments, and the French reluctantly withdrew at the end of October. One of the most serious crises arising from the European partitioning of African territory was peacefully settled on 21 March 1899, with the signing of the Anglo-French Declaration. With the reconquest of the Sudan, the Anglo-Egyptian Agreement was signed on 19 January 1899, providing for joint rule in the area. The Anglo-Egyptian Condominium was created, which lasted until 1956.[14]

In 1854, Frederick Douglass summed up the relationship that black Americans continued to have with North Africa even during the period under consideration. He claimed that "the desirableness of isolating the negro race and especially of separating them from the various peoples of Northern Africa, is too plain to need a remark."[15] Because of an attempt by whites to disclaim North Africa as belonging to the continent of Africa and its distinctly different religion and culture, Afro-Americans felt a greater ambivalence toward this area than any other region of the continent. Also, most of North Africa had been divided among the Europeans by the time of the formal partitioning. This could account for the paucity of information on the views of middle-class Afro-Americans toward the partitioning of North Africa.

In the discussion of the Maghrib countries of Algeria, Tunisia, Morocco, and Libya, the Afro-American press was the most vocal within the literate black community, and it was the leading group to respond to the partitioning. News items and articles of events in these countries can be found in many black newspapers, although editorial comment was scarce. The *Sentinel* (Trenton, New Jersey) and the *Huntsville Gazette* (Alabama), for example, contained a lot of information about North Africa in their columns "Foreign News" and "News and Notes," but most of these articles were reprints from white newspapers and white correspondents who discussed North African developments. Seemingly, the editors of these papers did not feel that North African events warranted their comment.

Algeria was briefly taken up in black newspapers after 1880, but much of this discussion centered around the "progress" made in this country under French rule. The building of railroads, the construction of telegraph lines, and the discovery of petroleum were briefly noted upon occasion. Not surprisingly, considering the constant troubles France had in the pacification of Algeria, revolts and insurrections were also mentioned.[16]

With the occupation of Tunisia in May of 1881, the black press emphasized the animosity between France and Italy for control of the area. The series of revolts by Tunisians against French rule also received attention. Basically, however, European interest and activity in Algeria and Tunisia warranted little comment from articulate Afro-Americans.[17]

Morocco received some notice in the black press early in the twentieth century. The sultan of Morocco was portrayed as a "little despot" who governed his people unsparingly and hated nonbelievers. The Algeciras Conference of 1906 was covered, and the *Savannah Tribune* predicted that "a supreme diplomatic struggle is eminent." Europe looked longingly at North Africa, the paper contended.[18] Walter F. Walker, in his column on Africa, warned in 1907 that the problems Europeans faced in Morocco were connected to a wider anti-European movement that was permeating all of North Africa. Morocco was seen as one of the principal areas of discontent.[19]

R. Henri Herbert, editor of the *Sentinel*, briefly discussed French and Italian rivalries in Libya. Herbert noted that France's renouncement of claims to or designs on Libya after its occupation of Tunisia involved no sacrifice of national pride, since Libya was not strategically or politically in the line of French conquest. Curiously, Afro-American newspapers did not discuss the acknowledged Italian protectorate over Libya in 1912.[20]

Generally, Afro-American responses to the events in Northeast Africa, and specifically in Egypt and the Sudan, received greater coverage in newspapers and more discussion outside of journalistic circles than incidents in the Maghrib North. Egypt, like Ethiopia, had a special place in the hearts of all black Americans. In the writings of Afro-Americans beginning in the early nineteenth century and throughout the period under discussion, Egypt functioned as a conspicuous refutation of the racist black inferiority argument. Egyptians were described as black or colored people. Egyptians and Ethiopians were viewed as cousins, of one and the same people. Africa, so the argument went, was the cradle of mankind, and the black man, born in the land of Egypt, was the father of civilization. Accordingly, Greece and Rome, and through them Europe, and North and South America, were settled by and received their civilization from descendants of the ancient Egyptians. Afro-Americans were thus descendants of the progenitors who ruled Egypt centuries ago. In an address in 1854, Douglass emphasized that "Egypt is in Africa" and the ancient Egyptians were not white people.[21]

With this framework, naturally blacks looked to events in this area more frequently, although it was again the newspapers that dominated the discussion. The *Washington Bee*, although not making any editorial comment, had continuous news items on events in Egypt, most relating to commercial developments in the country. The British bombardment of Egypt in 1882 was discussed by several newspapers. In an editorial, Herbert of the *Sentinel* satirized the British occupation. Herbert reported that the British guns had battered down the forts of Alexandria and taken possession of the remains of the city. To accomplish this, he maintained, "victorious England" had indirectly caused the murder of several hundred Christians and the destruction of millions of dollars of property, unsettled the tenuous peace of Europe, and precipitated a crisis in the British cabinet.[22]

The *Huntsville Gazette*, in its columns "Late News Items" and "News and Notes," also covered the British invasion of Egypt. These articles recounted British public opinion, which favored the seizure of Egypt, France's intention to send troops to Egypt to assist in the protection of the Suez Canal, and Arabi's surrender. It is not clear whether or not the editor had any say over the news items placed in these columns, but in one the idea was astutely advanced that the bombardment of Egypt could be regarded as the first step in the British military occupation of Egypt, which had the ultimate purpose of separating that country from the Ottoman empire and making it a British province.[23]

In a series of editorials, Charles Hendley, Jr., editor of the Republican *Gazette*, discussed the British invasion of Egypt. Hendley predicted that the conflict between the Egyptian and British forces would prove to be economically beneficial to the United States since it would increase the demand for and price of American cotton, presently in competition with Egypt's crop. The open country was

seen as a battleground where Arabi and his troops could fortify themselves. Hendley predicted that the bloody conflict was not over and
North Africa would eventually flow in blood before the struggle
ended.[24]

Douglass, the best-known black leader before 1895, in a trip to
Egypt in 1886, discussed the circumstances in that country as he had
observed them. He noted that he could understand why Great
Britain and France were so interested in making this area a colony.
These "two rival powers each jealous of the other" were vying for
domination over the resources of Egypt, he insisted. Douglass also
viewed the commercial and strategic position of the country as
significant. Primarily, he saw control of the Suez Canal as "the
motive and mainspring of English Egyptian occupation and of
English policy."[25]

After 1882, blacks seldom talked of British imperialism in Egypt
and made little mention of the affairs there. The *Cleveland Gazette*,
in 1900, in a rare article, mentioned the khedive of Egypt and
described him as intelligent and cultured.[26] Otherwise, there was little
attention given to Egypt in the black press. There was also no discussion of the declaration of a formal British protectorate over Egypt,
which was announced in December of 1914, but of course by this
time Afro-American interest was directed toward the European war.

Ironically, it was the events in the Sudan that received the greatest
attention from the Afro-American literate community. These blacks
were particularly interested in the Mahdi's fight against British rule.
The *Sentinel* noted the preaching of a "false prophet" a few months
after Muhammad Ahmad had proclaimed himself the Mahdi.[27]

In a series of editorials in the *Freeman* in 1885, T. Thomas Fortune
criticized British activity in the Sudan, claiming that, as usual, it was
foremost in planting itself in Africa. He praised the struggle of the
Mahdi against foreign rule and sympathized with the Sudanese fight
for independence. In July of 1885, after the death of the Mahdi, the
so-called false prophet of the Sudan, he described him as a great
man who "made it exceedingly warm for the British who desired to
gobble up Sudanese territory." Fortune noted that the British were
now finding the African less likely to accept colonial rule, as had been
demonstrated in the revolt in the Sudan and those throughout the
continent.[28]

During the years 1884 and 1885, the *Washington Bee* was filled with items on the Sudan. Activities of the Mahdi and his followers, evacuation of British forces in the Sudan, and the death of the Mahdi were disclosed. The Sudan was generally described as in a state of anarchy and chaos during these years.[29] Other papers mentioned these same issues.[30]

In 1898, black journalists discussed the British conquest of the Sudan. The British victory was seen as complete, the Khalifa's reign over, and Mahdism dead. The Anglo-French confrontation was also discussed. Most of these articles were reprints from London correspondents, however.[31]

In an editorial in 1899, Julius F. Taylor of the *Broad Ax* criticized British monopolistic activities in the Sudan and stated, "This is the natural outcome of the policy which aims at the complete control of the Nile from Uganda to Khartoum in the interest of Egypt and Great Britain." Taylor remarked that all of France's developments and investments in the Bahr-el-Ghazal would come to nothing unless it was willing to go to war with Great Britain over the territory.[32] Several newspapers noted and mentioned the problems the British were having getting other nations to respect the Anglo-Egyptian Agreement in the Sudan and told of the signing of the Anglo-French Declaration of 1899 delimiting frontiers in the Sudan.[33]

Finally, Afro-Americans in another capacity were interested in the Sudan. Tuskegee's methods and principles, which had been demonstrated in other areas of Africa, were also tried in the Anglo-Egyptian Sudan. Leigh Hunt, who helped to open up the cotton region in the Sudan, suggested that skilled blacks from the United States, such as blacksmiths, mechanics, and dairy and other farmers, who had been trained in American agricultural schools be used as technical demonstrators to the local Sudanese. Hunt, an American businessman, in cooperation with British associates, bought a tract of land on the banks of the Nile River with the idea of setting up a cotton plantation. A group of Tuskegee students were sent to the Sudan in 1906 to organize this project and to prepare for other black emigrants. But the experimental farm lasted only a few years because the students began to die and eventually all of them returned to the United States. Hunt soon withdrew his support, and Tuskegeans were not involved further in the scheme.[34]

Several explanations may elucidate why there was limited discussion of North African events in the black middle-class community during the years 1880 to 1914. First is the fact that much of North Africa was partitioned earlier that the other regions of Africa (France invaded Algeria in 1830, Tunisia was occupied by the French in 1881, and the British took over Egypt in 1882) and was not as prominent in the minds of blacks during the height of the partitioning. Second, because there were no opprobrious examples of maladministration or mistreatment, which would have attracted attention to this area as had the atrocities in the Congo, these blacks focused their attention on other events. Third, although black Americans identified with Egypt because of its historical longevity, generally middle-class blacks did not align themselves with Islamic North Africa. No black missionaries were stationed in this area before 1920, and much as with East Africa, few blacks had treveled to or were knowledgeable about this region. Finally, it is important to note that there were calculated and overt attempts by whites to disclaim North Africa as a part of the continent of Africa; it was seen instead as an integral sector of the Mediterranean world. This propaganda campaign presented a dilemma for blacks in their identification with Africa and accounts for their persistent hesitation in embracing North Africa. Thus, although a few middle-class blacks discussed the partitioning of North Africa, this area more than any other on the continent was left out of any in-depth Afro-American discussion of the European partitioning of Africa.

With the capitulation of North Africa, the partitioning of Africa was complete. The European imperialists began to implement their distinct systems of colonialism. By this time, only two African nations had escaped the rule of the European powers. Standing alone in Africa as the only independent countries, Ethiopia and Liberia were nonetheless constantly forced to protect their sovereignty against foreign control.

Notes

1. Jamil M. Abun-Nasr, *History of the Maghrib*, pp. 176, 235, 238, 240, 245-46, 258; Galbraith Welch, *North African Prelude*, p. 489; Charles F. Gallagher, *The United States and North Africa*, p. 64; Halford L. Hoskins,

European Imperialism in Africa, pp. 18, 20-21; and E. A. Ayandele, "The Magrib in the Nineteenth Century," pp. 184-85.

2. Abun-Nasr, *History of the Maghrib*, p. 235.

3. Ibid., pp. 189, 271, 276, 279; Hoskins, *European Imperialism in Africa*, pp. 47, 49-50; Gallagher, *The United States and North Africa*, pp. 70-71; Ayandele, "The Magrib in the Nineteenth Century," pp. 192-94; and Edward Freeman Gossett, "The American Protestant Missionary Endeavor in North Africa," p. 5.

4. Abun-Nasr, *History of the Maghrib*, pp. 297, 303; Hoskins, *European Imperialism in Africa*, pp. 90, 92, 94; Gallagher, *The United States and North Africa*, pp. 76-77, 79; Rupert Emerson, *Africa and United States Policy*, p. 16; and Edward W. Chester, *Clash of Titans*, pp. 113, 145, 162.

5. Abun-Nasr, *History of the Maghrib*, pp. 304, 308, 309, 311; and Hoskins, *European Imperialism in Africa*, pp. 85-89.

6. Lenoir Chambers Wright, *United States Toward Egypt, 1830-1914*, pp. 20-22, 24; Hoskins, *European Imperialism in Africa*, p. 22; and Welch, *North African Prelude*, p. 451.

7. Ronald Robinson and John Gallagher, *Africa and the Victorians*, pp. 76-77, 80, 83; Hoskins, *European Imperialism in Africa*, pp. 23, 25-26; and Wright, *United States Policy Toward Egypt, 1830-1914*, pp. 89, 103, 105-6.

8. Robert O. Collins and Robert L. Tignor, *Egypt and the Sudan*, p. 84; Hoskins, *European Imperialism in Africa*, pp. 27-28; Wright, *United States Policy Toward Egypt, 1830-1914*, pp. 107, 111-12, 114-16, 124-25, 133; and Robinson and Gallagher, *Africa and the Victorians*, pp. 87-88, 119.

9. Wright, *United States Policy Toward Egypt, 1830-1914*, p. 119; Robinson and Gallagher, *Africa and the Victorians*, p. 302; and Muhammad A. Al-Hajj, "The Nile Valley," p. 175.

10. Hoskins, *European Imperialism in Africa*, pp. 29-30; and Wright, *United States Policy Toward Egypt, 1830-1914*, pp. 133, 161.

11. Robert I. Rotberg, *A Political History of Tropical Africa*, p. 233; and Collins and Tignor, *Egypt and the Sudan*, pp. 67-68.

12. Robert O. Collins, *The Southern Sudan, 1883-1898*, pp. 19, 51; Richard L. Hill, *Egypt in the Sudan, 1820-1881*, p. 164; Peter M. Holt, *The Mahdist State in the Sudan, 1881-1898*, p. 45; Hoskins, *European Imperialism in Africa*, pp. 80-81; Robinson and Gallagher, *Africa and the Victorians*, pp. 132-33, 135; Collins and Tignor, *Egypt and the Sudan*, pp. 76-77, 79; and Al-Hajj, "The Nile Valley," pp. 178-79.

13. Hoskins, *European Imperialism in Africa*, pp. 29, 82; Robinson and Gallagher, *Africa and the Victorians*, pp. 346, 349; Collins, *The Southern Sudan, 1883-1898*, p. 180; and Holt, *The Mahdist State in the Sudan, 1881-1898*, pp. 223-24.

14. Hoskins, *European Imperialism in Africa*, pp. 81-83; Robinson and Gallagher, *Africa and the Victorians*, pp. 370, 374, 378; Collins, *The Southern Sudan, 1883-1898*, p. 180; Hill, *Egypt in the Sudan, 1820-1881*, p. 167; and Holt, *The Mahdist State in Sudan, 1881-1898*, p. 243.

15. Frederick Douglass, *Claims of the Negro*, p. 16.

16. See *Sentinel* (Trenton, New Jersey), "Foreign News," 11 June 1881, 25 June 1881, 17 September 1881, and 20 August 1881. Also consult, "African Affairs," *Washington Bee*, 2 November 1901.

17. See *Huntsville Gazette* (Alabama), "News and Notes," 2 July 1881 and 16 July 1881; *Sentinel*, "Foreign News," 14 May 1881, 21 May 1881, 28 May 1881, 4 June 1881, 25 June 1881, 2 July 1881, 9 July 1881, 20 August 1881, and 3 September 1881; and Editorial note (reprint from *Philadelphia Press*), *Sentinel*, 11 June 1881.

18. "Sultan of Morocco," *Washington Bee*, 13 April 1901; and "Morocco the Issue," *Savannah Tribune*, 16 January 1906 and 20 January 1906.

19. Walter F. Walker, "A Wider African Movement," *Alexander's Magazine* (October 1907): pp. 326-28.

20. Editorial note, *Sentinel*, 23 July 1881.

21. David Walker, *David Walker's Appeal* (1829), p. 8; Hosea Easton, *A Treatise on the Intellectual Character* (1837), pp. 8-9, 12-14; James W. C. Pennington, *Textbook of the Origin and History, & c. & c. of the Colored People* (1841), p. 21; Robert B. Lewis, *Light and Truth* (1844), pp. 2-3, 123, 129-37; Henry Highland Garnet, *The Past and Present Condition, and the Destiny of the Colored Race* (1848), p. 7; Douglass, *Claims of the Negro* (1854), p. 17; Rufus Lewis Perry, *The Cushite* (1883), p. 41; James M. Webb, *The Black Man the Father of Civilisation Proven by Biblical History* (1910), pp. 9-10, 13, 23, 27; and M. C. B. Mason, *Solving the Problem* (1917), pp. 131-32.

22. See *Sentinel*, 15 July 1882, "The War in Egypt" and Editorial, "Victorious England." For a discussion of Egypt in the *Washington Bee*, see 1882-83, passim.

23. See *Huntsville Gazette*, "Late News Items," 15 July 1882, 19 August 1882 and 14 October 1882; "News and Notes," 15 July 1882, 22 July 1882, 12 August 1882, 9 September 1882, 16 September 1882, 23 September 1882, and 30 September 1882; and "The Second Day," 22 July 1882.

24. See *Huntsville Gazette*, Editorial note, 15 July 1882, 22 July 1882, and 29 July 1882.

25. Frederick Douglass, *Life and Times of Frederick Douglass Written By Himself*, pp. 581, 703-5.

26. "The Khedive of Egypt," *Cleveland Gazette*, 25 August 1900.

27. "Foreign News," *Sentinel*, 27 August 1881.

28. See *New York Freeman*, Editorial, "The World in Africa," 14 February 1885; and Editorial, "An African Confederation," 18 July 1885.

29. See *Washington Bee*, "Foreign," 19 January 1884, 26 January 1884, 2 February 1884, 16 February 1884, 23 February 1884, 1 March 1884, 8 March 1884, 18 July 1885, and 25 July 1885.

30. "Foreign News" and "Topics of the Day," *Huntsville Gazette*, 4 July 1885; "Foreign Intelligence," *Arkansas Mansion* (Little Rock), 12 January 1884 and 19 January 1884; and "Foreign," *Grit* (Washington, D.C.), 2 February 1884, 9 February 1884, 16 February 1884, 23 February 1884, and 1 March 1884.

31. See *Richmond Planet*, "The Khalifa Put to Flight," 10 September 1898; and "Khalifa Still At Liberty," 10 September 1898; *Parsons Weekly Blade*, "Battle Believed to Be On," 3 September 1898; and "Fifteen Thousand Killed," 10 September 1898; *Topeka State Ledger*, "Khartoum Has Fallen," 10 September 1898; and "Army of Dervishes Routed," 8 October 1898; *Appeal* (St. Paul, Minnesota), "Campaign of Kitchener," 15 October 1898; "Dervishes and the British," 22 October 1898; and "Pen Picture of Omdurman," 29 October 1898; *American* (Coffeyville, Kansas), "French Saved By Kitchener," and "Army of Dervishes Routed," 1 October 1898; *Iowa State Bystander* (Des Moines), "Terrible Slaughter at Omdurman," 9 September 1898; and "English Flag Not Raised," "Stated That France Has Not Given Up Fashoda," and "Britain Seizes Fashoda," 30 September 1898; *Wisconsin Weekly Advocate*, "Rely on Kitchener," 22 September 1898; "Warning to France," 21 October 1898; and "Must Give Up Fashoda," 28 October 1898; and "Kitchener in London," *Topeka Weekly Call* (Kansas), 29 October 1898.

32. Editorial note, *Broad Ax*, 25 February 1899.

33. "Appoints Council to the Soudan in Spite of the British Position," *Iowa State Bystander*, 27 January 1899; and "France and England Agree," *Afro-American Sentinel* (Omaha, Nebraska), 25 March 1899.

34. Arthur Gaitskell, *Gezira*, pp. 51-52; Edwin S. Redkey, *The Meaning of Africa to Afro-Americans*, pp. 25-26; Kenneth James King, *Pan-Africanism and Education*, p. 14; and Louis R. Harlan, "Booker T. Washington and the White Man's Burden," pp. 447-48.

ETHIOPIA: VICTORY OVER EUROPEAN IMPERIALISTIC AGGRESSIONS, 1880–1914

9

Ethiopia shall soon stretch out her hands unto God.
Bible
Psalms 68:31

The Abyssinians [Ethiopians] are defending their homes and native land; they are perfectly right in expelling foreign aggressions. This over bearing spirit exercised by European nations over African natives should be stopped.
Editorial note, *Savannah Tribune*, 21 March 1896.
John H. Deveaux, ?-?

King Menelik is proving himself more than a match for civilization's trained and skilled warriors, with all their improved machinery of war. More power to him!
Editorial note, *Cleveland Gazette*, 21 March 1896.
Harry Clay Smith, 1863-1941

During the years of the partitioning of Africa among the European powers, two republics in Africa, Ethiopia and Liberia, were able to maintain their independence. Liberia remained independent because of American support, and Ethiopia was able to repulse European invasion. Faced with the threat of domination, Ethiopia was able to defeat Italian imperialistic aggressions through military force.

The Italians began their slow encroachment in East Africa in February of 1885, when they settled in the horn of Africa with the full knowledge and support of the British government, which preferred the weak Italians to their archenemy, France. This advance was initiated when the Massawa seaport in Eritrea, Ethiopia, on the Red Sea was seized. The Italians planned to use this port as their staging area for expansion and settlement in East Africa. They hoped to move inland from this point. The emperor of Ethiopia, although bothered by Italian action, did not formally object because the Italians possessed only a small area. Within a period of three years, however, the Italians had occupied a large section of the East African highlands in Eritrea and had plans for future colonization of the area.[1]

In 1889, Menelik II (Ethiopian: Minīlik), king of the Shoa region, acceded to the imperial crown of Ethiopia. Hoping to gain Italian support for his claim to the throne and not fully aware of Italian designs in East Africa, on 2 May 1889, Menelik signed the Treaty of Wichale (Italian: Uccialli). Because of its interest in Ethiopia, the Italian government reasoned that an agreement with the existing Ethiopian government might expedite its purposes there. Under the most important article of this Treaty of Perpetual Peace and Friendship, article 17, the Italian government claimed to have gained Menelik's permission to establish a protectorate over Ethiopia. This article led to an unresolvable dispute which set the stage for the Italo-Ethiopian War of 1895-96. The Treaty of Wichale, signed by Emperor Menelik and Count Pietro Antonelli, was ratified by King Umberto I of Italy on 29 September 1889.[2]

Since the General Act of the Berlin West African Conference had stipulated that any European nation establishing a protectorate over an African country should notify the other nations of Europe, on 11 October 1889, the Italian government announced its protectorate over Ethiopia along with Menelik's consent to conduct all diplomatic matters through the Italian government. Menelik, who did not feel that article 17 had restricted his diplomatic power, continued to write to the European heads of state. Queen Victoria of Great Britain later sent back a reply which contained the Italian version of article 17.[3] When the Italian and Amharic versions of the treaty were compared, mistranslations were discovered, and Menelik concluded that the Italian government had purposely tricked him.[4]

Article 17 of the Italian version of the treaty limited Ethiopian sovereignty and, in fact, made Ethiopia an Italian protectorate. The issue of the validity of Italy's protectorate over Ethiopia continued to dominate Italo-Ethiopian relations until the outcome of the war in 1896. Attempts to settle the conflict over the article failed, and on 12 February 1893, Menelik denounced the Treaty of Wichale and all of its articles and provisions. This act of denunciation helped to incite animosities, which led to confrontation in 1895. Italy had to defend its reputation in Europe, and Menelik felt that Ethiopia had been humiliated.[5]

One historian has stated that Menelik foresaw the possibility of war with Italy as early as 1893, when he denounced the Treaty of Wichale, and thus prepared himself militarily. A continuing stream of munitions from France came into Ethiopia through Djibouti on the Red Sea. Already by the early 1890s a nationwide feeling of hatred for whites, stimulated by a fear of conquest, had developed among Ethiopians, as the surrounding African territories were partitioned among the European powers.[6]

War was unavoidable. On 7 and 8 December 1895, Ras Makonnen, Menelik's cousin and general of the Ethiopian forces, was victorious over the Italians at Amba Alagi. The war took many directions, but the Italians were overconfident that their victory was inevitable and, consequently, underestimated the strength and determination of the Ethiopians.[7]

From the beginning of the war, Menelik had several advantages over the Italian invaders: he had the support not only of the chiefs of the provinces but also of the local population; he knew the terrain much better than his opponents; and he had a well-equipped, well-trained army. The people of Ethiopia understood clearly that their independence was at stake in this war, and their patriotism played a significant role in the Ethiopian victory. When Menelik issued his mobilization proclamation, "every hut and village in every far-off glen of Ethiopia [sent] out its warrior." In the areas of direct confrontation, the inhabitants helped Menelik's army by showing them the best paths and bringing them information on Italian movements. The Italians, on the other hand, were forced to use a trial-and-error technique. The Italian army found itself ill-prepared to face the determined efforts of Menelik and the Ethiopian people, who were willing to defend their independence at any cost.[8]

Under pressure from his government, General Oreste Baratieri, Italian governor of Eritrea, ordered an attack on the Ethiopian forces camped at Aduwa on 29 February 1896. The Italian army, numbering about 18,000 men and officers, of whom 10,596 were Europeans and the remainder African regular troops, had a firepower of 14,519 obsolescent rifles and 56 artillery and machine-gun units. The Ethiopian forces have been estimated at 120,000 men, composed of 80,000 riflemen, 8,600 cavalry, 42 artillery and machine-gun batteries, and about 20,000 hangers-on armed only with spears, lances, and swords but ready to take over the rifles of those who fell in battle. Having marched through the night, the tired Italian army faced massive numbers of Ethiopians at 6:00 A.M., 1 March 1896. By midday, the Italian army had been defeated. Italian casualties were approximately 7,500 or nearly 43 percent, while Ethiopian losses have been estimated at 17,000 killed and wounded, or 14 percent of the total army. Over 1,800 Italian officers and soldiers were captured. The Ethiopian victory was overwhelming.[9]

Ethiopia's victory over Italian imperialistic aggressions was a shock to the white man's confidence and forced the European nations to recognize Ethiopian sovereignty. The Italian defeat at Aduwa ended, for a time, all plans of Italian imperialism and schemes for settlement. During the next years, Menelik expanded and consolidated his empire.[10]

When the news of the Italian defeat reached Italy, excitement and riots ensued in the cities of that country. The defeat was seen as disastrous to Italian prestige in Africa and to Francesco Crispi's government in Italy. General Baratieri was brought to trial before a special court martial, while Crispi's government in Italy collapsed.[11]

On 26 October 1896, Menelik and the Italian government signed a treaty at Addis Ababa. By the terms of the peace agreement, Ethiopia's sovereign independence was affirmed and the Treaty of Wichale abolished. With the Ethiopian victory at Aduwa and the treaty of October 1896, Ethiopian integrity was preserved and Italian imperialism checked, and Ethiopia stood as the single successful example of Africans repulsing European aggressions and maintaining their independence in the midst of the encroaching colonization of Africa by whites. This event was one dramatic example of African resistance to the imposition of colonial rule.[12]

Future observers were to see the Italo-Ethiopian War of 1895-96 as one of the great events in the history of Ethiopia and of European imperialism in Africa.[13] The Battle of Aduwa represented a major defeat for whites in Africa during the partitioning of the continent. Surprisingly, however, the battle received little attention from contemporaries. European newspapers scarcely covered the war, discussing only the military campaigns and not dealing directly with the political consequences of the Italian defeat. American white newspapers did not regularly publicize the war until the beginning of 1896, and they ignored the implications behind the victory of this black African country over a white European one. The black American newspapers, because of the nature of their sources of international news during these years, contained basically the same general information about the war as the white newspapers. The diversity lay in the different interpretations these two groups gave to the events in Ethiopia.[14]

Historically, Ethiopia has held a certain mystique for Afro-Americans and occupied a special place in their hearts and minds. Ethiopia was a symbol of black independence and successful black self-government years before Menelik's victory over Italy. Blacks had long drawn inspiration from classical and modern Ethiopia as a symbol of black power and pride. The Ethiopian tradition found expression in the narratives, songs, and folklore of southern slaves. Antebellum blacks were soon exposed to the name of Ethiopia in their Bibles in the prophecy, "Ethiopia shall soon stretch out her hands unto God." This quotation was well known among free blacks and slaves in pre-Civil War America and was viewed as a prediction that Ethiopia, used as a synonym for the whole African continent, would once again rise to the level of its former greatness during ancient times. Black churches were established during this period with names such as Abyssinia, Ethiopian, and Kush. In 1858, the African Civilization Society quoted the full biblical verse in its constitution, with an interpretation by Henry Highland Garnet. The term "Ethiopianism" became popular in the 1890s throughout Africa and spurred the Ethiopian independent church movement in southern Africa. It was also no coincidence that later in the twentieth century the official anthem of Marcus Garvey's Universal Negro Improvement Association was entitled, "Ethiopia, Thou Land of Our Fathers."[15]

Black identification with Ethiopia reached a high point with the victory of the Ethiopians over the Italians in March of 1896. As a result, international attention was focused on Menelik and Ethiopia, both gaining a great deal of prestige. Menelik became a hero throughout the black world, and the defeat of a white European nation elicited reaction among black people everywhere. Black American interest in Africa in general, and in Ethiopia in particular, was heightened during these years. Their stronger attachment to Africa during this period, despite pressing domestic concerns, can probably be attributed to a need for racial identification. The Ethiopian victory at Aduwa served this purpose well and made a deep and permanent impression on blacks in their relationship with Africa. The tremendous response of Afro-Americans to the Italian invasion of Ethiopia in 1935 can probably be attributed to an attitude about the country that developed after 1896.

When the news of the battle reached the United States, Americans, both black and white, were shocked. Afro-Americans, like their Ethiopian brothers, understood the importance and significance of the Ethiopian victory. They could now point to Ethiopia as a strong African nation, able to maintain its independence and defend itself against the encroachment of European imperialism. Afro-Americans felt a personal sense of pride over the defeat of a white European power by a black African country. It seems likely that this victory held out the hope that other African countries might be able to resist European domination.

Years later, a leading Afro-American journalist, interviewed by Harold Isaacs, alleged that when he was a young boy he heard of the Italo-Ethiopian War of 1895-96. He pointed out, "Of course we all knew about Menelik's defeat of the Italian Army in 1896."[16] It appears that the Ethiopian victory over the Italians, like many events in the Afro-American experience, became a kind of folk story that was well known to all blacks and passed among individuals within the black community in beauty parlors and barber shops, at church congregations, at various meetings and gatherings, and in family circles.

Articles and editorials appeared in black newspapers immediately following the disclosure of the Italian defeat at Aduwa. Little discussion was given to the campaign before this period. The press was the one sector in the black community to react immediately, although it is likely that many church sermons on the Sunday following the battle dealt with the Ethiopian victory. In every black paper extant today there was a discussion of this event. It can be assumed that the extinct papers also discussed this great event in black history.

The disturbances in Italy caused by their humiliating defeat at Aduwa was reported by many black papers. These newspapers described the Italian position at the end of the war as one of desperation, dishonor, and chaos. The Ethiopian victory was seen as complete, having caused turmoil and disruption not only among the Italians at Aduwa but also in cities throughout Italy.[17]

The *Cleveland Gazette* reported that this "Italian Waterloo" had changed the tone of European politics and blamed the defeat on the colonial craze for territory and power. The paper believed that the Aduwa incident would lead to a readjustment of European politics in Africa.

Harry C. Smith commented that the conquest of Ethiopia had not proved to be an easy one and this could be taken as evidence that Africans would fight honorably for what was rightfully theirs. Menelik had shown the bravery of a leader determined to maintain independence for his people, Smith affirmed. He boasted, "King Menelik is proving himself more than a match for civilization's trained and skilled warriors, with all their improved machinery of war. More power to him!" In a later editorial note, Smith remarked that Menelik's triumph relieved Ethiopia from the "yoke of an Italian protectorate" and that the Ethiopians had shown the world that they could match the obstinacy of an arrogant European power.[18] The determination of the Ethiopian people and the organization of its well-trained army were constantly stressed by Afro-Americans in their comments about the Ethiopian victory in the war.

Smith's attitude best reflected Afro-American views on the Italo-Ethiopian War. Blacks viewed it as a senseless, useless war, depicted the Italians as aggressive, land-grabbing invaders, and represented the Ethiopians as a brave people defending their land and country. This same analogy was later used by white Americans to describe the British and the Boers in the Anglo-Boer War.

The *Savannah Tribune* predicted that the Italian upset could prove to be a disastrous indicator for Europeans in their penetration and colonization of Africa. If used as an example by other black Africans, the paper suggested, the event could have political reverberations throughout Africa. The full details of the battle and of Italy's defeat had not been disclosed, the *Tribune* reported, and the excitement and confusion in Italy showed few signs of diminishing.

In the final analysis, Afro-Americans viewed the Italo-Ethiopian War of 1895-96 as revealing the African struggle to maintain independence amidst the widening imperialistic intentions of Europeans. The Ethiopians had shown themselves equal to any emergency, and John H. Deveaux, editor of the *Tribune*, probably reflected the sentiment of most Afro-Americans when he proudly noted, "The Abyssinians [Ethiopians] are defending their homes and native land; they are perfectly right in expelling foreign aggressions. This overbearing spirit exercised by European nations over African nations should be stopped."[19]

George L. Knox of the *Freeman* congratulated Menelik and Ethiopia on their victory and commented, "They hit 'em hard in Abyssinia." The European overconfidence in their penetration of Africa had been destroyed, and Menelik had proven himself an able leader, Knox editorialized.[20]

Fred L. Jeltz of the *Topeka State Ledger* also praised Menelik's ability. Jeltz commented that Ethiopia, a land almost as historic as Egypt, had given the Italians a lesson in leadership. Noting that the nations of Europe now spoke of Ras Makonnen as the Napoleon of Africa, he explained that this was the highest token of European respect and admiration.[21]

Similarly, George A. Dudley, editor of the *American Citizen*, and Julius F. Taylor of the *Broad Ax* (published in Salt Lake City from August 1895 to July 1899, then moved to Chicago, where it was published until 1927) commended Ethiopia's prowess. Dudley commented, "King Menelik went to the primaries and gave the Italian machine somewhat of a surprise party."[22]

A. L. Graves, editor of the *Broad Axe* (St. Paul, Minnesota), claimed that the descendants of the ancient Romans had lost some of their old passion for conquest after their defeat at Aduwa. Italy would have to be content in its African colonial possessions to be without Ethiopia, the editor maintained. The loss of interest was understandable, Graves remarked, and no sensible person could blame the Italian change of heart after their degrading showing in Ethiopia. Graves's prediction that Italy would divert its attention elsewhere was accurate, as Italy refocused its attention on the conquest of Libya in North Africa.[23]

The *National Reflector* (Wichita, Kansas) discussed extensively the excitement in Italy caused by General Baratieri's defeat at Aduwa and its international significance. G. Wesley White, editor, satirically remarked, "Legs are more needed in fighting the Ethiopians than firearms," and Italians, obviously unable to enlist the necessary number of fighting men, should now retreat.[24]

In a letter to the *Parsons Weekly Blade* from Indian Territory (later, Oklahoma), H. Augustus Guess, a black educator, praised the courageous fight of the Ethiopians. Guess, who regularly wrote letters to the *Blade* from the region commenting on national and international events, predicted that the Italian army's defeat at the hands of the Ethiopians would signal a new day for Africa.[25]

Both Mifflin Gibbs and W. E. B. Du Bois later commented about the war. Arriving in Djibouti, on his way to Madagascar, in 1898, Gibbs referred to the recent conflict between Italy and Ethiopia and concluded that the "unpleasantness" had resulted unprofitably to the Italians. Du Bois spoke of 1896 as "that year Abyssinia vanquished Italy."[26]

Thus, the results of the Italo-Ethiopian War of 1895-96 were viewed by Afro-Americans as advantageous to blacks all over the world. Ethiopia's ability to repulse European encroachment was attributed not only to the efforts of a united and determined people but also to the longevity of its historical development.

After 1900, the U.S. government entered into a new relationship with Ethiopia. Before this date, American contacts with Ethiopia were commercial and limited. Official policy was nonexistent, since British, French, and Italian interests there were thought to have been paramount. In the early twentieth century, however, some American diplomats began to concern themselves with an alliance between the United States and Ethiopia. One such person was the American consul at Marseilles, France, Robert P. Skinner. Skinner realized that Ethiopia had trade potential which deserved American attention. He wrote to assistant secretary of state, David J. Hill, on 8 January 1900, suggesting America's entry into Africa, but the State Department was not interested in his recommendations. In March, he wrote Secretary of State Hay warning that it was only a matter of time before Ethiopia would become a European colony, shutting the United States out from any commercial relationship. Apparently, he was unaware of Ethiopia's victory over Italy in 1896. Skinner proposed in November that the Marseilles consulate be extended to include Ethiopia and that a commission be sent to Ethiopia to negotiate a commercial treaty. The State Department still made no attempt to implement his ideas.

Years passed, and again in May of 1903 Skinner wrote to the State Department. By this date, the State Department had altered its attitude, possibly because the U.S. government realized that Ethiopia's sovereignty was assured, and was more receptive to his recommendations that diplomatic relations be established. In the summer of 1903, President Roosevelt commissioned Skinner to negotiate a commercial treaty with Menelik. Skinner, the head of the first American diplomatic mission to Ethiopia, successfully concluded a commercial treaty with Menelik, signed on 27 December 1903.

The description of the trip and his stay in Ethiopia were later recorded along with details of the treaty by Skinner in a book published in 1906, *Abyssinia of Today*. The treaty of commerce was an agreement between Menelik and the United States to develop and regulate commercial relations between the two countries, and the document contained a "most-favored nation" clause. In article 4, Ethiopia and the United States agreed to receive representatives from the other government. The treaty was to last for ten years and then come up for renewal. On 12 March 1904, the treaty was ratified by the U.S. Senate and signed by the president on 17 March 1904. Notification was sent to Menelik on 2 August 1904, and the treaty was formally proclaimed on 30 September 1904.

An American consul to Ethiopia was not immediately delegated, and it was not until 1907 that a vice-consul was appointed. The vice-consul served until 1909, when a minister-resident position was established, which lasted one year. The minister-resident was succeeded by a vice-consul, who remained for four years. In 1914, John P. Ward negotiated another treaty, and afterward American interests were entrusted to the British legation at Ethiopia and the American consul at Aden, on the Arabian peninsula. There was no American diplomatic agent for Ethiopia again until 1928.[27]

The independent nations of Africa, Ethiopia and Liberia, evoked the most contradictory responses from the United States Government before 1920. Throughout the nineteenth century, commercial interests dominated America's relationship with Ethiopia, though trade with that country was of far less importance than with other African countries, for example, Zanzibar. After the treaty with Ethiopia was signed in 1903, the leader of the American anti-Ethiopian forces, Secretary of State Elihu Root, opposed the appointment of a minister to Ethiopia. Thus, a vice-consul was not appointed until 1907, and by 1914 the United States had withdrawn its minister.

The U.S. government did not follow a consistent strategy with either Ethiopia or Liberia, probably because such a policy with those black African nations would have endangered America's relationship with the European nations already in Africa and obviously because such a commitment would have placed American racial practices at home under scrutiny. Even during the Italo-Ethiopean War of 1935-36, the U.S. government remained neutral, much to the dismay of Afro-Americans.[28] It is apparent that, aside from trading rights, the U.S. government was not geniunely interested in Ethiopia before 1920 and did not really have what could be called a foreign policy for that country. Black Americans, though particularly excited about Ethiopia during the late nineteenth and early twentieth centuries, were unable to affect their government's position.

The *A.M.E. Church Review* discussed the sudden American interest in Ethiopia and the Skinner expedition. H. T. Kealing, editor from 1896 to 1912, reported that the recent attention was part of American imperialistic policy. Hightower Kealing, a native Texan, alternated between public school official and president of the African

Methodist Episcopal (AME) Church Paul Quinn College (founded in 1872 in Austin, Texas, later moved to Waco) between 1881 and 1895. After leaving the editorship of the *Church Review* in 1912, he became president of Western University in Quindaro, Kansas. Kealing was somewhat accommodating in his views but supported the Niagara Movement and the NAACP. He also approved of AME missions in Africa.

Kealing claimed that American overtures toward Ethiopia were stimulated by the interest of rival foreign investors in the wealth of the country. Kealing reminded the reading audience of Menelik's crushing defeat over Italy in 1896, characterizing him as aware of the land-grabbing proclivities of white nations and concerned only with the dignity and independence of his country. With reference to the Skinner expedition, Kealing remarked that it presumably was to secure commercial advantages for the United States. The periodical likewise noted that along with this offical action went the voluntary, informal, and unofficial visit of William Henry Ellis, a black multilingual businessman from San Antonio, Texas, who had previously attempted unsuccessfully a black emigration scheme in Mexico. Ellis had anticipated Skinner's errand and had led an expedition supported by Henry M. Turner to Ethiopia in 1903. Unlike Skinner's official mission, however, nothing came of the Ellis repatriation scheme, though he appears to have won the confidence of Menelik.[29]

John E. Bruce also discussed the Skinner expedition. Bruce, like Kealing, believed that the mission had selfish and ulterior motives. But he voiced the belief that American diplomats would not easily fool Menelik because he was perhaps the shrewdest and most sagacious ruler on the African continent.[30]

Although Afro-Americans continued to talk about the future of Ethiopia after 1900, most were not particularly interested in the Skinner expedition. They were generally more concerned with the maintenance of Ethiopian independence.[31] One incident that precipitated a small discussion by the Afro-American press was the death, in 1909, of General Ras Makonnen, military commander at the Battle of Aduwa. Makonnen was viewed as a great leader. The *Colored American Magazine* commented that it was through Makonnen's strategy and valor that the Italians were defeated and

Ethiopia remained completely free and independent.[32]

T. Thomas Fortune, of the *Age*, described Makonnen as one of the great generals of his time. According to Fortune, it was because of his courage that Ethiopia enjoyed international respect. "General Ras Makonnen," Fortune declared, "must go down in history as the savior of his country and a great general."[33]

Afro-Americans also saw the death of Menelik II, in December of 1913, as significant to Ethiopian relations with Europe. The *Crisis* reported that, since the Battle of Aduwa, Ethiopia had been unmolested by Europeans. Menelik's death left the future of Ethiopia uncertain, Du Bois warned, and marked the end of a significant period in the history of that country.[34] Smith of the *Cleveland Gazette* suggested that the Battle of Aduwa had only postponed European colonization of Ethiopia and Menelik's death might signal the acceleration of that process.[35]

Thus, by the beginning of World War I, the stability and security which had been won for Ethiopia as a result of its victory in the Italo-Ethiopian War was under serious consideration. The future of this independent African country, surrounded by European colonies, was uncertain. Although Ethiopia had successfully repulsed European imperialistic aggressions and survived in the struggle against foreign domination, its future was still not completely secure. As fate would have it, only Liberia would escape the grasp of the European powers completely, for in 1936 Ethiopia would lose its independence to the European country it had defeated forty years earlier.

Notes

1. Richard Pankhurst, "Italian Settlement Policy in Eritrea and Its Repercussions, 1889-1896," pp. 121-25; and Harold G. Marcus, "Imperialism and Expansionism in Ethiopia," p. 424. For a discussion of official Italian policy in Eritrea, see Donald A. Limoli, "Francesco Crispi's Quest for Empire," p. 112.

2. Marcus, "Imperialism and Expansionism in Ethiopia," p. 428; and Limoli, "Francesco Crispi's Quest for Empire," p. 119. See also Richard Pankhurst, "Ethiopia Emperor Menelik II Repulsed Italian Invasion, 1895," pp. 35-36; Harold G. Marcus, "A History of the Negotiations Concerning

the Border Between Ethiopia and British East Africa, 1897-1914," p. 264; and Sven Rubenson, "The Protectorate Paragraph of the Wichale Treaty," p. 243.

3. Marcus, "Imperialism and Expansionism in Ethiopia," pp. 429-30; and Pankhurst, "Ethiopian Emperor Menelik II Repulsed Italian Invasion, 1895," p. 36.

4. This article has caused serious debate among historians. The difference in meaning of the Italian and Amharic versions of article 17 of the treaty was considerable. In the Italian version of the text, it read: "His Majesty the King of Kings of Ethiopia consents to avail himself of the government of His Majesty the King of Italy for all negotiations of affairs which he might have with other powers or governments." The Amharic version read: "The King of Kings of Ethiopia, with the kings of Europe for all the matters which he wants, it shall be possible for him to communicate with the assistance of the Italian government." A discussion of article 17 of the Treaty of Wichale can be found in Rubenson, "The Protectorate Paragraph of the Wichale Treaty," pp. 243-44, 249-50.

5. Marcus, "Imperialism and Expansionism in Ethiopia," p. 430; and Rubenson, "The Protectorate Paragraph of the Wichale Treaty" pp. 244, 251. Pankhurst's "Italian Settlement Policy in Eritrea and Its Repercussions, 1889-1896," p. 149, also makes this point.

6. Marcus, "Imperialism and Expansionism in Ethiopia," pp. 433-34.

7. A detailed military description of the war can be found in George Berkeley, *The Campaign of Adowa and the Rise of Menelik*, passim. See also, Pankhurst's "Ethiopian Emperor Menelik II Repulsed Italian Invasion, 1895," p. 38; and his "Italian Settlement Policy in Eritrea and Its Repercussions, 1889-1896," pp. 150-51.

8. Ernest Work, *Ethiopia*, p. 154; Pankhurst, "Ethiopian Emperor Menelik II Repulsed Italian Invasion, 1895," pp. 35, 38; Pankhurst, "Italian Settlement Policy in Eritrea and Its Repercussions, 1889-1896," p. 121; Marcus, "Imperialism and Expansionism in Ethiopia," p. 435; and Felix Aucaigne, "Italy and Abyssinia," p. 247.

9. Berkeley, *The Campaign of Adowa and the Rise of Menelik*, pp. 345-46; Augustus B. Wylde, "The Battle of Adowa," pp. 121-22; Sven Rubenson, "Adowa 1896," pp. 113, 126; Pankhurst, "Ethiopian Emperor Menelik II Repulsed Italian Invasion, 1895," p. 39; Marcus, "Imperialism and Expansionism in Ethiopia," pp. 435-37. See also Harold G. Marcus, "The Black Men Who Turned White," pp. 160-62.

10. Pankhurst, "Italian Settlement Policy in Eritrea and Its Repercussions,

1889-1896," p. 121; and Marcus, "Imperialism and Expansionism in Ethiopia," p. 454. A similar interpretation is given in Robert O. Collins, *The Partition of Africa*, introduction, p. 19.

11. Limoli, "Francesco Crispi's Quest for Empire," p. 123; Aucaigne, "Italy and Abyssinia," p. 247; and "Italy's Terrible Defeat," *New York Times*, 4 March 1896.

12. Collins, *The Partition of Africa*, introduction, p. 20; Harold Isaacs, *The New World of Negro Americans*, p. 150; and Marcus, "Imperialism and Expansionism in Ethiopia," p. 438.

13. Both Lewis M. Gann and Peter Duignan's *Burden of Empire*, pp. 35-36, and R. A. Caulk's "Firearms and Princely Power in Ethiopia in the Nineteenth Century," p. 625, described this as significant in its impact on colonial expansion.

14. See, for example, *New York Times*, "Abyssinians Around Makalle," 23 January 1896; and "Italians Will Have to Fight," 23 January 1896. See also, *Times* (London), "The Italians in Africa," 26 July 1895; "The Italians in Africa," 27 July 1895; "The Italian Reverse in Abyssinia," 13 December 1895; "Abyssinia," 24 January 1896; "The Italians in Abyssinia," 27 January 1896; "Italian Reverse in Abyssinia," 3 March 1896; "The Italian Disaster in Abyssinia," 4 March 1896; "The Italian Disaster," 5 March 1896; and "The Italian Crisis," 6 March 1896.

15. For discussion of this earlier identification with Ethiopia, see Robert G. Weisbord, *Ebony Kinship*, pp. 89-90; St. Clair Drake, *The Redemption of Africa and Black Religion*, pp. 9-11, 73; and Wilson Jeremiah Moses, *The Golden Age of Black Nationalism*, pp. 10, 23. William Scott's "A Study of Afro-American and Ethiopian Relations, 1896-1941," is an excellent study of the interactions between those two groups in the years between the Italo-Ethiopian War of 1895-96 and the Italo-Ethiopian War of 1935-36. See also Wilson J. Moses, "The Poetics of Ethiopianism," pp. 411-12, 420; Clarence G. Contee, "Ethiopia and the Pan-African Movement Before 1945," p. 43; William R. Scott, "Black Nationalism and the Italo-Ethiopian Conflict," pp. 118-19; Robert Weisbord, "Black America and the Italian-Ethiopian Crisis," p. 230; and George Shepperson, "Ethiopianism and African Nationalism," pp. 249-50.

16. Isaacs, *The New World of Negro Americans*, p. 185.

17. See, for example, *Washington Bee*, "More Rioting in Italy," 14 March 1896; "No Fetes on the King's Birthday," 21 March 1896; "More Rioting in Italy," 21 March 1896; Note, 4 April 1896; and Note, 11 April 1896. Or, see

Leavenworth Herald (Kansas City, Kansas), "Italians Defeated," 7 March 1896 and "Late News Notes," 7 March 1896, 14 March 1896, 21 March 1896, 28 March 1896, and 4 April 1896. Italy's problems were also discussed in "Italians Raising Funds," *Enterprise* (Omaha, Nebraska), 7 March 1896; and "Italians Defeated," *Topeka Weekly Call*, 7 March 1896.

18. See *Cleveland Gazette*, Editorial note, 21 March 1896; "The Battle of Adowa," 28 March 1896; and Editorial note, 21 November 1896.

19. See *Savannah Tribune*, "Italy's Troubles," 14 March 1896; "Italians Routed," 14 March 1896; and Editorial note, 21 March 1896.

20. See Editorial notes, *Indianapolis Freeman*, 14 March 1896.

21. See *Topeka State Ledger*, Editorial note, 20 March 1896; and "News in Brief," 20 March 1896.

22. Editorial note, *American Citizen*, 15 May 1896. See also, *Broad Ax* (Salt Lake City), Editorial notes, 4 April 1896, and 25 April 1896.

23. See *Broad Axe* (St. Paul, Minnesota), "War in Abyssinia," 19 March 1896; and Editorial note, 16 April 1896.

24. See *National Reflector* (Wichita, Kansas), "Turmoil in Italy," 7 March 1896; "Late News Notes," 7 March 1896, and 21 March 1896; and Editorial note, 2 May 1896.

25. "Letter No. 4," *Parsons Weekly Blade*, 14 March 1896.

26. Mifflin Wistar Gibbs, *Shadow and Light*, p. 238. See also, W. E. B. Du Bois, *Dusk of Dawn*, p. 57; and *The Autobiography of W. E. B. Du Bois*, p. 192.

27. Robert P. Skinner, *Abyssinia of Today*, pp. 1, 223-26; Frank J. Manheim, "The United States and Ethiopia," pp. 141-50; and Marcus, "Imperialism and Expansionism in Ethiopia," p. 454.

28. Edward W. Chester, *Clash of Titans*, pp. 3, 55, 173-74, 198.

29. August Meier, *Negro Thought in America*, pp. 233, 266; and Editorial, "Menelik, the Negus," *A.M.E. Church Review* (January 1904): 302.

30. J. E. Bruce, "Dusky Kings of Africa and the Islands of the Sea," *Voice of the Negro* (August 1905): 573-75.

31. "Menelik, Emperor of Abyssinia," *Colored American Magazine* (December 1900): 149-53. See also, *Alexander's Magazine*, "The Christianity of Menelik of Abyssinia," 15 September 1907, pp. 256-57; and "Constitutional Government for Aybssinia [*sic*]," 15 November 1907, p. 19.

32. "Political," *Colored American Magazine* (September 1909): 168.

33. Editorial, "Italian Conqueror Dead," *New York Age*, 5 August 1909.

34. Editorial, "Menelik," *Crisis* (February 1914): 185.

35. Editorial, "Menelik and Abyssinia," *Cleveland Gazette*, 1 March 1914.

LIBERIA: STRUGGLE AGAINST EUROPEAN DOMINATION, 1880–1914

10

They [Liberians] deserve all the assistance and encouragement which it may be in the power of the [American] government to render, in view of the intimate relations which a portion of the Negro race bears to the United States.

Letter to Mr. Evarts, 12 February 1880, *Foreign Relations of the United States*, 1880, p. 702.

John Henry Smyth, 1844-1908

The colored people in every part of this country are . . . deeply interested in saving and helping Liberia.

Letter to Henry Cabot Lodge, 10 April 1910, Booker T. Washington Papers (411).

Booker Taliaferro Washington, 1856-1915

There never was a time perhaps, more than now, when this little Republic [Liberia] struggling for existence between two great and formidable European Powers [Great Britain and France] stood in greater need of the active assistance of the Government of the United States.

Letter to Secretary of State, 21 November 1906 (#177), U.S. Department of State, Record Group 59, Numerical File (1906-1910), Cases 3513-3536, roll #326.

Ernest Lyon, 1860-1938

In the late nineteenth century, when Ethiopia was repulsing Italian aggressions, Liberia was also struggling against European domination. Although Liberia was able to survive the European partitioning of Africa, it was not left completely untouched. Throughout the period from 1880 to 1914, Liberia was constantly threatened with the encroachment of British, French, and Germans upon its territory. While Liberia and Ethiopia faced a similar threat of European imperialism, the two independent African countries dealt with the problem differently. Because of these diverging approaches, the Europeans' attitudes and behavior toward the two countries varied. Without the military strength of Ethiopia, Liberia was compelled to negotiate with the Europeans in a more passive manner, through treaty making. Realizing its weakness, the republic depended upon international morality to play a role in maintaining its independence. This failed to give Liberia any political advantage, and, as a result, Europeans slowly acquired more and more of Liberian territory. Surrounded by the British colony of Sierra Leone to the west and French West Africa to the north and east, Liberia was boxed in by the European colonialists. Notwithstanding this handicap, Liberia still was able to preserve its independence during the scramble for African territory and resources.

Liberia's future, from its inception, was uncertain. The Republic of Liberia, which was organized in 1822, issued a Declaration of Independence on 26 July 1847. The next year, Great Britain recognized the new nation, and other European governments followed suit. Although founded by the American Colonization Society, there was hardly what could be called a consistent American concern for or interest in Liberian development. Thus, U.S. government did not formally recognize Liberian independence until 1862. In that year, a treaty of commerce and navigation was concluded between the two countries, and in 1863, an American embassy was established with a diplomatic agent with the rank of commissioner and consul general. This was the designation from 1863 to 1866, and from 1866 to 1931, it was minister-resident and consul general.[1]

Throughout the nineteenth century, American involvement in Liberia was primarily humanitarian. The United States was never prepared to take over Liberia as a colony, or even as a protectorate. At the same time, the U.S. government was not willing to see the

European powers completely take advantage of Liberia's weakness.

Circumstances in the United States during the first half of the nineteenth century had made the founding of Liberia possible. The desire to rid the country of free blacks and the philanthropic interest of the American Colonization Society forced the U.S. government to assume a large responsibility in the funding of this republic. Between 1819 and 1869, governmental expenditure in Liberia was $2,338,000. During these years the society spent $2,588,907. The U.S. government and the American Colonization Society were in reality the co-founders of Liberia. It was largely because of southern opposition that the United States waited fifteen years after its declaration before recognizing Liberian independence.

America did not claim a protectorate over Liberia, but, since it was founded under its fostering care, the American government saw itself "as the next friend of Liberia" and claimed that it would aid in preventing the encroachment of any foreign power upon its territorial sovereignty. In 1843, the Upshur statement, formulated by Secretary of State Abel P. Upshur, became the basis of the relationship between the two countries. He noted that Liberia had not been established under the authority of the U.S. government but by the voluntary association of American citizens, and thus its activities were not subject to American jurisdiction. He then went on to say that nonetheless the State Department was prepared to interpose its good offices to prevent any encroachment on the colony by foreign nations.

In spite of this high-sounding proclamation, during the years under study American policy toward Liberia remained erratic, and the U.S. government continued to maintain a hands-off policy. It is difficult to explain why the State Department failed to develop a consistent policy toward Liberia. But throughout the century following its establishment, this same inconsistency prevails. On the one hand, the United States seemed interested in the future of Liberia and protested when any European nation threatened the country's sovereignty; on the other hand, it did nothing to prevent encroachment upon Liberian territory. Perhaps again the U.S. government did not want to become involved in "entangling alliances" with foreign countries, but it is more likely that Liberia's status as an independent black African country plagued the government and explains America's ambiguous stance.[2]

Liberia, although never a colony of any European power, did not escape the partitioning of Africa unharmed. Unable to protect its outlying territories and powerless to check the aggressiveness of its European neighbors, Liberia slowly gave up thousands of miles of territory, eventually losing almost one-half of its original territory, in order to prevent a confrontation with one of the European powers. Great Britain and France were the two European countries presenting the greatest threat to Liberian independence.

The boundary disputes between Liberia and its colonial neighbors lasted for over five decades. Liberia's first boundary dispute with Great Britain centered around the territory along the western coast. The disagreement lasted from 1860 to 1883 and resulted in a treaty whereby Great Britain gained much of the contested territory.[3] In its dealings with Great Britain, not only was Liberia faced with the threat of British encroachment upon its territory, but the greatest fears arose from British loans and the resulting financial controls that were imposed. From its beginning, Liberia had had difficulties with fiscal policy. A loan that Liberia received from Great Britain in 1871 for the financial rehabilitation of the country, which was renegotiated in 1898, posed a serious threat to Liberian sovereignty in the early twentieth century.[4]

Liberia was confronted with the same basic problems in its relations with France. In 1879, France offered to place Liberia under its protection, but the U.S. government discouraged such a move, and Liberia itself was uninterested in becoming a French protectorate.[5] France seriously challenged Liberia's territorial claims in the early 1890s. In a treaty signed on 8 December 1892, and another on 18 September 1907, Liberia was forced to hand over to the French extensive territory which had for years been looked upon as part of its original domain.[6]

Liberian independence was only preserved during these years of mounting European imperialism because of a lack of agreement among the European countries. Great Britain and France, in their struggle for territorial supremacy in West Africa, were unable to agree between themselves as to the policy to follow in Liberia. Thus, to a certain extent, Liberia was spared by the lack of a European consensus. More importantly, the silent role of the United States in Liberian affairs could also account for the choice by the European powers of diplomatic aggression in Liberia rather than military attack. This was the situation that Liberia faced until the crisis of 1908.[7]

On 11 March 1863, a white man was appointed as commissioner and consul general to Liberia. The first black minister-resident and consul general went there in 1871; James Milton Turner was designated on 1 March. Thereafter, the post of minister to Liberia was held continuously by black men into the twentieth century. Although the ministers were usually not the most prominent black leaders, those chosen were educated and had some influence within the black community. Upon their return to the United States, they lectured and wrote about their experiences in Africa and affected black attitudes and opinions toward the continent. Also, according to one historian, their reaction to Africa better represented the thought of the masses of the people rather than the intellectual elite.[8]

It was this segment of the Afro-American community that was closest to the activity of Europeans in Liberia. Because they were black and could easily identify with Liberia's struggle against white domination, these ministers strongly empathized with the little republic's fight to maintain its independence.

Upon his arrival in Liberia in 1871, Turner was immediately faced with the issue of the threat of European encroachment on territory in that country. The question over the northwest boundary was the source of a problem between Liberia and Great Britain which had lingered on for over a decade. Turner suggested that if Great Britain would not abandon the territory—and it was unlikely to because of commercial interests there—Liberia should be willing to accept pecuniary compensation. He feared that any Liberian belligerence in the affair might result in military confrontation.[9]

Turner took a leave of absence from Liberia on 7 May 1878, and did not return. John Henry Smyth was commissioned on 23 May 1878, left his post on 22 December 1881, was recommissioned on 12 April 1882, and dispatched his final communique on 17 December 1885. Smyth is considered one of America's most outstanding ministers to Liberia and a militant spokesman for nineteenth-century Pan-African thought. Free-born near Richmond, Virginia, he later attended and graduated from the Philadelphia Institute for Colored Youth in 1862 and Howard University Law School in 1871. Smyth supported emigration and saw Africa as the fatherland and natural home of Afro-Americans. During his seven years' stay in Liberia, he served successfully. He was recalled in 1881 and replaced with the appointment of Henry Highland Garnet. Garnet, however, died after less than two months at his post, and Smyth, who was still in Liberia, resumed the position as minister. Smyth was awarded the LL.D. by Liberia College and appointed Knight Commander of the Liberia Order of African Redemption by the Liberian president, Hilary Richard Wright Johnson. Upon his return to the United States, Smyth resumed his law practice in Washington, D.C.[10]

As a result of the continued dispute over the northwest boundary, a meeting between Liberia and Great Britain convened in 1879 to attempt to settle the question. The British commissioner refused to accede to Liberia's claim, and the meeting was adjourned. Smyth commented in a dispatch that, because of the British refusal to compromise, there was some uneasiness among Liberian leaders.[11]

As if British encroachment was not presenting enough problems to this struggling republic, Smyth later reported the same year that the French government had initiated action suggesting that it wanted to make Liberia a colony and had offered to place Liberia under its protection. The sentiment of the people and the administration, however, was against intervention by France or any foreign country, Smyth asserted.[12]

Because of these constant aggressions, Smyth finally came to the conclusion that the British and French governments, which had purported for so long to be interested in "development" in Africa, were not influenced by humanitarian or "civilizing" motives at all but were interested solely in the acquisition of territory on the continent. In conjunction with this, he argued, was the purpose of exploring and developing Africa for the prospective wealth that these governments would gain. It was, therefore, not surprising that the Europeans desired Liberia as a colony, Smyth emphasized, in view of the commercial resources there.[13]

Throughout his assignment in Liberia, Smyth constantly urged the U.S. government to establish commercial relations with Liberia because he felt that if Great Britain, France, and Germany completed their occupation of West Africa the American relationship with Liberia would be secondary to these powers. Liberia would also be unable to resist their demands if Great Britain, France, and Germany reduced it to a protectorate, Smyth cautioned.[14]

The debate between Liberia and Great Britain over the northwest territory continued. By 1882, the British were claiming additional territory, up to and including the Manna River. A. E. Aenmey, acting minister in charge of the Liberian legation between the death of Garnet and the reappointment of Smyth, commented that the Manna River claim that the British government had made against the northwest territory was entirely unexpected by the Liberian government. Liberians feared that the British would use force to recover what they considered to be their territory.[15]

A few months later, the British government insisted that the Republic of Liberia conclude and ratify the 1879 convention on the basis of the Manna River boundary line. Aenmey warned that if the Liberians refused the British would immediately demand restitution for their claims against the territory, and this would create a problem since Liberia did not have the funds for such payment.[16]

Finally, in 1883, the British seized and occupied the disputed northwest territory of Liberia. A proclamation was issued giving notice to Liberia, in particular, and the world, in general, that Great Britain had annexed this portion of Liberia to its colony of Sierra Leone, although there was a clause promising to pay for all the money that Liberia had paid to the interior peoples for the disputed territory. The reappointed minister, Smyth, contended, "This whole matter appears to be a fraudulent sale, if a sale be possible, in which there is but one party to it." He disapproved of the manner in which Great Britain had gone about obtaining this territory, stating, "These subsidiary acts which led up to the seizure of the territory, all have their precedents specially with the dealing of Her Majesty's Government with African races." Smyth explained that the proclamation mentioned taking only one-half of the territory from the river, but there was no doubt in his mind that within a short time the British would possess all of the surrounding country, and each time with less formality than in this instance.[17]

Liberians protested to the American government about the action taken by the British authorities in the northwest territory of the Republic. As a result of American recommendations concerning the border dispute, the Liberian government reluctantly accepted the proposal made by Great Britain fixing the northwest boundary of

Liberia at the Manna River. At this time, the United States apparently was unwilling to assume any great responsibility for Liberia. Liberians hoped that this would be the end of the dispute with the British.[18]

Unfortunately, however, this was not the case. In 1887, the British government insisted that the southwest boundary of Liberia be fixed according to the demands of the French. Minister Charles Henry James Taylor remarked, "Nothing can save this country, except two or three thousand Negro emigrants from the United States."[19]

This comment was strangely out of character for Taylor since even before he arrived in Liberia he was an anti-emigrationist. During his short stay in Liberia, Taylor never left the capital, Monrovia, and even the Liberian government complained of his shallow reports, designed to discourage Afro-American colonization. He was apparently uninterested in or unconcerned with Liberia or its people and accomplished little in the diplomatic field, although during his appointment there were many problems to be settled. Taylor remained in Liberia less than a year; he was commissioned in March of 1887 and left in September, quitting in the United States in November with a 115-page resignation. After his return to the United States, he adamantly lectured and demonstrated against emigration, claiming that Liberia would cause "the destruction and burial of American Negroes." Taylor, referring to Liberia as "an independent farce" and "that dark, disagreeable, and death giving country," suggested that the U.S. government claim the country as a dependency. Known for his accommodationist attitude, Taylor advocated less politics and more land for blacks and called for them to remain in the United States and learn their duties as American citizens.[20]

In 1892, Liberia concluded an agreement with France settling the question of the delimitation of territories of the Republic of Liberia and the French possessions in West Africa. The United States, concerned that Liberia was being forced to sign, interceded in behalf of the little republic before confirmation by that government. The Liberian government did not desire ratification of the treaty, but France claimed certain portions of territory owned by Liberia. Liberia did not feel that it would be able to defend the area.

Vice-Consul General Beverly Yates Payne explained in late 1893 that, since the Liberian government had only the moral support of the United States government, it felt incapable of contending with a nation such as France and accepted the proposed pact rather than have France simply take the territory. "If the Government of the United States would protect and defend Liberia . . . against French encroachments in case the treaty is not ratified," Payne insisted, Liberia would be less likely to sign.[21]

Payne was close to Liberian feelings toward European imperial initiatives since by this date he had already been stationed in Liberia for six years. He was in charge of the Liberian legation from October 1887 to July 1888; May 1890 to November 1890; June 1891 to March 1892; and May 1893 to May 1895. Payne had also served as vice-consul general under Ezekiel Ezra Smith, from 1888 to 1890; Alexander Clark, 1890 to 1891; and William D. McCoy, 1892 to 1893.

Payne later informed the American government that the Delimitation Treaty of 8 December 1892 between Liberia and France had been ratified. The president of the republic recommended acceptance of the settlement because he feared that France was preparing to take more aggressive steps if Liberia continued to delay any longer.[22]

A few years later, in 1895, the French occupied territory four miles beyond the boundary of their possessions as defined by the Delimitation Treaty of 1892. Minister William Harrison Heard subsequently declared that the French had violated their own treaty. The real problem was in the interior, he maintained, because the Liberian government had no frontier force to guard the area.[23]

Heard was a member of the college-educated elite. He had studied at the University of South Carolina, Clarke University, and Atlanta University. He served as a member of the South Carolina legislature for one session, from 1876 to 1877, before he was unseated. It was here that he met and became a life-long friend of Henry McNeal Turner. In 1880 he entered the ministry of the African Methodist Episcopal (AME) Church and was elected a bishop in 1908. With the assistance of Bishop Turner, he was appointed minister to Liberia in 1895, a position he held until 1898.

Heard was a convinced emigrationist and praised Liberia. When he arrived in Liberia and met the black president and cabinet, he stated, "I was so impressed that the Negro had a future that I determined to spend my life in trying to brighten that future." He later remarked that his travels in Africa had given him knowledge that he could never have learned in books. While in Liberia, he purchased land and built the first AME church in Monrovia, the Elias Turner Memorial Chapel. After his return to the United States in 1898, he praised Liberian "progress." He was on the executive board of the Bostonian Liberian Development Association for emigration to Liberia, organized by Charles Alexander, Francis Warren, and Walter Walker in 1907. In January 1909, Heard, his wife, and eight black missionaries from the AME Church sailed to Sierra Leone, held a conference, and then went on to hold a second conference in Liberia. He remained in West Africa for eight years, serving as bishop of the AME Church.[24]

Even the German government threatened Liberian sovereignty. In 1898, the German Diplomatic Representative to Liberia presented a letter from his government suggesting that Germany make Liberia a protectorate to avoid damages for the destruction of property of German citizens. Heard commented that it appeared that Germany, along with Great Britain and France, was determined to crush Liberia.[25]

At the beginning of the twentieth century, there was an intensification of the rivalry between the European powers in Liberia. By this time, Great Britain and France were negotiating between themselves a joint protectorate over Liberia, but they were unable to agree on the details.

In 1900, the French again made encroachments upon the northeastern frontier of Liberia, which had been previously fixed by the Franco-Liberian Treaty of 1892. Minister Owen L. W. Smith of North Carolina asked the U.S. government to appoint a commission to act with one from France and Great Britain to fix, once and for all, the eastern boundary between the French and Liberian possessions.[26]

The commission was not appointed, and the debate continued. The French contended that Liberia had no right to this section. Two Liberian representatives went to France to negotiate the boundary question, but nothing was accomplished.[27] Ernest Lyon, U.S. minister to Liberia from 1903 to 1911, reported in 1905 that the encroachments of the French government upon Liberian land had reached serious proportions. The French had established outposts extending one hundred miles into territory that Liberia had been granted by the Treaty of 1892.[28]

Lyon was born in Belize, British Honduras, in 1860, and became a naturalized citizen of the United States in 1894. He was educated at New Orleans University, where he received the bachelor's and master's degrees, and Union Theological Seminary in New York. In 1882, he was ordained a Methodist Episcopal minister and continued this occupation for nineteen years. A protégé of Booker T. Washington, he founded the Maryland Industrial and Agricultural Institution for the Education of Colored Youths. It was during his term as minister that Liberia faced the most serious threat to its independent survival. He realized this and made every attempt to gain American support for the struggling republic. After his appointment as minister ended, he served from 1911 to 1913 as consul general for Liberia at Washington. In 1913 he returned to Maryland. Lyon was a practical man whose attitude toward emigration was realistic; he believed that only those who could support themselves and contribute to development should go to Africa.[29]

Lyon consistently emphasized to the U.S. government that the British and French would not attempt to steal Liberian territory if it was strong enough to repel the invaders. Like previous ministers, he requested that the United States intervene in the matter. Lyon announced in 1906, "From our observation on the ground there never was a time perhaps, more than now when this little Republic struggling for existence between two great and formidable European Powers stood in greater need of the active assistance of the Government of the United States."[30] The United States did not intervene in behalf of Liberia, but, as a result of this critical situation, negotiations were begun between Liberia and France to settle the matter. In September of 1907, a new Delimitation Agreement was reached and ratified by the Liberian legislature.[31]

While France was encroaching upon Liberian territory in the east, Great Britain was claiming areas on the western border. Great Britain, which feared that any advantage gained by France would jeopardize its interests, aggressively pursued efforts to control large regions of the Liberian interior for commercial purposes. Lyon again warned in 1906 that these attempts to extend the boundary beyond the point agreed upon by Liberia and Great Britain was "but one of the many

secret attempts which are constantly being made for the dismember-
ment of Liberia."[32]

In January of 1908, a British officer arrived in Liberia to take
charge of the frontier force in the interior of Liberia. Great Britain had
insisted that Liberia "put her house in order," and this was one of the
stipulations upon which it had insisted. In a letter to President Arthur
Barclay, Braithwait Wallis, consul for Great Britain, warned Liberia
that it "must not lose a moment in settling herself seriously to work to
put her house in order, or be prepared, at no distant date, to disap-
pear from the catalogue of independent countries." The British
claimed that they were not threatening the independence of the
republic but only desired, "a stable and effective government as a
neighbor." Along with the frontier force, Britain insisted that Liberia
place its finances in the hands of a European financial expert, reform
the Liberian judiciary, and settle the boundary dispute with France.
Wallis concluded that the British government would like these reforms carried into effect within six months, and if Liberia refused to
take British advice it would be necessary to take steps to safeguard
British interests.[33] America's lack of interference at this time to safeguard the maintenance of Liberian sovereignty implied a tacit agreement with the British attitude that reform was essential in that
country.[34]

Lyon implored the U.S. government to act immediately. Liberian
matters were approaching a dangerous crisis, he warned, because of
the demands made upon the government by both the British and
French. The British Foreign Office was insisting not only that Liberia
make these immediate reforms in its government, Lyon stated, but
also that it give up a piece of valuable territory in exchange for one
that was barren and unpopulated. Lyon declared, "The loss of this
territory together with the one-sixth taken by France according to the
stipulations of the last treaty will greatly embarass the little Republic."[35]

Thus, by the beginning of 1908, Liberia, having already signed
several treaties with Great Britain and France in an attempt to maintain its sovereignty, and having relinquished 100,000 square miles to
these powers, was still not secure. In fact, by this date Liberia faced
the greatest threat to its independence since the declaration in 1847.
Its sovereignty was indeed in jeopardy. Unfortunately for Liberia, it

was a pawn juxtaposed between two European nations flexing their power in Africa. It is unlikely that Liberia would have had the problems it did if the Europeans had not been vying for African territory.

During the years before 1908, several Afro-Americans visited and worked in Liberia, reporting on their impressions of developments there. Like the diplomats, they were closer than other black Americans to Liberia's situation and could assess the urgency of the problem.

George Washington Williams, traveling in Africa in 1890, warned that it was inevitable that Liberia would eventually fall to the British. Because of Liberia's debt and administrative problems, he contended, Liberia would soon become a protectorate of Great Britain, despite the subtle efforts of the United States to maintain Liberian sovereignty.[36]

Bishop Turner, while in Liberia establishing an AME Church Conference in 1891, expressed Williams's fear that the day when Liberia would come under some form of European control was not far away. Great Britain, France, and Germany were reaping millions of dollars in Liberia, Turner affirmed, that the black man rightfully ought to have. But Turner considered France Liberia's greatest enemy. Believing that the French were the most oppressive and outrageous in their dealings with Liberia, Turner observed that the French, because they had the power, were seizing hundreds of miles of Liberian territory. "I fear the results," Turner remarked, "because Liberia would be unable to stand against France."[37]

A few years later in a letter to the editor of the *Savannah Tribune*, the AME missionary Alfred Lee Ridgel declared that West Africa was rapidly passing under the control of the European powers and would soon be filled with those imperialists. Liberia, he maintained, would be surrounded. Ridgel saw Great Britain and France as great rivals for territory in Liberia and also feared the possible results to Liberian autonomy.[38]

T. McCants Stewart, who had just returned from Liberia, emphasized that Liberia's situation was grave. He suggested that the U.S. government show a greater interest in the development and independence of Liberia so as to spare it from European aggressions. Stewart advised that Liberia needed men and capital to maintain its sovereignty from European imperialists.[39]

Black Americans who had not visited Liberia were also aware of the threat that the European powers were presenting to Liberia. They viewed these events in Liberia with a personal interest. Journalists were particularly prominent in the discussion before 1908.

Early in the events threatening Liberian sovereignty, in 1886, T. Thomas Fortune noted that there already was a crisis in Liberia because the European nations were ready to blot Liberia from the map of Africa. Fortune insisted that loans were creating Liberia's problems. He asked the U.S. government to show friendly interest in Liberia and save "the struggling African Republic from the 'roaring lion seeking whom he may devour.'" Fortune stated that black Americans would be happy for any American initiative. The *New York Freeman* and *Age* mentioned all of the black appointees to Liberia, and both were concerned with the country's future, although Fortune himself never considered the position of minister to Liberia.[40]

George L. Knox also discussed the problems that Liberians were facing in the *Indianapolis Freeman*. He warned that Liberia was in great danger of being gobbled up by the foreign powers of Europe. Liberia needed money, he asserted, and the United States should look upon Liberia as a protégé and not wait until the country was involved in an international dispute over finances before stepping in to aid it. It should be done while the country was still intact and free from the greed of Great Britain, France, and Germany, Knox suggested.[41]

Early in 1907, *Alexander's Magazine* described the future of Liberia as bright, in spite of the problems that the country was facing. The magazine believed that Liberia would maintain its independence, despite European aggressions, and saw the country as progressing. The American black had a particular interest in Liberia, one article in the magazine insisted. As an experiment in self-government, this writer saw Liberia, despite the comments of its critics, as a successful, independent state.

In late 1907, the magazine reported that Liberia was again facing problems concerning the boundary question with Great Britain and France. These countries had continually encroached upon Liberian territory, *Alexander's Magazine* explained, but with the conclusion of the recent treaties with the British and the French, Liberian sovereignty was maintained. The magazine naively believed that Liberia's battle against European domination was over.[42]

Beginning in August of 1907, *Alexander's Magazine* began a section entitled "Important News About Africa," which the next month was renamed "News About Liberia and Africa Generally." The column, written by Walter F. Walker, Alexander's assistant, was designed to give "accurate and reliable information of Africa in general and the republic of Liberia in particular." The articles that followed discussed the idea of the destiny of black Americans to return to Liberia for the "upbuilding" of that country. In the first issues of the magazine, Walker, a Boston University student, had written an article on "Scientific Redemption of Africa." At this time, he did not endorse African emigration, but by January of 1907 he had made an about-face. Walker was excited about the idea of going to Liberia and learning about the country, thus the initiation of the section in *Alexander's Magazine*. Late in 1907, he was involved in the organization of the Liberian Development Association. Walker, the association's secretary, went to Liberia in 1908 "to spy out the land" and to advise on emigration. Walker's report, which appeared in the August 1908 issue of *Alexander's Magazine*, described Liberian affairs as not conducive to Afro-American emigration. His column ended when he left for Liberia, and his report was the last item on emigration to Liberia that appeared in the magazine. Walker remained in Liberia as a Methodist missionary.[43]

Fortune did not view the conditions in Liberia as positively as *Alexander's Magazine*. In 1906, he insisted that although Liberia's failure as a prosperous and successful government did not weaken his faith in the development of black nations, he doubted that Liberia could recover from its present "sad condition." As his friend Stewart had emphasized earlier, Fortune believed that what Liberia needed was greater industrial and commercial activity. Only economic stability could save the republic, he maintained.[44]

Fred R. Moore of the *Colored American Magazine* was also concerned with the maintenance of Liberian sovereignty because he believed it represented the first stage in the realization of "Africa for the Africans." Liberia and Ethiopia stood as symbols of black independence in Africa. Moore even suggested that, since the white man was dividing up Africa, "Liberia get ready to demand at least a portion of the great African continent. . . ."[45]

Fear that Great Britain and France would break their previous pattern of being unable to come to an accord coupled with the belief that American assistance would be less likely to jeopardize its independence prompted Liberia to send a three-man delegation led by Vice President James J. Dossen to the United States in May of 1908 to request American arbitration of treaties in behalf of the country and to aid in bringing about reform of the customs, postal, educational, military, and agricultural departments. The years from 1908 to 1914 were characterized by continued European encroachment on Liberian territory and active Liberian and Afro-American attempts to gain U.S. governmental support.[46]

Black Americans were extremely interested in the visit of the Liberian envoys. The press, which reported the visit, again stressed the importance for Afro-Americans that Liberia remain an independent country. Fortune stated that Afro-Americans regretted the fact that Liberia had become so entangled with the European powers. By this time, he was not sure whether Liberia would be able to maintain its independence.

In acknowledging the visit of the Liberian commission, Fortune argued that the menacing attitude of the Europeans toward Liberia made immediate action imperative. The United States should do everything in its power to protect Liberia from the European governments, Fortune concluded, and black Americans should exert pressure on the U.S. government to let them know that Liberian interests were the concern of Afro-Americans.[47]

W. Calvin Chase commended the Liberian government for sending the emissaries to the United States. In an editorial in the *Bee*, Chase recommended a closer union between Liberia and the United States so as to repulse the threatened encroachments by Great Britain, France, and Germany on Liberian territory.[48]

Alexander's Magazine noted that these three European countries, through gradual encroachment, had indeed endangered the integrity of Liberia and that the United States should lend its moral assistance to this struggling country. Charles Alexander, the editor, also believed that Afro-Americans should play a role and advised, "Let the American Negroes combine and aid these less fortunate brethren in West Africa to the best of their ability."[49] The *Colored American Magazine* predicted that good will would result from the visit of the Liberian commission to the United States.[50] The Liberian envoys left the United States, however, with no definite commitment from the U.S. government.

Booker T. Washington's impact on the question of United States' diplomatic policy toward Liberia was significant during this period. Washington also wished to see Liberia tied to the U.S. government in some way because of his fear that Great Britain or France, already encroaching upon Liberian territory, would eventually force the republic into a colonial status.[51]

When news reached the United States in early 1908 that Liberia was sending a commission to America to discuss foreign encroachments upon its territory, Washington began almost immediately to pressure the U.S. government to respond favorably to Liberia's request for aid. He asked that the U.S. government treat the delegates with the customary diplomatic courtesy because, "Whatever is done, or is not done, will attract a good deal of attention and result in wide comment among the Colored people" of this country.[52] Ernest Lyon even suggested, in a letter to Washington, that the Liberian question be used as an issue in the upcoming presidential election and that blacks use their vote to pressure the U.S. government to help Liberia in its request.[53] Consistent with his interest in Africa, Washington assisted the Liberian commission throughout its stay in the United States.[54]

Immediately after the commission's departure from the United States, Washington began to campaign feverishly for representatives from the U.S. government to investigate the conditions in Liberia. Washington attempted to persuade President William Taft and Secretary of State P. C. Knox of the necessity for American involvement in Liberia in order to enable that country, in its struggle against foreign domination, to maintain its sovereignty. He asked the government to establish and send, as soon as possible, a delegation to Liberia.[55]

On 4 March 1909, the U.S. Congress appropriated $30,000 for an investigating committee, appointed by the president, to examine the conditions in Liberia. The new secretary of state, Elihu Root, considered Washington an indispensable member of the Liberian commission, but when William Howard Taft became president, in

March of 1909, he had insisted that Washington remain in the United States during the first months of his term as his advisor on black and southern affairs. Washington, therefore, made arrangements for his personal secretary, Emmett J. Scott, to substitute for him. The American commission to Liberia, which consisted of Roland P. Falkner, former superintendent of education in Puerto Rico, as chairman, George Sale, superintendent of Baptist mission schools in Puerto Rico and Cuba, and Scott, left in May of 1909. The American representatives submitted their report to the Department of State on 9 October 1909. They recommended that the U.S. government extend aid to Liberia in order to settle boundary disputes, assist in the reform of the finances, and organize and drill a frontier force, and that it consider establishing a coaling station in Liberia.[56]

When the American commission returned from Liberia, Washington urged the United States to consider the recommendations of the delegation and act as friend to the Liberian government. He hoped that the American government would aid in straightening out Liberia's financial affairs and warned that if something was not done to help the country it would be in a worse diplomatic and financial condition than before the commission went. In a letter to Henry Cabot Lodge, chairman of the Senate Foreign Relations Committee, Washington declared, "The colored people in every part of this country are . . . deeply interested in saving and helping Liberia." Washington was optimistic about the outcome of the discussion and confided to Lyon that he was surprised at the deep interest most congressmen were expressing in Liberia. Washington was able to influence the Senate's final decision to approve a loan for Liberia through the assistance of Secrtary of State Root and Senator Lodge.[57]

Washington was deeply concerned and involved in the fight to save Liberia from foreign rule. His actions indicated a strong desire for the continuation of the sovereignty of the two remaining independent countries in Africa as examples that black Americans could look to and with which they could identify.[58]

The Afro-American press was very much interested in the appointment and recommendations of the delegation. Knox, of the *Indianapolis Freeman*, commented in March 1909, before the departure of the American representatives, that the visit of the Liberian envoys had not been in vain and recommended that Congress appropriate all the necessary funds to send the American commission to Liberia.[59]

Throughout 1909, the *Freeman* urged American interest in Liberia. The paper suggested, however, that if Liberia could not remain a prosperous sovereign country financial assistance from the European countries might be necessary. The paper contended that Africa, in general, could probably solve its own problems if the European nations would just leave it alone.[60]

The *Age* also discussed, in depth, the activities of the American commission. Fortune commended the U.S. government for its interest in Liberia while criticizing the actions of the European governments there. "England and France seem to halt at no act, however vicious, that would give them a hold in Liberia," Fortune maintained. Fortune felt that American blacks had a great chance to show their racial loyalty and that they should stand by Liberia and let no opportunity pass in which they did not impress upon President Taft and his Cabinet their interest in the country. America could hardly afford not to give its assistance to Liberia, he insisted, because of the African descendants within the United States. Liberia was making a "manly appeal" for America's help in maintaining its independence, Fortune concluded, and America should grant it.[61]

The *Bee* concurred with Fortune's statement concerning the role America should play in maintaining Liberia's independence. Chase pointed out that in a sense Liberia was a ward of this country and that the United States should grant its appeals for support.[62] *Alexander's Magazine* also praised the United States for sending the commission to Liberia to investigate the affairs of the country. Alexander stated that this was obviously needed since it was clear that Liberia was on the verge of failure as a sovereign state unless it received American assistance.[63]

Other black newspapers similarly expressed the belief that the American commission to Liberia was a necessity for maintaining Liberian independence. The United States had an obligation to aid in strengthening the Liberian government, these papers contended.[64] George W. Harris, who had become editor of the *Colored American Magazine* in October 1907 when Moore left to edit the *Age*, maintained that Liberian affairs were in bad shape. He commended this country for stepping in rather than allowing some European nation to take charge. Viewing American intentions in Liberia very optimistically, Harris asserted that it was a fine example of good feeling in the United States toward blacks that the government would become interested enough to send out a commission of inquiry.[65] Harris subsequently concluded that, although in the past Great Britain and France had seized Liberian territory and had attempted to overthrow the republic, now "it is evident that this brave little Government of hardy black men under American tutelage and protection for a few years will go forward."[66]

In an article in the *Colored American Magazine*, Scott, the black representative on the American commission to Liberia, discussed the results of the inquiry. Scott contended that the Liberians felt that the United States had failed to exercise a friendly interest in the development of their country and that fear of losing their independence had encouraged them to have as little contact with Europeans as possible.[67]

Emmett Jay Scott was born in 1873 in Houston, Texas, and educated at Wiley University (Marshall, Texas) and Wilberforce University. From 1891 to 1894 he worked as a journalist on a white newspaper, the *Houston Daily Post*, and from 1894 to 1897 as editor of the *Texas Freeman*, a black paper. In 1897 he joined the Tuskegee staff as personal secretary to Washington. Though poorly paid and overworked, with no prospect of improving his position at Tuskegee, he was entirely loyal to Washington, serving as his alter ego. During World War I, he served as special assistant in matters relating to black troops to Secretary of War Newton D. Baker. In 1919, four years after Washington's death, he was appointed secretary-treasurer (registrar) of Howard University, a post he held until his death in 1940. Scott was a Marcus Garvey convert and awarded the rank of Knight Commander of the Distinguished Order of the Nile.[68]

Just before and immediately after his return to the United States as a member of the American commission to Liberia, Scott, who had always questioned the activities of the British, French, and Germans in Liberia, in conjunction with Washington pushed to maintain Liberian sovereignty. In the early Senate deliberations concerning the recommendations made by the commission, Scott confided to Lyon that he feared the Senate Committee on Foreign Relations would suggest that the United States "enter into a compact with Great Britain, Fraince and Germany to preserve the territorial integrity of the little Republic." But he commented that "even this is something." Presumably, Scott was basically concerned that Liberia not become a colony of any single European power.[69]

A few weeks later, Scott wrote to Lyon that he was beginning to wonder if the Senate committee was going to do anything officially for Liberia. He informed Lyon that he was nevertheless using his influence to arouse public opinion in support of the recommenda- tions. However, "if the United States is not going to do anything, itself," Scott wrote, "it would seem that it ought to be disposed to have some of the capitalists who are interested in Liberia to take hold of the situation." Apparently, Scott believed that European involve- ment in bringing about reforms in Liberian affairs should only be used as a last resort.[70]

Scott's opinion of European activity in Liberia was obvious from the comments that he made in many of his letters to friends. He referred to the Europeans, particularly the British, as "malefactors who [had] despoiled Liberia under the loan agreements" and con- fided to Falkner, chairman of the commission, "The Europeans who have handled matters for the Liberians have been . . . rascally." Scott thus agreed with most black Americans of the period that the United States alone could save the Liberian Republic.[71]

In 1911, Liberia was spared from a British, French, or German takeover, although the country was left virtually a colony of the United States. In exchange for recognizing American control over Liberian finances, Great Britain, France, and Germany received generous trading concessions, and their previous annexations of Liberian territory were left intact. An international loan of $1.7 million at 5 percent interest was approved for Liberia and backed by a consortium of bankers in the United States, Great Britain, France, and Germany; an American receiver-general was appointed with broad powers over customs collection, and he also served as finan- cial advisor to the Liberian government; and three black retired U.S. Army officers, under the leadership of Colonel Charles Young, senior ranking Afro-American officer in the army, were to assist Libe- ria in organizing a frontier force. The U.S. Senate approved the loan, the Liberian legislature ratified it on 19 November 1911, and it became effective in 1912.[72]

The Afro-American press, in discussing the loan, commended the American government for its praiseworthy action. The administration deserved the gratitude of all those interested in the preservation of the sovereignty of Liberia, one paper maintained.[73] In considering the future of Liberia, the *Cleveland Gazette* felt that rehabilitation was now assured and Liberia was on a sure footing. The Liberian "experiment" had contributed a chapter in the history of black people of which Afro-Americans could be proud, the paper boasted. The *Gazette* concluded this discussion with the observation, "All of its [Africa's] vast territory has been divided among the European powers, with the exception of Liberia on the west coast,"[74] and, of course, Ethiopia in the east.

Within the literate black community, then, there were three distinct segments that commented on the events occurring in Liberia from the 1880s to 1914: the diplomats stationed in Liberia and personally involved in the activities there; the travelers and missionaries in Liberia who observed conditions in the country and returned to the United States, many times not fully understanding the diplomatic implications behind the incidents they had observed; and those Afro-Americans who learned about Liberia's situation from the reports that came back from that country. Nonetheless, regardless of how they learned of Liberian circumstances, most Afro-Americans perceived European activity there as a threat to Liberian sovereignty and insisted upon the maintenance of Liberian independence. They all held basically the same positions, believing that European aggressions in Liberia were an extension of their efforts throughout the continent to acquire territory and monopolize resources. Because of a fear that Liberia would eventually fall under European domination, black Americans constantly insisted that the U.S. government intervene on behalf of this struggling republic which American efforts had brought into existence. It was in Liberia that almost all elements of the Afro-American community united behind the cry of "Africa for the Africans."

With these events and other incidents that were constantly occurring throughout Africa it was not surprising that by 1914 black American perspectives on European imperialism focused less on the humanitarian and religious aspects of the "civilizing mission" and more on the exploitative elements that had kept blacks throughout Africa in an inferior position since the arrival of the Europeans on that continent. By this time, black Americans were beginning to call for alternatives to the colonial system that had become entrenched in Africa.

Thus it was that by 1914, with the exception of Ethiopia and Liberia, all of Africa was under the control of the European powers. European imperialism in Africa was at its zenith. With the coming of World War I and the redivision of the German colonies at its conclusion, the scramble for African territory was complete. The two remaining independent countries in Africa were surrounded by the colonies of the European imperialist powers.

Notes

1. Raymond W. Bixler, *The Foreign Policy of the United States in Liberia*, pp. 12-13; J. H. Mower, "The Republic of Liberia," p. 268; Roland Falkner, "The United States and Liberia," p. 539; and James A. Padgett, "The Ministers to Liberia and Their Diplomacy," p. 50.

2. Rupert Emerson, *Africa and United States Policy*, p. 16; Bixler, *The Foreign Policy of the United States in Liberia*, pp. 9-13, 19; Edward W. Chester, *Clash of Titans*, pp. 2, 130-31, 169; and Roy Olton, "Problems of American Foreign Relations in the African Area During the Nineteenth Century," pp. 6-7.

3. Nnamdi Azikiwe, *Liberia*, pp. 100-1; and Falkner, "The United States and Liberia," pp. 540-41.

4. Bixler, *The Foreign Policy of the United States in Liberia*, pp. 22-23; and Azikiwe, *Liberia*, pp. 111, 113.

5. Mower, "The Republic of Liberia," p. 270.

6. Azikiwe, *Liberia*, p. 106; John D. Hargreaves, "Liberia," p. 5; and Falkner, "The United States and Liberia," p. 542.

7. Bixler, *The Foreign Policy of the United States in Liberia*, p. 22; and Hargreaves, "Liberia," p. 15.

8. Walter L. Williams, "Nineteenth Century Pan-Africanist," pp. 18-19; and Padgett, "The Ministers to Liberia and Their Diplomacy," p. 50.

9. J. Milton Turner to William M. Evarts, 30 August 1877, Department of State, Record Group 59, Despatches from U.S. Ministers to Liberia, 1863-1906, roll 6, National Archives. (Hereafter cited DS, Despatches from Liberia.)

10. Williams, "Nineteenth Century Pan-Africanist," pp. 18-25.

11. John H. Smyth to William M. Evarts, 7 January 1879, 5 March 1879, and 12 May 1879, DS, Despatches from Liberia, roll 7.

12. See U.S., Department of State, *Foreign Relations of the United States*, 1879, Smyth to Evarts, 30 May 1879, p. 718; and Hunter to Smyth, 8 September 1879, p. 727. Also examine John H. Smyth to William M. Evarts, 18 November 1879, DS, Despatches from Liberia, roll 7.

13. See *Foreign Relations of the United States*, 1879, Smyth to Seward, 7 August 1879, pp. 722-23; and 1880, Smyth to Evarts, 18 November 1879, p. 693.

14. Smyth to Seward, n.d., *Foreign Relations of the United States*, 1879, p. 723.

15. A. E. Aenmey to Second Assistant Secretary of State, 28 March 1882, Department of State, Record Group 59, Despatches from U.S. Consuls in Monrovia, 1852-1906, roll 3, National Archives.

16. A. E. Aenmey to Fred Frelinghuysen, 23 June 1882, DS, Despatches from Liberia, roll 9.

17. John H. Smyth to Fred Frelinghuysen, 30 March 1883, 31 March 1883, and 7 April 1883, DS, Despatches from Liberia, roll 9.

18. John H. Smyth to Fred Frelinghuysen, 28 April 1883, 25 May 1883, and 24 August 1883, DS, Despatches from Liberia, roll 9. See also, John H. Smyth to T. F. Bayard, 21 November 1885, and 4 December 1885, DS, Despatches from Liberia, roll 10.

19. Charles H. J. Taylor to T. F. Bayard, 31 August 1887, DS, Despatches from Liberia, roll 10.

20. Taylor made his position on emigration clear in *Whites and Blacks or the Question Settled*, pp. 32-33, 39. See also, Edwin S. Redkey, *Black Exodus*, p. 54; and Padgett, "The Ministers to Liberia and Their Diplomacy," pp. 74-75.

21. William D. McCoy to Secretary of State, 1 February 1893, and 11 March 1893; and Beverly Y. Payne to Walter Gresham, 24 October 1893, DS, Despatches from Liberia, roll 11.

22. Beverly Y. Payne to Walter Gresham, 13 January 1894, and 18 August 1894, DS, Despatches from Liberia, roll 11.

23. Beverly Payne to Walter Gresham, 21 May 1895, DS, Despatches from Liberia, roll 11; and William H. Heard to John Sherman, 15 April 1897, DS, Despatches from Liberia, roll 12.

24. See William H. Heard, *The Bright Side of African Life*, p. 9; and his *From Slavery to the Bishopric in the A.M.E. Church*, pp. 37-38, 44-45, 78-79, 83-84.

25. William H. Heard to John Sherman, 27 January 1898, DS, Despatches from Liberia, roll 12.

26. Owen L. W. Smith to John Hay, 4 September 1900, DS, Despatches from Liberia, roll 12.

27. Ernest Lyon to Francis B. Loomis, 25 February 1904; Ernest Lyon to John Hay, 26 May 1904, and 25 April 1905; and George W. Ellis to Alvey A. Adee, 28 September 1904, DS, Despatches from Liberia, roll 14.

28. Ernest Lyon to John Hay, 21 June 1905, DS, Despatches from Liberia, roll 14.

29. Padgett, "The Ministers to Liberia and Their Diplomacy," pp. 80-83.

30. Ernest Lyon to Secretary of State, 21 November 1906; and Arthur Barclay to Ernest Lyon, 9 August 1907, enclosed in Ernest Lyon to Secretary of State, 9 August 1907, Department of State, Record Group 59, Numerical File (1906-10), Cases 3513-36, roll 326. National Archives. Hereafter cited DS, with numerical case number.

31. Ernest Lyon to Secretary of State, 12 August 1907, and 4 January 1908; Ernest Lyon to Elihu Root, 22 April 1907, DS, 3513-3536, roll 326; and Ernest Lyon to Secretary of State, 3 December 1907, DS, 4676-4695, roll 405.

32. Ernest Lyon to John Hay, 8 December 1903, DS, Despatches from Liberia, roll 13. See also Ernest Lyon to Robert Bacon, 21 August 1906, DS, 1352-1379, roll 161; and Ernest Lyon to Secretary of State, 29 November 1906, DS, 3513-3536, roll 326.

33. Ernest Lyon to Secretary of State, 4 January 1908, DS, 4676-4695, roll 405; and Braithwait Wallis to President of Liberia, 14 January 1908, enclosed in Ernest Lyon to Secretary of State, 25 January 1908, DS, 3513-3536, roll 326.

34. Lloyd N. Beecher, Jr., "The State Department and Liberia, 1908-1941," p. 6.

35. Ernest Lyon to Secretary of State, 25 January 1908, DS, 3513-3536, roll 326.

36. George Washington Williams to Robert Terrell, 14 October 1890, R. H. Terrell Papers (1).

37. Edwin S. Redkey, ed., *Respect Black*, pp. 122, 141; and Letter to the Editor, "Bishop H. M. Turner's Travels in Africa," *Christian Recorder*, 11 February 1892, p. 1.

38. Letter to the Editor, "Letter from Africa," *Savannah Tribune*, 20 October 1894.

39. T. McCants Stewart, *Liberia*, pp. 105-7.

40. Editorial, "The Crisis in Liberia," *New York Freeman*, 6 February 1886.

41. Editorial, "Liberia's Future Menaced," *Indianapolis Freeman*, 16 July 1898.

42. See *Alexander's Magazine*, Editorial, "Future of Liberia," 15 January

1907, p. 127; "The Upbuilding of Liberia," 15 February 1907, p. 183; "A Letter to the Editor," 15 July 1907, p. 173; "Echoes from Africa," 15 August 1907, p. 198; and "The Negro as Ruler," 15 October 1907, p. 331.

43. See *Alexander's Magazine*, "Scientific Redemption of Africa," 15 August 1905, pp. 3-5; "Important News About Africa," 15 August 1907, pp. 198-99; and "News About Liberia and Africa Generally," 15 September 1907, pp. 254-55. Redkey discusses Walker in *Black Exodus*, pp. 281, 284-85. For his report, see Walter F. Walker, "Liberia and Emigration," *Alexander's Magazine*, 15 August 1908, pp. 162-65.

44. See *New York Age*, Editorial, "Liberia's Sad Condition," 9 August 1906; and Editorial, "What Liberia Needs," 29 August 1907.

45. Editorial, "Liberia's Opportunity," *Colored American Magazine* (March 1907): 167.

46. Ernest Lyon to Secretary of State, 28 January 1908; and F. E. R. Johnson to Ernest Lyon, 13 February 1908, enclosed in Ernest Lyon to Secretary of State, 14 February 1908, DS, 12075-12083/150, book 794.

47. See *New York Age*, Editorial, "Is Liberian Independence Jeopardized," 30 April 1908; "Commissioners from Republic of Liberia," 4 June 1908; and Editorial, "Envoys from Liberia," 4 June 1908.

48. See *Washington Bee*, Editorial, "Liberian Envoys," 30 May 1908; and Editorial, "The Liberian Envoys," 20 June 1908. A similar discussion is also given in "Envoys See President," *Indianapolis Freeman*, 20 June 1908.

49. Editorial, "The Liberian Commission Here!," *Alexander's Magazine*, 15 June 1908, p. 86.

50. "Distinguished Liberians Visit the United States," *Colored American Magazine* (July 1908): 411.

51. Booker T. Washington to Theodore Roosevelt, 19 September 1907, Washington Papers (7).

52. Booker T. Washington to Theodore Roosevelt, 21 March 1908, Washington Papers (7).

53. Ernest Lyon to Booker T. Washington, 15 April 1908, Washington Papers (375).

54. See, for example, Booker T. Washington to J. J. Dossen, 20 May 1908; and Booker T. Washington to Ernest Lyon, 23 May 1908, 25 May 1908, and 27 May 1908, Washington Papers (375).

55. See Booker T. Washington to Elihu Root, 14 December 1908, and 15 December 1908, Washington Papers (895).

56. For a discussion of the American Commission to Liberia, see Huntington Wilson to Emmett J. Scott, 24 March 1909; P. C. Knox to Ernest Lyon, 24 March 1909; Emmett J. Scott to Huntington Wilson, 25 March 1909,

DS, 12075-12083/150, book 794; P. C. Knox to Messrs. W. Morgan Shuster, George Sale, and Emmett J. Scott, 13 April 1909; Huntington Wilson to Ernest Lyon, 20 April 1909; Ernest Lyon to Secretary of State, 13 May 1909, DS, 12083/151-12083/260, book 795; and Ernest Lyon to Secretary of State, 8 June 1909, DS 4966-4984, roll 423. See also, Azikiwe, *Liberia*, pp. 99-100, 116; and Louis R. Harlan, "Booker T. Washington and the White Man's Burden," p. 455.

57. Booker T. Washington to J. J. Dossen, 10 April 1910, Washington Papers (404). See also Booker T. Washington to Henry Cabot Lodge, 10 April 1910; and Booker T. Washington to Ernest Lyon, 21 April 1910, Washington Papers (411).

58. There is an extensive discussion of Washington's interest and involvement in the Liberian crisis contained within his manuscript collection. See, for example, folders on Liberia in boxes 404, 411, and 895.

59. See *Indianapolis Freeman*, Editorial, "Liberia," 6 March 1909; and Edtorial, "In the Interest of Liberia," 20 March 1909.

60. See *Indianapolis Freeman*, "Liberia," 3 April 1909; and "Why Roosevelt Is in Africa," 11 December 1909.

61. See *New York Age*, "Liberia Conditions," 8 April 1909; "Liberian Commission," 29 April 1909; "Liberian Commission," 20 May 1909; "Liberian Commission," 17 June 1909; Editorial, "Liberians Not Despairing," 17 June 1909; Editorial, "Liberia Again," 1 July 1909; "Commission to Liberia," 8 July 1909; and Editorial, "Liberia's Manly Appeal," 15 July 1909.

62. See *Washington Bee*, Editorial, "Hear Liberia's Cry," 27 February 1909; Editorial, "Liberian Commission," 6 March 1909; Editorial, "The Liberian Commission," 27 March 1909; Editorial, "The Liberian Commission," 19 June 1909; and "Liberia Redeemed," 19 June 1909.

63. See *Alexander's Magazine*, Editorial, "Liberia," January 1909, pp. 108-9; and Editorial, "Commissioner Scott" (March-April 1909): 225.

64. See, for example, Editorial note, *Savannah Tribune*, 1 May 1909; and "Liberians Call for Aid," *Wichita Searchlight*, 30 January 1909.

65. Editorial, "The Commission to Liberia," *Colored American Magazine* (May 1909): 315.

66. See *Colored American Magazine*, "In Behalf of the Negro" (February 1909): 69; "The Liberian Crisis" (April 1909): 209-12; "Political" (June 1909): 331; "Grab for Liberia" (August 1909): 118-22; and Editorial, "Liberia's Manly Appeal" (September 1909): 223.

67. Emmett J. Scott, "The Commissioners to Liberia," *Colored American Magazine* (September 1909): 204-10. See also "Is the Republic of Liberia Worth Saving," *Cleveland Gazette*, 8 March 1911.

68. Emma Lou Thornbrough, *T. Thomas Fortune*, pp. 150, 357-58; and Martin Kilson and Adelaide Cromwell Hill, comps. and eds., *Apropos of Africa*, pp. 375-76.

69. Emmett J. Scott to Ernest Lyon, 9 April 1910, Washington Papers (908).

70. Emmett J. Scott to Ernest Lyon, 21 April 1910, Washington Papers (908).

71. See Emmett J. Scott to Bishop I. B. Scott, 26 September 1910, Washington Papers (408); Emmett J. Scott to J. J. Dossen, 30 September 1910, Washington Papers (905); and Emmett J. Scott to Roland Falkner, 13 December 1910, Washington Papers (905), for a discussion of Scott's views on the Europeans in Liberia and his attempts to maintain American public interest in the Liberian crisis.

72. Charles Morrow Wilson, *Liberia*, p. 109; Azikiwe, *Liberia*, pp. 117, 119; Bixler, *The Foreign Policy of the United States in Liberia*, pp. 26-28, 30, 33; Edwin S. Redkey, *The Meaning of Africa to Afro-Americans, 1890-1914*, p. 26; Falkner, "The United States and Liberia," p. 544; Mower, "The Republic of Liberia," pp. 274-75; and Charles A. Bodie, "The Images of Africa in the Black American Press, 1890-1930," p. 67.

73. "Liberia, Victim of British Greed!" *Cleveland Gazette*, 2 April 1910; Editorial, "President Taft and Liberia," *New York Age*, 23 June 1910; Editorial, "Liberian Problem Solved," *New York Age*, 28 July 1910; and "The Negro Problem in Liberia," *Wichita Searchlight*, 24 September 1910.

74. See *Cleveland Gazette*, "Clear Sailing for Liberia," 15 April 1911; "The Republic of Liberia," 13 May 1911; "U. S. Takes Charge of Liberian Finances," 26 August 1911; and "Liberia's Crying Need is Education," 28 October 1911.

AFRICA, WORLD WAR I, AND THE PARIS PEACE SETTLEMENT, 1914–1920

11

The question of Africa is an international question; it belongs at the peace table.
"Africa and the World," *NAACP Annual Conference, 1919,* p. 331.
James Weldon Johnson, 1871-1938

In truth, the hour has come, in my opinion, when the world should declare that not only are these colonies not to be turned back to Germany, *but to no other nations as well.*
Address, Carnegie Hall, New York City, 2 November 1918; Emmett J. Scott Papers (93).
Emmett Jay Scott, 1873-1940

After all they have won in this great continent and after all they have suffered in the war, it is not likely that England and France will voluntarily withdraw from Africa at any time in the near future or suffer such a disposition of the German colonies as would endanger themselves.
Africa and the War, p. 38.
Benjamin Brawley, 1882-1939

By the outbreak of World War I, in 1914, Europeans ruled throughout Africa. Remarkably, they were able to divide the continent among themselves without resort to arms. This is singularly important since during the period of the scramble for and partitioning of Africa Europeans placed a great deal of emphasis on the acquisition of African territory. However, despite a few incidents that flared up before 1914 concerning occupation and boundaries which threatened amity, there had been no war between the colonial powers over the division of Africa.[1]

Historians and political experts have interpreted the European war of 1914-18 from various perspectives. Some have seen it as the culmination of European worldwide imperialistic competition and expansion. Vladimir Lenin described it as "a war for the division of the world, for the partition and repartition of colonies."[2] David Lloyd George, prime minister of Great Britain, admitted to Colonel Edward H. House, Woodrow Wilson's confidential secretary, that the conflict was an imperialist war and that capturing German colonies was one of the Allied war aims.[3] Some observers have contended that World War I had its origins in the chain of events that had begun with the partitioning of Africa in the 1880s and were influenced by the imperialistic relations between the European powers.[4] Other writers affirmed that the underlying cause of the war was neither the inherent contradictions of imperialism nor the economic competition among the major European nations but the rival aspirations of less powerful states attempting to gain greater political influence within Europe.[5] Regardless of how they viewed the war, however, most commentators agreed that the impulse for imperialistic expansion was a factor in the coming of the war. By 1914, Africa had been completely partitioned among the European powers for all practical purposes. At the end of World War I, the question of the repartition of the German African colonies revived interest in that continent.[6]

The war was very much a reality for Africa and Africans. These years brought immense and significant changes that would have repercussions in the years that followed. The direct and obvious impact of World War I on Africa included: the East African campaign, the recruitment of Africans, the emphasis on war production, and the transfer of the German African colonies after the war to the League of Nations' mandate system.[7]

In the late summer of 1914, the European Allies met to discuss strategies to conquer Germany's colonial possessions. The African territories particularly were seen as valuable pawns that could be used in the peace settlement. The Allies thus began a concentrated campaign to relieve Germany of her colonies in Africa.

They first launched an offensive in West Africa. The least protected German area was Togo, and the colony was easily captured early in the war, by August of 1914. The other German West African colony, the Cameroons, was taken with less ease, but by February 1916 the Allied campaign had also ended there. Both Togo and the Cameroons were captured through the united efforts of British, French, and Belgian troops.

In German Southwest Africa and German East Africa, the Allied seizure required much more attention. German Southwest Africa was finally subdued, with some difficulty, in July 1915, with the assistance of about sixty thousand white soldiers from the Union of South Africa. This, of course, explains the annexation of Southwest Africa to South Africa, under the mandate system, at the end of the war. After their campaign in Southwest Africa, fifty thousand of the South African troops shifted to the contest in German East Africa. There the South African forces were joined by the British, Belgians, and Portuguese. German East Africa was surrendered by the Germans in late November 1918, two weeks after the armistice had been signed. With this capitulation, all of the German colonial possessions in Africa came into the hands of the Allies.

Both the British and the German administrators between 1914 and 1918, in preparing for the struggle in Africa, drafted Africans for military service. In all instances, these colonial powers organized the human and material resources of their African colonies to assist the wider war effort.[8]

In the fall of 1917, when it became evident that the Allies would win the war, President Wilson asked Colonel House to create an American commission of inquiry to gather information and report on every possible problem that might be discussed at the peace conference. The question of the fate of the German colonies was seen as one of the most important matters that would concern the powers assembled at the conference. By the end of the war it was a foregone conclusion that, for both moral and political reasons, the captured colonies could not be returned to Germany.

In a message to Congress on 8 January 1918, Wilson presented a fourteen-point program for a just peace. Of the Fourteen Points, the fifth referred to the colonies and arranged for "a free, open-minded, and absolutely impartial adjustment of all colonial claims, based upon a strict observance of the principle that in determining all such questions of sovereignty the interests of the populations concerned must have equal weight with the equitable claims of the government whose title is to be determined." Without direct reference to the German colonies, Wilson had pronounced the principle of self-determination for colonial peoples. In the negotiations that led up to the armistice of 11 November 1918, it was agreed that the future peace treaty would be concluded on the basis of Wilson's Fourteen Points. But Wilson had never intended to apply the principle of self-determination to non-European peoples and definitely not to the inhabitants of the African colonies.[9]

At the end of World War I, Africa was still not a major American concern. Probably the most notable act of American diplomacy relative to Africa during the years between 1914 and 1920 was the successful attempt by President Wilson to preclude annexation of the German African colonies by the European powers. As a compromise, these powers agreed to place the disputed territories under the mandate system. Although Wilson's role has been minimized, he must be credited with arranging the final settlement relative to the colonies. American troops did not fight in Africa during World War I, though they did participate in the campaign in North Africa and Liberia during World War II. It was only with the coming of World War II that the U.S. government became interested in the African continent, and then largely as a source of raw materials.

World War I reviewed the scramble for Africa. The Allies could not afford to overlook the opportunity that the settlement of the war offered them to acquire additional colonial territory. One of the consequences of the war and the peace settlement for Africa was the disappearance of the German flag from the continent and the distribution of its colonies as mandates among the victorious Allied powers. The peace conference of 1919 renewed the imperialist urge of the European powers.[10]

According to George Louis Beer, the American colonial delegate to the peace conference, the primary consideration in the settlement of the colonial questions at the Paris Peace Conference was the "welfare" of the indigenous populations. By article 119 of the Treaty of Versailles, "Germany renounces in favor of the Principal Allied and Associated Powers all her rights and titles over her overseas possessions."

Although it seems likely that territorial acquisition was the Europeans' main interest, President Wilson tried to prevent the imperialistic powers of Great Britain, France, Belgium, and South Africa from directly annexing the German colonies. Regardless of what may be said about Wilson's "lost peace" at the Paris conference, he was instrumental in safeguarding the German colonies from the expansionist aspirations of the European powers. At another time in European history the German colonies might have been annexed outright.

The final compromise resulted in the mandate system, which attempted to reconcile those who advocated annexation with the supporters of international administration of the colonial territories. The mandates were intended to serve the same basic purposes as the Berlin Act of 1885: to protect the welfare of the indigenous populations and to ensure free trade, although both fell far short of these goals.

The concept behind the mandate system was that the powers were to act as custodians and were not to benefit from their trusts, seemingly a reflection of the conferees' concern that humanitarian rather than commercial considerations prevail. The Mandatory Commission came into being as a result of article 22 in the Covenant of the League of Nations. The mandatory system was unique from any previous such international arrangement in that the league possessed intervening powers. The former German colonies in Africa, which were assigned mandates on 7 May 1919, were divided into "B" and "C" mandates.[11]

Countries that held B mandates for the German African colonies were obliged to "respect the rights and safeguard the native population" and to maintain an "open door" policy. In Africa, only German Southwest Africa received a C mandate. The mandate was granted to the Union of South Africa, its conqueror, which allowed for the incorporation of Southwest Africa into the administrative system of the Union, a disguised form of annexation. The underlying idea behind the B and C mandates for Africa was that the colonies were placed under permanent tutelage.[12] Rayford W. Logan has contended that it was obvious from the structure of the mandate system that "Africa was never expected to 'grow up.'" Sovereignty did not rest with the mandated colonies.[13]

In the final division of the former German African colonies, 42 percent were placed under the guardianship of Great Britain, 33 percent under France, and 25 percent under Belgium. The mandate system went into effect on 10 January 1920, by ratification of the Treaty of Versailles, which contained article 22 of the covenant.[14]

By the outbreak of World War I, many black Americans who had earlier supported the "civilizing mission" in Africa to aid in the "development" of that continent had come to question seriously the motives of the Europeans there. World War I augmented Afro-Americans' international awareness. Some called for African sovereignty at the end of the war, believing that African independence from European tutelage was justified as a result of the economic, political, religious, and educational "progress" that had been made under the European colonial powers up to that date. In formulating their ideas about the war and the future status of Africa at the end of the war, black Americans viewed each colonial power according to the advances that had been made in its colonies.

Of particular interest to blacks, because of the role of Germany in the war, was the future of the German colonies. Afro-American opinions on German imperialism in Africa, of course, had been formed years before the war, and by the beginning of World War I most blacks viewed German imperialism as exploitative and supported African rebellion against German rule. Because of this perspective on German imperialism in Africa before the war and German activities during the war black Americans were against Germany in the war and after the war opposed to returning the African colonies to Germany.

From 1914 to 1918, black Americans discussed the possible impact of World War I on Africa and Africans of the diaspora. The three major Afro-American groups to debate the war were journalists, religious leaders, and educators. By this time, also, the largest civil rights organization, the National Association for the

Advancement of Colored People (NAACP), had become involved in the plight of blacks in Africa.

From the very beginning of the war, the Afro-American press as well as other segments of the black community viewed the war, as did many of their white contemporaries, within the context of racism and imperialism. W. E. B. Du Bois declared in November of 1914 that the war was due to color prejudice.[15] In May 1915 Du Bois gave a more extended analysis of the causes of the war. He maintained that greed over the partitioning and exploitation of African land, labor, and resources had led to the world war. The methods by which Africa had been stolen were contemptible and dishonest, he asserted, and "lying treaties, rivers of rum, murder, assassination, mutilation, rape, and torture have marked the progress of [the] Englishman, German, Frenchman, and Belgian on the dark continent." Pointing to the economic resources of Africa, Du Bois declared that Africa was the continent of the twentieth century and depicted European activity there as the "rape of a continent."[16]

William Edward Burghardt Du Bois was undoubtedly one of the greatest Afro-American intellectuals the twentieth century has known thus far. Born in Great Barrington, Massachusetts, in 1868, he became correspondent and agent for the *New York Globe* at the age of sixteen. He attended Fisk University from 1885 to 1888, and Harvard University from 1888 to 1890, graduating *cum laude*. He received a Master's degree from Harvard in 1892 and a Ph.D. in 1896. From 1894 to 1896, he worked at Wilberforce University. He spent the next year in Philadelphia writing *The Philadelphia Negro*, the first systematic study of blacks. In 1897 he accepted a position at Atlanta University to head the department of history and economics, where he worked until 1910. From 1910 to 1934, Du Bois held the position of director of publications and research for the newly formed NAACP (founded in 1909). In November 1910 the first issue of the *Crisis*, the official organ of the NAACP, was published with Du Bois as editor. During these years, Du Bois not only edited the *Crisis* but also organized four Pan-African congresses, traveled extensively, lectured nationwide, and wrote numerous articles and four books. Because of a change in leadership in the NAACP and a shift in his politics, on 11 June 1934, Du Bois, sixty-six years old, submitted his resignation as editor of the *Crisis* and as a member of the NAACP.

Du Bois returned to Atlanta University, where he worked until 1944, when he was retired, at the age of seventy-six, by the university's board of trustees. He was then restored by the NAACP, where he remained for four years. He attended the fifth Pan-African Congress in Manchester in 1945. After he was fired from the NAACP in 1948, he became honorary vice-chairman of the Council of African Affairs, an organization which disseminated information about Africa in America. From 1948 until his death in 1963, Du Bois worked with the Council on African Affairs, chaired the Peace Information Center, and continued to travel and lecture while his writings and speeches became more imbued with Marxism, as socialism became primary in his thought. A recent article on the evolution of Du Bois's thought and philosophies, however, characterizes Du Bois as early attracted to socialism but eventually repelled by its racism, and implies that Du Bois never completely subordinated racial loyalty to socialism. In October 1961, at the age of ninety-three, Du Bois left the United States for Ghana. He spent the last years of his life in Ghana working on one of his oldest projects, the *Encyclopedia Africana*. In 1963 he became a Ghanaian citizen. On 27 August 1963, Du Bois, the "father of Pan-Africanism," died in Ghana at the age of ninety-five.

Du Bois would become the best-known twentieth-century black intellectual to protest against colonialism in Africa. In the late 1880s he had not questioned the prevalent view that Europeans in Africa represented the advance of "civilization." He admitted that he was "blithely European and imperialist in outlook." By the mid-1890s, however, Du Bois came to realize that there was a need for some kind of unity among blacks of the world and to recognize the parallel oppressive nature of colonialism in Africa and segregation in the United States.[17]

During World War I, Du Bois viewed France as the best colonial power in Africa. The record of Germany as a colonizer of darker people was the most barbarous of any people, he contended, while Belgium ranked a close second. Great Britain was fair in its treatment of black people, Du Bois explained, but France was by far the most kindly of all the European nations in its personal relations with indigenous Africans. Du Bois failed to see the commonality of all the colonial powers in Africa: a contempt for blacks.[18]

Du Bois hoped that the war would result in the establishment of an

independent black Central African state under international guarantees and control. The *Crisis* predicted that exploitation of Africa
would cease at the end of the hostilities because Africans returning
from fighting would begin to assert themselves more than they had in
the past.[19]

At the beginning of the struggle, the *New York Age* declared that
power and domination over black people in Africa was the underlying cause.[20] As the war picked up momentum, Fred R. Moore
reported that the readers of the *Age* also supported the French
because it was believed that they had been more generous in their
dealings with Africans in their colonies. In addition to the question of
the treatment of the indigenous Africans by the European powers,
black journalists also backed the parties according to their use of Africans as soldiers. Moore again praised the French for allowing Africans to fight.

In supporting the use of Africans as soldiers in "this white man's
war," Moore suggested that the conflict would prove to be the
medium of change in Africa because the knowledge and experience
gained by the African soldiers would later prove to be a leaven in
inspiring them to gain their share of the democracy for which they
were fighting. The African troops would return from Europe with a
new hope for bettering the conditions of the people of Africa, he
predicted, because they would bring back with them the incentive to
fight for their own rights.[21] The question of democracy was bound to
become an issue in Africa, he explained later, and autonomy and
home rule would eventually prevail.[22] In this prognostication, Moore
came very close to predicting future nationalistic developments on
the continent.

Throughout the war, the Afro-American community attempted to
foretell the possible effect that it would have on the future of German
Africa, particularly considering news of the Allied capture of these
colonies. In an editorial, Moore expressed the hope that the oppressed peoples of the world would come out of the contest as the
only victors. He hoped that Africans would be given an opportunity
to rule themselves.[23]

George L. Knox of the *Indianapolis Freeman* questioned Du Bois's
thesis on the origins of the war. Knox pointed out that although the
quest for territory in Africa could have entered into the jealousies of

the European nations, there had been little ill feeling among Europeans on account of Africa since the settlement of the Anglo-Boer War. He also argued that Africans were making "headway" under "European civilization."[24]

W. Calvin Chase criticized the British refusal to allow Africans to offer their services in the war. It is not sure why Chase believed that Great Britain did not employ Africans, since it did. The only explanation that can be given is that he possibly objected to the British policy of segregation in the armed forces. Chase contended that Great Britain, which boasted of its humane treatment of its colonial subjects, had proved that it too did not practice equal treatment of Africans. He compared the discriminatory treatment of Africans by the British with that of Afro-Americans by southern whites. In concluding, Chase declared that if the European war was "for whites only," then the white man should do all the fighting.[25]

Like Du Bois, A. Phillip Randolph and Chandler Owen, editors of the *Messenger*, also contended that rivalry for rich lands and abundant labor that could be easily supplied in Africa were the causes of the conflict. The delicate balance of power that had been maintained carefully before 1914 had been destroyed, the editors claimed, and this had resulted in a contest for domination.[26]

The *Messenger* first appeared in 1917 in New York City with Randolph and Owen as editors. Beginning as a social organ of hotel bellmen, it soon became known for its socialistic leanings. It appealed directly to workers, both white and black, but particularly to blacks. Later the *Messenger* became the official organ of Randolph's Brotherhood of Sleeping Car Porters, organized in 1925.[27]

Like other newspapers, the Chicago *Broad Ax* presented the view that Africa would demand its rights at the end of the war. The paper explained that the African possessions and protectorates of the European powers were more than three times as large as Europe, and Africans would begin to take advantage of this asset.[28]

In 1918, in New York City, journalist John E. Bruce delivered a speech on "The Destiny of the Darker Races." He stated, "I think we may very safely conclude now that the allies have won this war, that the darker races the wide world over will be in no position, despite their prominence on the firing line, to exact any demands from the victors." Bruce predicted that blacks would be unrepresented at the peace conference and that when "all the warring nations assemble around the council table, there will probably be no black or colored man there, *and* no white man there will be quite as interested in the questions in which the vital interests of the black and colored races are involved as would have been a black or colored man, had one been there." He urged black people worldwide to think of their common destiny and unite to influence the decisions of the white nations represented at the meeting.[29]

Elements of the religious community also saw a need for blacks everywhere to unite. Lewis G. Jordan compared the position of Africans and Afro-Americans in their societies. In an address to Baptist ministers in Louisville, Kentucky, Jordan affirmed that since the war was affecting Africans, there were bound to be reverberations for blacks the world over.[30] He believed that World War I would bring about major changes on the continent. With African troops fighting, he declared, it could never again be possible to make Africans docile creatures driven by their European oppressors.[31]

Lewis Garnett Jordan was born a slave in Mississippi in 1858. On 12 September 1873, he was licensed to preach by the Baptist ministry. He received the degree of Doctor of Divinity from the Baptist Natchez College (Natchez, Mississippi) in 1880. In February of 1885 he made his first trip to Africa. Jordan visited Africa three times, the last time in 1920. He made Africa his special study for thirty-five years and wrote two books on the subject, *Pebbles From an African Beach* and *On Two Hemispheres*. He served as corresponding secretary of the Foreign Mission Board of the National Baptist Convention for twenty-five years, beginning in 1896. Jordan also founded and edited the Baptist *Mission Herald* and served in the Afro-American Council.[32]

Other segments of the Afro-American community aside from the press and religious leaders likewise addressed themselves to the causes of the conflict. Benjamin Brawley, in a book written during the war, maintained that the overwhelming question of World War I was the possession of the continent of Africa. Brawley contended that the cry of "Africa for the Africans" would go unheeded by the European powers because, as a result of their economic advantage there, it was unlikely that they would voluntarily withdraw from the continent at any time in the near future.

Brawley, who espoused the idea of a special "Negro Genius" for the arts, was graduated from Morehouse College with an A.B. in 1901. He received another A.B. from Chicago University in 1906 and a Master's degree from Harvard University in 1908. Later, he taught English at Shaw College, Howard University, and Morehouse College. Brawley had a concept of a black soul and an interest in African origins. He made pleas for literature based on the black racial experience. He wrote dozens of essays, short stories, poems, and literary and social histories.[33]

Other Afro-Americans saw a connection between the position of Africans during the war and the possible effect that it could have on the future status of blacks in the United States. According to James Weldon Johnson, field secretary of the NAACP, Afro-Americans viewed the war as crucial to their struggle for greater civil rights. The elevation of blacks in Africa could result in the advancement of blacks in America, and he asserted that Afro-Americans should join hands with Africans in their common struggle.[34]

By mid-1918, with the end of World War I in sight, blacks began to debate the possible settlement that would be equitable for all concerned. They continued this discussion until the first months of 1919, when their attention turned to the effects of the actual peace settlement. In anticipation of the impending peace settlement, Afro-Americans supported the right of self-determination, suggesting "internationalization" as a possible solution to the question of the disposition of the former German African colonies. Blacks hoped that this proposal would eventually lead to an Africa ruled by Africans. Before the final settlement of this issue, however, blacks offered several solutions for the future status of the German colonies.

The press again was prominent in the unsettled question of the future of the German African colonies. In June 1918, on behalf of the War Department and the Committee on Public Information, Emmett J. Scott called a conference in Washington, D.C., of some thirty-one black newspaper editors. For three days they pondered issues affecting American blacks and Africa. The recommendations of this meeting were embodied in a "Bill of Particulars." A formal letter of protest was also sent to Scott, as assistant secretary of war, denouncing the restoration to Germany of its colonies in Africa. These editors called for the appointment of an international commission to govern the colonies. Their request was reiterated again and again by blacks during these years.[35]

John Mitchell of the *Richmond Planet* later argued that self-determination should be the policy regarding the former German African territories. Mitchell explained that it was only fair that since black people had been fighting in the war they should also be at the peace table. Although he knew this would not be the case, he nonetheless felt that blacks should make enough noise to attract attention to their cause.[36]

The impending peace conference concerned not only blacks in Africa, Moore of the *Age* contended, but also blacks in America. The cause of all black people of the world should be brought to the attention of those who were to make the peace settlement, he insisted, and suggested that blacks use this conference as a forum to express their grievances. Moore believed that Afro-Americans were interested in the outcome of the negotiations both in behalf of themselves and their brethren in Africa. He also emphasized that the only plan that would fit in with the stated aim of the war was to internationalize these colonies and govern them only for the benefit of Africans.[37]

Africa was at the bottom of the cause of the World War, the *Age* asserted, and unless the African question was settled wisely and justly there could be no guarantees of future peace. One of the most important questions to be settled at the peace conference, Moore explained, was the disposition of the German African colonies.[38]

Harry C. Smith of the *Gazette* condemned whites who were attempting to discourage blacks from attending the peace conference. Surprisingly, Smith, who had always been concerned with the plight of Africans, seemed more interested in presenting the cause of American blacks to the conference than that of Africans. He criticized Du Bois for presenting a "memorandum" pleading for self-determination for blacks in the German, Belgian, and Portuguese colonies in Africa. Smith contended that black Americans could not depend upon Du Bois to represent them in Paris. This antagonism toward Du Bois for attempting to see that Africans were treated fairly in the peace settlement seemed to be somewhat contradictory to the position that Smith had taken in previous years concerning the duty of Afro-Americans to concern themselves with the events that affected

Africa, though probably this had nothing to do with Du Bois but was more a result of his own declining political career. Believing that this was the perfect opportunity for Afro-Americans to present their cause to the world and that America's "domestic issue" was not just confined to the United States, Smith pushed for this matter to be presented at the peace table.[39]

The *Afro-American* (Baltimore) reported in late December of 1918 that the NAACP had issued a memorial pleading for the privilege of self-determination for blacks in the German, Belgian, and Portuguese colonies. Reiterating a perspective generally held by articulate blacks, the paper was convinced that the German African colonies should not be returned to that country.[40]

The religious community also discussed the question of internalization of the German African colonies. In a letter to Scott, J. W. E. Bowen, vice president of Gammon Theological Seminary in Atlanta, urged him to make a plea on behalf of the black people of the world that the former German West African colony of Togo be organized into a new black international republic under the protection of the United States, Great Britain, and France. This republic could be protected, fostered, and built up for blacks in Africa and America, Bowen suggested. He declared, "Why not now make the great Peace Table, that is coming, the turning point in Africa's history, and the history of the American Negro."[41]

Bowen, although accommodating toward southern disfranchisement of blacks and echoing early in his career Booker T. Washington's position of economics before politics, was concerned nevertheless with bettering the position of blacks throughout the world. He believed that excellence and industry would be important in black progress. Born a slave in New Orleans, he graduated from the Methodist New Orleans University with an A.B. in 1878. He later took the course in theology and received the B.D. in 1885 and the Ph.D. in 1887 from Boston University. Bowen was a professor of ancient languages at Central Tennessee College in Nashville from 1878 to 1882. From 1882 to 1888, he served as a Methodist pastor in churches in Boston and Newark, New Jersey. In 1888, he went to Morgan College in Baltimore as professor of church history and systematic theology, and from 1891 to 1892 he taught Hebrew at Howard University in Washington, D.C. He became a professor of historical theology at Gammon Theological Seminary in 1893, and acted as librarian and secretary of the Stewart Missionary Foundation for Africa. He was president of Gammon from 1906 to 1912, and vice president for several years. He also served as secretary and agent of the Methodist Episcopal Foreign Mission Society.[42]

Another religious leader, E. C. Morris, likewise supported the proposal of an international commission to govern the former German colonies. Elias Camp Morris was born a slave in northern Georgia and never acquired more than a secondary education. He was ordained in 1879, and was pastor of the Centennial Baptist College in Helena, Arkansas, from 1879 until his death in 1922. He founded Arkansas Baptist Church in Little Rock in 1884. In 1895, Morris brought together three separate Baptist organizations to create a national group; the American National Convention joined the Foreign Mission Convention and the National Education Convention to form the National Baptist Convention of America. Morris, as organizer of the convention, was its first president and remained at its head until his death. In a letter to Emmett J. Scott in November 1918, Morris asked that Scott "push the matter about the release of the African colonies from German tyranny."[43]

The Negro Ministerial Council of Dallas, Texas was in accord with the general consensus among Afro-American clergymen that the African colonies should not be returned to Germany. In a letter to President Wilson, the council maintained,

> We note with satisfaction, that one of the conditions of the Armistice terms requires that Germany relinquish her possessions in Africa, we earnestly ask no agreement shall be arrived at during the sitting of the Peace Council which shall operate to return these holdings to German rule; but in keeping with the policy of self-determination, as the proposed policy for dealing with the weaker people shall find no exception in its application to Africa.[44]

In early 1919, the *Star of Zion* contended that nothing could be more dangerous and retarding to the "civilization" of Africa than to be under the rule of the Germans, since they had no interest in the "progress" of the African people. But the *Star* also reported, in anticipation of the mandate system, that the African colonies were not sufficiently "developed" for self-government and should be placed under the protectorate of one or more of the Allied nations.[45]

Aside from the press and the religious community, other black leaders were also interested in the fate of the German African colonies. Emmett Scott agreed with most Afro-Americans that the colonies could not be returned to Germany and made this point in a speech given on 2 November 1918, at Carnegie Hall in New York. "In truth," he declared, "the hour has come, in my opinion, when the world should declare that not only are these colonies not to be turned back to Germany, *but to no other nations as well.*"[46]

Scott agreed that the peace conference should establish an international commission to govern these colonies, with one black American member sitting on the panel.[47] Scott received many letters from Afro-Americans supporting his proposal of an international commission to administer the former German colonies. Some even suggested that Belgium not be allowed to keep its African colony either because its treatment of Africans had been no better than that of Germany. One writer echoed Scott's belief that blacks should have representation at the international conference, "not only to look after our own interests but also to see that a just and equitable line of policy and government is accorded to our more unfortunate Race members in Africa." Most also hoped that Scott would do his best to gain a larger freedom for American blacks from the peace settlement. However, blacks tended to magnify Scott's influence with the U.S. government concerning Africa and the settlement.[48]

There was a mass meeting sponsored by the NAACP in New York on 6 January 1919, where the subject "Africa in the World Democracy" was discussed. The general tone of the meeting was that Africa should ultimately be returned to Africans.[49] At this meeting, James Weldon Johnson discussed "Africa at the Peace Table and the Descendants of Africans in Our American Democracy."

Johnson, born in Jacksonville, Florida, in 1871, attended Atlanta University, graduating in 1894. He was admitted as an attorney in the courts of the state of Florida in 1897. He wrote the words to the black national anthem, "Lift Every Voice and Sing," and his brother, Rosamond, set the poem to music. He later moved to New York and wrote musical comedy. From 1906 to 1909 he served as U.S. Consul at Puerto Cabello, Venezuela, and from 1909 to 1913 as

Consul at Corinto, Nicaragua. Johnson wrote editorials for the *New York Age* for ten years, from 1914 to 1924. In 1916, he began work as the NAACP field secretary and remained in this position until 1930. Johnson constantly emphasized the need for blacks to retain their racial identity.[50]

At the 1919 meeting, Johnson asserted that the NAACP was interested in African democracy because "that too means the liberation of the Negroes and the elevation of the Negro in the public mind." This, in essence, was the core of the brotherhood theme. Johnson, who throughout the war had maintained that Africa was at the root of the hostilities, noted that the powers of the world could form all the leagues of nations that could be formed, but if the African question was not settled justly there would be more wars. The question of the future of Africa had focused international attention on the just claims of blacks all over the world, Johnson astutely declared.[51]

As a result of this mass meeting, a resolution was passed which resulted in the sending of a cablegram to President Wilson pledging the loyal support of the NAACP in his efforts toward establishing a universal league of free nations which would have among its duties the protection and "development" of the peoples of Africa. A similar communication was sent to the president of the Senate.[52]

The NAACP stood upon the platform drawn up by Du Bois. This program asked that the German colonies in Africa not be returned to Germany; that the "barter" of colonies without regard to the wishes or welfare of the inhabitants not be tolerated; and that the reorganization of Africa be made under the guidance of an organized body.[53]

The solution to the question of the status of the former German African colonies was reached early in the peace settlement. By January of 1919, the Allied powers had agreed informally upon the disposition of the former German colonies and elements of the mandate system. After this date, black Americans speculated on the effect that this agreement would have upon their own status in the United States and the status of Africans on the continent. The press was again in the forefront of the discussion.

Moore of the *Age* contended that if the fight for democracy for Africa was won, blacks in the United States would reap many of the benefits of the victory. He noted that, historically, powerful nations had justified taking lands belonging to other people by declaring that they did it in order to carry "civilization" to "benighted" people. The ability to find a "moral" principle to justify whatever you want to do was of tremendous advantage to a nation, Moore asserted, and, in the name of such a "lofty" principle as the spread of "Christianity" and "civilization," anything might be done.

After the signing of the peace treaty by the Allied powers, Moore expressed his disappointment with the issues that the powers agreed upon. The main source of the trouble between the European nations had not been touched, he maintained, and "there stands Africa, as she was before, exploited, robbed, and oppressed." When the U.S. Senate failed to ratify the peace treaty, Moore commented that Afro-Americans had no regrets since there were no benefits that would come from it for blacks of the world.[54]

Throughout the peace settlement the *Savannah Tribune* advocated the principle of self-determination. Africa, because of its "undevelopment," had been the main object of exploitation and colonization for the past century, Sol C. Johnson, the editor, contended, and competition for trade and political supremacy in Africa had caused jealousies to arise among the powerful nations of the world and lay at the root of the war. Accordingly, the principle of self-determination should have been applied to the African colonies, Johnson maintained. He concluded that the goal of "Africa for the Africans" was as inevitable as it had been in the history of all other nationalities.[55]

The *Washington Bee* presented an answer to the question of the fate of the German colonies somewhat different from the solution of its contemporaries. According to Chase, the settlement commission should adopt the proposition, Africa in the future for Africans. He proposed that the German African colonies should either be restored to the Africans or transferred to the United States, to be held in trust for black people. The *Bee* demanded the right of self-determination for Africans as part of the peace plans. With the United States as trustee, Africans could be guided toward eventual independence, Chase contended.[56]

In an extended discussion of the deliberations of the peace conference concerning Africa, Katherine E. Williams-Irvin, editor of the *Half-Century Magazine*, which first appeared in 1910 in Chicago with Anthony Overton as editor, warned early in 1919 that Africa would emerge badly tattered when "the wolves" at the peace conference were finished "nibbling" on it. Although also believing that Africa was not yet prepared for self-government, Williams-Irvin asserted that "she [Africa] will never be ready if the heel of oppression rests on her head forever." Williams-Irvin pointed out that the Europeans had gone into Africa to "poach" upon the ignorance of the indigenous peoples. She saw the Germans and the Belgians as the biggest exploiters of African resources, and announced, "They [Germany and Belgium] have bled that continent [Africa] for generations, and the shame that rises out of their oppression will mar the pages of history." She insisted that the African colonies should not be returned to Germany because "a return of the lost German provinces to Germany will mark a backward step in civilization's progress."[57]

Also criticizing the League of Nations, Williams-Irvin maintained that it did not represent every people or every country and was autocratic and would eventually stifle and oppress the darker peoples of the world. She viewed the league as a "skeleton in armor." The "scramble" that the peace envoys were staging behind closed doors indicated another fight for power, Williams-Irvin asserted. Whites were continuing to plot the exploitation of Africa, she continued, and "the principle of self-determination . . . does not apply when Africa is considered."[58]

Williams-Irvin reported late in 1919 that, by the final terms of the peace treaty, German interests in Africa were lost. Removing these African colonies from German control was a wise move, she argued, but if they were going to be placed under the control of powers who would give them even worse treatment they had reaped no benefit from their years of bloodshed. Williams-Irvin severely criticized the transfer of a part of the former German colonies to Belgium because of "the days of the anarchist King Leopold." "Africa must be freed from all forms of vandalism," she declared, and "the European nations are on trial."[59]

Randolph and Owen of the *Messenger* agreed that there could be no more "Congo massacres" of innocent Africans by Belgians, and they also questioned the assignment of a part of the former German colonies to Belgium. The editors consistently contended throughout the peace conference that in order to free Africa the Africans must be consulted about their future.[60]

Du Bois continued to question the very presence of the Europeans in Africa. He implored, "Is a civilization naturally backward because it is different?" He insisted that there was no vice in Africa which could begin to touch the horrors thrust upon it by the white imperialists. "Who shall say that any civilization is in itself so superior that it must be superimposed upon another nation without the expressed and intelligent consent of the people most concerned?" he asked. Du Bois believed that the Europeans in Africa were not interested in spreading European "civilization" but in having a field for exploitation. "Greed—naked, pitiless lust for wealth and power, lie back of all Europe's interest in Africa," he claimed. The interests of Africans should be considered, and a form of government should be established based on the concept that Africa was for the Africans. Black Americans would benefit from such a plan, he reported, because there would be a chance for them to emigrate. "The world-fight for black rights is on!" Du Bois announced.[61]

In *Darkwater*, Du Bois contended that black Americans should demand that the conquered German African colonies not be returned to Germany and not be held by the Allies. He saw this as an opportunity for the establishment of an African nation. Believing that European colonial aggrandizement explained the war, Du Bois emphasized that Europeans could not continue to decide the future of Africa.[62] At the end of the war, Du Bois felt that blacks should use the idealism expressed throughout the conflict to their advantage. Here was an opportunity for blacks to benefit from the ideals of democracy, anti-imperialism, and anticolonialism, he maintained.[63]

Mary Church Terrell was another black leader concerned about the future of Africa after the settlement of the peace conference. Terrell was "interested in all African questions." At the International Congress of Women for Permanent Peace, held in Zurich, Switzerland, on 12-17 May 1919, she advocated the idea of permanent world peace and asserted that this could only be brought about by settling the question of the fate of Africa and the issue of European domination on that continent.[64]

Mary Church was a champion of women's rights and civil rights. She was graduated from Oberlin College with the A.B. degree in 1884. From 1885 to 1887 she taught at Wilberforce University. She then went to teach at the black high school in Washington, D.C., Dunbar, and here she met her future husband, Robert Herberton Terrell.

She became the first president of the National Association of Colored Women's Clubs (the National Federation of Afro-American Women merged with the League of Colored Women in 1897). Terrell was also a member of the Washington Board of Education from 1895 to 1901 and 1906 to 1911. In 1904 she was a representative to the International Congress of Women held in Berlin. As a delegate to the International Congress of Women in 1919, she stated, "For the second time in my life it was my privilege to represent, not only the colored women of the United States, but the whole continent of Africa as well." She appealed for justice and fair play for all the darker peoples of the world.[65]

Similarly, other Afro-American leaders were also concerned with European rule in Africa after the peace conference. In an article on Africa in 1919, James W. Johnson contended, "The question of Africa is an international question; it belongs at the peace table." Since he believed that Africa was at the bottom of the war, he warned that there would be more wars if the African question was not settled justly. Johnson held that the black man in America was very interested in the future of Africa, not only because this was his blood brother in Africa who was suffering wrongs against him but also because the white man had attempted to strip blacks all over the world of any historical significance.[66]

In a book published after the settlement of peace, Scott also stressed that Afro-Americans expected the League of Nations to secure opportunities for social, economic, and political "development" for Africans. The time had come, he noted, when Africans would cry out for their right to choose their own destinies under an acceptable tutelage rather than under oppressive and cruel colonial rulers.[67]

Some Afro-Americans agreed with Scott that, through the League of Nations, Africans could improve "their physical, mental, moral, economic, and political conditions, so that sooner or later they will become self-governing peoples."[68] Charles Young from the U.S. legation in Liberia warned, however, that in spite of the establishment of the League of Nations, Africa was still in the throes of the world's unrest and only God knew where it would lead. One thing was certain, though, Young declared, and that was that it would never again be as easy for the white man to oppress Africans.[69]

Within the Afro-American religious community after 1919 Africa's future was seen as dismal. These blacks viewed the League of Nations as discriminatory because one-half of the world's people had been excluded as participants from "Mr. Wilson's league," and they believed that an international organization such as was proposed should represent all the people of the world.[70]

One event during the discussion of the peace settlement that helped to influence a few black opinions on the policy to be pursued by the world powers in regard to the future of Africa was the first Pan-African Congress held in 1919. Du Bois took advantage of the convening of the Paris Peace Conference to attract international attention to the plight of blacks throughout the world by arranging for the first Pan-African Congress to assemble at Paris in February of 1919. Du Bois, representing the NAACP, organized the congress for the purpose of presenting to the powers at the peace conference matters affecting the African colonies. When Du Bois was asked to go to France by the NAACP, he admitted that he and a number of blacks in the United States talked of the advisability and necessity of having American blacks and blacks all over the world represented in some way at the peace conference. Although the problems of Africa were to be discussed, there was no provision to allow blacks to speak for themselves, and therefore he was determined to call a Pan-African meeting. The congress hoped to impress upon the peace delegates the need for internationalization of the former German colonies in Africa. Other Afro-Americans who attended the congress were Dr. Robert R. Moton, former secretary of the NAACP and Booker T. Washington's successor at Tuskegee Institute, Nathan Hunt, Moton's traveling secretary, Lester Walton, managing editor of the *New York Age*, and William H. Jernagin, pastor of Mt. Carmel Baptist Church in Washington, D.C.[71]

In preparation for the congress, Du Bois wrote Newton D. Baker, secretary of war, asking that he approach Wilson about the feasibility of such a meeting being held in the United States. "It seems to me," Du Bois contended, "it would be a calamity for the two hundred million of black people to be absolutely without voice or representation at this great transformation of the world." In an attached memorandum on the future of Africa, he emphasized that the barter of colonies without regard to the wishes or welfare of the indigenous peoples must cease and suggested that the former German colonies be internationalized.[72]

The U.S. and British governments were opposed to the conference and tried to prevent it from being held. The U.S. State Department refused passports to many American blacks who planned to attend the Pan-African Congress. Great Britain followed the same policy, refusing to allow Africans to travel from British colonies to Paris for the congress. Georges Clemenceau, prime minister of France, eventually gave permission for the meeting to be held in Paris.

The Pan-African Congress was held from 19 to 21 February 1919, at the Grand Hotel, Boulevard des Capucines. Fifty-seven delegates from fifteen countries attended. The United States had sixteen representatives, the French West Indies (Martinique and Guadaloupe) thirteen, Haiti and France seven each, and Africa twelve. Belgium and Portugal were represented by officials. The resolutions that emerged from the congress demanded that Africa be ruled by the consent of Africans. There was, however, no drive by the congress for changes in colonial policy other than those that would give equal justice to Africans. Du Bois admitted that the results of the congress were small but did have some influence on the final peace treaty. In fact, the meeting had no impact on the peace conference, and its significance lies only in the fact that it helped solidify an international consciousness among black people throughout the world.[73]

The Pan-African Congress was scantly covered by black journalists in the United States. The *Crisis*, naturally, gave coverage to the event. The magazine emphasized that blacks should involve themselves not only in the peace settlement but also in the Pan-African movement, which was attempting to influence the question of the reapportionment of the former German colonies in Africa. Du Bois recounted that the resolutions of the Pan-African Congress set up a code of laws for international protection of Africans.[74]

In reporting the demands of the congress, the *Washington Bee* agreed that Africans should have the right to participate in their government as fast as their "development" permitted and that the present colonial government existed for the Africans and not vice versa. The *Bee* saw the goals of the congress as praiseworthy, since it was asking for a "square deal" for Africa.[75]

The *Savannah Tribune* also commended the efforts of the Pan-African Congress. Johnson contended that Du Bois and those with him understood their relation to the peace conference and the duty they had to perform. The congress was bound to make a significant impact on African peoples, he maintained, and the effect would be felt by blacks all over the world.[76]

It was terribly ironic that while world leaders at Versailles and blacks in Paris were both discussing the future of Africa, Africans, and blacks the world over, the United States was suffering the worst outbreak of racial violence it had yet endured. During 1919, seventy-seven blacks were lynched. It appeared that the status of blacks in the United States and throughout the world had not been dramatically altered by the high-sounding democratic ideals of World War I. The war was basically inseparable from imperialism and empire and, in a sense, completed colonialism and initiated the period of colonial rule proper. International public opinion was on the side of European imperialism and colonialism and not on the side of self-determination for black people worldwide.[77]

The Treaty of Versailles, which came into force on 10 January 1920, marked the close of a major chapter in the history of Europeans in Africa. After the settlement, Europeans devoted their attention to the formulation of administrative colonial policies.[78]

In many respects, the peace settlement also initiated a new era in Afro-American-African relations. With the revival of organizational Pan-Africanism in 1919, the years that followed witnessed an increased interest among all Afro-Americans in the unity of blacks throughout the world. The omnipresent theme of brotherhood among Africans and blacks of the diaspora was more readily accepted by a greater number of Afro-Americans, and found expression in the next two and a half decades in such activities as the Garvey movement, a continuation of the Pan-African congresses, and the black American outcry at the Italian invasion of Ethiopia in 1935. The new relationship between Afro-Americans and Africa that had been evolving during the three centuries before World War I blossomed after this date, as blacks began to see their future directly related to the fate of Africa and Africans. Their regard for Africa's position after the war was the result of a greater awareness of how the destiny of these two were intricately entwined. Black Americans, concerned with Africa from the beginning of their experiences in the United States, again struggled to maintain the African link, and their concern and militancy helped contribute to the modern African nationalist movement, which gained momentum after 1920, and which resulted in the ultimate independence of almost all the nations on the continent.

Notes

1. Robert O. Collins, *Europeans in Africa*, pp. 97-98; and Halford L. Hoskins, *European Imperialism in Africa*, p. 97.

2. Vladimir Lenin, *Imperialism, the Highest Stage of Capitalism*, p. 4.

3. Richard Rathbone, "World War I and Africa," p. 4.

4. George Padmore, *Africa and World Peace*, p. 43; and Hoskins, *European Imperialism in Africa*, pp. 98-101.

5. Parker Thomas Moon, *Imperialism and World Politics*, p. 460; and Lewis H. Gann and Peter Duignan, *Burden of Empire*, p. 53.

6. Frank H. Tucker, *The White Conscience*, pp. 105-6; Oliver and Fage, *A Short History of Africa*, p. 195; and Gann and Duignan, *Burden of Empire*, pp. 205-6.

7. Rathbone, "World War I and Africa," pp. 1, 9. The *Journal of African History* 19, no. 1 (1978), brought together a number of articles originally presented at a conference on World War I and Africa held in April 1977, at the School of Oriental and African Studies, London.

8. James E. Edmonds, *A Short History of World War I*, pp. 394-408; Hoskins, *European Imperialism in Africa*, pp. 98-99; Collins, *Europeans in Africa*, p. 125; and Mary E. Townsend, *The Rise and Fall of Germany's Colonial Empire 1884-1918*, pp. 365-68.

9. Harold W. V. Temperley, ed., *A History of the Peace Conference of Paris* 2: 226; George Louis Beer, *African Questions at the Paris Peace Conference*, p. xi; Hoskins, *European Imperialism in Africa*, p. 99; and Immanuel Geiss, *The Pan-African Movement*, p. 237.

10. Temperley, ed., *A History of the Peace Conference of Paris*, 6: 500; Hoskins, *European Imperialism in Africa*, p. 99; Edward W. Chester, *Clash of Titans*, pp. 3-4, 179, 181-82, 198. See also Grace P. Hayes, *World War I*, p. 154; and William Roger Louis, "The United States and the African Peace Settlement of 1919," p. 143.

11. See Rayford W. Logan, *The African Mandates in World Politics*, pp. 2-7; idem. "The Operation of the Mandate System in Africa," p. 429; and idem, "The Historical Aspects of Pan-Africanism, 1900-1945," p. 41. Also consult Lawrence E. Gelfand, *The Inquiry*, p. 235; Beer, *African Questions at the Paris Peace Conference*, pp. 431, 471-73; Temperly, ed. *History of the Peace Conference of Paris*, 2: 230-36, 6: 503; Chester, *Clash of Titans*, p. 181; Hoskins, *European Imperialism in Africa*, p. 100; and Louis, "The United States and the African Peace Settlement of 1919," p. 413.

12. Beer, *African Questions at the Paris Peace Conference*, pp. 433-43; and Temperly, ed., *History of the Peace Conference of Paris*, 2: 230, 234-35, 240-41, 243, 6: 503-4.

13. Logan, "The Operation of the Mandate System in Africa," pp. 431-33. See also Gelfand, *The Inquiry*, p. 240.

14. Temperley, ed. *History of the Peace Conference of Paris*, 2: 244, 6: 505, 523; Logan, "The Operation of the Mandate System in Africa," p. 426; and Louis, "The United States and the African Peace Settlement," p. 433.

15. Editorial, "World War and the Color Line," *Crisis* (November 1914): 28-30.

16. W. E. Burghardt Du Bois, "The African Roots of War," pp. 708, 710-11, 713.

17. Julius Lester, ed., *The Thought and Writings of W. E. B. Du Bois, The Seventh Son*, 1: 3-152, passim; W. E. B. Du Bois, *The Autobiography of W. E. B. Du Bois*, pp. 126, 143; idem, *Dusk of Dawn*, pp. 32, 41, 196, 261; Edwin S. Redkey, *The Meaning of Africa to Afro-Americans*, pp. 20, 22-23; and Joel Williamson, "W. E. B. Du Bois as a Hegelian," p. 44.

18. Editorial, "World War and the Color Line," *Crisis* (November 1914): 28-30; and Lester, *The Thought and Writings of W. E. B. Du Bois*, p. 69.

19. See *Crisis*, Editorial, "The Future of Africa" (January 1918): 114; and "Africa" (April 1918): 290-92.

20. "Europe at War to Rule Africa," *New York Age*, 10 December 1914.

21. See *New York Age*, Editorial, "African Troops in the War," 3 September 1914; and Editorial, "Africans in the War," 23 February 1918.

22. Editorial, "The Indirect Results of the War," *New York Age*, 27 April 1918.

23. See *New York Age*, Editorial, "The After Results of the Great War," 15 October 1914; and Editorial, "Africa After the War," 26 January 1918.

24. Editorial, "Africa and the Negroes," *Indianapolis Freeman*, 5 June 1915.

25. Editorial, "White Man's War," *Washington Bee*, 26 December 1914.

26. Editorial, "Negroes to be at Peace Conference in Europe," *Messenger* (January 1918): 6.

27. Lewis H. Fenderson, "Development of the Negro Press, 1827-1948," p. 32.

28. "African Colonies," *Broad Ax*, 17 October 1914.

29. Peter Gilbert, *The Selected Writings of John Edward Bruce*, pp. 142-44.

30. Editorial note, *Indianapolis Freeman*, 21 November 1914.

31. Lewis Garnett Jordan, *Pebbles From an African Beach*, p. 2.

32. Lewis Garnett Jordan, *On Two Hemispheres*, passim.

33. Benjamin G. Brawley, *Africa and the War*, pp. 3, 38; "Benjamin Brawley," p. 757; and John W. Parker, "Benjamin Brawley," *Crisis* (May 1939): 144.

34. George Shepperson, "Negro American Influences on the Emergence of African Nationalism," p. 308.

35. Protest by Conference of Editors of Colored Newspapers in the United States, Washington, D.C., 21-23 June 1918, Emmett J. Scott Papers (93).

36. Editorial note, *Richmond Planet*, 23 November 1918.

37. See *New York Age*, Editorial, "The Race Issue at the Peace Table," 20 November 1918; and Editorial, "Colored Peoples in the Peace Settlement," 7 December 1918.

38. Editorial, "The Negro at the Peace Table," *New York Age*, 11 January 1919.

39. See *Cleveland Gazette*, Editorial, "Du Bois Ignores Our Cause," 28 December 1918; and Editorial, "The Peace Conference and the American Negro," 25 January 1919.

40. "N.A.A.C.P. Head Asks Internationalization of Africa," *Afro-American* (Baltimore), 20 December 1918.

41. J. W. E. Bowen to Emmett J. Scott, 18 November 1918, Scott Papers (112).

42. *Who's Who in America* 14 (1926-27): 313.

43. E. C. Morris to Emmett J. Scott, 13 November 1918, Scott Papers (112).

44. Negro Ministerial Council to Woodrow Wilson, 25 November 1918, Scott Papers (93).

45. Editorial, "Not Ready for Self-Government—Should Be Under Protectorate," *Star of Zion*, 9 January 1919.

46. Excerpt from Address of Emmett J. Scott at Meeting in Carnegie Hall, N.Y., 2 November 1918, Scott Papers (93).

47. Emmett J. Scott, *Scott's Official History of the American Negro in the World War*, p. 469.

48. Letter, James B. Dudley, President of Negro Agricultural and Technical College of North Carolina, Greensboro, n. d.; Letter, National Association of Loyal Negroes, Peace Aims, n. d.; and Charles B. Wickham, Grand Chancellor Knights of Pythias, to Emmett J. Scott, 28 November 1918, Scott Papers (93). See also P. S. L. Hutchins to Emmett J. Scott, 16 November 1918, Scott Papers (112); and Editorial "Will Germany Get Her Colonies Back," *Echo* (Red Bank, New Jersey), 16 November 1918.

49. Announcement of NAACP Meeting, National Association for the Advancement of Colored People (NAACP) Papers (C-64).

50. James Weldon Johnson, *Along This Way*, passim; and Eugene Levy, *James Weldon Johnson*, passim.

51. James Weldon Johnson, "Africa in the World Democracy," 6 January 1919, NAACP Papers (C-332).

52. Press Service of the NAACP, 10 January 1919, NAACP Papers (A-23); and "Africa and the World Democracy," *Crisis* (February 1919): 173-76.

53. See *Crisis*, "The Future of Africa—A Platform" (January 1919): 119; and "Africa and the World Democracy" (February 1919): 173-76.

54. See *New York Age*, "Clash Over African Colonies," 1 February 1919; Editorial, "Civilizing the 'Backward' Races," 22 March 1919; and Editorial, "The Peace Treaty," 5 July 1919.

55. Editorial, "Self-Determination," *Savannah Tribune*, 15 February 1919.

56. See *Washington Bee*, "The Settlement," 16 November 1918, and 23 November 1918; Editorial, "German African Colonies," 4 January 1919; and "The League of Nations," 8 March 1919.

57. See *Half-Century Magazine*, Editorial, "Nibbling on Africa" (February 1919): 3; and Editorial, "Grinding Down Africa" (March 1919): 3.

58. See *Half-Century Magazine*, Editorial, "The League of Nations a Skeleton in Armor" (May 1919): 3; and Editorial, "Africa, the Mint of Gold" (May 1919): 3.

59. See *Half-Century Magazine*, Editorial, "Africa Unbenefited by World War" (September 1919): 3, and Editorial, "The Burdens of Africans Increased" (February 1920): 3.

60. See *Messenger*, Editorial, "Peace Conference" (March 1919): 5; Editorial, "The Peace Treaty" (August 1919): 5; and Editorial, "Africa for the Africans" (September 1920): 84.

61. See *Crisis*, Editorial, "Reconstruction and Africa" (February 1919): 105-6; and W. E. B. Du Bois, "Opinion" (May 1919): 7-9.

62. W. E. B. Du Bois, *Darkwater*, pp. 41, 61.

63. Du Bois, *An ABC of Color*, p. 103; and Clarence G. Contee, "Du Bois, the NAACP, and the Pan-American Congress of 1919," p. 25.

64. John H. Harris to J. H. Wymans, 18 June 1919, Trip Abroad, 1919, Mary Church Terrell Papers (21).

65. Mary Church Terrell, *A Colored Woman in a White World*, pp. 331-35.

66. James W. Johnson, "Africa and the World," *NAACP Annual Conference, 1919*, pp. 331-32.

67. Scott, *The American Negro in the World War*, pp. 469-70.

68. Walter W. Delsarte, *The Negro, Democracy and the War*, pp. 18, 21, 24.

69. Colonel Charles Young to C. S. Cuney, 15 May 1920, Carter G. Woodson Papers (12).

70. See, for example, Editorial, "The Prophet Isaiah on League of Nations," *A.M.E. Church Review* 35 (April 1919): 232.

71. Du Bois, *Dusk of Dawn*, p. 260; Secretary John R. Shillady to Robert J. Victor, 9 January 1919, NAACP Papers (C-1); Press Service of the NAACP, 30 January 1919, NAACP Papers (A-19); and Contee, "Du Bois, the NAACP and the Pan-African Congress of 1919," p. 15.

72. W. E. B. Du Bois to Newton D. Baker, 27 November 1918, Scott Papers (112).

73. W. E. B. Du Bois, *The World and Africa*, p. 11; Elliott Rudwick, *W. E. B. Du Bois*, p. 25; Du Bois, *Dusk of Dawn*, pp. 261-62; Du Bois, *The Autobiography of W. E. B. Du Bois*, p. 271; Lester, *The Thought and Writings of W. E. B. Du Bois*, pp. 81-83; Chester, *Clash of Titans*, p. 183; Logan, *African Mandates in World Politics*, pp. iv, 42; Beer, *African Questions at the Paris Peace Conference*, pp. 285-86; "Du Bois Memorandum," 1 January 1919, and "Resolutions of the Pan-African Congress," in *A Documentary History of the Negro People in the United States*, ed. Herbert Aptheker, 2:249-51; "Memorandum to B. Diagne and Others on a Pan African Congress to be Held in Paris in February, 1919," *Crisis* (March 1919): 224-25. See also Geiss, *The Pan-African Movement*, pp. 233-39; Davis, "Black Americans and U.S. Policy Toward Africa," p. 239; Shepperson, "Negro American Influences on the Emergence of African Nationalism," p. 308; and Contee, "Du Bois, the NAACP, and the Pan-African Congress of

1919," p. 25.

74. Clarence G. Contee, "Afro-Americans and Early Pan-Africanism," p. 26; and Rayford Logan, "The American Negro's View of Africa," p. 219. See also *Crisis*, Editorial, "Africa" (February 1919): 164-65; and W. E. B. Du Bois, "The Pan-African Congress" (April 1919): 271-74.

75. See *Washington Bee*, "Pan-African Congress," 1 March 1919; "Pan-African Conference," 29 March 1919; and "Pan-Africans Ask Peace Council for Square Deal," 29 March 1919.

76. Editorial, "Pan-African Conference," *Savannah Tribune*, 8 February 1919.

77. Stephen R. Fox, *The Guardian of Boston*, p. 231; Du Bois, *Dusk of Dawn*, pp. 263-64; Rathbone, "World War I and Africa," p. 4; and Contee, "The Emergence of Du Bois as an African Nationalist," p. 59.

78. Gann and Duignan, *Burden of Empire*, p. 206; and Chester, *Clash of Titans*, p. 180.

CONCLUSION:
THE AFRICAN NEXUS

12

The psychological moment has, I believe, arrived for Negroes and colored men the world over to get together and to fight for every right with all our might . . . for Negroes all over the world to begin to touch elbows and exchange ideas.

Speech, "The Sons of Africa," New York City, 1913, in Peter Gilbert, comp. and ed., *The Selected Writings of John Edward Bruce*, p. 102.

John Edward Bruce, 1856-1924

We [the Negro world in Africa and America and the Islands of the Sea] have organized the 'Pan-African Congress' as a permanent organization. . . . The world-fight for black rights is on!

"Opinion," *Crisis*, May 1919, pp. 7, 9.

William Edward Burghardt Du Bois, 1868-1963

If the Negro is interested in Africa, he should be interested in the whole of Africa; if he is to link himself up again with his past and his kin, he must link himself up with all of the African people.

"Apropos of Africa," Martin Kilson and Adelaide Cromwell Hill, comp. and ed., p. 412.

Alain Locke, 1886-1954

Africa has continuously held a certain attraction for many Afro-Americans. Regardless of their attitudes toward and perceptions of Africa, these black Americans have felt a racial attachment to their ancestral homeland. During the period 1880-1920, black interest in the future of Africa and the European partitioning of the continent resulted in their expression of concern for events there. Those blacks who addressed themselves to the impact of European activity in Africa most frequently consisted of a small segment of the articulate Afro-American community who were familiar with international issues and enunciated their views on these incidents.

The partitioning of Africa was the inevitable consequence of the late nineteenth-century belief in the duty and destiny of the Western powers to conquer the world for "civilization." Afro-Americans generally agreed that there were many things that Europeans could bring to Africa. Themselves a product of Westernization, most middle-class blacks believed that Africa was in need of Western "development." In viewing the entrance of the Europeans into Africa, these blacks initially supported the economic, social, political, educational, and religious advantages that could be gained from the "civilizing mission" on the continent. In the early years of this study, they adhered to almost all aspects of the "civilizing mission" as a justification for Europeans in Africa. At this time, these blacks perceived European imperialism in Africa as humanitarian and philanthropic. Thus, the period from 1880 to 1900 witnessed an endorsement among most American middle-class blacks of European activity in Africa as a catalyst for African "progress" and "development."

Furthermore, the Spanish-American War aroused interest among Afro-Americans in the "white man's burden" and brought closer to home the possible results of imperialistic expansion. Extremely optimistic at the beginning of the war and believing that American humanitarian interests toward the people in Cuba, the Philippines, and the other areas of the Spanish empire would have positive reverberations within the United States for them, black Americans were nonetheless completely disillusioned by the end of the conflict. This disenchantment with American imperialism also affected Afro-American perspectives on European imperialism in Africa. Hence, the confidence in European activity in Africa expressed before 1900 came under serious consideration by literate blacks after that date, and by the turn of the century these Afro-Americans began to question seriously the motives of the Europeans in Africa. As a result of their direct exposure to some of the consequences of American imperialism and because of a greater discussion and publication in the American media of some of the more exploitative elements of colonialism in Africa, blacks began to doubt the advantages of European imperialism. In many instances, Africans were abused and refused their natural rights. When blacks realized that the European colonialists had not only humanitarian intentions in Africa but were also concerned with commercial, economic, and political advantage, a period of black protest against European imperialism began which would continue throughout the period under discussion.

By the end of World War I, and with the question of the future of the German African colonies being concluded, Afro-Americans began militantly to propagate the slogan "African for Africans," which they had adopted many years earlier. They saw self-determination as the only possible future for Africa and felt that Europeans had failed in their purpose in Africa: the "civilizing and Christianizing" of the continent. Although blacks did not advocate the immediate control of Africa by Africans, they envisioned eventual African independence as a process that could be accomplished within decades under the guidance of the European powers in Africa and, more importantly, with the assistance of middle-class blacks in America.

The various segments of the literate Afro-American community reacted somewhat differently to the Europeans in Africa. Afro-American newspapers gave extensive coverage to this issue and how it influenced Africans as well as how it might affect American blacks. Throughout the period 1880-1920, Afro-American editors were the severest critics of European imperialism. They tended to focus more on the economic, political, and commercial elements of imperialism than any other group within the Afro-American community.

The Afro-American religious community, conversely, was initially the strongest supporter of imperialism because of the benefits, particularly social and religious, that they felt would accrue to Africans because of their contact with Western culture and "civilization." Generally speaking, except in obvious cases of oppression and exploitation, as in the Congo Free State or South Africa, this sector maintained a certain degree of confidence throughout the years studied in the professed humanitarian motives of the Europeans in Africa.

In the other sectors of the Afro-American community, the range of attitudes varied between the optimism expressed by the religious community and the pessimism exhibited by the Afro-American press. Afro-American diplomats in Liberia, because of their involvement in the affairs of that country and because of their day-to-day contact with the colonization process, probably understood better than any other segment of the Afro-American community, except perhaps the missionaries, the impact Europeans were having on African society. These blacks were therefore skeptical about the intentions of the Europeans in Africa and viewed European objectives as essentially exploitative because they discouraged African traditional growth. Travelers and visitors to Africa were also dubious about European intentions in Africa.

The more prominent black leaders held various different views on the European partitioning of Africa. Some, like Booker T. Washington, who believed that Africans were "uncivilized," adhered to almost all the tenets of the "civilizing mission." Others, like W. E. B. Du Bois, for example, rejected many elements of the "civilizing mission" concept and depicted European imperialism on the continent as "the rape of Africa." The seeming confusion and lack of consensus about the partitioning displayed by middle-class blacks was more a reflection of the uncertainty they felt about their own declining status and their differing philosophies and strategies on survival in white America than a major difference of opinion over the impact of European colonialism.

In the final analysis, it appears that perspectives on the European colonization of Africa did not vary greatly within the literate Afro-American community. These Afro-Americans, although they may have viewed the different elements of imperialism in various ways, generally believed that, as long as the interests of the indigenous African population were considered, European activity on that continent would be beneficial. Thus, it can be concluded that middle-class black Americans, on the whole, tended to support the European partitioning of Africa as long as exploitation was not the only goal of the European powers there. Although the masses of blacks left little documentation to demonstrate how they felt about the partitioning, it seems apparent from the evidence that does exist that they were at least aware of specific incidents in the partitioning, such as the Ethiopian victory over Italy, the Congo atrocities, and the Liberian crisis, though they may not have known about the debate within the black middle-class community over the effects of the partitioning.

In some instances, black Americans emphasized the same issues as white Americans; in others, blacks presented different positions on the partitioning. Blacks interpreted European imperialism in Africa more personally than whites did because it was another example of white oppression over blacks. Thus, the same attitudes were not always expressed, even though in many cases information about an event came from the same sources. Afro-Americans took this information and interpreted for themselves the meaning it would have for them.

During the Congo controversy, for instance, both blacks and whites agreed that reforms should be made in the Leopoldian administration. Although blacks seemed to have identified a little more with the plight of the Congolese, they offered the same solutions as whites, strongly recommending Belgian annexation, and only advocated violence at the end of the debate. In the Anglo-Boer War, however, whites supported the Boers while blacks stood almost unanimously behind the British cause. Blacks depicted the Boers as oppressive and thus favored British rule, which they felt had proved more humane and just to Africans in the past. In the case of the Italo-Ethiopian War, blacks tended to attach substantial importance to the Ethiopian victory and magnified its possible impact on the course of the partitioning of Africa. White Americans, on the other hand, simply did not discuss the implications the Ethiopian victory held for international diplomatic relations.

During the period 1880-1920, black perspectives on the European colonialists themselves also gradually changed. Throughout these years, the European powers in Africa were viewed differently by Afro-Americans. Generally, blacks viewed the British and French as the most liberal colonizers while the other imperialists were viewed with various degrees of contempt. Because of the constant uprisings throughout the German colonies and the atrocities committed in the

Belgian areas, Germany and Belgium were seen as the least desirable for the "progress" and "development" of Africa.

In the cases of the two independent countries, Ethiopia and Liberia, blacks focused their attention on the necessity of maintaining the sovereignty of these countries. Afro-Americans severely condemned encroaching imperialism in these areas.

It appears that the U.S. and European governments were only rarely affected by pressure from the Afro-American community. In the United States, blacks sometimes were able to influence American policy toward Liberia. This was to a great extent due to the lack of a consistent American policy toward Liberia, which in turn allowed for some degree of flexibility. In conjunction with white American and European pressure, blacks were able to influence indirectly American policy toward the Congo in the early twentieth century as well as contribute to the final decision of annexation by Belgium. On several occasions, blacks petitioned the U.S. government as well as the European governments. Because of his influence with both the black and white communities, Booker T. Washington was constantly being approached by the European powers attempting to get him to endorse their policies in Africa. In addition, Afro-Americans attempted to help "develop" Africa in humanitarian terms through missionary involvement with the African population, but this came to be considered so disruptive by the colonialists that early in the twentieth century Afro-American misionaries were discouraged from working in Africa. These were the only changes that can be seen concerning Afro-American public persuasion over American or European policy in Africa. Actually, discernible Afro-American impact on America's relationship with Africa did not occur until after World War I, and blacks were thwarted in their efforts to effect change before this date.

Black American attitudes toward the European partitioning of Africa were affected primarily by events in the United States and only secondarily by activities on the continent. During periods of severe oppression in America, Afro-Americans diverted their attention from Africa and concentrated on improving their status at home. Also, in the final analysis, most middle-class blacks fully realized that they could not dramatically alter the European partitioning process and thus understood that denunciation of imperial policy had its inherent limitations. Nonetheless, these blacks likewise knew that the exploitation of Africans could result in the continual justification for degradation of black people throughout the world. Since the years covered in this study found American blacks themselves subjected to the severest forms of discrimination, it was easy for them to empathize with the oppressive conditions of Africans under Euopean rule.

Because of this similarity in white domination and exploitation of blacks, throughout the period discussed Afro-Americans emphasized the need for brotherhood among blacks of the world. Afro-Americans related directly to the experiences of Africans under colonial rule and frequently compared this situation to their position in American society. They saw a common plight among blacks and therefore a need for unity. Thus, it is obvious that the idea of Pan-Africanism, which appeared as a theoretical concept in 1900, existed within the black community many years earlier. This expression was an informal precept which evolved out of the black experience in America. Further research in this area has revealed that racial ideologies analogous to the concept of Pan Africanism have been with blacks since their beginnings in the United States.

Believing that Africa needed to be "civilized and Christianized," most middle-class blacks during this period suggested that it was the duty of Afro-Americans to assume this responsibility for African "development." Therefore, individuals within all sectors of the black community advocated Afro-American involvement in the religious, economic, commercial, social, cultural, educational, and political training of Africans.

Throughout the period from 1880 to 1920, then, black American perspectives on the European partitioning of Africa generally varied from tacit approval to partial rejection. However, throughout this period, one factor in Afro-American relations with Africa remained constant. Many black Americans subscribed to the concept of a common brotherhood among blacks the world over and saw the need to maintain the African nexus.

BIBLIOGRAPHY

Primary Materials

MANUSCRIPT COLLECTIONS

The Historical Foundation of the Presbyterian and Reformed Churches,
     Montreat, North Carolina.
          William Henry Sheppard Papers.
Library of Congress, Washington, D.C.
          John Hay Papers.
          John Tyler Morgan Papers.
          National Association for the Advancement of Colored People Papers.
          Elihu Root Papers.
          Mary Church Terrell Papers.
          Robert H. Terrell Papers.
          Booker T. Washington Papers.
          Carter G. Woodson Papers.
Moorland-Spingarn Research Center, Howard University, Washington, D.C.
          Mary Ann Shadd Cary Papers.
          Archibald H. Grimke Papers.
          William H. Hunt Papers.
Morgan State University Library, Baltimore.
          Emmett J. Scott Papers.
Schomburg Center for Research in Black Culture, New York.
          John Edward Bruce Papers.
          Alexander Crummell Papers.

GOVERNMENT DOCUMENTS

U.S. Congress. House. *House Joint Resolutions*, 56th Cong., 1st sess., no.
     84; 56th Cong., 1st sess., no. 193; 57th Cong., 1st sess., no. 27;

57th Cong., 1st sess., no. 137; 57th Cong., 1st sess., no. 167; and 57th Cong., 1st sess., no. 170.

———. *House Resolutions*, 57th Cong., 1st sess., no. 186.

U.S. Congress. Senate. *Senate Documents*, 59th Cong., 2d sess., no. 139.

———. *Senate Executive Documents*, 49th Cong., 1st sess., no. 196.

———. *Senate Resolutions*, 56th Cong., 1st sess., no. 56; and 59th Cong., 2d sess., no. 194.

U.S. Congress. Record Group 46. Records of the U.S. Congress, 58th Congress. Committee on Foreign Relation Papers Related to Affairs in the Congo.

U.S. Department of Commerce. Bureau of the Census. *Negro Population, 1790-1915*. Washington, D.C.: Government Printing Office, 1918.

———. *Negroes in the U.S., 1920-1932*. Washington, D.C.: Government Printing Office, 1935.

U.S. Department of State. *Foreign Relations of the United States*, 1879, 1895. Washington, D.C.: Government Printing Office, 1934.

———. Record Group 59. Decimal File (1910-1929). Box 1755. National Archives, Washington, D.C.

———. Record Group 59. Despatches from U.S. Consuls in Monrovia, Liberia, 1852-1906. Roll 3. National Archives, Washington, D.C.

———. Record Group 59. Despatches from U.S. Ministers to Liberia, 1863-1906. Rolls 6-7, 9-14. National Archives, Washington, D.C.

———. Record Group 59. Numerical File (1906-1910). National Archives, Washington, D.C.

Cases 1352-1379. Roll 161 (Liberia).
Cases 2911-2927. Roll 281 (Congo).
Cases 3513-3536. Roll 326 (Liberia).
Cases 4676-4695. Roll 405 (Liberia).
Cases 4966-4984. Roll 423 (Liberia).
Cases 7872-7910. Roll 584 (Congo).
Cases 12024-12053/60. Book 792 (Congo).
Cases 12053/61-12074. Book 793 (Congo).
Cases 12075-12083/150. Book 794 (Liberia).
Cases 12083/151-12083/260. Book 795 (Liberia).

———. Record Group 84. Despatches from U.S. Consulate at Cape Town, South Africa, 1899. National Archives, Washington, D.C.

———. Minor File (1906-1910). Vols. 32, 33, 34. National Archives, Washington, D.C.

———. Miscellaneous Letters of the Department of State. Roll 1182. National Archives, Washington, D.C.

U.S. Presidents. Messages and Papers. *A Compilation of the Messages and Papers of the Presidents.* Vols. 10, 11, 13, 14. New York: Bureau of National Literature, 1897-1927.

A Report of the Commission of Inquiry Appointed by the Congo Free State Government. New York: G. P. Putnam's Sons, 1906.

AUTOBIOGRAPHIES, MEMOIRS, AND TRAVELERS' ACCOUNTS

Beer, George Louis. *African Questions at the Paris Peace Conference.* Reprint. London: Dawsons of Pall Mall, 1968.

Boone, Clinton C. *Congo As I Saw It.* New York: J. J. Little and Ives, 1927.

Campbell, Robert. *A Pilgrimage to My Motherland: An Account of a Journey Among the Egbas and Yorubas of Central Africa, In 1859-60.* New York: Thomas Hamilton, 1861.

Coppin, Levi Jenkins. *Observations of Persons and Things in South Africa, 1900-1904: Letters From South Africa.* Philadelphia: A.M.E. Book Concern, n. d.

Corrothers, James D. *In Spite of the Handicap, An Autobiography.* New York: George H. Doran, 1916.

Dean, Harry. *The Pedro Gorino: The Adventure of a Negro Sea-Captain in Africa and on the Seven Seas in His Attempts to Found an Ethiopian Empire, An Autobiographical Narrative.* New York: Houghton and Mifflin, 1929.

Delany, Martin R. *Official Report of the Niger Valley Exploring Party.* New York: T. Hamilton, 1861.

Delsarte, Walter W. *The Negro, Democracy and the War.* Detroit: Wolverine, 1919.

Douglass, Frederick. *Life and Times of Frederick Douglass Written by Himself.* Boston: De Wolfe, Fiske, 1892.

Du Bois, W. E. B. *The Autobiography of W. E. B. Du Bois: A Soliloquy on Viewing My Life From the Last Decade of Its First Century.* New York: International, 1968.

———. *Darkwater: Voices From Within the Veil.* New York: Harcourt, Brace and Howe, 1920.

———. *Dusk of Dawn: An Essay Toward An Autobiography of a Race Concept.* New York: Harcourt, Brace, 1940.

Gibbs, Mifflin Wistar. *Shadow and Light: An Autobiography with Reminiscences of the Last and Present Century.* Washington, D.C.: The Author, 1902.

Heard, William H. *From Slavery to the Bishopric in the A.M.E. Church, An Autobiography.* Philadelphia: A.M.E. Book Concern, 1924.

Johnson, James Weldon. *Along This Way.* New York: Viking Press, 1933.

Jordan, Lewis Garnett. *On Two Hemispheres: Bits From the Life Story of Lewis G. Jordan, As Told by Himself.* Nashville, Tenn.: A.M.E. Sunday School Union [1935].

―――. *Pebbles From an African Beach.* Philadelphia: Lide-Carey Press, 1918.

Roosevelt, Theodore. *African Game Trails.* New York: Charles Scribner's Sons, 1924.

Sheppard, William H. *Presbyterian Pioneers in Congo.* Richmond, Va.: Presbyterian Committee of Publication, 1917.

Skinner, Robert P. *Abyssinia of Today: An Account of the First Mission Sent by the American Government to the Court of the King of Kings (1903-1904).* New York: Longmans, Green, 1906.

Smith, Charles Spencer. *Glimpses of Africa, West and Southwest Coast, Containing the Author's Impressions and Observations During a Voyage of Six Thousand Miles From Sierra Leone, St. Paul de Loanda and Return, Including the Rio del Ray and Cameroons River, and the Congo River, From Its Mouth to Matadi.* Nashville, Tenn.: A.M.E. Church Sunday School Union, 1895.

Stewart, T. McCants. *Liberia: The Americo-African Republic.* New York: Edward O. Jenkins' Sons, 1886.

Terrell, Mary Church. *A Colored Woman in a White World.* Washington, D.C.: Ransdell, 1940.

Turner, Henry McNeal. *African Letters.* Nashville, Tenn.: A.M.E. Sunday School Union, 1893.

Walters, Alexander. *My Life and Work.* New York: Fleming H. Revell, 1917.

CONTEMPORARY ARTICLES, BOOKS, LETTERS, PAMPHLETS, PROCEEDINGS, REPORTS, SPEECHES, AND EDITED COLLECTIONS

Alexander, William T. *History of the Colored Race in America.* Kansas City, Mo.: Palmetto, 1887.

Alger, R. A. "America's Attitude Toward England." *North American Review* 170 (March 1900): 332-34.

Allen, Richard. "Address to the Free People of Colour of These United

States." In *Constitution of the American Society of Free Persons of Colour*, pp. 9-12. Philadelphia: Printed by J. W. Allen, 1831.

The American Negro Academy Occasional Papers. Nos. 1-22, 1897-1924. New York: Arno Press and *New York Times*, 1969.

Aptheker, Herbert. *A Documentary History of the Negro People in the United States*, 2 vols. New York: The Citadel Press, 1968.

Aucaigne, Felix. "Italy and Abyssinia." *Harper's Weekly*, 14 March 1896, p. 247.

Barber, J. Max. *How They Became Distinguished*. Atlanta: Hertel, Jenkins, n.d.

Bell, Howard. *A Survey of the Negro Convention Movement, 1830-1861*. New York: Arno Press, 1969.

"The Boer Cause in American Politics." *The American Monthly Review of Reviews* 22 (August 1900): 145.

Bowen, J. W. E., ed. *Africa and the American Negro*. Atlanta: Gammon Theological Seminary, 1896.

Brawley, Benjamin G. *Africa and the War*. New York: Duffield, 1918.

———. *A Social History of the American Negro*. New York: Macmillan, 1921.

Brooks, Sydney. "America and the War." *North American Review* 170 (March 1900): 337-47.

Coppin, Levi J. "The American Negro's Religion for the African Negro's Soul." *Independent*, 27 March 1902, pp. 748-50.

———. "The Negro's Part in the Redemption of Africa." In *Masterpieces of Negro Eloquence*, edited by Alice Moore Dunbar, pp. 243-50. New York: Bookery, 1914.

Cromwell, J. W. *History of the Bethel Literary and Historical Association*. Washington, D.C.: Press of R. L. Pendleton, 1896.

Crummell, Alexander. "Address Before the American Geographical Society, On the King of Belgium's Congo State." In *Africa and America: Addresses and Discourses*, ed. Alexander Crummell, pp. 307-23. Reprint. New York: Negro Universities Press, 1969.

The Duty of a Rising Christian State to Contribute to the World's Well-Being and Civilization and the Means By Which It May Perform the Same. London: Wertheim & MacIntosh, 1856.

———. "The Progress of Civilization Along the West Coast of Africa." In *The Future of Africa; Being Addresses, Sermons, Etc. Delivered in the Republic of Liberia*, pp. 105-29. New York: C. Scribner, 1862.

———. "The Regeneration of Africa." In *Africa and America; Addresses and Discourses*, pp. 431-53. Reprint. New York: Negro Universities Press, 1969.

———. To Charles B. Dunbar, 1 September 1860. "The Relations and Duties of Free Colored Men in America to Africa." In *The Future of Africa; Being Addresses, Sermons, Etc. Delivered in the Republic of Liberia*, ed. Alexander Crummell, pp. 215-81. New York: C. Scribner, 1862.

Delany, Martin R. *The Condition, Elevation, Emigration and Destiny of the Colored People of the United States*. Philadelphia: Reprint. New York: Arno Press and *New York Times*, 1968.

———, and Campbell, Robert. *Search for a Place, Black Separatism and Africa, 1860*. Ann Arbor: University of Michigan Press, 1969.

Douglass, Frederick. *The Claims of the Negro Ethnologically Considered*. An Address Before the Literary Societies of Western Reserve College, at Commencement, 12 July 1854. Rochester, N.Y.: Lee, Mann, 1854.

Dube, John L. "Are Negroes Better Off in South Africa?" *The Missionary Review* 17 (August 1904): 583-86.

Du Bois, W. E. Burghardt. "The African Roots of War." *Atlantic Monthly* (May 1915): 707-14.

Easton, Hosea. *A Treatise on the Intellectual Character and Civil and Political Condition of the Colored People of the United States*. Boston: Isaac Knapp, 1837.

Falkner, Roland. "The United States and Liberia." *American Journal of International Law* 4 (1910): 529-45.

Fortune, T. Thomas. *Black and White: Land, Labor and Politics in the South*. New York: Fords, Howard, & Hulbert, 1884.

———. "The Nationalization of Africa." In *Africa and the American Negro*, edited by J. W. E. Bowen, pp. 199-204. Atlanta: Gammon Theological Seminary, 1896.

Garnet, Henry Highland. *The Past and Present Condition, and the Destiny of the Colored Race*. Troy, N.Y.: Steam Press of J. C. Kneeland, 1848.

———. "Speech Delivered at Cooper's Institute, New York City, 1860." In *"Let your Motto Be Resistance," The Life and Thought of Henry Highland Garnet*, compiled by Earl Ofari, pp. 183-87. Boston: Beacon Press, 1972.

Gilbert, Peter, comp. and ed. *The Selected Writings of John Edward Bruce: Militant Black Journalist*. New York: Arno Press and *New York Times*, 1971.

Grimke, Archibald. "The Opening Up of Africa." *The New Deal* 3 (July-August 1890): 355-56.

Hammond, E. W. S. "Africa in Its Relation to Christian Civilization." In *Africa and the American Negro*, edited by J. W. E. Bowen, pp. 205-10. Atlanta: Gammon Theological Seminary, 1896.

Heard, William H. *The Bright Side of African Life*. Philadelphia: A.M.E., 1898.

Johnson, H. T. "The Black Man's Burden." Speech delivered at the Nova Scotia Conference, Halifax, 21 August 1899. [Philadelphia]: n.p. [1899].

Johnson, James W. "Africa and the World." *NAACP Annual Conference 1919*, pp. 13-23.

Kilson, Martin, and Hill, Adelaide Cromwell, comps. and eds. *Apropos of Africa, Afro-American Leaders and the Romance of Africa*. Garden City, N.Y.: Doubleday, 1971.

Lester, Julius, ed. *The Thought and Writings of W. E. B. Du Bois, The Seventh Son*. 2 vols. New York: Random House, 1971.

Lewis, Robert B. *Light and Truth; Collected From the Bible and Ancient and Modern History*. Boston: Benjamin F. Roberts, 1844.

Marks, George P., III. *The Black Press Views American Imperialism (1898-1900)*. New York: Arno Press and *New York Times*, 1971.

Marsh, J. B. T. *The Story of the Jubilee Singers. Cleveland:* The Cleveland Printing, 1892.

Mason, M. C. B. "The Methodist Episcopal Church and the Evangelization of Africa." In *Africa and the American Negro*, edited by J. W. E. Bowen, pp. 143-48. Atlanta: Gammon Theological Seminary, 1896.

———. *Solving the Problem: A Series of Lectures*. Mt. Morris, Ill.: Kable Brothers, 1917.

Maxeke, Marshal. "Black Man's Side in the Transvaal War." *Independent*, 7 December 1899, pp. 3286-87.

———. "How the Boers Treat the Natives." *Independent*, 2 November 1899, pp. 2946-48.

Morris, Charles S. "A Work for American Negroes." *Ecumenical Conference Report, 1900*. New York: American Tract Society, 1900.

Nash, F. B. "America and the Transvaal War." *Saturday Review*, 24 February 1900, pp. 236-37.

National Association for the Advancement of Colored People. *Thirty Years of Lynching in the United States, 1889-1918.* New York: National Association for the Advancement of Colored People, 1919.

"Native Unrest in South Africa." *Independent*, 30 November 1899, pp. 3240-41.

Peck, Harry T. "American Opinion on the South African War." *Bookman* 10 (February 1900): 527-32.

Pennington, James W. C. *A Textbook of the Origin and History, & c. & c. of the Colored People.* Hartford: L. Skinner, 1841.

Perry, Rufus Lewis. *The Cushite; or the Descendants of Ham.* Springfield, Mass.: Willey, 1893.

Proceedings of the Colored National Convention, 1853. Rochester: Printed at the Office of *Frederick Douglass' Paper*, 1853.

Redkey, Edwin S., ed. *Respect Black: The Writings and Speeches of Henry McNeal Turner.* New York: Arno Press, 1971.

Scott, Emmett J. *Negro Migration During the War.* New York: Oxford University Press, 1920.

―――. *Scott's Official History of the American Negro in the World War.* Chicago: Homewood Press, 1919.

Scott, Horatio L. *The Truth of Africa.* Oakland, Calif.: The Press of Wm. H. Day, 1901.

Smyth, John H. "The African in Africa, and the African in America." In *Africa and the American Negro*, edited by J. W. E. Bowen, pp. 69-83. Atlanta: Gammon Theological Seminary, 1896.

Taylor, C. H. J. *Whites and Blacks or the Question Settled.* Atlanta: Jas. P. Harrison, 1889.

Turner, H. M. "The American Negro and His Fatherland." In *Africa and the American Negro*, edited by J. W. E. Bowen, pp. 195-98. Atlanta: Gammon Theological Seminary, 1896.

Walker, David. *David Walker's Appeal.* New York: Hill and Wang, 1965.

Washington, Booker T. "Cruelty in the Congo Country." *Outlook* 8 (October 1904): 375-77.

―――. *The Future of the American Negro.* Boston: Small, Maynard, 1899.

―――. "The Future of Congo Reform." *Congo News Letter* (August 1906): 9-10.

Webb, James M. *The Black Man the Father of Civilisation Proven by Biblical History.* Seattle: n.p., 1910.

Wilcox, W. C. "How the English Treat the Natives." *Independent*, 7 December 1899, pp. 3288-89.

Williams, George Washington. *History of the Negro Race in America.* 2 vols. New York: G. P. Putnam's Sons, 1883.

―――. "An Open Letter to His Serene Majesty Leopold II, King of the Belgians and Sovereign of the Independent State of Congo by Colonel, The Honorable George W. Williams, of the United States of America." In *Apropos of Africa: Sentiments of Negro Leaders on Africa From the 1800s to the 1950s,* edited by Martin Kilson and Adelaide Hill, pp. 98-107. London: Cass, 1969.

Woodson, Carter G., ed. *The Mind of the Negro as Reflected in Letters Written During the Crisis, 1800-1860.* Washington, D.C.: Association for the Study of Negro Life and History, 1926.

CONTEMPORARY NEWSPAPERS AND PERIODICALS

Newspapers, Black

Afro-American (Baltimore).
Afro-American Sentinel (Omaha, Nebraska).
American (Coffeyville, Kansas).
American Citizen (Kansas City, Kansas).
Appeal (St. Paul, Minnesota).
Arkansas Mansion (Little Rock).
Boston Guardian.
Broad Ax (Chicago).
Broad Ax (Salt Lake City).
Borad Axe (St. Paul, Minnesota).
Cleveland Gazette.
Colored American (Washington, D.C.).
Detroit Informer.
Echo (Red Bank, New Jersey).
Enterprise (Omaha, Nebraska).
Frederick Douglass' Paper (Rochester, New York).
Grit (Washington, D.C.).
Huntsville Gazette (Alabama).
Indianapolis Freeman (Indiana).
Indianapolis Recorder (Indiana).
Iowa State Bystander (Des Moines).
Leavenworth Herald (Kansas City, Kansas).

National Reflector (Wichita, Kansas).
New York Age.
New York Freeman.
North Star (Rochester, New York).
Parsons Weekly Blade (Kansas).
People's Advocate (Washington, D.C.).
Portland New Age (Oregon).
Richmond Planet (Virginia).
Rising Sun (Kansas City, Kansas).
St. Louis Palladium.
San Francisco Elevator.
Savannah Tribune (Georgia).
Sentinel (Trenton, New Jersey).
Statesman (Colorado Springs).
Topeka Colored Citizen (Kansas).
Topeka State Ledger (Kansas).
Topeka Weekly Call (Kansas).
Washington Bee (Washington, D.C.).
Western Enterprise (Colorado Springs).
Wichita Searchlight (Kansas).
Wisconsin Weekly Advocate (Milwaukee).

Newspapers, White

Baltimore Sun.
Boston Herald.
New York American.
New York Daily Tribune.
New York Times.
Springfield Republican (Massachusetts).
Times (London).
Washington Evening Star (Washington, D.C.).

Periodicals, Black

A.M.E. Church Review.
African Times and Orient Review.
Alexander's Magazine.
Christian Recorder.
Colored American Magazine.

Crisis.
Douglass' Monthly.
Fisk Herald.
Half Century Magazine.
Horizon.
Kassai Herald.
Messenger.
Star of Zion.
Voice of Missions.
Voice of the Negro.

Periodicals, White

African Repository.
Missionary Herald.
Our Day.
Southern Workman.

Secondary Materials

BOOKS

Abun-Nasr, Jamil M. *A History of the Maghrib.* Cambridge: Cambridge University Press, 1971.

Anderson, John D. *West Africa and East Africa in the Nineteenth and Twentieth Centuries.* London: Heinemann Educational Books, 1972.

Azikiwe, Nnamdi. *Liberia in World Politics.* London: Arthur H. Stockwell, 1934.

Bedinger, Robert D. *Triumphs of the Gospel in the Belgian Congo.* Richmond, Va.: Presbyterian Committee of Publications, 1920.

Bennett, Norman R. *Africa and Europe: From Roman Times to the Present.* New York: Africana, 1975.

Berkeley, George. *The Campaign of Adowa and the Rise of Menelik.* Westminister: Archibald Constable, 1902.

Bittle, William E., and Geis, Gilbert. *The Longest Way Home: Chief Alfred C. Sam's Back-to-Africa Movement.* Detroit: Wayne State University Press, 1964.

Bixler, Raymond W. *The Foreign Policy of the United States in Liberia.* New York: Pageant Press, 1957.

British Imperialism in East Africa. Colonial Series no. 1. London: Labour
    Research Department, 1926.

Carlson, Lewis H., and Colburn, George A., eds. *In Their Place: White
    America Defines Her Minorities, 1850-1950*. New York: John Wiley
    and Sons, 1972.

Chester, Edward W. *Clash of Titans: Africa and U.S. Foreign Policy*. Mary-
    knoll, N.Y.: Orbis Books, 1974.

Clendenen, Clarence; Collins, Robert; and Duignan, Peter. *Americans in
    Africa, 1865-1900*. Stanford, Calif.: Hoover Institution on War,
    Revolution, and Peace, Stanford University, 1966.

Coan, Josephus R. *Daniel Alexander Payne Christian Educator*. Philadel-
    phia: A.M.E. Book Concern, 1935.

Collins, Robert O. *Europeans in Africa*. New York: Knopf, 1971.

———. *King Leopold, England, and the Upper Nile, 1899-1909*. New
    Haven: Yale University Press, 1968.

———. *The Southern Sudan, 1883-1898, A Struggle for Control*. New
    Haven: Yale University Press, 1962.

———, ed. *The Partition of Africa: Illusion or Necessity?* New York: J.
    Wiley, 1969.

———, and Tignor, Robert L. *Egypt and the Sudan*. Englewood Cliffs, N.J.:
    Prentice-Hall, 1967.

Contee, Clarence G. *Henry Sylvester Williams and Origins of Organizational
    Pan-Africanism, 1897-1902*. Washington, D.C.: Department of His-
    tory, Howard University, 1973.

Cookey, Sylvanus J. S. *Britain and the Congo Question, 1885-1913*. Lon-
    don: Longmans, 1968.

Coupland, Reginald. *The Exploitation of East Africa, 1856-1890: The Slave
    Trade and the Scramble*. Evanston, Ill.: Northwestern University
    Press, 1967.

Crowder, Michael. *West Africa Under Colonial Rule*. Evanston, Ill.: North-
    western University Press, 1968.

Crowe, Sybil. *The Berlin West African Conference, 1884-1885*. London:
    Longmans, Green, 1942.

Cruse, Harold. *The Crisis of the Negro Intellectual*. New York: William Mor-
    row, 1967.

Davidson, Basil. *East and Central Africa to the late Nineteenth Century*.
    London: Longmans, 1967.

Dennis, Alfred L. P. *Adventures in American Diplomacy, 1896-1906*. New
    York: E. P. Dutton, 1928.

Detweiler, Frederick. *The Negro Press in the United States*. Chicago: University of Chicago Press, 1922.

Drachler, Jacob, ed. *Black Homeland/Black Diaspora: Cross-Currents of the African Relationship*. Port Washington, N.Y.: Kennikat Press, 1975.

Drake, St. Clair. *The Redemption of Africa and Black Religion*. Chicago: Third World Press, 1970.

Du Bois, W. E. B. *An ABC of Color, Selections Chosen By the Author From Over a Half Century of His Writings*. Berlin: Seven Seas, 1963.

———. *The World and Africa: Inquiry into the Part which Africa Has Played in World History*. New York: International, 1968.

Edmonds, James E. *A Short History of World War I*. London: Oxford University Press, 1951.

Emerson, Rupert. *Africa and United States Policy*. Englewood Cliffs, N.J.: Prentice-Hall, 1967.

Ferguson, John H. *American Diplomacy and the Boer War*. Philadelphia: University of Pennsylvania Press, 1939.

Fox, Stephen R. *The Guardian of Boston: William Monroe Trotter*. New York: Atheneum, 1970.

Franklin, John H. *George Washington Williams and Africa*. Washington, D.C.: Department of History, Howard University, 1971.

Fredrickson, George M. *The Black Image in the White Mind: The Debate on Afro-American Character and Destiny, 1817-1914*. New York: Harper & Row, 1971.

Gaitskell, Arthur. *Gezira: A Study of Development in the Sudan*. London, 1959.

Gallagher, Charles F. *The United States and North Africa: Morocco, Algeria, and Tunisia*. Cambridge: Harvard University Press, 1963.

Gann, Lewis H., and Duignan, Peter. *Burden of Empire: An Appraisal of Western Colonialism in Africa South of the Sahara*. New York: Praeger, 1967.

Gatewood, Willard B., Jr. *Black Americans and the White Man's Burden, 1898-1903*. Urbana: University of Illinois Press, 1975.

Geiss, Immanuel. *The Pan-African Movement*. Translated by Ann Keep. London: Methuen, 1974.

Gelfand, Lawrence E. *The Inquiry, American Preparations for Peace, 1917-1919*. New Haven: Yale University Press, 1963.

Hargreaves, John D. *Prelude to the Partition of West Africa*. New York: St. Martin's Press, 1963.

Harris, Sheldon H. *Paul Cuffee: Black America and the African Return*. New York: Simon and Schuster, 1972.

Hayes, Grace P. *World War I: A Compact History*. New York: Hawthorn Books, 1972.

Healy, David. *US Expansionism, the Imperialist Urge in the 1890s*. Madison: University of Wisconsin Press, 1970.

Helmreich, William B., comp. *Afro-Americans and Africa, Black Nationalism at the Crossroads*. Westport, Conn.: Greenwood Press, 1977.

Herskovits, Melville J. *The American Negro: A Study in Racial Crossing*. New York: Knopf, 1928.

Hill, Richard L. *Egypt in the Sudan, 1820-1881*. London: Oxford University Press, 1959.

Hirshson, Stanley P. *Farewell to the Bloody Shirt: Northern Republicans and the Southern Negro, 1877-1893*. Bloomington: Indiana University Press, 1962.

Holt, Peter M. *The Mahdist State in the Sudan, 1881-1898: A Study of Its Origins, Development, and Overthrow*. Oxford: Clarendon Press, 1958.

Hoskins, Halford L. *European Imperialism in Africa*. New York: H. Holt, 1930.

Isaacs, Harold. *The New World of Negro Americans*. New York: John Day, 1963.

Isichei, Elizabeth. *History of West Africa Since 1800*. New York: Africana, 1977.

Johnston, Harry H. *George Grenfell and the Congo*. Reprint. New York: Negro Universities Press, 1969.

Keith, Arthur B. *The Belgian Congo and the Berlin Act*. Oxford: Clarendon Press, 1919.

King, Kenneth James. *Pan-Africanism and Education: A Study of Race Philanthropy and Education in the Southern States of America and East Africa*. Oxford: Clarendon Press, 1971.

Kronus, Sidney. *The Black Middle Class*. Columbus, O.: Charles E. Merrill, 1971.

Kruger, Rayne. *Good-Bye Dolly Gray: The Story of the Boer War*. London: Cassell, 1959.

Lenin, Vladimir. *Imperialism, the Highest Stage of Capitalism: A Popular Outline*. Reprint. Peking: Foreign Languages Press, 1970.

Levy, Eugene. *James Weldon Johnson: Black Leader, Black Voice*. Chicago: University of Chicago Press, 1973.

Logan, Rayford W. *The African Mandates in World Politics*. Washington, D.C.: Public Affairs Press, 1948.

————. *The Betrayal of the Negro From Rutherford B. Hayes to Woodrow Wilson*. New York: Collier Books, 1965.

Louis, William Roger, and Stengers, Jean, eds. *E. D. Morel's History of the Congo Reform Movement*. Oxford: Clarendon Press, 1968.

Lugard, Frederick. *The Dual Mandate in British Tropical Africa*. London: W. Blackwood and Sons, 1922.

Lynch, Hollis R. *Edward Wilmont Blyden. Pan-Negro Patriot, 1832-1912*. London: Oxford University Press, 1967.

Marquard, Leo. *The Story of South Africa*. London: Faber and Faber, 1968.

Marsh, Zoe, and Kingsnorth, G. W. *An Introduction to the History of East Africa*. Cambridge: Cambridge University Press, 1961.

Martelli, George. *Leopold to Lumumba: A History of the Belgian Congo, 1877-1960*. London: Chapman & Hall, 1962.

Mathurin, Owen Charles. *Henry Sylvester Williams and the Origins of the Pan-African Movement, 1869-1911*. Westport, Conn.: Greenwood Press, 1976.

Meier, August. *Negro Thought in America, 1880-1915. Racial Ideologies in the Age of Booker T. Washington*. Ann Arbor: University of Michigan Press, 1963.

————, and Rudwick, Elliott. *From Plantation to Ghetto: An Interpretive History of American Negroes*. New York: Hill and Wang, 1966.

Moon, Parker Thomas. *Imperialism and World Politics*. Reprint. New York: Garland, Inc., 1973.

Moses, Wilson Jeremiah. *The Golden Age of Black Nationalism, 1850-1925*. Hamden, Conn.: Archon Books, 1978.

Okoye, Felix Nwabueze. *The American Image of Africa: Myth and Reality*. Buffalo, N.Y.: Black Academy Press, 1971.

Oliver, Roland, and Atmore, Anthony. *Africa Since 1800*. Cambridge: Cambridge University Press, 1967.

Oliver, Roland, and Fage, John. *A Short History of Africa*. Harmondsworth: Penguin, 1966.

Oliver, Roland, and Mathew, Gervase. *History of East Africa*, 1. Oxford: Clarendon Press, 1963.

Padmore, George. *Africa and World Peace*. London: Martin Secken and Warburg, 1937.

Painter, Nell I. *Exodusters: Black Migration to Kansas After Reconstruction*. New York: Knopf, 1977.

Penn, I. Garland. *The Afro-American Press and Its Editors.* Springfield, Mass.: Willey, 1891.

Perkins, Bradford. *The Great Rapprochement: England and the United States 1859-1914.* New York: Atheneum, 1968.

Porter, Bernard. *Critics of Empire: British Radical Attitudes to Colonialism in Africa, 1895-1914.* London: Macmillan, 1968.

Porter, Kirk H., and Johnson, Donald B., comps. *National Party Platforms, 1840-1956.* Urbana: University of Illinois Press, 1956.

Redkey, Edwin S. *Black Exodus: Black Nationalist and Back to Africa Movements, 1890-1910.* New Haven: Yale University Press, 1969.

―――. *The Meaning of Africa to Afro-Americans, 1890-1914.* Buffalo, N.Y.: Special Studies Council on International Studies, 1971.

Reeves, Jesse S. *The International Beginning of the Congo Free State.* Baltimore: Johns Hopkins University Press, 1894.

Robinson, Ronald, and Gallagher, John. *Africa and the Victorians—The Climax of Imperialism in the Dark Continent.* New York: St. Martin's Press, 1961.

Rosenthal, Eric. *Stars and Stripes in Africa.* London: G. Routledge and Sons, Ltd., 1938.

Rotberg, Robert I. *A Political History of Tropical Africa.* New York: Harcourt, Brace and World, 1965.

Rudwick, Elliott. *W. E. B. Du Bois: Propagandist of the Negro Protest.* New York: Atheneum, 1968.

Schor, Joel. *Henry Highland Garnet: A Voice of Black Radicalism in the Nineteenth Century.* Westport, Conn.: Greenwood Press, 1977.

Schuman, Frederick L. *War and Diplomacy in the French Republic.* New York: Whittlesey House, 1931.

Shaloff, Stanley. *Reform in Leopold's Congo.* Richmond, Va.: John Knox Press, 1970.

Slade, Ruth M. *King Leopold's Congo: Aspects of the Development of Race Relations in the Congo Independent State.* London: Oxford University, Press, 1962.

Smith, Edwin W. *Aggrey of Africa: A Study in Black and White.* New York: Richard R. Smith, 1930.

Staudenraus, P. J. *The African Colonization Movement, 1816-1865.* New York: Columbia University Press, 1961.

Stuckey, Sterling. *The Ideological Origins of Black Nationalism.* Boston: Beacon Press, 1972.

Sundkler, Bengt G. M. *Bantu Prophets in South Africa.* London: Oxford University Press, 1961.

Taylor, Arnold H. *Travail and Triumph: Black Life and Culture in the South Since the Civil War.* Westport, Conn.: Greenwood Press, 1976.

Temperley, Harold W. V., ed. *A History of the Peace Conference of Paris.* 5 vols. London: H. Frowde, and Hodder & Stoughton, 1920-24.

Thompson, L. M. *The Unification of South Africa, 1902-1910.* Oxford: Clarendon Press. 1960.

Thornbrough, Emma Lou. *The Negro in Indiana: A Study of a Minority.* Indianapolis: Indiana Historical Bureau, 1957.

———. *T. Thomas Fortune, Militant Journalist.* Chicago: University of Chicago Press, 1972.

Thwaite, Daniel. *The Seething African Pot: A Study of Black Nationalism, 1882-1935.* London: Constable, 1936.

Townsend, Mary E. *The Rise and Fall of Germany's Colonial Empire, 1884-1918.* New York: MacMillan, 1930.

Tucker, Frank H. *The White Conscience.* New York: Frederick Ungar, 1968.

Tupper, Henry Allen. *Foreign Missions of the Southern Baptist Convention.* Philadelphia: American Baptist Publication Society, 1880.

Ullman, Victor. *Martin R. Delany, The Beginnings of Black Nationalism.* Boston: Beacon Press, 1971.

Uya, Okon Edet. *Black Brotherhood. Afro-Americans and Africa.* Lexington: D.C. Heath and Company, 1971.

Walker, Eric A. *A History of Southern Africa.* London: Longmans, Green, 1928.

Webster, J. B., and Boahen, A. A. *History of West Africa, The Revolutionary Years — 1815 to Independence.* New York: Praeger, 1970.

Weisbord, Robert G. *Ebony Kinship: Africa, Africans and the Afro-American.* Westport, Conn.: Greenwood Press, 1973.

Welch, Galbraith. *North African Prelude: The First Seven Thousand Years.* New York: W. Morrow, 1949.

Wellington, John H. *Southwest Africa and Its Human Issues.* Oxford: Clarendon Press, 1967.

Wesley, Charles. *Richard Allen: Apostle of Freedom.* Washington, D.C.: Associated, 1935.

Weston, Rubin. *Racism in U.S. Imperialism: The Influence of Racial Assumptions on American Foreign Policy, 1893-1946.* Columbia: University of South Carolina Press, 1972.

Who's Who in America. Vol. 14. Chicago: A. N. Marquis, 1926-27.

Wilson, Charles Morrow. *Liberia: Black Africa in Microcosm*. New York: Harper & Row, 1971.

Winks, Robbin W. *The Blacks in Canada: A History*. New Haven: Yale University Press, 1971.

Woodward, C. Vann. *The Strange Career of Jim Crow*. London: Oxford University Press, 1955.

Work, Ernest. *Ethiopia, A Pawn in European Diplomacy*. New Concord, O.: The Author, 1935.

Wright, Lenoir Chambers. *United States Policy Toward Egypt, 1830-1914*. New York: Exposition Press, 1969.

ARTICLES

Abramowitz, J. "Crossroads of Negro Thought: 1890-1895." *Social Education* 18 (March 1954): 117-20.

Al-Hajj, Muhammad A. "The Nile Valley: Egypt and the Sudan in the Nineteenth Century." In *Africa in the Nineteenth and Twentieth Centuries*, edited by Joseph C. Anene and Godfrey N. Brown, pp. 163-80. Ibadan: Ibadan University Press, 1966.

Ayandele, E. A. "The Magrib in the Nineteenth Century." In *Africa in the Nineteenth and Twentieth Centuries*, edited by Joseph C. Anene and Godfrey N. Brown, pp. 181-98. Ibadan: Ibadan University Press, 1966.

Baylen, Joseph O. "Senator John Tyler Morgan, E. D. Morel, and the Congo Reform Association." *Alabama Review* 15 (April 1962): 117-32.

Bell, Howard H. "Negro Nationalism: A Factor in Emigration Projects, 1858-1861." *Journal of Negro History* 47 (January 1962): 42-53.

"Benjamin Brawley." In *The Negro Caravan*, edited by Sterling A. Brown, Arthur P. Davis, and Ulysses Lee, p. 757. New York: Dryden Press, 1941.

"Black Is Black? A Selected and Introductory Bibliographical Guide to Current Resources on Relations Between the Black American and the African." *A Current Bibliography on African Affairs* 1 (May 1968): 5-9.

Blakely, Allison. "The John L. Waller Affair, 1895-1896." *Negro History Bulletin* 37 (February-March 1974): 216-18.

Bond, Horace Mann. "Howe and Isaacs in the Bush: The Ram in the Thicket." *Negro History Bulletin* 25 (December 1961):67-70, 72.

Boyd, Willis Dolmond. "Negro Colonization in the Reconstruction Era, 1865-1870." *Georgia Historical Quarterly* 40 (December 1956): 360-82.

Caulk, R. A. "Firearms and Princely Power in Ethiopia in the Nineteenth Century." *Journal of African History* 13 (1972): 609-30.

Clarke, John Henrik. "Africa and the American Negro Press." *Journal of Negro Education* 30 (Winter 1961): 64-68.

Contee, Clarence G. "Afro-Americans and Early Pan-Africanism." *Negro Digest* (February 1970): 24-30.

———. "Du Bois, the NAACP, and the Pan-African Congress of 1919." *Journal of Negro History* 57 (January 1972): 13-28.

———. "The Emergence of Du Bois as an African Nationalist." *Journal of Negro History* 54 (January 1969): 48-63.

———. "Ethiopia and the Pan-African Movement Before 1945." *Black World* 21 (February 1972): 41-45, 79-83.

Davis, John A. "Black Americans and United States Policy Toward Africa." *Journal of International Affairs* 23 (1969): 236-49.

Drake, St. Clair. "The American Negro's Reaction to Africa." *Africa Today* 14 (December 1967): 12-15.

———. "Hide My Face?—On Pan-Africanism and Negritude." In *Soon One Morning*, edited by Herbert Hill, pp. 78-105. New York: Knopf, 1963.

Drimmer, Melvin. "Review Article—*Black Exodus*." *Journal of American Studies* 4 (1970): 249-56.

Du Bois, W. E. B. "Of Our Spiritual Strivings." In *The Souls of Black Folk*, by W. E. Burghardt Du Bois, pp. 15-22. Greenwich, Conn.: Fawcett, 1953.

Fisher, Miles Mark. "Lott Cary, the Colonizing Missionary." *Journal of Negro History* 7 (October 1922): 380-418.

Fleming, Walter L. "'Pap' Singleton, the Moses of the Colored Exodus." *American Journal of Sociology* 15 (July 1909): 61-82.

Foster, Badi G. "United States Foreign Policy Toward Africa: An Afro-American Perspective." *Issue* (Summer 1972): 45-51.

Franklin, John H. "George Washington Williams, Historian." *Journal of Negro History* 31 (January 1946): 60-90.

Garvin, Roy. "Benjamin or 'Pap' Singleton and His Followers." *Journal of Negro History* 33 (January 1948): 7-23.

Gatewood, Willard B., Jr. "Black Americans and the Boer War, 1899-1902." *The South Atlantic Quarterly* 75 (Spring 1976): 226-44.

———. "Black Americans and the Quest for Empire, 1898-1903." *Journal of Southern History* 38 (November 1972): 545-66.

———. "A Negro Editor on Imperialism: John Mitchell, 1898-1901." *Journalism Quarterly* 49 (Spring 1972): 43-50.

Gillard, D. R. "Salisbury's African Policy and the Heligoland Offer of 1890." *English Historical Review* 75 (October 1960): 631-53.

Hallett, Robin. "Changing European Attitudes to Africa." In *The Cambridge History of Africa*, edited by John E. Flint, 5: 458-96. Cambridge: Cambridge University Press, 1976.

Hammond, Harold E. "American Interest in the Exploration of the Dark Continent." *The Historian* 18 (Spring 1956): 202-29.

Hargreaves, John D. "The European Partition of West Africa." In *History of West Africa*, edited by J. F. A. Ajayi and Michael Crowder, 2: 402-23. New York: Columbia University Press, 1973.

———. "Liberia: The Price of Independence." *Odu: A Journal of West African Studies* 6 (October 1971): 3-20.

Harlan, Louis R. "Booker T. Washington and the White Man's Burden." *American Historical Review* 71 (January 1966): 441-67.

Keto, Clement T. "Black Americans and South Africa, 1890-1910." *A Current Bibliography on African Affairs* 5 (July 1972): 383-406.

King, Kenneth J. "The American Negro as Missionary to East Africa: A Critical Aspect of African Evangelism." *African Historical Studies* 3 (1970): 5-22.

Kirk-Greene, A. H. M. "America in the Niger Valley: A Colonization Centenary." *Phylon* 23 (Fall 1962): 225-39.

Limoli, Donald A. "Francesco Crispi's Quest for Empire—and Victories—in Ethiopia." In *The Partition of Africa: Illusion or Necessity?*, edited by Robert O. Collins, pp. 111-23. New York: John Wiley & Sons, 1969.

Logan, Rayford. "The American Negro's View of Africa." In *Africa Seen by American Negroes*, edited by John A. Davis, pp. 218-22. New York: American Society of African Culture, 1958.

———. "The Historical Aspects of Pan-Africanism, 1900-1945." In *Pan Africanism Reconsidered.*, edited by the American Society of African Cultures, pp. 37-52. Berkeley: University of California, 1962.

———. "The Operation of the Mandate System in Africa." *Journal of Negro History* 13 (October 1928): 423-77.

Louis, William Roger. "Roger Casement and the Congo." *Journal of African History* 5 (1964): 99-120.

―――. "The Triumph of the Congo Reform Movement, 1905-1908." In *Boston University Papers on Africa*, edited by Jeffrey Butler, 2: 267-302. Boston: Boston University Press, 1966.

―――. "The United States and the African Peace Settlement of 1919: The Pilgrimage of George Louis Beer." *Journal of African History* 4 (1963): 413-33.

Lynch, Hollis R. "Pan-Negro Nationalism in the New World Before 1862." In *Boston University Papers on Africa*, edited by Jeffrey Butler, 2: 147-79. Boston: Boston University Press, 1966.

MacMaster, Richard K. "Henry Highland Garnet and the African Civilization Society." *Journal of Presbyterian History* 48 (Summer 1970): 95-112.

Manheim, Frank J. "The United States and Ethiopia: A Study in American Imperialism." *Journal of Negro History* 17 (April 1932): 141-55.

Marcus, Harold G. "The Black Men Who Turned White: European Attitudes Towards Ethiopians, 1850-1900." *Archiv Orientalni* 39 (1971): 155-66.

―――. "A History of the Negotiations Concerning the Border Between Ethiopia and British East Africa, 1897-1914." In *Boston University Papers on Africa*, edited by Jeffrey Butler, 2: 237-65. Boston: Boston University Press, 1966.

―――. "Imperialism and Expansionism in Ethiopia From 1865 to 1900." In *The History and Politics of Colonialism, 1870-1914*, edited by L. H. Gann and Peter Duignan, pp. 420-61. Cambridge: Cambridge University Press, 1969.

Matthews, Fred H. "Robert Park, Congo Reform and Tuskegee: The Molding of a Race Relations Expert, 1905-1913." *Canadian Journal of History* 8 (March 1973): 37-65.

Mbata, J. Congress. "Race and Resistance in South Africa." In *The African Experience*, edited by John N. Paden and Edward W. Soja, pp. 210-32. Evanston, Ill.: Northwestern University Press, 1970.

Meier, August. "Negro Class Structure and Ideology in the Age of Booker T. Washington." *Phylon* 23 (Fall 1962): 258-66.

Moses, Wilson J. "Civilizing Missionary: A Study of Alexander Crummell." *Journal of Negro History* 60 (April 1975): 229-51.

―――. "The Poetics of Ethiopianism: W. E. B. Du Bois and Literary Black

Nationalism." *American Literature* 47 (November 1975): 411-26.

Mower, J. H. "The Republic of Liberia." *Journal of Negro History* 32 (July 1947): 265-306.

Murray, Percy E. "Crusading Editor, Harry Clay Smith." *Blacks in Ohio History* 4 (1976): 31-38.

O'Connor, James. "The Meaning of Economic Imperialism." In *Imperialism and Underdevelopment: A Reader*, edited by Robert I. Rhodes, pp. 101-50. New York: Monthly Review Press, 1971.

Padgett, James A. "The Ministers to Liberia and Their Diplomacy." *Journal of Negro History* 22 (January 1937): 50-92.

Pankhurst, Richard. "Ethiopia Emperor Menelik II Repulsed Italian Invasion, 1895." In *The Africa Reader: Colonial Africa*, edited by Wilfred Cartey and Martin Kilson, pp. 33-39. New York: Vantage Books, 1970.

———. "Italian Settlement Policy in Eritrea and Its Repercussions, 1889-1896." In *Boston University Papers on Africa*, edited by Jeffrey Butler, 1: 119-56. Boston: Boston University Press, 1964.

Rathbone, Richard. "World War I and Africa: Introduction." *Journal of African History* 19 (1978): 1-9.

Record, Wilson. "Negro Intellectuals and Negro Movements in Historical Perspective." *American Quarterly* 8 (Spring 1956): 3-20.

Redkey, Edwin S. "Bishop Turner's African Dream." *Journal of American History* 54 (September 1967): 271-90.

———. "The Meaning of Africa to Afro-Americans, 1890-1914." *Black Academy Review* (Spring-Summer 1972): 5-37.

Reid, Inez Smith. "Black Americans and Africa." In *The Black American Reference Book*, edited by Mabel M. Smythe, pp. 648-83. Englewood Cliffs, N.J.: Prentice-Hall, 1976.

Rubenson, Sven. "Adwa 1896: The Resounding Protest." In *Protest and Power in Black Africa*, edited by Robert I. Rotberg and Ali A. Mazrui, pp. 113-42. New York: Oxford University Press, 1970.

———. "The Protectorate Paragraph of the Wichale Treaty." *Journal of African History* 5 (1964): 242-83.

Scott, Clifford. "Up the Congo Without a Paddle: Images of Blackest Africa in American Fiction." *North Dakota Quarterly* 40 (Autumn 1972): 7-19.

Scott, William R. "Black Nationalism and the Italo-Ethiopian Conflict, 1934-1936." *Journal of Negro History* 63 (April 1978): 118-34.

Shepperson, George. "The American Negro and Africa." *British Association for American Studies* 8 (June 1964): 3-20.

―――. "Ethiopianism and African Nationalism." *Phylon* 14 (Spring 1953): 9-18.

―――. "Notes on Negro American Influences on the Emergence of African Nationalism." *Journal of African History* 1 (1960): 299-312.

Sherwood, Henry Noble. "Paul Cuffe." *Journal of Negro History* 8 (April 1923): 153-229.

―――. "Paul Cuffe and His Contribution to the American Colonization Society." *Proceedings of the Mississippi Valley Historical Association for the Year 1912-1913*, 6 (1913): 371-402.

Spivey, Donald. "The African Crusade for Black Industrial Schooling." *Journal of Negro History* 63 (January 1978): 1-17.

Stengers, Jean. "The Congo Free State and the Belgian Congo Before 1914." In *The History and Politics of Colonialism, 1870-1914*, edited by L. H. Gann and Peter Duignan, pp. 261-92. Cambridge: Cambridge University Press, 1969.

―――. "The Place of Leopold II in the History of Colonization." In *The Partition of Africa: Illusion or Necessity*, edited by Robert O. Collins, pp. 28-43. New York: John Wiley & Sons, 1969.

Thornbrough, Emma Lou. "American Negro Newspapers, 1880-1914." *Business History Review* 40 (Winter 1966): 467-90.

Thorpe, Earl E. "Africa in the Thought of Negro Americans." *Negro History Bulletin* 23 (October 1959): 5-10, 22.

Toll, William. "Free Men, Freedmen, and Race: Black Social Theory in the Gilded Age." *Journal of Southern History* (November 1978): 573-96.

Wahle, Kathleen. "Alexander Crummell: Black Evangelist and Pan-Negro Nationalist." *Phylon* (Fourth Quarter 1968): 388-95.

Weisbord, Robert. "Africa, Africans, and the Afro-American: Images and Identities in Transition." *Race* 10 (January 1969): 305-21.

―――. "Black America and the Italian-Ethiopian Crisis: An Episode in Pan-Negroism." *The Historian* 34 (1972): 230-41.

Williams, Walter L. "Black American Attitudes Towards Africa, 1877-1900." *Pan-African Journal* 4 (Spring 1971): 173-94.

―――. "Black Journalism's Opinions About Africa During the Late Nineteenth Century." *Phylon* 34 (September 1973): 224-35.

―――. "Nineteenth Century Pan-Africanist: John Henry Smyth, United

States Minister to Liberia, 1878-1885." *Journal of Negro History* 63 (January 1978): 18-25.

Williamson, Joel. "W. E. B. Du Bois as a Hegelian." In *What Was Freedom's Price?* edited by David G. Sansing, pp. 21-49. Jackson: University Press of Mississippi, 1978.

Woods, Randall B. "Black America's Challenge to European Colonialism: The Waller Affair, 1891-95." *Journal of Black Studies* 7 (September 1976): 57-77.

Wylde, Augustus B. "The Battle of Adowa." In *Travellers in Ethiopia*, edited by Richard Pankhurst, pp. 121-27. London: Oxford University Press, 1965.

DISSERTATIONS

Beecher, Lloyd N., Jr. "The State Department and Liberia, 1908-1941: A Heterogeneous Record." Ph.D. dissertation, University of Georgia, 1970.

Bodie, Charles A. "The Images of Africa in the Black American Press, 1890-1930." Ph.D. dissertation, Indiana University, 1975.

Booth, Alan R. "Americans in South Africa, 1784-1870." Ph.D. dissertation, Boston University, 1964.

Coan, Josephus R. "The Expansion of Missions of the African Methodist Episcopal Church in South Africa, 1896-1908." Ph.D. dissertation, Hartford Seminary Foundation, 1961.

Fenderson, Lewis H. "Development of the Negro Press, 1827-1948." Ph.D. dissertation, University of Pittsburgh, 1948.

Goldstein, Myra S. "The Genesis of Modern American Relations with South Africa, 1895-1914." Ph.D. dissertation, State University of New York at Buffalo, 1972.

Gossett, Edward F. "The American Protestant Missionary Endeavor in North Africa From Its Origin to 1939." Ph.D. dissertation, University of California at Los Angeles, 1960.

Haney, James E. "Theodore Roosevelt and Afro-Americans, 1901-1912." Ph.D. dissertation, Kent State University, 1971.

Karanja, Josphat N. "United States Attitudes and Policy Toward the International African Association, 1876-1886." Ph.D. dissertation, Princeton University, 1962.

Keto, Clement. "American Involvement in South Africa, 1870-1915: The Role of Americans in the Creation of Modern South Africa." Ph.D. dissertation, Georgetown University, 1972.

McStallworth, Paul. "The United States and the Congo Question, 1884-
    1914." Ph.D. dissertation, Ohio State University, 1954.
Magubane, Bernard. "The American Negro's Conception of Africa: A Study
    in the Ideology of Pride and Prejudice." Ph.D. dissertation, University
    of California at Los Angeles, 1967.
Noer, Thomas J. "The United States and South Africa, 1870-1914." Ph.D.
    dissertation, University of Minnesota, 1972.
Olton, Roy. "Problems of American Foreign Relations in the African Area
    During the Nineteenth Century." Ph.D. dissertation, Fletcher School
    of Law and Diplomacy, Tufts University, 1954.
Scott, Clifford H. "American Images of Sub-Sahara Africa, 1900-1939."
    Ph.D. dissertation, University of Iowa, 1968.
Scott, William. "A Study of Afro-American and Ethiopian Relations, 1896-
    1941." Ph.D. dissertation, Princeton University, 1971.
Stuckey, Ples Sterling. "The Spell of Africa: The Development of Black
    Nationalist Theory, 1829-1945." Ph.D. dissertation, Northwestern
    University, 1973.

INDEX

Abyssinia of Today (Skinner), 197
Adams, Henry, 11
Address to the Slaves (Garnet), 25
Aduwa. *See* Battle of Aduwa
Aenmey, A. E., 212
Africa: Afro-American ambivalence towards, 5-6, 7, 21, 58, 148, 160, 178, 183; Afro-American commercial interest in, 48, 49, 52, 71, 75, 85, 121, 153, 220; Afro-American developmental projects in, 7; and Afro-American diplomats, 23-24, 26, 46, 47, 70-71, 75, 78, 94, 127-30, 196, 210-17, 219, 226, 271; and Afro-American educators, 49, 75, 241; Afro-American identification with, 10, 12, 19, 21, 27, 75, 93, 183, 193, 269; and Afro-American intellectuals, 19-20, 23, 26, 49, 242, 243; Afro-American knowledge of, 6; and Afro-American leaders, 6, 7, 26, 27, 40-41, 49, 58, 99, 251, 255, 256; and the Afro-American masses, 6, 7, 9, 10, 13, 24, 30, 38, 39, 43, 49, 78, 104, 194, 210, 271-72; and the Afro-American middle class, 7, 10, 13, 19-20, 23, 28, 30, 38-39, 47, 49, 58, 68-69, 104, 142, 148-49, 152, 156, 160-61, 178, 183, 269, 270, 271, 272, 273, 274; and Afro-American missionaries, 7, 10, 22-23, 39, 41, 46, 69, 77, 78, 95, 96, 102-103, 122, 123, 142, 144, 156-58, 159, 183, 215, 218, 226, 271, 273; and the Afro-American press, 10, 42-43, 46, 47, 48, 89, 92, 94, 96, 103, 125, 126, 143, 146, 151, 154, 155, 178-79, 180, 182, 194, 219, 223, 226, 241, 242, 244, 246, 247-48, 251, 252, 270, 271; and the Afro-American religious community, 10, 21-22, 39, 42, 69, 89, 95, 96-97, 123-24, 143, 146, 156-57, 192-93, 194, 241, 246, 249, 251, 257, 270-71; and Afro-American travelers, 9, 78, 151-52, 218, 226, 271; and the Afro-American upper class, 11, 13, 23; and American organizations, 6, 99; and antebellum free blacks, 3, 6, 8, 9, 20, 24, 30, 192, 208; commercial companies in, 117-18, 119; and European and white American authors, 5; European and white American stereotypes of, 5; forced labor in, 84, 92, 100, 103, 121; and industrial education, 49, 75-77, 130; and pro-Boer sentiment among Afro-Americans, 146, 149, 150-51; slaves and, 6, 9, 20, 30, 192; "special duty" of Afro-Americans to, 10, 19, 21, 23, 30, 32, 38, 39, 42, 51, 58, 69, 71, 90, 104, 248, 274; white American commercial interest in, 142, 197. *See also* African uprisings; Africans of the diaspora; Afro-American-African relations; Emigration; Imperialism in Africa; Slavery in Africa
"Africa and the Descendants of Africa" (speech), 41
"Africa at the Peace Table and the Descendants of Africans in Our American Democracy" (speech), 251

"Africa for the Africans" (slogan and movement), 17, 27, 28, 71, 86, 125-26, 143, 157, 158, 220, 227, 246, 247, 253, 255, 270
"Africa in the World Democracy" (speech), 251
African Association, 55, 57
African Civilization Society, 25, 26, 27, 193
"African Experiences" (speech), 52
"African in Africa, and the African in America, The" (speech), 47
African Methodist Episcopal Church, 10, 22, 39-40, 41, 96, 143-44, 157-58, 199, 214, 215
African Methodist Episcopal Zion Church, 55
African nexus, 5-6, 10, 12-13, 39, 260, 267, 274
African personality, 22
African Repository, 24
African Times, 48
African uprisings, 121, 124, 125-26, 156-58, 175, 179, 181, 241, 272
Africans of the diaspora, 6, 20, 241, 259
Afrikaner National party, 160
Afro-American: promotion of term, 44
Afro-American-African relations, 5, 259
Afro-American Council, 55, 56, 246
Afro-American Press Association, 149
Afro-American relations. *See* Africa; United States
Aggrey, James E. K., 76
Ahmad, Muhammad (the Mahdi), 176-77, 181, 182
Akim Trading Company, 12
Alexander, Charles, 91, 95, 215, 220, 221, 224
Alexander, William T., 39
Alexander's Magazine, 91, 219-20, 221, 224
Algeciras Conference (1906), 173, 179
Ali, Muhammad, 175, 176
Allen, Richard, 22
Allen University, 50

Allied campaign, 124, 237, 238, 239, 244, 245
Al-Marsa Convention (1883), 173
Alsace-Lorraine, 172, 173
AME Church Review, 44, 70, 144, 198, 199
AME Women's Home and Foreign Missionary Society, 69
American Baptist Foreign Mission Society of Boston, 96
American Baptist Free Mission Society, 70
American Baptist Missionary Convention, 70
American Colonization Society, 8, 9, 22, 24, 69, 207, 208
American commission to Liberia, 222-24, 225
American Congo Company, 101
American Congo lobby, 101
American Educational Association, 70
American Episcopal Church, 71
American Geographical Society, 29
American Missionary Association, 41
American Negro Academy, 22, 51, 52
Anglo-Boer War, 56, 138-54, 156, 159, 161, 195, 245, 272; fate of Africans in, 147-48, 154
Anglo-Egyptian Agreement (1889), 178, 182
Anglo-French contests in Northeast Africa, 174, 175, 177-78, 182
Anglo-French Declaration (1899), 173, 178, 182
Anglo-German Agreement (1886), 117
Anglo-German contest for East Africa, 117, 118
Anglo-Portuguese Treaty (1884), 83
Anti-emigration sentiment, 7, 213
Anti-German sentiment: Afro-American, 125-27, 241, 272
Anti-imperialism and anti-expansionism, 31, 44, 139, 255
Antonelli, Pietro (Count), 189
Apartheid, 160

Arabi, Ahmad (Colonel), 175-76, 181
"Are the Present Inhabitants of Egypt
    Identical with the Ancient Egyptians?"
    (paper), 52
Armistice (World War I), 238, 239
Arnett, Benjamin William, 35, 41
Associated Literary Press of the United
    States, 85
Associated Negro Press, 43
Associated Press, 43
Association for the Study of Negro Life
    and History, 48
Atlanta compromise speech, 49
Atlanta pogrom (1906), 92
Atlanta University, 214, 242, 243, 251
Avery College, 26

Back-to-Africa sentiment, 7, 9, 42, 69,
    143
Baker, Newton D., 225, 257
Baltimore *Afro-American*, 249
Baratieri, Oreste (General), 191, 196
Barber, Jesse Max, 81, 92-93, 95, 126
Barclay, Arthur, 217
Barnet, Claude A., 43
Barnett, Ferdinand, 42
Battle of Aduwa, 191, 192, 193, 194,
    196, 199, 200
Beauchamp, Earl, 87
Beer, George Louis, 239-40
Bennett College, 49
Berlin West African Conference (1884-
    85), 28, 31, 65, 67-68, 70, 71, 72,
    73, 74, 81, 83-84, 86, 87, 92, 96,
    101, 116, 117, 177, 189, 240
Bethel Literary and Historical Society,
    52-53
Bismarck, Otto von (Chancellor), 67,
    118, 172
Black experience in America, The, 5,
    12, 194, 260, 274
Blackshear, Edward L., 97-98
Blyden, Edward Wilmot, 22
Boer Relief Fund, 140
Bonaparte, Napoleon, 174-75, 195

Booker T. Washington Agricultural and
    Industrial Institute, 76
Boone, Clinton C., 95-96
Boston Guardian, 91, 126
Boston Literary and Historical Associa-
    tion, 51
Boston University, 220, 249
Bowen, J. W. E., 249-50
Brawley, Benjamin, 235, 246-47
British Church Missionary Society, 116
British East African Association, 117
British South Africa Company, 118, 153
Brooklyn *National Monitor*, 70
Brooklyn *Sunbeam*, 70
Brotherhood of Sleeping Car Porters,
    245
Brotherhood theme, 58, 69, 94, 99,
    252, 259, 274
Bruce, John Edward [pseud. Bruce
    Grit], 48, 49, 52, 74, 152, 199,
    245-46, 267
Brussels Anti-Slavery Conference
    (1890), 76
Brussels Conference (1876), 28-30
Bryan, William Jennings, 141
Buckner, George W., 94

Calloway, James Nathan, 76
Campbell, Robert, 26-27, 28
Caprivi, Graf von, 118
Carey, Lott, 3
Carter, James G., 130
Cary, Mary Ann Shadd, 21, 27
Casement, Roger, 87
Centennial Baptist College, 250
Central Africa. *See* Congo
Central Tennessee College, 249
Chaltin, Louis Napoleon, 102
Chase, W. Calvin, 42, 54, 135, 148-49,
    221, 224, 245, 253
Chatham *Provincial Freedom*, 21
Cheeks, R. M., 52
Chicago *Broad Ax*, 150-51, 182, 195,
    245
Chicago Conservator, 42, 51

Chicago University, 247
Chicago World's Fair (1893), 41
Christian Educator, 46
Christian Recorder, 40, 69, 145
Cincinnati Law School, 85
Civil War, 9, 38, 39, 45, 142
"Civilizing mission" in Africa, 10, 13, 19, 20, 22, 24, 29, 30, 31, 32, 37, 42, 46, 51, 53, 58, 86, 90, 98, 104, 129, 144, 211, 227, 241, 269, 271
Clark, Alexander, 214
Clark University, 87
Clarke University, 214
Clemenceau, Georges, 258
Cleveland Gazette, 42, 48, 54, 73, 90-91, 124, 126, 150, 181, 194, 200, 226, 248
Cleveland, Grover, 51, 68, 84
Colored American Magazine, 93-94, 103, 125, 155, 159, 199-200, 220, 221-22, 224-25
Colored Citizen (Boston), 91
Colored National Convention (1853), 25
Columbus *People's Journal*, 70
Commission of inquiry, 96, 102
Committee on Foreign Affairs (House), 140
Committee on Foreign Relations (Senate), 93, 96, 140, 223, 225
Committee on Public Information, 247
Concessionary companies, 84, 87, 102, 119
Congo, 81-105; atrocities, 84, 86, 87, 88, 91, 93, 94, 95, 97, 98, 101, 103, 104, 105, 183, 254, 272-73; controversy, 87, 89, 93, 94, 97, 98, 102, 103, 104, 272; Free State, 84, 85, 86, 87, 88, 89, 97, 102; reform movement, 88, 95, 97, 98, 100
Congo News Letter, The, 100
Congo Reform Association, 87-88, 89, 90, 92, 93, 97, 98, 99, 100, 101, 102, 104
Congress of Berlin (1878), 172, 174
Congress on Africa (1895), 46-48, 73

Cook, George W., 97
Cooper, Anna J., 57
Cooper, E. E., 43, 45, 53-54, 129, 147, 148
Coopers' Institute, 26
Coppin, Fanny Jackson, 144
Coppin, Levi Jenkins, 135, 144
Council on African Affairs, 243
Crisis, The, 200, 242, 244, 258
Crispi, Francesco, 191
Crowe, Sybil, 67
"Cruelty in the Congo Country" (Washington), 99
Crummell, Alexander, 22-23, 24, 29, 42, 53
Cuffee, Paul, 7-8, 122

Darkwater (Du Bois), 255
Dean, Harry, 113, 122-23, 127, 152-53, 154
De Brazza, Savorgnan, 37
Delany, Martin Robison, 17, 26-28, 71, 121-22, 125, 127
Delimitation Treaty: (1892), 213-14, 215; (1907), 216, 217, 219-20
"Destiny of the Darker Races, The" (speech), 245
Deveaux, John H., 42, 187, 195
Dossen, James J., 221
Douglass, Frederick, 3, 20-21, 25, 26, 48, 178, 180, 181
Douglass' Monthly, 21
"Dual mandate," 31
Dube, John L., 158
Du Bois, W. E. B., 12, 48, 56-57, 90, 95, 196, 200, 242-44, 245, 248, 249, 252, 254-55, 257-59, 267, 271
Dudley, George A., 195-96

"Early Christianity in Africa" (address), 85
East Africa, 113-33; and European colonization, 115-16; and the German East Africa Company, 118, 119; and the Imperial British East Africa Com-

pany, 119; as possible colony for Afro-Americans, 121-24; and the Afro-American press, 24-27; strategic considerations, 115, 237. *See also* Anglo-German Contest for East Africa

Ecumenical Missionary Conference (1900), 145

Egypt: Afro-American identification with, 179-80, 183

Elias Turner Memorial Chapel, 215

Elliot, Robert Brown, 50

Ellis, William Henry, 199

Emigration: Afro-Americans and Africa, 3-4, 7, 8, 9, 10, 11, 12, 13, 19, 20-21, 22, 23, 24, 25, 26, 27, 30, 38, 39, 40, 41, 44, 47, 49, 50, 52, 53, 55, 69, 72, 75, 85, 90, 91, 104, 121-23, 127, 129, 143, 145, 148, 149, 153, 210, 213, 214-15, 216, 220, 255; Afro-Americans and British West Indies, 8; Afro-Americans and Canada, 8, 22, 27; Afro-Americans and the Congo, 88; Afro-Americans and Cuba, 129; Afro-Americans and East Africa, 121-22, 123, 127-29; Afro-Americans and Ghana, 12, 243; Afro-Americans and Haiti, 8, 22, 71; Afro-Americans and the insular possessions, 54, 75; Afro-Americans and Liberia, 8, 9, 10, 11, 19, 71, 75, 91, 215; Afro-Americans and Madagascar, 127-29; Afro-Americans and Mexico, 199; Afro-Americans and Mozambique (Portuguese East Africa), 122-23; Afro-Americans and the Niger area, 26-28; Afro-Americans and Sierra Leone, 8; slave petitions and, 7

Encyclopedia Africana, 243

Entente of 1904, 176

Ethiopia, 187-203, 207; Afro-American identification with, 192-93, 220; and the Afro-American press, 194-96; and the Italian hostility, 189-92; U.S. policy towards, 197-99. *See also*

Battle of Aduwa; Italo-Ethiopian War of 1895-96 and of 1935-36; and Menelik II (King)

"Ethiopia, Thou Land of Our Fathers" (anthem), 193

"Ethiopian" empire, 122-23

Ethiopianism: in South Africa, 125, 143, 144, 157, 193

"The Ethiopians—Who Were They?" (paper), 52

"Exodusters," 11

Falkner, Roland P., 223, 225

Firestone Rubber Company, 76

Fisk Herald, 122

Fisk University, 76, 152, 242

Foreign Slave Trade Act (1808), 6

Fortune, T. Thomas, 42, 44-45, 46, 47, 48, 52, 54, 55, 73, 74, 75, 90, 94-95, 113, 124, 126, 155-56, 160, 181, 200, 219, 220, 221, 224

Fourteen Points, 239

Franco-German War (1870-71), 172

Frederick Douglass' Paper, 21, 27

Free African Society, 7, 22

Freedmen's Aid and Southern Education Society, 46

Fugitive Slave Act (1850), 8

Gammon Theological Seminary, 46, 249, 250

Garnet, Henry Highland, 17, 22, 25-26, 27, 28, 193, 211, 212

Garvey, Marcus, 9, 45, 48, 193, 225, 259

George, David Lloyd, 237

German Colonization Society, 118

German East African Company, 118, 119

Germany: unification of (1871), 116

Gibbs, Ida, 130

Gibbs, Mifflin Wistar, 113, 129-30, 196

Gibson, E. D., 151

Gold Coast Aborigines, 48

Gordon, Charles George, 176, 177

Grandison, Charles Nelson, 49-50
Graves, A. L., 196
Gray, Henry Clay, 45
Gray's Inn, 55
Grimke, Archibald Henry, 51
Groton Academy, 130
Guess, H. Augustus, 196

Haiti: Afro-American diplomats in, 85;
    Afro-American missionaries in, 70, 71
Haley, Alex, 6
Half-Century Magazine, 253
Hall, G. Stanley, 87
Hammond, E. W. S., 47
Hampton Institute, 49, 89
Harris, George W., 224-25
Harrison, Benjamin, 85, 127
Harvard University, 27, 51, 242, 247
Hawkins, Henry P., 96
Hay, John, 101, 139, 141, 197
Heard, William Harrison, 214-15
Hearst, William Randolph, 88, 93
Hedgeman, Ethel O., 97
Heligoland Treaty (1890), 117, 118,
    124
Hendley, Charles Jr., 65, 73, 180-81
Herbert, R. Henri, 169, 179, 180
Hertzog, James B. M., 160
Hicks, Pasha, 177
Hill, David J., 197
History of the African Methodist
    Episcopal Church (Payne), 39
History of the African Methodist
    Episcopal Church, A (Smith), 73
History of the Colored Race in America
    (Alexander), 39
History of the Negro Race in America
    (Williams), 30
Holly, Theodore, 27, 71-72
Hood, Solomon Porter, 70-71
Horizon: A Journal of the Color Line, 95
House, Edward H., 237, 238
Houston Daily Post, 225
Howard University, 50, 70, 74, 97, 210,
    225, 247, 249
Hunt, Leigh, 182

Hunt, Nathan, 257
Hunt, William Henry, 130
Huntington, Collis P., 85
Huntsville Gazette, 73, 178, 180-81

Imperial British East Africa Company,
    117, 118
Imperialism in Africa: European justifica-
    tion of, 10, 13, 26, 31, 49, 269
Indianapolis Colored World, 147
Indianapolis Freeman, 40, 43, 45, 126,
    146, 147, 153, 181, 195, 219,
    223-24, 244
Indianapolis Recorder, 146-47
Indianapolis World, 147
International Association for the Explora-
    tion and Civilization of Africa (Interna-
    tional African Association, later
    International Association of the Congo),
    29, 68, 83-84, 85, 96, 116
International Committee of Colored
    Men's Young Men's Christian Associ-
    ation (YMCA), 124
International Conference on the Negro
    (1912), 77
International Congress of Women
    (1904), 256
International Congress of Women for
    Permanent Peace (1919), 255, 256
International Education Board, 76
International Peace Congress (1904),
    87, 98
Isaacs, Harold, 104, 193
Ismail Pasha (Khedive of Egypt), 175
Ismail Pasha (son of Muhammad Ali),
    176
Italo-Ethiopian War: of 1895-96, 120,
    174, 177-189, 190-91, 192-93, 195,
    196, 200, 272; of 1935-36, 198, 200,
    259. See also Ethiopia

Jeltz, Fred L., 149, 150, 195
Jernagin, William H., 257
Jim Crow, 142
Johnson, Henry Theodore, 145
Johnson, Hilary Richard Wright, 211

Johnson, James Weldon, 235, 247, 251-52, 256
Johnson, Rosamond, 251
Johnson, Sol C., 253, 259
Johnston, Harry, 117
Jones, Absalom, 22
Jordan, Lewis G., 246
Jubilee Singers, 152

Kansas City *Western Recorder*, 127
Kasai Company (Compagnie du Kasai), 86, 102-103
Kassai Herald, 76, 86, 96, 103
Kealing, H. T., 198-99
Kipling, Rudyard, 37
Knight Commander of the Distinguished Order of the Nile, 225
Knight Commander of the Liberia Order of African Redemption, 211
Knights of Pythias, 149
Knox, George L., 35, 43, 45, 146, 147, 195, 219, 223, 244-45
Knox, P. C., 222
Kruger, Paul, 137

Lagos Weekly Record, 48
"Land of Our Fathers, The" (article), 50
Lapsley, Samuel, 86
League of Nations, 100, 237, 240, 252, 254, 256, 257
Lee, Benjamin F., 40
Lenin, Vladimir, 237
Leopold II (King), 28-29, 37, 67, 81, 83-85, 86, 87, 88, 89, 92, 93, 94-95, 96, 98, 99, 100, 101, 102, 103, 104, 116, 254, 272
Liberia, 189, 205-33; Afro-American identification with, 205, 220, 221; and Afro-American press, 219-22, 223-26; boundary disputes of, 209, 211, 212, 213; and Delcaration of Independence, 207, 208, 217; and the European threat, 207-208, 209, 211; and France, 211, 213-16; and Great Britain, 207, 209, 211-13, 215, 216,

217; U.S. policy towards, 207-208, 210, 211, 213, 222-25. *See also* American commission to Liberia
Liberia College, 74, 211
Liberian commission to the United States, 221-22, 223-24. *See also* Liberia, U.S. policy towards
Liberian Development Association, 91, 215, 220
Lisbon Geographical Society, 119
Lide, A. E., 150
"Lift Every Voice and Sing" (anthem), 251
Lincoln Institute (later Lincoln University), 24, 51, 70
Livingstone College, 76
Locke, Alain, 267
Lodge, Henry Cabot, 93, 223
Logan, Rayford W., 241
Lott Carey Baptist Home and Foreign Mission Convention, 95-96
Loudin, Frederick J., 57, 135, 152
Loyal Order of the Sons of Africa, 74
Lugard, Frederick, 31, 119
Lynch, Hollis, 9
Lyon, Ernest, 205, 215-17, 222, 223, 225

McCormick, H. P., 99
McCoy, William D., 214
McKinley, William, 41, 130, 138, 139, 140, 141, 147, 149, 150
Mackinnon, William, 117
Mahdism, 176-77, 182
Maji-Maji Rebellion (1905-1907), 121
Makoko, 37
Makonnen (General), 190, 195, 199-200
Mandate system, 100, 237, 238, 239, 240-41, 250, 252
Maryland Industrial and Agricultural Institution for the Education of Colored Youths, 216
Mason, M. C. B., 46-47
Maxeke, Marshal, 139
Mechanics Savings Bank, 149

Menelik II (King), 189-92, 193, 194,
    195, 196, 197-98, 199, 200
Messenger, 245, 254
Methodist Episcopal Church, 47, 216,
    250
"Methodist Episcopal Church and the
    Evangelization of Africa, The"
    (speech), 46
Migration of Afro-Americans within the
    United States, 10-12, 127
Mission Herald, 246
"Missionary tokenism," 39
Mitchell, John P. Jr., 43, 54, 149-50,
    248
Moore, Fred R., 44, 90, 93-94, 95, 125,
    220-21, 224, 244, 248, 252-53
Morehouse College, 247
Morel, Edmund D., 87, 89, 101
Morgan College, 249
Morgan, John T., 88
Morris Brown University, 69
Morris, Charles S., 145-46
Morris, E. C., 250
Morrison, William M., 102, 103
Moton, Robert R., 257
Muckraking journalism, 88
Muhammad, Abdallahi ibn (Khalifa),
    177, 182
Mwanga, 118, 119

Natchez College, 246
National Association for the Advance-
    ment of Colored People (NAACP),
    47, 57, 199, 241-42, 243, 247, 249,
    251-52, 257
National Association for Colored
    Women's Clubs, 256
National Baptist Convention, 100, 145,
    246, 250
National Emigration Convention, 27-28,
    71
Nationalism, 8, 9, 13, 25, 260
Native Carrier Corps, 124
Natives Land Act (1913), 160
Negative propaganda about Africa, 7
Negritude, 22
"Negro genius," 247

Negro Historical Society, 52
Negro Ministerial Council, 250
"Negro Nationality," 27, 71
Negro Society for Historical Research,
    48
Negro World, The, 45
Negro Young People's Christian and
    Educational Congress, 158
New Orleans University, 46, 216, 249
New York Age, 42, 44, 45, 48, 54, 94,
    97, 102, 126, 156, 158, 200, 219,
    224, 244, 248, 252, 257
New York American, 88, 93
New York *American Baptist* (later the
    Baptist Weekly), 70
New York *Amsterdam News*, 45
New York *Anglo-African*, 26
New York Central College, 70
New York Colonization Society, 76
New York Freeman, 42, 44, 74, 219
New York Globe, 42, 44, 242
New York *Rumor*, 44
Newton Theological Seminary, 85
Niagara Movement, 57, 95, 199
Nicaragua: Afro-American diplomats in,
    252
Niger Expedition (1859-60), 27-28
Norfolk Journal and Guide, 45
Nova Scotia Conference (1899), 145

Oberlin College, 23, 129, 130, 255
On Two Hemispheres (Jordan), 246
Oneida Institute, 25
Ottoman empire, 171, 172, 173, 174,
    175, 176
Outlook, 99
Overton, Anthony, 253
Owen, Chandler, 245, 254

Pan-African Conference (1900), 50, 55-
    57, 73, 152
Pan-African Congress (1919), 130, 257-
    59, 267
Pan-African Congresses (1919, 1921,
    1923, 1927, 1945), 57, 242, 243,
    259

Pan-Africanism, 6, 13, 22, 44, 55, 57, 210, 243, 258, 259, 274
Paris Exposition (1900), 56
Park, Robert E., 99, 100
Parsons Weekly Blade, 150, 196
Pass system. *See* South Africa, pass system in
Paul Quinn College, 199
Payne, Beverly Yates, 213-14
Payne, Daniel Alexander, 39, 40, 52
Peace Conference (1919), 239, 240, 245, 248, 250, 251, 253-54, 255, 257, 259
Peace Information Center, 243
Pebbles from an African Beach (Jordan), 246
Pedro Gorino (ship), 154
Pennington, James W. C., 17, 25
Pennsylvania University, 69
Perry, Rufus Lewis, 70-71
Petitions to the United States government, 96-97, 98, 99, 151, 152, 252, 273
Phelps-Stokes Fund, 76
Philadelphia Institute for Colored Youth, 26, 210
Philadelphia Negro, The (Du Bois), 242
Philadelphia Tribune, 45
"Pile on the Black Man's Burden" (poem), 145
Pittsburgh *Mystery*, 27
Prairie View State Normal and Industrial College, 97
Presidential election: of 1900, 54-55, 151; of 1908, 222
Pride, Armistead, 42
Princeton College (later University), 74
"Project for an Expedition of Adventure to the Eastern Coast of Africa," 121
"Providential design": theory of, 23

Quaker African repatriation scheme (1713), 7
Queen's College, 22

Race riots: of 1919, 259
Randolph, A. Phillip, 245, 254

Rape of Africa Concept, 242, 271
Reconstruction, 9, 37, 38, 72, 142
Redkey, Edwin S., 7
Reeve, John Bunyan, 70-71
Reeves, Jesse, 84
"Relations of the Scriptures to Africa, The" (paper), 53
"Religious crusade" in Africa, 69
Republican National Committee, 46
Revolutionary War, 7
Rhodes, Cecil, 153
Richmond Planet, 43, 54, 149, 248
Richmond *Reformer*, 47
Ridgel, Alfred Lee, 35, 41, 218
Robinson, John W., 76
Rochester *North Star*, 21, 27
Rockefeller Foundation, 76
Roosevelt, Theodore, 55, 99, 101, 141, 197
Root, Elihu, 97, 101, 198, 222, 223
Rust Institute, 73

St. Louis Palladium, 93
St. Paul *Broad Axe*, 196
Sale, George, 223
Sam, Alfred Charles [pseud. "Chief Sam"], 12
San Francisco Elevator, 24
Savannah *Colored Tribune*, 42
Savannah Tribune, 42, 103, 147-48, 149, 179, 195, 218, 253, 259
Scarborough, William Sanders, 55, 98
Schomburg, Arthur A., 48
"Scientific Redemption of Africa" (article), 220
Scott, Emmett J., 223, 225, 235, 247, 249, 250, 256
Scott, Horatio L., 153-54
"Scramble" for Africa, 28-29, 37, 73, 78, 83, 116, 118, 123, 171, 237, 254
Self-determination: principle of, 239, 247, 248, 249, 250, 253, 254, 259, 270
Self-help philosophy, 22, 38, 41, 94, 159
Shaw College (later University), 124, 247

Sheppard, William H., 81, 85, 86-87, 95, 98, 102-103

Sierra Leone Weekly News, 48

Singleton, Benjamin "Pap," 11, 127

Skinner, Robert P., 197, 198, 199

Slavery in Africa, 26, 58, 68, 77, 84, 94, 117, 125, 137, 146

Smith, Charles Spencer, 65, 72-73, 158

Smith, E. E., 214

Smith, H. A., 153

Smith, Harry C., 43, 54, 90, 124-25, 150, 187, 194-95, 200, 248-49

Smith, Owen L. W., 215

Smith, Robert J., 52

Smyth, John H., 47, 50, 52, 205, 210-12

Social Darwinism, 38

Society for the Collection of Negro Folk Lore, 52

South Africa, 135-68; and the Afro-American press, 147-51; and British-Boer struggle, 137-41; diamond mining in, 137; gold fields in, 137; pass system in, 137; unification, 157, 159-60, 161. *See also* Anglo-Boer War

South Carolina State Agricultural College, 74

South Carolina University, 74

Southern Christian Recorder, 69

Southern Presbyterian Church, 96

Southern Workman, 89

Southwestern Christian Advocate, 47

Spanish-American War, 53-54, 89, 104, 138, 269

Speke, John Hanning, 115

Stanley, Henry Morton, 83, 116

Star of Zion, 250-51

Stengers, Jean, 84

Stewart, George P., 146

Stewart Missionary Foundation for Africa, 46, 250

Stewart, T. McCants, 50, 65, 74-75, 218, 220

"Story of the Congo Free State, The" (article), 91

Straker, D. Augustus, 50-51, 55, 74

Suez Canal, 37, 115, 116, 174, 175, 181

Sultan of Morocco, 179

Sultan of Zanzibar, 115, 117, 118

Taft, William H., 222-23, 224

Tawfiq, 175

Taylor, C. H. J., 213

Taylor, Julius F., 169, 182, 195

Taylor, S. Coleridge, 57

Terrell, Mary C., 255-56

Terrell, Robert H., 255

Topeka *American Citizen*, 46, 127, 195

Topeka State Ledger, 149, 195

Trader Horn, 122

Treaty of Bardo (1881), 173

Treaty of Fez (1912), 173

Treaty of Lausanne (1912), 174

Treaty of Versailles (1920), 240, 241, 259

Treaty of Wichale (1889), 189, 190, 192

Trenton *Sentinel*, 178, 179, 180, 181

"Tribal system": abolishment, 137

Trotter, William M., 91

Troy *Clarion*, 26

Troy *National Watchman*, 26

Truth of Africa, The (Scott), 153

Turkiya, 176, 177

Turner, Henry M., 3-4, 10, 23, 40, 41, 44, 49, 52, 54, 55, 69-70, 143, 199, 214, 218

Turner, James M., 23-24, 210

Tuskegee "captains of industry," 76, 123, 182

Tuskegee Institute, 49, 51, 76-77, 91, 123, 182, 225

Umberto I (King), 189

Union Theological Seminary, 70, 216

United States: African policy, 31, 57-58, 68, 100-101, 127-28, 137, 138, 141, 173, 196-98, 207-208, 222, 239, 273; Far East policy, 31

United Trans-Atlantic Company, 11

Universal Negro Improvement Association, 193
University of Heidelberg, 25
University of South Carolina, 214
Upshur, Abel P., 208

Venezuela: Afro-American diplomats in, 251
Victoria (Queen), 56, 190
Voice of Missions, 40, 69, 96, 145
Voice of the Negro, 92, 98, 125-26

Walker, Walter F., 91-92, 169, 179, 215, 220
Waller, John L., 46, 127-29, 130
Wallis, Braithwait, 217
Walters, Alexander, 55-57
Walton, Lester, 257
Ward, John P., 198
Warren, Francis H., 91, 215
Washington Bee, 42, 54, 148, 180, 182, 221, 224, 253, 258
Washington, Booker T., 44, 45, 48, 49, 50, 51, 52, 54, 55, 76-77, 88, 90, 91, 94, 97, 98-100, 101, 123, 147, 158-59, 205, 216, 222-23, 225, 249, 257, 271, 273
Washington *Colored American*, 53, 129-30, 147, 151
Washington, George, 31
Washington *People's Advocate*, 30
Washington Sun, 45
Wells-Barnett, Ida B., 51-52
West Africa, 65-80; AME and European partitioning of, 69; attitudes of Afro-American press towards, 73-74; interest of Afro-American diplomats and educators, 75-76
West African Conference. *See* Berlin West African Conference (1884-85)
Western University, 199

"What Causes Are in Operation for the Redemption of Egypt?" (paper), 52
White, G. Wesley, 196
"White man's burden," 23, 31, 37, 48, 53, 58, 70, 74, 98, 269
"White superiority": ideology of, 5, 19, 31, 37, 38, 50, 54
"Who Were the Ancient Egyptians and What Did They Accomplish?" (paper), 52
Wichita *National Reflector*, 196
Wichita Searchlight, 158
Wilberforce University, 39, 40, 69, 98, 139, 225, 242, 255
Wiley University, 225
Williams College, 130
Williams, George Washington, 10, 29-30, 81, 85-86, 87, 218
Williams, Henry Sylvester, 50, 55-57
Williams-Irvin, Katherine E., 253-54
Wilson, Woodrow, 237, 238, 239, 240, 252, 257
Woodson, Carter G., 48
"Work for American Negroes, A" (speech), 145
World Christian Endeavor Conference (1900), 56
World War I, 123-24, 126, 172, 175, 176, 181, 200, 225, 227, 237-41, 259, 270, 273
World War II, 239
World's Congress on Africa (1893), 41-42, 46

Yerby, William J., 75
Yergan, Max, 124
Young, Charles, 226, 256

Zulu Christian Industrial School, 158
Zulu (Bambata) Rebellion (1906), 156, 157
Zulu War (1879), 138

About the Author

SYLVIA M. JACOBS is an associate professor of history at North Carolina Central University at Durham and a specialist in Afro-American relations with Africa. Professor Jacobs has contributed also to the *Dictionary of American Negro Biography*.

Recent Titles in
Contributions in Afro-American and African Studies
Series Adviser: *Hollis R. Lynch*

The Slave Drivers: Black Agricultural Labor Supervisors in the Antebellum South
William L. Van Deburg

The Black Rural Landowner—Endangered Species: Social, Political, and Economic Implications
Leo McGee and Robert Boone, editors

"Keep A-Inchin' Along": Selected Writings of Carl Van Vechten about Black Arts and Letters
Bruce Kellner, editor

Witnessing Slavery: The Development of Ante-bellum Slave Narratives
Frances Smith Foster

Africans and Creeks: From the Colonial Period to the Civil War
Daniel F. Littlefield, Jr.

Decolonization and Dependency: Problems of Development of African Societies
Aquibou Y. Yansané, editor

The American Slave: A Composite Autobiography
Supplement, Series 2
George P. Rawick, editor

The Second Black Renaissance: Essays in Black Literature
C.W.E. Bigsby

Advice Among Masters: The Ideal in Slave Management in the Old South
James O. Breeden, editor

Towards African Literary Independence: A Dialogue with Contemporary African Writers
Phanuel Akubueze Egejuru

The Chickasaw Freedmen: A People Without a Country
Daniel F. Littlefield, Jr.